Migrating to the C

Migrating to the Cloud
Oracle Client/Server
Modernization

Tom Laszewski

Prakash Nauduri

Technical Editor

Ward Spangenberg

AMSTERDAM • BOSTON • HEIDELBERG • LONDON
NEW YORK • OXFORD • PARIS • SAN DIEGO
SAN FRANCISCO • SINGAPORE • SYDNEY • TOKYO

Syngress is an imprint of Elsevier

SYNGRESS

Acquiring Editor: Chris Katsaropoulos
Development Editor: Matt Cater
Project Manager: Jessica Vaughan
Designer: Alisa Andreola

Syngress is an imprint of Elsevier
225 Wyman Street, Waltham, MA 02451, USA

Notices

Knowledge and best practice in this field are constantly changing. As new research and experience broaden our
understanding, changes in research methods or professional practices may become necessary.
Practitioners and researchers must always rely on their own experience and knowledge in evaluating and using
any information or methods described herein. In using such information or methods they should be mindful of
their own safety and the safety of others, including parties for whom they have a professional responsibility.

To the fullest extent of the law, neither the Publisher nor the authors, contributors, or editors, assume any liability
for any injury and/or damage to persons or property as a matter of products liability, negligence or otherwise,
or from any use or operation of any methods, products, instructions, or ideas contained in the material herein.

Library of Congress Cataloging-in-Publication Data
Laszewski, Tom.
  Migrating to the cloud : Oracle client/server modernization / Tom Laszewski, Prakash Nauduri.
    p. cm.
  ISBN 978-1-59749-647-6
  1. Cloud computing. 2. Systems migration. 3. Oracle (Computer file) 4. Client/server computing.
  I. Nauduri, Prakash. II. Title.
  QA76.585.L38 2012
  004.6782—dc23

                              2011029908

British Library Cataloguing-in-Publication Data
A catalogue record for this book is available from the British Library.

ISBN: 978-1-59749-647-6

Printed in the United States of America

12 13 14 15 16   10 9 8 7 6 5 4 3 2 1

Working together to grow
libraries in developing countries

www.elsevier.com | www.bookaid.org | www.sabre.org

ELSEVIER   BOOK AID International   Sabre Foundation

For information on all Syngress publications visit our
website at www.syngress.com

Contents

About the Authors

Tom Laszewski has more than 20 years of experience in databases, middleware, software development, management, and building strong technical partnerships. He is currently the director of cloud migrations in the Oracle Platform Migrations Group. His main responsibility is successful completion of cloud migration projects initiated through the Oracle partner ecosystem and Oracle Sales. These migration projects involve mainframe service enablement and integration, mainframe rehost and rearchitecture, and Sybase, DB2, SQL Server, Informix, and other relational database migrations. Tom works on a daily basis with TCS, Infosys, and niche migration system integrators, customer technical architectures, CTOs and CIOs, and Oracle account managers to ensure the success of migration projects. Tom also works with cloud service providers to assist in their migration of current non-Oracle-based offerings to an Oracle-based platform. This work involves solution architecture of Oracle-based cloud solutions utilizing Oracle Exadata, Oracle Virtual Server, and Oracle Enterprise Linux.

Before Oracle, Tom held technical and project management positions at Sybase and EDS. He has provided strategic and technical advice to several startup companies in the database, blade, XML, and storage areas. Tom holds a master of science degree in computer information systems from Boston University.

Prakash Nauduri has more than 19 years of experience working with databases, middleware, and development tools/technologies. In his current role as technical director in the Platform Migrations Group at Oracle, he is responsible for promoting adoption of Oracle products such as Oracle Exadata, Exalogic, Oracle Database, and Fusion Middleware in non-Oracle-to-Oracle platform migrations as well as assisting cloud service providers in development of Oracle-based cloud offerings. Before joining Oracle, Prakash worked with automotive companies in India, namely Hero Group and Eicher Tractors Ltd., as developer/database administrator/system analyst. He holds a bachelor of science degree from Berhampur University in Orissa, India.

About the Technical Editor

Ward Spangenberg (CISSP, CISA) is the director of Security Response for Zynga Inc. Ward manages three divisions for Zynga: Incident Response, eDiscovery/Forensics, and eCrime. His teams are responsible for helping to maintain the safety and security of more than 200 million daily active players.

As a security professional with more than 15 years of real-world IT experience, Ward is an expert in many areas of IT security, specializing in security engineering, compliance, cloud research, and security integration. He has provided security services across industries including defense, law enforcement, finance, and health care.

Introduction

INFORMATION IN THIS CHAPTER:

- Book Overview
- Audience
- Book Layout

BOOK OVERVIEW

Cloud computing is being adopted at a rapid rate by both large and small companies. Cloud computing is all about moving from departmental, distributed computing to rapidly provisioned and Internet-accessible shared resources. Shared resources are centralized resources that typically involve consolidation and migration projects.

Migrations from mainframe and midrange systems have been occurring for decades. The legacy migration marketplace is a multimillion-dollar-per-year business, yet there are only around 15,000 mainframes in the world. This pales in comparison to the number of servers that are running relational databases and the number of PCs running client/server applications that access these relational databases. One major financial services institution is running 600 UNIX servers with more than 1,000 Sybase databases and tens of thousands of client/server applications on user desktops. Another Fortune 1000 company is running a Citrix server farmer of 1,000 servers for a PowerBuilder application. This company would incur significant savings if it could move this legacy client/server application to an Oracle cloud infrastructure. This book will provide readers with the knowledge and insight to successfully migrate client/server applications to the cloud.

The main purpose of this book is to serve as a reference guide as you plan, determine effort and budget, design your Oracle cloud infrastructure, execute the migration, and move your Oracle cloud environment into production. In order to achieve this objective, this book covers a range of topics, from Oracle application and database cloud offerings, to the migration of your infrastructure to the cloud. Database and application migrations can become a complicated exercise if they are not planned and executed carefully. Understanding various migration approaches and choosing the appropriate approach is key to successful execution of a migration project. Many migration tools and technologies are available to ease the migration effort that will be covered in this book. Useful code snippets as well as step-by-step instructions in database migrations are included to assist database administrators and developers in executing migration projects. Also included are four case studies that highlight the business and technical challenges, processes, and results achieved by Oracle and its partner ecosystem. The customer success case studies cover service enablement of DOS-based applications, Sybase to

Oracle, Forms to Java EE, and PowerBuilder to APEX. Finally, future trends in migration technologies as well as cloud computing to prepare the audience for the future are also discussed in this book.

AUDIENCE

This book is a definitive guide on database and application migrations and deployment of applications/databases in a cloud environment suitable for most IT professionals including developers, database administrators, architects, IT project managers, and executives. This book contains a wealth of information for database administrators, developers, and architects on databases, application migration challenges and solutions, differences among database platforms, and more. This book can also be a valuable tool for IT project managers and executives as well as lead architects in understanding/scoping out migration efforts, developing migration strategies and best practices, and selecting appropriate solutions.

Architects and database administrators working in a cloud environment can gain insight into various Oracle products that can be leveraged for deploying an Oracle platform-based cloud offering.

BOOK LAYOUT

This book is organized into 14 chapters, nine of which are dedicated to various topics related to database and application migrations, infrastructure planning, cloud computing, and other aspects of migrating to the Oracle cloud, and the last chapter, which discusses current challenges and advances in technology around cloud computing and client/server migrations. The remaining four chapters highlight successful service enablement and application and database migrations to the Oracle cloud. Various migration tasks such as schema, data, stored procedures, and application migration are covered individually in Chapters 4 through 8, with code samples where appropriate, and, in some cases, step-by-step guidance in using the free migration tool from Oracle, Oracle SQL Developer. For data and application migration, there are recommendations on what approach and tools to use.

The subsections that follow provide details on each chapter in the book.

Chapter 1: Migrating to the Cloud: Client/Server Migrations to the Oracle Cloud

In this chapter, readers will learn about the evolution of various computing archi-tectures and the basics of cloud computing deployment models: public, private, hybrid, and community. The chapter covers the cloud computing delivery models: Infrastructure as a Service (IaaS), Platform as a Service (PaaS), and Software as a Service (SaaS). Also covered in this chapter are topics such as virtualization techniques, Oracle products enabling cloud computing, and cloud migration approaches and strategies.

Chapter 2: Identifying the Level of Effort and Cost

This chapter contains information on how to identify the level of effort and cost involved in database and application migrations. This chapter also discusses the best practices for defining complexity levels of a database and application migration. Effort and resource estimates for each phase in a migration project, such as analysis and design, schema and data migration, application migration, and production rollout, are discussed in depth.

Chapter 3: Methodology and Design

It is important that any migration project include some time in the beginning to finalize the migration options and methodology, and to perform an in-depth analysis of differences between the source(s) and target Oracle databases. This chapter includes the most common differences between non-Oracle relational databases such as Sybase, SQL Server, DB2, Informix, and Oracle. It also includes guidance on how to address the differences from other databases to an Oracle database.

Chapter 4: Relational Migration Tools

This chapter focuses on the various tools available from Oracle and its partners for performing relational database migrations. This includes products such as Oracle GoldenGate for production rollout of the new environment, and Oracle Enterprise Manager Tuning and Diagnostics packs for performance acceptance testing.

Chapter 5: Database Schema and Data Migration

This chapter covers database schema migration tools as well as database schema and data migration tasks in detail. Data migration in large database environments can become a complex task, so this chapter discusses various methodologies and options to migrate large databases to Oracle. A step-by-step example on migrating a sample Sybase database to Oracle is included.

Chapter 6: Database Stored Object Migration

Oracle SQL Developer offers full support for migrating stored procedures, triggers, and views from databases such as SQL Server, Sybase, and MySQL to Oracle. Oracle's SQL Developer tool is covered in detail. This chapter also discusses the differences in SQL language implementation between Oracle and other databases, and provides code snippets illustrating the differences. In addition, the chapter highlights some of the shortcomings in SQL Developer and how best to address those shortcomings.

Chapter 7: Application Migration/Porting Due to Database Migration

Database migration has an impact on every application that performs database Create, Read, Update, and Delete (CRUD) operations and all the interfaces that interact with it. Changes must be carried out in applications, batch processes, scripts, and integration interfaces with respect to changes in the SQL statement migration, database API, and command-line interface (CLI). This chapter discusses the changes required when keeping the application languages and tools the same.

Chapter 8: Migrating Applications to the Cloud

Many options and tools are available for migrating applications from one language to another or from one development platform to another. Application rationalization options, migration of 3GL- and 4GL-based applications, potential target languages and environments, and hardware and software stacks are discussed in this chapter. The chapter also covers the cloud application infrastructure environments on which the target application can run.

Chapter 9: Service Enablement of Client/Server Applications

This chapter discusses Web service enablement of a client/server application using Oracle partner Rocket Software's LegaSuite application modernization software. A step-by-step example walks you through the process of service-enabling a client/ server application. In addition to covering the service-enablement process, this chapter includes deployment-related information for LegaSuite in conjunction with Oracle Fusion Middleware products and the cloud. Three case studies highlight, at a high level, successful client/server application Web service enablement, and a fourth case study details how LegaSuite helped a nonprofit organization in California to modernize its public assistance enrollment process.

Chapter 9 was written by Patrycja Grzesznik, a product manager at Rocket Software. Patrycja has more than 15 years of experience in product management and software development. Currently, she is a research and development team lead at Rocket Software with a focus on service-oriented architecture (SOA), integration, and user interface generation.

Chapter 10: Oracle Database Cloud Infrastructure Planning and Implementation

This chapter focuses on Oracle database cloud infrastructure implementation topics such as server and workload consolidation and virtualization. It also covers aspects of the target infrastructure such as platform sizing considerations including database server sizing, storage sizing, Exadata sizing, backup and recovery, disaster recovery, and more.

Chapter 11: Sybase Migrations from a Systems Integrator Perspective, and Case Study

This chapter presents a case study from a preferred Oracle partner, mLogica, highlighting a successful Sybase-to-Oracle database migration. It also discusses topics such as business justification for migration, target system sizing, and work-load consolidation. The chapter highlights the many challenges that mLogica has encountered during migration projects and how the company successfully addressed those challenges.

Founded by a former head of Sybase Worldwide Strategic Services, mLogica is a specialized database consulting firm with deep expertise in Sybase technologies. mLogica has extensive database migration and data server consolidation experience in the Oracle platform. mLogica also provides managed Sybase pre- and post-sales database administrators and implementation experts to more than 200 active clients worldwide.

Chapter 12: Application Migration: Oracle Forms to Oracle Application Development Framework 11g

This chapter presents a migration approach and case study from an Oracle partner, Vgo Software. Vgo Software has expertise in migrating Oracle Forms-based applications to J2EE and SOA-based applications. This chapter provides an over-view of Oracle Application Development Framework (ADF) v11g, a high-level process overview for modernizing Oracle forms, and how Forms application components map to ADF 11g. Also provided is a case study that brings the presented ADF overview, process, and mappings to light.

Vgo Software is a leader in the application modernization industry, delivering modernization services using a combination of proprietary tools and bespoke modernization processes. Vgo fosters a holistic approach to modernization, ensuring that the demands of the business, organization, and technology are met. Vgo has worked with companies around the world in modernizing their business operations and platforms.

Chapter 13: Application Migration: PowerBuilder to Oracle APEX

This chapter covers the process of migrating a PowerBuilder application to Oracle Application Express (APEX). The Oracle partner that wrote this chapter, JSA^2 Solutions, has significant expertise in migrating client/server applications to APEX. The approach involved for a large-scale, mission-critical Carter's PowerBuilder application migration to APEX along with the migration, challenges, and solutions are discussed in depth. The chapter also covers the reasons why APEX is a "cloud-ready" product for both cloud development and deployment.

JSA^2 Solutions works with clients to extend their enterprise resource planning (ERP) solutions and modernize legacy business applications. The company provides expertise in business domain, application modernization, Oracle APEX, SOA, and

Java EE knowledge areas. JSA[2] helps clients from concept to delivery of applications to meet unique business requirements and extend the life of their systems.

Chapter 14: Challenges and Emerging Trends

Innovation in the IT industry is usually driven by current challenges and advances in technology. This chapter takes stock of current challenges in application and database migrations and how these challenges can be met, as well as adoption of cloud computing in general. The ironic aspect about this chapter is that cloud computing is essentially a rebranding of an old concept dating back to the 1960s of time sharing on centralized mainframe computers. Instead of calling it "cloud computing," hosting companies such as EDS and CSC called it "outsourcing." So, what is old is new and innovative again.

CONCLUSION

Migrating to the cloud involves migrating your databases, applications, and infrastructure. The goal of this book is to cover all these areas of cloud migrations. However, this book will be helpful for anyone migrating just database(s), just applications, or just infrastructure to the Oracle cloud. Migrating to the cloud is more an art than a science, but we have attempted to demystify the art by sharing our experiences and knowledge and by including Oracle partner experiences and case studies.

We are pleased to have the opportunity to share our knowledge and passion of migrating to the cloud with you. We hope you enjoy reading the book as much as we enjoyed writing it. We wish you luck in your current or future cloud migration endeavors.

Migrating to the Cloud: Client/Server Migrations to the Oracle Cloud

IT departments at many companies today are maintaining systems that were developed over the past 40 years. Initially, these systems were based on monolithic architectures using languages such as Assembler, COBOL, and C, and a central server was responsible for all data processing activities. Users and clients accessed these servers via unintelligent terminals (a.k.a. dumb terminals). Many of these systems exploited the latest technologies available at the time, but were not able to evolve as technology evolved. Some of these applications are still around today and are accessed via terminal emulators.

With the advent of desktop computers, client/server computing took off in a big way in the late 1980s and early 1990s. Client/server computing helped to offload some data processing activities from central servers to client desktops. The downside of client/server computing was that IT departments had to manage hundreds, and sometimes thousands, of desktop computers to periodically update the applications that clients developed in languages such as C++, PowerBuilder, Visual Basic, and Delphi. These client/server applications were attractive to users because of the rich graphical user interfaces (GUIs) they provided instead of traditional "green screens."

In the late 1990s, the next revolution in computing occurred, and it enabled users to access data and information using Internet browsers on personal computers, smartphones, and other digital devices. No other software was required on these devices to access applications over the Internet. Internet computing also heralded an era of openness and the proliferation of standards allowing seamless access to data and information over the Internet (e.g., SOAP/XML), resulting in development of service-oriented architecture (SOA) standards. Eventually, SOA became overhyped to the point that every software vendor started to claim support for SOA standards in some shape or form, even if their products had nothing to do with SOA.

Increased adoption of client/server and Internet computing architectures resulted in the proliferation of a large number of servers in data centers. Use of packaged business applications such as customer relationship management (CRM) and enterprise resource planning (ERP) also contributed to an increase in the use of siloed systems within data centers, with each application environment depending on a unique configuration of servers, storage, and software.

Over time, IT departments and organizations began to incur huge costs in terms of capital and operational expenditures to maintain these IT systems and infrastructure. They were required to anticipate future growth in demand for IT resources, and they had to plan for and acquire the necessary hardware and software and configure them accordingly. Similarly, every few years they had to plan for hardware and software upgrades to incorporate newer technology into their infrastructures. Even in difficult economic climates in which companies were forced to cut costs, IT departments received increasing pressure to trim their budgets and increase their utilization of these expensive resources. To address these concerns and challenges, in the early 2000s the concept of grid computing began to take shape. With grid computing, groups of inexpensive networked servers functioned as one large server. This meant IT departments no longer had to acquire large and expensive servers to meet existing or anticipated workload requirements. Moreover, capacity could be added to existing infrastructure by simply adding new servers and systems. Grid computing also enabled data-center consolidation via server clustering.

WHAT IS CLOUD COMPUTING?

With grid computing driving data-center consolidation and resource sharing, the need to further cut the cost of operating data centers filled with disparate systems led to an evolution known as cloud computing. Cloud computing is poised to become the next big wave in the IT revolution. The National Institute of Standards and Technology (NIST) defines cloud computing as follows [1]:

> *Cloud computing is a model for enabling convenient, on-demand network access to a shared pool of configurable computing resources (e.g., networks, servers, storage, applications, and services) that can be rapidly provisioned and released with minimal management effort or service provider interaction.*

The basic premise of cloud computing is that users can get access to any IT resource, including storage, CPU resources, memory, and software, over the Internet whenever they want, and can pay for their actual use of the resource rather than incurring capital and operational expenditures in order to own and operate the IT infrastructure. This computing scheme closely mimics the way households pay for utilities such as electricity and gas on metered usage. The NIST cloud computing model is composed of five unique characteristics, three service models, and four deployment models. The five characteristics associated with this model mainly enable easier availability of metered, scalable, elastic computing resources that can be provisioned via self-service and can be accessed from any thin or thick client over the network.

Cloud Computing Service Models

Cloud computing service models indicate the type of service that is being offered (i.e., hardware/software infrastructure, or application development, testing, and deployment platform, or enterprise software ready for use by subscription). The three service models that are essential components of cloud computing standards are:

- **Software as a Service (SaaS)**   Applications delivered as a service to end users over the Internet. This model is the earliest model of cloud computing in which software companies started to sell their solutions to businesses based on the number of users with a given set of service-level requirements. The major players in this field are Oracle (with its CRM on Demand solution), Salesforce.com, and Google (with its Google Apps).
- **Platform as a Service (PaaS)**   Application development and deployment platform (comprising application servers, databases, etc.) delivered as a service. Amazon Elastic Compute Cloud (EC2) and Savvis are the prominent providers of this model of cloud service.
- **Infrastructure as a Service (IaaS)**   Server, storage, and network hardware and associated software delivered as a service. Amazon EC2 is the prominent provider of this model of cloud service.

Key technologies that have enabled cloud computing in general are virtualization and clustering.

Virtualization

Virtualization allows users to overcome the restrictions associated with sharing physical computing resources such as servers, storage, and networks. For example, virtualization of servers allows users to run multiple operating system images on a single server. Virtualization of network infrastructure allows users to share network bandwidth by creating virtual local area networks (VLANs). Virtualization in cloud computing typically involves deploying many operating system images (virtual machines or VMs) on a single server sharing available CPU resources and memory. Being able to deploy many VMs also allows users to pay only for the resources they use instead of paying for all the installed capacity on the servers. This also facilitates monitoring of resource consumption by individual VMs for use by charge-back systems later.

Most of the virtualization software that is available today is based on hypervisor technology. IBM introduced hypervisor technology in the 1960s with a mainframe-based product called CP/CMS, which evolved into a product known as z/VM. Using hypervisor technology for server virtualization is more popular than using hardware partitioning or OS partitioning (host OS based), for the following reasons:

- **Ease of deployment**   VMs can be quickly deployed or undeployed with a click of a button.

- **Isolation**   Since each VM provides a complete image of the operating environment, including the choice of operating system and applications, it provides excellent isolation capabilities for users sharing the same servers.
- **Multiplatform support**   Hypervisor-based virtualization technologies support a wide range of platforms, making them very popular. They can also support different operating systems, unlike traditional server partitioning methods such as hardware partitioning. This is a key requirement for cloud providers because they need to support the most popular operating systems, databases, middleware, and applications.

Two types of hypervisors are available today. The first, which is the most widely used and is known as a "bare-metal" or "native" hypervisor, is directly deployed on a server. Therefore, it interacts directly with the hardware to provide virtualization support. Many software vendors, including Oracle, leverage a bare-metal hypervisor for performance reasons. The most popular virtualization software in this category is Oracle VM, VMware VSphere, Microsoft Hyper-V, and the IBM pSeries PR/SM. The second type of hypervisor, known as a "hosted" hypervisor, is deployed on top of an operating system (hosted) on a server. Products such as Oracle VirtualBox (formerly Sun), VMware Server/Client, and Microsoft Virtual PC fall into this category.

Bare-metal hypervisor-based virtualization offerings primarily differ from one another in terms of the following factors:

- **Hypervisor used**   Some vendors, such as VMware, developed their own hypervisors (VMware's is called ESX), whereas others, such as Oracle with its Oracle VM, leverage the open source Xen hypervisor as the foundation for their solution.
- **Full virtualization**   Products such as those from VMware support full virtualization; that is, they run a binary image of the OS and emulate real I/O device drivers. Other offerings that support full virtualization are KVM and Xen-HVM.
- **Paravirtualization**   Products that support paravirtualization, such as Oracle VM, run OSes that are ported to specific hardware architecture and are hypervisor-aware. As such, they use generic device drivers to perform regular system functions.

Virtualization is essential for cloud providers to be able to provide end users with computing resources at a lower cost. Virtualization also helps cloud providers to maximize utilization of resources and reduce capital expenditures by avoiding implementation of siloed IT infrastructure.

Clustering

Clustering allows multiple systems to function as one large system by using software and networking technologies such as shared file systems, high-speed interconnects (for servers), and similar technology. This, in turn, helps users to scale out their applications easily by adding more systems to an existing cluster to overcome the limits of physical resources (CPU and memory) in a single server. It also makes the applications highly available by allowing them to run on multiple servers in an active-active fashion to avoid single points of failure. Grid computing, as discussed earlier, was all about clustering commercially available, off-the-shelf hardware technologies to create powerful, scalable computing infrastructure. In some ways, grid computing was an early form of cloud computing in that it ensured availability of applications and masked the servers which executed specific requests in the grid.

Cloud Computing Deployment Models

Cloud deployment models indicate how the cloud services are made available to users. The four deployment models associated with cloud computing are as follows:

- **Public cloud**   As the name suggests, this type of cloud deployment model supports all users who want to make use of a computing resource, such as hardware (OS, CPU, memory, storage) or software (application server, database) on a subscription basis. Most common uses of public clouds are for application development and testing, non-mission-critical tasks such as file-sharing, and e-mail service.
- **Private cloud**   True to its name, a private cloud is typically infrastructure used by a single organization. Such infrastructure may be managed by the organization itself to support various user groups, or it could be managed by a service provider that takes care of it either on-site or off-site. Private clouds are more expensive than public clouds due to the capital expenditure involved in acquiring and maintaining them. However, private clouds are better able to address the security and privacy concerns of organizations today.
- **Hybrid cloud**   In a hybrid cloud, an organization makes use of interconnected private and public cloud infrastructure. Many organizations make use of this model when they need to scale up their IT infrastructure rapidly, such as when leveraging public clouds to supplement the capacity available within a private cloud. For example, if an online retailer needs more computing resources to run its Web applications during the holiday season it may attain those resources via public clouds.
- **Community cloud**   This deployment model supports multiple organizations sharing computing resources that are part of a community; examples include universities cooperating in certain areas of research, or police departments within a county or state sharing computing resources. Access to a community cloud environment is typically restricted to the members of the community.

With public clouds, the cost is typically low for the end user and there is no capital expenditure involved. Use of private clouds involves capital expenditure, but the expenditure is still lower than the cost of owning and operating the infrastructure due to private clouds' greater level of consolidation and resource pooling. Private clouds also offer more security and compliance support than public clouds. As such, some organizations may choose to use private clouds for their more mission-critical, secure applications and public clouds for basic tasks such as application development and testing environments, and e-mail services.

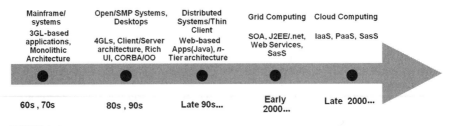

FIGURE 1.1

Evolution of Computing Architectures

> **TIP**
>
> Using hypervisor-based virtualization software to provide isolation between different customer environments can lead to increased utilization of system resources such as CPU and memory. Using native virtualization technologies offered by hardware vendors, such as Solaris Zones when using the Oracle Solaris operating system, can be much more effective and efficient depending on the customer environment. Native virtualization technologies offered by hardware vendors are more restrictive in terms of what is supported than hypervisor-based virtualization software.

Figure 1.1 summarizes the computing architecture evolution.

As Figure 1.1 shows, cloud computing primarily impacts how IT infrastructure and platforms are set up, deployed, and provisioned from an end-user perspective. The applications running in a cloud environment should be able to seamlessly interact with the cloud ecosystem, including other applications within or outside the cloud environment.

Table 1.1 highlights the pros and cons of different computing architectures.

To take advantage of cloud computing, legacy applications such as those developed using mainframe client/server technologies need to be adapted or migrated to modern languages and APIs so that they can interact with other applications regardless of where they are deployed. Cloud-enabling an application requires that the application be able to interact with databases, middleware, and other applications using standards-based mechanisms such as Web services. Most legacy and client/server applications today do not have this capability natively. Typically, these legacy applications require adapters and wrapper software to make them accessible via Web services.

THE ORACLE CLOUD

In an effort to keep up with the pace of evolution in computing architectures, including Internet computing, grid computing, and cloud computing, Oracle continues to deliver innovations in the enterprise software and hardware arena, increasing data-center efficiency by increasing resource utilization, automation

Table 1.1 Pros and Cons of Different Computing Architectures

Architecture	Pros	Cons
Mainframe/ proprietary systems	• Mostly third-generation language (3GL)-based applications • Very efficient • Easier to secure/manage (only one large server) • Fewer moving parts	• Outdated/proprietary technology • Difficult to maintain due to declining skill sets • Expensive • Less agile
Client/server computing	• Supports different operating systems (including open source) • Different languages, fourth-generation languages (4GLs) used for application development • Many options for software and hardware vendors • Cheaper than mainframes	• Many systems to manage and secure • Performance bottlenecks • Unique environment for each application, resulting in silos of systems
Internet computing (*n*-tier) architecture	• Separation between applications, business process orchestration, rules, and data and application services • Agility • Interoperability using standard mechanism such as Web services • Support for compliance requirements • Globalization	• Many servers to manage • Many software components to integrate
Cloud computing	• Self-contained environment • Interoperability between applications and environments using standard interfaces • Cheaper to acquire and operate for end users	• Security • Compliance • Performance (public clouds) • Emerging patterns • Mostly used for development and testing environments • Most legacy client/server applications need to be rewritten and/or adapted to make them cloud-ready

in provisioning, management and monitoring, scalability, and the leveraging of off-the-shelf components and technologies.

Oracle's strategy is to support various cloud computing service and deployment models with open, complete, and integrated sets of products from application to disk. Oracle offers the following products and technologies for various cloud service models:

- **SaaS**   Oracle has long been providing SaaS capability with its Siebel CRM solution, which it provides on demand and on a subscription basis. Other software vendors offer their solutions in a similar way (e.g., Salesforce.com).
- **IaaS**   Oracle's IaaS products include Oracle Database 11g and the Oracle Fusion Middleware 11g family of products which are available on most public cloud service providers including Amazon EC2 and Savvis.
- **PaaS**   Oracle offers a wide range of products to support deployment of cloud infrastructure for cloud providers as well as enterprises that are planning to build their own private clouds. With Oracle hardware and software technology, users can choose to adopt a "cloud in a box" strategy that involves very little effort in terms of infrastructure configuration and deployment, or they can choose to build the complete infrastructure from the ground up by installing and configuring their desired hardware, storage, and networking products. This "cloud in a box" approach is best suited for deploying private clouds as it is purpose-built to run Oracle software-based workloads in an optimized fashion and it helps organizations to standardize on hardware and software platforms while delivering extreme performance and driving data-center consolidation efforts. The DIY (do it yourself) option is best suited for cloud providers who are interested in deploying public cloud infrastructure and who wish to deploy a wide range of operating systems, database and middleware products leveraging blade servers based on SPARC and x86 chips, and storage and network switches. The following Oracle products enable cloud computing:

  - **Oracle Exadata Database Machine**   This product combines Sun hardware, Oracle Database 11g Release 2, and Oracle Exadata Storage Server software and is targeted at data warehousing and online transaction processing (OLTP) applications, making it a good platform for consolidating databases. It is a prefabricated system consisting of the latest Sun servers using Intel x86-64 chips, storage, networking (InfiniBand), and choice of operating system (Solaris or Oracle Enterprise Linux). With Oracle Exadata Database Machine, organizations can reportedly reduce IT costs through consolidation, manage more databases and data (increased density), and improve the performance of all Oracle database-based applications.
  - **Oracle Exalogic Elastic Cloud**   Like Oracle Exadata Database Machine, Oracle Exalogic Elastic Cloud is engineered, tested, and tuned by Oracle to run Java and other applications in the middle tier. This machine provides a high-performance compute platform for deploying applications in a private cloud environment or consolidation of a wide range of Java and non-Java application workloads, and meets the most demanding service-level requirements. It is also optimized for integration with Oracle Exadata Database Machine as both can share the InfiniBand network fabric for all database and application communications. In addition, it exploits recent advances in storage, networking, and

server technologies, including solid state disks. Customers reportedly can expect significant performance improvements when deploying existing Java applications running on Oracle WebLogic Server to Oracle Exalogic Elastic Cloud. This system also supports running the Solaris or Oracle Enterprise Linux (OEL) operating system.

* **Oracle VM**   In addition to high-performance platforms for running applications and databases, Oracle also offers free server virtualization software called Oracle VM to support both Oracle and non-Oracle applications running on Windows, Linux, and Solaris operating systems. Oracle VM allows creation of VM templates that are VM images containing preinstalled, configured enterprise software images such as Oracle Database and Oracle Fusion Middleware to develop and deploy applications rapidly. VM templates reduce and/or eliminate the effort needed to install and configure software.

* **Oracle Assembly Builder**   This product helps in creating assemblies containing all the components required for running an application, including a VM, operating system, enterprise software, distributed applications, and start-up sequences. These assemblies resemble an appliance of shared services that can be deployed in both public and private cloud environments.

* **Oracle Enterprise Manager**   Playing an important role in providing complete cloud computing life cycle management capability, Oracle Enterprise Manager (OEM) can be used to provision and deploy Oracle VM software, VM templates, and assemblies built using assembly builders. OEM can also be used to set up policies for how the VMs and applications are placed within the server pool and started in a cloud environment. In addition, it can be used to patch, monitor, and scale up/down resources in the cloud.

Figure 1.2 illustrates a timeline highlighting Oracle's offerings over the years.

Oracle has continually invested in research and development of new technologies to meet the needs of the business community as requirements changed and computing architectures evolved over time.

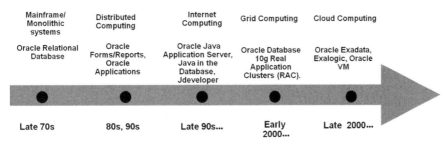

FIGURE 1.2

Oracle Computing Architectures and Paradigms

LEGACY CLIENT/SERVER DATABASES AND APPLICATIONS

What is a legacy IT system? We typically think of hardware such as the DEC VAX, HP 300, and iSeries; languages such as COBOL and RPG; scripting languages such as Rexx and JCL; and databases such as VSAM, IDMS, Datacom and IMS as legacy products. However, a legacy system is anything that has outlived its useful life. Client/server systems which were considered "newer age" when compared to legacy systems from the 1960s and 1970s are increasingly joining the ranks of legacy systems because, in most cases, they are developed using proprietary technologies, e.g., client/server systems such as those developed in PowerBuilder running against a Sybase database, Visual Basic applications that use MS SQL Server, PHP applications that use MySQL, or an application based on MS Access database. Databases such as Progress DB, Ingres, and Btrieve barely exist today. Sybase and Informix are on the verge of becoming legacy databases. Application languages such as Forte and Informix-4GL are almost nonexistent. People are looking to move off of Visual Basic (VB), PowerBuilder (PB), and Oracle Forms as part of an effort to take advantage of the latest innovations in information technology.

These newer-age systems have outlived their usefulness for a variety of reasons:

- The application does not have the scalability, reliability, and performance characteristics that were required as organizations have grown. Client/server applications traditionally suffer from these constraints.
- It is very difficult to maintain client/server applications, especially when they are installed on hundreds of desktop computers.
- Most client/server legacy applications do not support mobile users which is a very common scenario these days.
- The availability of skill sets is declining for many languages and technologies such as Delphi, Btrieve, and Informix-4GL.
- There is an increasing desire to implement new technologies, software designs and patterns, and standards in computing, such as SOA, BPM (Business Process Management), Web services, and cloud computing.
- Database vendors are pressuring customers with increased support and licensing costs.
- Database vendors are tied to one OS platform that is no longer strategic for an organization.
- Database platforms are being consolidated to one or two vendors.
- Companies are moving toward packaged applications that run better on an Oracle database.

The aforementioned reasons notwithstanding, perhaps the most important reason newer-age systems have outlived their usefulness is because client/server applications are not flexible enough to interact with other applications using standards-based technologies, or they need special software to make them accessible remotely. In most cases, these legacy applications need to be upgraded to their latest versions, and may also require use of an additional layer of software to enable them to interact with other applications in the cloud.

NOTE

The easiest way to modernize a client/server application is to make it Web service-enabled so that it can be deployed in cloud environments. Similarly, replatforming/rehosting enables users to switch from one platform to another relatively quickly compared to more time-consuming alternatives such as rearchitecting or completely rewriting the application.

WHY MIGRATE?

Many organizations adopt a "don't fix it if it's not broken" approach when it comes to adopting the latest technologies and architectures. The main reasons behind this approach are cost, uncertainty, and fear of failure. Some organizations also think that new systems and architectures cannot match or outperform their current systems. In adopting this approach, these organizations miss out on many important advances in software and hardware technology, as well as the advantages offered by the latest standards and architectures.

Not adopting new technologies, platforms, and standards can result in the following:

- **Less agility**   Significant effort is required to make changes to existing applications.
- **Longer time to market**   It takes longer to roll out new services and features to support business expansion and acquisitions.
- **Cost of maintenance**   Over the years, it becomes expensive to maintain staff for ongoing system maintenance and routine updates. Legacy software vendors also incur increased costs in supporting the very large number of customers using their products.
- **Difficult to integrate**   Integrating legacy applications with newer and modern standards-based applications, special tools, and services is necessary, but difficult.
- **Ease of access/globalization**   Legacy applications, especially client/server applications, require client software to be installed on desktop computers so that users can access the applications. This, in turn, forces organizations to develop plans to push periodic upgrades to the desktop whenever changes are made to the software.

Despite these disadvantages, there are many advantages to migrating to newer systems, technologies, and architectures:

- **Faster, more efficient hardware**   Technology is improving at a faster rate, resulting in systems on the market today that are exponentially faster than their predecessors. Therefore, organizations can benefit from periodically updating their systems by having similar or smaller hardware configurations delivering the same level of performance.

- **Leveraging of the latest standards**   It becomes much easier to integrate and exploit the latest trends in software and hardware technologies, such as SOA and cloud computing. This can result in standardization of application architecture and leveraging of business rule engines, business process management methodologies, and Web services.

- **Reduced total cost of ownership**   Migrating to newer software and hardware platforms can result in consolidation, therefore reducing the number of disparate environments that must be maintained in the future. It may also result in higher utilization of IT resources such as CPUs and storage. Consolidating existing applications into one or two platforms using standard software can cut down on management costs and enable organizations to get better prices from software vendors as their usage grows. Organizations can also take advantage of open source software such as operating systems and development tools to reduce their total cost of ownership. Newer systems based on off-the-shelf components, such as x86-based systems with open source operating systems (e.g., Linux), can reduce the cost of ownership significantly.

- **Increased agility**   It becomes easier to modify a business rule, alter a business process, or change a business service on the fly as doing so does not require unnecessary system downtime. Having a clear separation of application user interface, business logic, business process orchestration, and business rules makes it easier to enhance the system when required.

- **Governance/compliance**   In older technologies, it is very difficult to implement new requirements concerning governance and compliance. Newer software products have out-of-the-box features to support these requirements, such as extensive auditing, logging, monitoring, and security features.

- **Longer shelf life**   Newer technologies have a longer shelf life, so organizations don't need to pay exorbitant fees for maintenance.

The cost of a migration project is a major source of concern for most organizations. They need to have a solid business case to justify the up-front investment in a migration project and be able to show a significant return on investment later. A typical cost breakdown for a migration project can be as follows:

- **Initial discovery/assessment**   Typically, organizations need to take at least a few weeks to assess their current portfolio of applications and analyze the impact of migration. This might require engaging a system integrator or in-house IT staff. Most system integrators provide this type of service for a fee.

- **Migration tools, hardware, and software**   Depending on the current portfolio of applications and the target platform, it may be necessary to acquire special migration tools and technologies that can assist with migration.

- **Migration services**   Most organizations do not have the skill set to perform migrations, as this is not their core competency and it is a one-time effort for them. As a result, they may need to hire a system integrator to perform the migration task. The cost of such a service depends on factors such as complexity, scope, and the number and size of applications and databases involved.

- **Hardware, software, and storage** For the target platform, new hardware, software, and storage may need to be acquired. The cost of hardware, software, network technology, and storage can also vary based on size, performance, and vendor, among other factors.
- **Testing and production rollout** Usually, testing and production rollout are required for any migration. These tasks are performed by system integrators in most cases.

Of these costs, the cost of acquiring hardware and software for the target platform can be avoided if organizations have spare hardware and possess licenses for software. Investing in automated migration tools can help to reduce overall migration costs and increase the quality of conversions in some cases. Investing in creating appropriate documentation for the new system should also be considered. In most cases, system integrators or migration service providers perform the task of documenting the new system as part of the migration effort.

Why Oracle?

Many vendors today offer databases, application servers, development tools, and platforms. In the cloud computing space, many vendors offer similar capabilities. So, what sets Oracle apart from these other vendors? Key differentiators between Oracle and other software and hardware vendors include the following:

- Oracle is the only company that offers a full range of products comprising business applications, enterprise software (e.g., databases), application servers, and hardware systems including servers, storage, and networking tools.
- Oracle is the first company to offer a highly optimized database platform and compute platforms by combining the latest in hardware and software technologies (Oracle Exadata, Exalogic). It also brought to the forefront the notion of balanced configurations. A balanced configuration approach ensures that when computing resources are required they can be added in a modular fashion to existing infrastructure. In other words, CPU resources, network and I/O bandwidth, and storage capacity are all added proportionately so that all resources are evenly configured.
- Oracle has a history of bringing important technologies to the realm of mainstream workloads, such as the use of encryption, compression by regular OLTP, and data warehousing applications. Typically, using these features involves a significant performance overhead. With Oracle Exadata, compression can be enabled even for high-performance OLTP applications in addition to data warehousing applications.
- Oracle has had a history of providing enterprise software that enables consolidation, scalability, and capacity on demand (e.g., Oracle Database Real Application Clusters or RAC) since the release of Oracle Database 10g and Oracle Application Server 10g in early 2000.

- Oracle offers out-of-the-box integration of various features and functionalities in its software offerings. Examples include Oracle Business Intelligence Enterprise Edition (OBIEE), which combines an application server, common metadata models, E-T-L (Extract-Transform-Load) tools, technologies and dashboards, and reporting tools; and Oracle Database, which offers full support for database-wide encryption and compression out of the box.
- Oracle software products offer unique features, such as:
  - Oracle Database row-level locking, which avoids locking rows of data in tables when reading them. For all other relational databases, this is a nightmare, as they have to enable row locking even for a brief period, or enable "dirty reads" to avoid locking, which has its own side effects, such as reading uncommitted data.
  - Oracle Database 10g Real Application clusters, which allow active-active clustering of multiple instances accessing a single Oracle database. Recently, other database vendors have begun to offer this type of solution as well.
- Organizations use an array of tools and technologies to manage and monitor different layers of IT systems. Oracle's consolidated management software, Oracle Enterprise Manager (OEM) Grid Control, can monitor and manage all components in a data center. OEM also offers a simple Web-based user interface that can be accessed from any device, such as a PDA, laptop/desktop, or mobile phone.

Table 1.2 highlights the primary differences between Oracle and other software and hardware vendors in the cloud infrastructure/platform space.

Table 1.2 Comparison of Oracle with Other Cloud Platform Vendors

Oracle	Other Vendors
Engineered systems (hardware and software)	Usually hardware- or software-only solution
Out-of-the-box integrated Oracle products and features	Varying degrees of integration required based on vendor products used
Superior performance, cost/performance out of the box	Performance dependent on optimization of all layers
Supports all types of workloads (OLTP, DW/DSS)	Appliances exist for specific workloads, mostly concentrating on DW/BI analytics
Reduced total cost of ownership due to use of standard x86-based architecture, high-performance characteristics, and engineered system requiring less maintenance effort	Total cost of ownership varies depending on configuration used
Unified management infrastructure with applications to disk monitoring capabilities	Requires multiple products to manage and monitor the full stack

Why the Oracle Database?

As this book is focused on migration of applications and databases to the Oracle platform, it is essential for readers to understand why they should choose Oracle as a database platform over other vendors' products. The Oracle database offers many advantages over its competitors. According to Gartner Inc.'s "Market Share: RDBMS Software by Operating System, Worldwide, 2009" report [2], Oracle leads the database market with more than 50 percent of the market share, more than its four closest competitors combined. Oracle also differs from other database vendors in features and functionalities offered. Table 1.3 compares key features and functions of Oracle Database and other relational databases.

Many organizations wonder why they should migrate to Oracle instead of to Microsoft SQL Server or IBM DB2, as sometimes it may appear to be much easier to migrate to these other databases than to Oracle. As Table 1.3 illustrates, Oracle is the only database that truly offers significant technological advantages over others, such as row-level locking, scalability, support for clustering, and virtualization. All other databases are technically very similar and do not offer any real advantages over one another. So, it may not be worthwhile migrating to these databases, considering the effort involved in the migration process.

Table 1.3 Oracle Database Feature Comparison with Other Databases

Database Feature/ Functionality	Oracle Database	DB2	SQL Server	Sybase	Informix
Row-level locking	Yes	Yes (with isolation levels)	No	Yes	No
Active-active clustering	Yes	Yes (DB2 PureScale)	No	Yes (via Cluster edition)	No
Integration with in-memory cache database and flash cache	Yes	No	No	No	No
Compression	Yes (OLTP/DW/ Archive)	Partial	No	No	No
Transparent database encryption	Yes	Partial	No	No	No
Unified management capability	Yes	No	No	No	No (command-line utilities)

Migration Strategies

Migrating a legacy application and database to a newer platform can be a lengthy process. The effort involved depends on a number of factors, including the amount of code that needs to be converted, separation of the data access layer from the user interface layer, use of legacy technologies such as Informix-4GL, and availability of migration tools depending on the source technology.

The most common approaches to migrating legacy applications are as follows:

- Rewriting the application, targeting Oracle as the platform.
- Converting legacy applications to a newer language/platform, such as Java/Oracle, using automated conversion tools.
- Migrating legacy databases to Oracle as part of the data migration (or modernization) process. Migrating legacy databases is easier than migrating applications. This approach will get users onto the Oracle cloud platform (Exadata) as a first step.
- Replatforming C/C++/COBOL applications to run on UNIX/Linux environments under Oracle Tuxedo, which is part of Oracle Fusion Middleware. Applications running in Oracle Tuxedo can easily integrate with other applications via Web services/Java APIs.
- Replatforming Java applications running IBM WebSphere, JBoss, and other application servers to run on Oracle WebLogic, which is the first logical step toward moving to the Oracle cloud (Exalogic).
- Using emulation/wrapper technologies to Web service-enable legacy applications (SOA) and integrate them with other applications.
- Taking a hybrid approach involving any of the previously mentioned approaches to migrate complex applications. This could involve any of the following options:
  a. Using the rewriting strategy to develop new user interfaces with a clear separation between the data access layer, user interface, and business process orchestration layer (*n*-tier architecture) in a modern language, while converting noncritical backend processes such as batch jobs using automated tools or replatforming them to Tuxedo where appropriate.
  b. Migrating the frontend applications, such as the user interaction layer, to Web technologies using automated conversion tools and rewriting/rearchitecting the business logic processing to take advantage of SOA and implement business rules, workflows, and so on. This is the first step 90 percent of the time.
  c. Starting with database modernization and SOA enablement for the application. SOA enablement can provide the opportunity for modernizing applications in a phased manner without taking a "big bang" approach to application migration.

Migration approaches have pros and cons, just like other options and strategies. Table 1.4 compares different migration approaches and the pros and cons of each.

Table 1.4 Comparison of Different Approaches for Legacy Application Migration

Migration Approach/ Option	Pros	Cons	Recommendation
Rewrite/ rearchitect legacy applications	• Takes advantage of latest technologies and standards • Increased agility • Quicker time to market • Simplifies application maintenance/ upgrade processes in the future	• Requires a lot of effort (usually takes at least 18 months for an average application) • Expensive due to the time and different technologies involved • Can take about 24 months to realize return on investment	• Use this approach to migrate the most complex/ brittle application components, such as the business logic processing tier, proprietary messaging systems, etc. • Any application that requires frequent changes due to a change in business rules and needs quicker time to market is a good candidate for this approach.
Replatform applications to Oracle (Tuxedo or WebLogic Server)	• Processes are easier to execute • Keeps the current business logic intact • Gets to the cloud platform more quickly • Less testing effort required • Quicker ROI than the rewriting/ rearchitecting approaches	• No optimization in business processes/logic is achieved • May require additional training/education for existing staff	• This is a good strategy for migrating to the Oracle cloud platform quickly. • This is ideal for applications/ modules that undergo few changes (e.g., backend reporting processes). • This can be used to migrate applications for which rewriting the business logic is considered too risky.
Automated conversions using tools	• Moves to a new platform quickly • Keeps the current business logic and rules intact	• Generated code may be difficult to maintain/ manage • No optimization of business	• This is ideal for moving to new platforms under a tight deadline. • This is good for applications that

(Continued)

Table 1.4 Comparison of Different Approaches for Legacy Application Migration *(Continued)*

Migration Approach/ Option	Pros	Cons	Recommendation
	• Quicker ROI	processes/logic is achieved • May need extensive testing • Performance may not be on par with the source system	are mostly static or rarely updated. • The user interface layer may be the best candidate.
Emulation (SOA enablement/ Web services, screen scraping)	• Ideal for integration of legacy applications in modern environments • Does not require extensive changes to legacy applications • Increases lifespan of legacy applications • Enables phased migration of legacy applications	• Does not improve agility of legacy applications • Adds to cost of maintaining existing environment • May require some changes to the application	• This is ideal for reusing business logic embedded in legacy applications. • This enables phased migrations of legacy applications at a later date. • This enables standards-based integration (Web services) between applications.
Data modernization	• Migrates to Oracle cloud (Exadata) • Takes advantage of enhanced capabilities in areas of business intelligence, data warehousing, reporting, etc. • Easier than application migration	• Applications depending on legacy databases may be impacted if legacy database is retired • May require some porting effort for existing applications	• This could be the first phase of legacy application/ database migration. • This offers a quicker ROI. • This enables rapid information integration.

As illustrated in Table 1.4, adopting a hybrid approach to application migration may be desired in most cases because of the reduced risk of such migrations and the fact that a quicker ROI is achieved from such efforts. Before embarking on a migration project of any kind, it is always a good idea to analyze your application portfolio so that you fully understand how the components in your infrastructure are linked, along with any complexities involved. This will help you to formulate a strategy for achieving a successful migration.

We will discuss how to implement these strategies in detail in Chapters 5 through 9. Additionally, readers will get firsthand experience with these strategies in the four use cases described in Chapters 9, 11, 12, and 13.

> **WARNING**
>
> Using screen scraping technologies for making legacy applications available as Web services can lead to a very rigid integration pattern as screen scraping technologies are heavily tied to the legacy applications' user interface (UI) layout. Any changes to the UI layout in the legacy applications will require changes to Web services built using screen scraping technology for Web service enabling the legacy applications. This is the least preferred option for Web service enabling a legacy application.

SUMMARY

Adoption of cloud computing can be beneficial to organizations, even as the technology behind it is maturing. Organizations should consider evaluating different cloud models suitable for their business requirements. The biggest inhibitor to adopting cloud computing will be the large number of legacy applications that take up a significant proportion of a typical company's IT budget, are not agile, and are difficult to maintain. Organizations should start to develop plans for eventual migration of these applications to newer and better technologies.

This book will guide readers through the process of migrating to the cloud, starting with a focus on scoping and estimating the migration effort in Chapter 2. Chapters 3 through 8 describe the database and application migration process along with the tools and technologies that can be used to aid in this effort. The last four chapters of the book provide case studies involving successful migrations to the cloud, including migrations from a service-oriented enablement perspective, database migration, and two case studies on application migration.

Endnotes

[1]   Mell P, Grance T. The NIST Definition of Cloud Computing. Available from: www.nist .gov/itl/cloud/upload/cloud-def-v15.pdf.

[2]   Gartner Inc. Market Share: RDBMS Software by Operating System, Worldwide, 2009. Available from: www.gartner.com/DisplayDocument?id=1362234.

Identifying the Level of Effort and Cost

2

INFORMATION IN THIS CHAPTER:

- Complexity of Database and Application SQL Migration Defined
- Overall Estimating and Scoping Approach
- Analysis and Design
- Database Migration
- Application Migration
- Integration Architecture
- Infrastructure Products, Utilities, and Tools
- Hardware and Software
- System, Customer Acceptance, and Performance Testing
- Moving to Production
- Other Things to Consider
- Project Management and Enterprise Architect
- Migration Effort Examples

Often, the first step in a cloud migration project is creation of a rough estimate. At this point, customers, independent software vendors (ISVs), and system integrators are looking for insight as to whether the project will cost $100,000, $1 million, or $5 million or more. They want to know whether the effort will require two resources or 20 resources, and whether they will need outside assistance. They want to know how long the project will take—a couple of weeks, three months, or several years. The cost and resource requirements of a project depend on the number of database servers and the size of the databases being migrated. It is not uncommon for large organizations to consider moving hundreds of databases, applications, and hardware servers to the cloud.

Typically, the rough estimate is performed by a migration specialist and can be 60 percent to 70 percent accurate. To complete the estimate quickly, the migration specialist does not analyze every issue in detail, nor does he provide a solution for any problems he encounters. Instead, he identifies the top 10 issues and documents potential ways to resolve them. The rough estimate usually requires a one- to three-day on-site analysis, after which the migration specialist compiles the estimate in one to two weeks. After receiving the rough estimate, customers receive a refined estimate that narrows down the expected duration of the project, along with the number of resources and types of resources to be migrated. A refined estimate usually takes two to three weeks of analysis and up to a one-week on-site visit with the IT staff. This would produce an estimate that is 70 percent to 80 percent accurate; the higher accuracy is achieved by identifying solutions or possible solutions to all database and application migration issues. These estimates are not a replacement for a complete analysis and design of the migration project, but are intended to provide IT and business decision makers with the ability to quickly determine whether to proceed with the project.

In this chapter, we will cover all the components of a cloud migration project, from the database to the hardware and software. We will assume you are moving your database from a non-Oracle Linux/UNIX/Windows platform to an Oracle database. We will also assume you will be moving to the Oracle Exadata and Exalogic platform for your hardware, as these "preengineered" software machines are the foundation of the Oracle cloud.

Your top three considerations when migrating to the Oracle cloud are as follows:

1. Database and application migration is only one component of the overall migration cost. You must also consider the cost of operating the new platform and acquiring the necessary hardware and software.
2. Testing will be the largest component of your migration cost. This includes unit, system, customer acceptance, and performance testing. You can reduce this cost if you have an extensive suite of automated regression testing software.
3. Initial hardware and software costs, ongoing hardware and software operating costs, and personnel costs comprise a large portion of the overall migration cost. You should consider reducing these costs if possible. If your company is in a hardware refresh cycle, your ROI business case will be much more attractive.

NOTE

The approach and the numbers provided in this chapter are the result of the authors' more than 14 years of experience and the experience of migration partners. Your project may have different characteristics or your organization may have different goals than those of the typical cloud migration covered in this chapter. For example, your focus may be to migrate from an old and unsupported version of PowerBuilder, or you may want to consolidate your database hardware infrastructure to Oracle Exadata.

Figure 2.1 shows a breakdown of the phases of a typical migration project.

Figure 2.1 depicts the typical migration cost estimate for each major phase of the project as follows:

- **Testing (25 percent)**   This includes system, integration, customer acceptance, and performance testing. The system and customer acceptance tests are a major component of this phase.
- **Database migration (20 percent)**   This assumes you have thousands of objects stored in your database. If there are no stored procedures, views, or triggers in

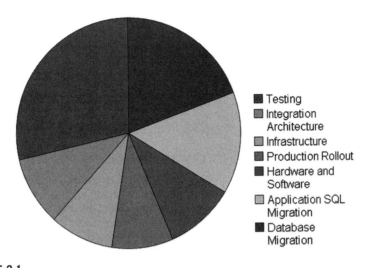

FIGURE 2.1

Migration Phases, with Percentage of Total Migration for Each Phase

your database, database migration is a trivial exercise. Databases with a limited number of stored objects and less than 500 GB of data can be migrated in days or weeks.

- **Application SQL migration (20 percent)**   This assumes the application language will remain the same, but some of the SQL in the application will need to change.
- **Hardware and software (10 percent)**   This assumes no operating system migration is required. We will discuss how to reduce this time using Oracle cloud hardware and software solutions later in this chapter.
- **Integration architecture (10 percent)**   Most applications have integration software such as message brokers, extract-transform-load (ETL) products, information integration buses, or, in many cases, custom data and application integration software.
- **Infrastructure products and solutions (5 percent)**   These can be anything from custom script-based database management and monitoring solutions to vendor database development tools.
- **Production rollout (10 percent)**   The production rollout time is a factor of the database size. Smaller databases can be migrated in a few hours and testing can be completed so that a production rollout can occur in the course of a weekend.

A migration project with no database stored objects would have a different split on the time required to perform application SQL migration and database migration. The database phase would require only 5 percent of the effort, whereas the application SQL phase would require 25 percent and testing would require 40 percent as it is more difficult to perform system and performance testing when SQL is spread throughout the application.

> **NOTE**
>
> The percentages for each phase of the migration are not published or "certified" by Oracle or any third-party migration company. These percentages are based on hundreds of migration projects from relational databases such as DB2, Sybase, SQL Server, and Informix to an Oracle database performed by service providers specializing in database migrations to Oracle. The numbers do not include application language transforms, operating system migrations, or cloud infrastructure configuration and installation, all of which may need to occur when migrating to an Oracle private cloud environment.

COMPLEXITY OF DATABASE AND APPLICATION SQL MIGRATION DEFINED

In this chapter, we will discuss database, infrastructure, and application complexity. So, before we get into the details, we need to define *complexity* as it is a major component of how long a migration project will take. Realizing that many variables influence the complexity of a project, we will operate from a simplified version of complexity and place migrations into four "complexity buckets":

1. **Easy**   Java, Java EE, Visual Basic, PowerBuilder, or C/C++ applications using Java Database Connectivity (JDBC), Open Database Connectivity (ODBC), Hibernate, TopLink, or another form of open standard database connectivity. Ninety percent of the application SQL follows the American National Standards Institute (ANSI) standard. No stored procedures, triggers, or views are involved in the migration.

2. **Medium**   Java, Java EE, Visual Basic, PowerBuilder, or C/C++ applications using JDBC, ODBC, Hibernate, TopLink, or another form of open standard database connectivity. Eighty percent of the application SQL follows the ANSI standard. Fewer than 2,000 stored procedures, triggers, and views are involved in the migration.

3. **Complex**   Java, Java EE, Visual Basic, PowerBuilder, or C/C++ applications using JDBC, ODBC, Hibernate, TopLink, or another form of open standard database connectivity, or a C/C++ or COBOL application with embedded SQL calls. Sixty percent of the application SQL follows the ANSI standard. Fewer than 6,000 stored procedures, triggers, and views are involved in the migration.

4. **Very complex**   The complexity items in numbers 1, 2, and 3, with the addition of proprietary vendor features such as the C/C++ DB Library or Open Client, Sybase Replication, Sybase Open Server, Microsoft Data Transformation

Services (DTS), or Microsoft SSIS. SQL or stored procedure generators can be written in any language.

OVERALL ESTIMATING AND SCOPING APPROACH

The overall estimating and scoping approach we will use assumes that you have already completed the preliminary business case investigation and believe there is a business case for investigating cloud migration in more detail. The estimating and scoping approach used by Oracle, global system integrators, and niche migration vendors is tool-assisted but relies heavily on best practices, questionnaires, face-to-face interviews, on-site visits, and spreadsheet-based estimating models.

You don't want to turn this into a multimonth architecture discovery and Oracle architecture build-out exercise. Oracle migration specialists have seen many cases in which customers get discouraged because the migration scope and estimate turns into a six-month project focusing on the best way to architect the Oracle solution and which features and options to use from Oracle. The scoping effort should be simple and straightforward, and should follow these guidelines:

- It should determine the migration cost with 70 percent to 80 percent accuracy, and should determine how much you will save by operating your new infrastructure. Do not attempt to get a perfect estimate or scope at this time. This will only delay your decision and bring "scope creep" into the migration project very early on.
- This should be an "as is" migration effort. Do not try to reengineer the database model, application architecture, or business processes. This will lengthen the scoping and estimating effort from a few weeks to several months.
- When moving to the cloud choose Oracle Database as your software and Oracle Exadata and Oracle Exalogic as your hardware, or choose hardware that supports the Oracle VM Server for x86. Don't make the process of choosing the software and hardware architecture a project unto itself.
- Avoid operating system migrations whenever possible. Migrating operating systems requires effort that is as intensive and extensive as migrating a database. Not only do you have to install and configure the new OS, but you also need to migrate the application, integration, database management, and other infrastructure utilities, as well as infrastructure products, to the new OS. It is strongly recommended that any OS migration be done in phase two of your migration to the cloud.

Questionnaires

The first step in the estimation process is completion of the migration questionnaire. Oracle has specific questionnaires for Sybase, SQL Server, Informix, and DB2 databases; a generic database and application migration questionnaire is available for Sybase IQ, Ingres, Progress, PostgreSQL, and relational databases. The objective of this questionnaire is to elicit relevant information about the scale and complexity of your planned database migration project.

The questionnaire covers major areas of the project, including database, application, testing, integration solutions, third-party products, and infrastructure. The 14 key questions with the biggest impact on the database migration effort are as follows:

1. **Database version, operating system type and version, and hardware vendor and specification**   The database version is required, as it determines which tools from Oracle can be used to automate the process. The operating system type and version will determine if the current release of Oracle is compatible or if an OS upgrade may be required. The hardware vendor and hardware specifications will help you to determine the overall magnitude of the migration project. Generally, the more powerful the hardware is, the more sophisticated the database and application will be.

2. **Online transaction processing (OLTP) or data warehousing**   As a rule of thumb, data warehousing applications are easier to migrate; this is because the data model is typically simpler, the usage of database stored objects is limited, and the application only does queries which are easier to migrate. OLTP systems usually take longer to test, but data warehouses usually take longer for data migration and production rollout because data volumes are larger.

3. **Number of users, peak transaction rate per second, and daily data volumes**   This information will help you to estimate how long it will take for performance testing.

4. **Database size**   This will affect the production rollout and influence the times for testing.

5. **Number of stored procedures and total lines of code**   Stored procedures are written in vendor-specific language and will need to be migrated to Oracle PL/SQL, the Oracle database procedural programming language. The number of stored procedures and total lines of stored procedure code has the biggest impact on the database migration effort.

6. **Number of triggers and total lines of code**   Triggers, like stored procedures, will require a migration from your vendor's database-specific language to Oracle PL/SQL. Triggers are usually not as complicated to migrate as stored procedures.

7. **Number of views and total lines of code**   Views are just SQL. Although SQL is an ANSI standard followed by all major database vendors, this does not mean SQL is completely compatible across vendors. In most cases, 70 percent to 90 percent of the views will migrate to Oracle with minor changes.

8. **Application languages and database connectivity layer**   The most important aspect of the language is the database connectivity layer. This will most likely be ODBC, JDBC, ASP.NET, or .NET.

9. **Number of SQL statements in the application**   Typically, 80 percent to 90 percent of the SQL in the application will be ANSI-standard SQL and will not

need to change. Java-based object-oriented, relational mapping solutions such as Hibernate and TopLink make it easy to migrate applications to work with an Oracle database as the SQL is generated for the target database by Hibernate and TopLink.

10. **DBA scripts (language and total number of lines)**   These scripts contain database-vendor-specific calls which will need to change.

11. **Replication server or products used**   Replication products such as Sybase Replication Server and Oracle GoldenGate are often used. The product will need to move to Oracle GoldenGate.

12. **ETL product usage**   Most applications have some form of ETL technology. This will need to be migrated to an Oracle solution or be changed to work with Oracle.

13. **Backup and recover and disaster recovery solutions**   Each database vendor has its own backup and recover and disaster recovery solution, or a third-party product is used. The database-vendor-specific solution will need to be migrated to Oracle, or the third-party solution will need to be verified to work with Oracle.

14. **Sybase Open Server, IBM MQ Series, Microsoft SSIS, or other vendor-specific products**   These products will need to be migrated to Oracle-equivalent products unless the solution offers Oracle support.

The questionnaire really just opens the discussion. It is a starting point to a high-level view into the database and application. The next steps in the scoping approach uncover the details that will lead to an educated estimate.

First-Pass Migration with Oracle SQL Developer

Oracle SQL Developer is used to uncover the details of the database, and quickly determine the magnitude of the database migration. Oracle SQL Developer can directly connect the source database or be used in offline capture mode. Offline capture mode is often used in the estimating process as the offline capture can be sent to whoever is doing the project estimating and scoping. We will learn more about the capabilities of Oracle SQL Developer in Chapter 4.

On-site Visit or Web Conference(s)

Thanks to the questionnaire, along with the offline capture and today's sophis-ticated Web conferencing capabilities (such as whiteboarding and the ability to take control of someone else's desktop) the estimate can be completed without an on-site visit. However, if the database and application details cannot be suffi-ciently captured and in-person whiteboarding is required, a one- to two-day on-site visit may be necessary. If hundreds of databases are being migrated, the estimating process will require an on-site visit of several weeks, along with weeks or months of analysis, before a comprehensive migration scope can be delivered.

The key to the on-site visit or Web conference(s) is to have the correct, most knowledgeable database and application owners on the phone or in the room. The following folks are most important:

- Technical architect, to answer the following questions: What does the current architecture look like end to end? What are all the data and information integration interfaces to the system? How do the business users use the system? What is the future direction of the system? What are all the user interfaces into the system?
- Lead database administrator, to answer the following questions: How much is stored in the database in terms of tables, images, or text? How large is the database? What are the database column types and how many database objects does the database contain? How many lines of code are stored in the object code? What database administrator tools, scripts, and utilities are used?
- Lead developer, to provide information regarding user interfaces, ETL process, workflow processes, languages used, development tools, database interfaces, and ad hoc query tools.
- System administrator, to provide information regarding hardware vendors and version numbers, database server CPU utilization, overall disk I/O configuration, usage patterns by day, month, and year, and overall hardware configuration.

Migration Workshop

The more the customer understands about the migration process, migration challenges, tools, the Oracle database, and migration best practices, the more accurate the estimate will be. Therefore, a half-day, one-day, or two-day workshop at the customer's location is often part of the estimating and scoping process.

Scope Deliverables

The scope deliverable is usually a PowerPoint presentation and a document with the estimated effort and cost of the migration. PowerPoint is a great format and typically the customer's point of contact will use the presentation to deliver the scope and estimate to executives. The key sections of the PowerPoint are the business objectives, a summary of findings, technical challenges and proposed solutions, risks, out-of-scope items, assumptions, and resource and time estimates for each phase of the migration. The text document will also include this information, along with a cost estimate, approach, and high-level project plan.

ANALYSIS AND DESIGN

No matter how small the migration effort is, it needs to be preceded by an analysis and design phase. This phase will define the technical details regarding how the migration will take place. This phase is much shorter than it would be for developing

Table 2.1 Analysis and Design Level of Effort Based upon Migration Complexity

Complexity	Time Estimate
Simple	4–7 days
Medium	7–13 days
Complex	13–20 days
Very complex	20–30 days

a custom application, because the core technical architecture and business logic are already in place. Therefore, the analysis and design are not included in the normal business user Joint Application Design (JAD), business requirements definition, database modeling, architecture design, or other phases in a typical "green field" development effort. The business and technical requirements, database model, and architecture are part of the system that is being migrated. The estimate for analysis and design is a function of complexity, as shown in Table 2.1.

DATABASE MIGRATION

The amount of time it will take to migrate the database depends on the amount of data involved and the number and size of stored procedures, triggers, and views. The number of indexes, tables, users, and data types plays a very small role in the time required to migrate the database.

Schema and Data

The Oracle SQL Developer Migration Workbench can be used to migrate the data. This tool will also automatically migrate Data Definition Language (DDL) statements with close to 98 percent accuracy, as DDL is very predictable in nature. Typically, DDL migrations take between two days and two weeks, including unit testing, depending on the number of tables and indexes and any potential data type changes. The migration process will include a lot of "babysitting" (unloading and loading of data) as the database increases in size. The level of effort outlined in Table 2.2 includes two test migrations and one mock production migration of data.

Data migration volumes and migration times are quickly moving targets as disk speeds increase and interconnects become faster. At the time of this writing, simple to very complex database migrations and their equivalent volumes are as follows:

- Simple: less than 100 GB of data
- Medium: less than 500 GB of data
- Complex: less than 2 TB of data
- Very complex: more than 2 TB of data

Table 2.2 Data Migration Based upon Migration Complexity

Complexity	Time Estimate
Simple	1–2 days
Medium	2–4 days
Complex	5–8 days
Very complex	8–12 days

Stored Procedures

Stored procedures will be migrated using the SQL Developer Migration Workbench, which will significantly reduce the migration of stored procedures. Stored procedures of simple or medium complexity will migrate and produce correct results, requiring no changes, 95 percent of the time. This means all that needs to be done is a quick unit test. Assuming a unit test will take an average of 10 minutes once test harnesses have been written and test plans have been created, the levels of effort shown in Table 2.3 apply.

It's important to note that what constitutes a complex item is difficult to specify because SQL Developer continues to support more and more vendor-specific functions, SQL syntax, extensions such as *@@rowcount* and *@@procid* (Sybase and SQL Server), and system table accesses.

Triggers

Triggers will be migrated using the SQL Developer Migration Workbench. Like stored procedures, triggers of simple and medium complexity will migrate over and produce the correct results, requiring no changes, 95 percent of the time. Unlike stored procedures, which typically have 400 to 1,500 lines of code, triggers usually have 30 to 50 lines of code. This means trigger fixes and unit testing will occur much more quickly. Assuming that a unit test will take an average of five minutes once test harnesses have been written and test plans have been created, the levels of effort shown in Table 2.4 apply.

Table 2.3 Stored Procedure Migration Level of Effort Based upon Migration Complexity

Complexity	Time Estimate
Simple: no complex items	40–50 per day, per person
Medium: one to two complex items	20–30 per day, per person
Complex: two to four complex items	4–8 per day, per person
Very complex: all items are complex	2–4 per day, per person

Table 2.4 Trigger Migration Level of Effort Based upon Migration Complexity

Complexity	Time Estimate
Simple: no complex items	80–100 per day
Medium: one complex item	50–70 per day
Complex: two complex items	10–20 per day
Very complex: all items are complex	5–10 per day

The most common complex items in triggers are commit statements, DDL statements in the trigger, and triggers that call system stored procedures or access database system tables.

Views

Views are migrated via the SQL Developer Migration Workbench and achieve higher levels of automated migration success as they don't contain vendor-specific database procedural language in them. They are simply a SQL statement that is persisted in the database. This means the complexity is only a factor of the SQL extensions the database vendor offers, or accesses to system tables, variables, or stored procedures. Assuming a unit test will take an average of five minutes once test harnesses have been written and test plans have been created, the levels of effort shown in Table 2.5 apply.

View complexities are the same as SQL complexity in an application, as views are simply a SQL statement. These include vendor-specific functions (date or math functions), SQL extensions, and performance hints for the database optimizer.

Stored Procedures and SQL Generation Tools

Stored procedures and SQL generators are not common, but they do occur often enough to merit mentioning, as they can make a simple migration become quite complex. Code generators for stored procedures, SQL, and sometimes even triggers and views can be written in any programming or database language. Migration specialists at Oracle and Oracle partners have encountered these generators written in Java, C, C++, Perl, .NET, and T-SQL.

Table 2.5 View Migration Level of Effort Based upon Migration Complexity

Complexity	Time Estimate
Simple: no complex items	80–100 per day
Medium: one complex item	50–70 per day
Complex: two complex items	10–20 per day
Very complex: all items are complex	5–10 per day

Here are a couple of examples to highlight how long it may take to migrate a code generator:

- C++ code to generate Oracle PL/SQL and Oracle SQL: 100 person days to migrate, generates about 3,000 stored procedures
- PERL code to generate Oracle PL/SQL and Oracle SQL: 55 person days to migrate, generates about 200 stored procedures

APPLICATION MIGRATION

When migrating an application you generally have one of two choices: Keep the application the same and modify the SQL, or actually migrate the application language. Twenty percent of the migration effort, as mentioned in this chapter's introduction, will be consumed by application migration if you choose to migrate the application SQL and keep the application the same.

SQL Only

Because we are keeping the application the same, we will only need to be concerned with the database connection string and vendor-specific SQL. It is a very good assumption that 80 percent to 90 percent of SQL code will not need to change. The SQL code will fail due to vendor-specific functions, SQL performance hints, database system table access, or vendor-specific SQL syntax. Manually scanning the application code or using UNIX commands such as GREP and then making the SQL change will add one to two hours to the migration for each SQL statement that needs to change.

The amount of time estimated for each SQL statement (one to two hours) includes any unit testing that needs to be done. The unit testing will involve executing the application against both the source database and the Oracle database and comparing the results, and then making any changes and retesting. Using a third-party migration partner that has expertise in database migrations and the application language can reduce this time to 30 minutes to one hour per SQL statement.

> **NOTE**
> Obviously, some SQL statements will not require any changes. However, all application SQL statements will need to be unit tested. Therefore, some application SQL statements will take literally seconds to migrate (amount of time to execute application) and others could involve any number of changes and retesting. As tools for scanning and automatically migrating application SQL become more sophisticated, the effort required for this activity will be reduced dramatically.

SQL Migration Scanning Tools

One way to significantly reduce the time it takes to migrate application SQL code is to use a tool that both identifies the SQL in the application and makes the appropriate change. Oracle SQL Developer includes such an automated tool. It currently supports SQL migration in C, C++, and Java EE applications. This tool has not been in production long, but it is anticipated that each SQL statement that needs to be migrated will only take 30 minutes to an hour to migrate, as only unit testing will need to occur.

> **TIP**
>
> Installation and configuration of Oracle SQL Developer takes less than 30 minutes. It is a great tool for validating the level of effort for a database migration. Sometimes customers do not want to go through the effort of getting approvals to connect to the source database, finding a machine and hard disk space to perform a trial database migration, or allowing a migration specialist to have access to database objects. You can get a good estimate by using the questionnaire, and talking with lead architects, developers, operations staff, and database administrators. However, no conversations or questionnaire can replace actually connecting to the source database and conducting a trial migration. Once the connection to the source database has been made, SQL Developer can provide real data in hours on the effort to migrate database objects. It is time well spent.

Language Migration

Migrating an application language is typically three to 10 times more time-consuming, and therefore more costly, than migrating a relational database. The standard estimate for migrating code from one language to another is based on the software industry-accepted measurement that the average developer produces 10 lines of code per day [1]. This may seem extremely low, but you have to take into account changing business requirements, changing technical specifications, unit testing, bug fixing, compile time, build time, and other factors. This makes it extremely important in an application language migration that as much of the legacy client/server code as possible is refactored and code migration tools are leveraged.

Some tool vendors provide automated tools to migrate PowerBuilder, Visual Basic, Forte, and Informix-4GL. We will discuss these in detail in Chapter 8. In Chapters 12 and 13, we will provide two case studies which will go into detail regarding the approach, cost, and technical details of application migration.

Language Migration: Sybase and SQL Server C/C++ APIs

Migration of proprietary Sybase and SQL Server C/C++ Open Client and DB-Library has traditionally required a rewrite to Oracle Call Interface (OCI). Oracle SQL Developer has been enhanced to migrate these database APIs to OCI automatically. However, some constructs will not migrate automatically (error handling may also need to change), and some unit testing will need to be completed. Even with the tool, you could plan for two to three weeks for the first C/C++ module and then one week for each additional module.

Service Enablement

Another option for language migration (which we describe via a case study in Chapter 9) is to service-enable the Windows, Java applet, or HTML-based application. Most modern languages, including Java EE and Microsoft .NET, allow Web service enablement as a part of their framework. However, older DOS applications written in C/C++ or even older versions of Oracle Forms, PowerBuilder, or Visual Basic do not offer Web service enablement out of the box. With vendor tools from Seagull Software and OpenSpan, it can take hours to Web-enable legacy client/server application modules.

INTEGRATION ARCHITECTURE

Standard tools such as IBM WebSphere Information Integrator, Tibco, and Informatica are database-vendor-neutral data and information integration products. Changes to these tools involve changing database drivers, migrating vendor-specific extensions, and unit testing. These products may require additional system and performance testing as the database may need to be tuned to gain the same performance and the integration product will need to be system-tested in the context of the entire application. Another option, which is more time-consuming and costly, is to migrate the vendor solution to an Oracle product such as Oracle Data Integrator (ODI), Oracle Warehouse Builder (OWB), or Oracle Service Bus (OSB).

Most applications also contain some type of custom script based on SQL or a vendor database language-specific ETL and File Transfer Protocol (FTP) integration layer. These custom scripts will contain SQL that will need to be migrated, just like the application SQL needs to be migrated. Also, vendor-specific integration solutions such as Sybase Replication Server require weeks or months to migrate. Therefore, integration and ETL tool migration consumes about 10 percent of the overall migration effort.

INFRASTRUCTURE PRODUCTS, UTILITIES, AND TOOLS

A wide variety of infrastructure tools are available today, including job schedulers, database and application server management and monitoring tools, testing tools such as Load Runner, and even database and application deployment scripts. If these solutions are custom-written, they will take more time to migrate than vendor tools. In some cases, utilities such as charge back and metering tools will need to be implemented when moving to the cloud as these solutions are not typically used in client/server environments. On average, infrastructure utilities and tools will consume 10 percent of the total migration effort.

Application Server Migration to Oracle WebLogic

A complete migration to the Oracle cloud infrastructure includes migrating to an Oracle database and Oracle WebLogic Server. Just as ANSI SQL usage in database application does not guarantee an application can be moved from one database vendor to another with zero changes, the Java EE standard is not implemented identically across vendor application servers. The two most common Java EE application servers besides Oracle WebLogic are JBoss and WebSphere. Migrating from these application servers to Oracle WebLogic can take weeks or months, depending on the level of vendor-specific Java classes used in the Java EE application.

The other components that may need to be migrated when migrating to WebLogic are Business Process Execution Language (BPEL) process managers, portal servers, messaging systems, enterprise service buses, business intelligence products, security servers such as single sign-on, Lightweight Directory Access Protocol (LDAP), virtual directories, and other service-oriented architecture (SOA) vendor solutions. These products all need to be considered on a case-by-case basis in terms of how much effort they will take to migrate.

HARDWARE AND SOFTWARE

A company that is going through a hardware refresh can produce a much more attractive migration ROI. For such companies, Oracle offers two solutions when moving to the cloud. The first option is to use the "cloud in a box," which is a combination of Oracle Exadata for the database and Oracle Exalogic for all your applications. A hardware refresh makes it more attractive to move to the Oracle "cloud in a box" cloud as this involves the purchase of a new hardware/software platform. If you are not going through a hardware refresh or prefer to use another hardware platform or Oracle Sun hardware, you have the option of using Oracle VM Server and Oracle Enterprise Linux (OEL). OEL is optional in this configuration as Oracle VM Server can be a host for Linux, Windows, or Solaris. This may be a more viable option for Microsoft SQL Server customers as Oracle Exadata and Exalogic do not support Windows. It also gives you the flexibility of doing a phased migration to the integrated hardware, software applications, and operating system solution that Exadata and Exalogic provide.

Exadata and Exalogic: Database and Middleware Hardware and Software

The Exadata and Exalogic install processes have been perfected over the past year and, in most cases, perform within the advertised time, which is two to three days for a full rack machine. In many cases, a week is allocated for this activity.

The cost of the initial purchase is one aspect of the overall cost to migrate hardware. There is also the cost of installation and configuration, storage assembly, networking, and installation of the operating system, database, and application software. It has been projected to cost five times less to use Oracle Exadata or Exalogic than to use conventional hardware and software for this task.

Oracle Virtualization and Oracle Enterprise Linux: Database and Middleware Hardware and Software

Oracle VM is server virtualization software that fully supports both Oracle and non-Oracle applications. Combined with OEL, Oracle VM provides a single point of enterprise-class support for your company's entire virtualization environment, including Oracle Database, Fusion Middleware, and Oracle Applications which are certified with Oracle VM. It is not a complete, integrated hardware, software, operating system, and application solution like Exadata and Exalogic, but it does provide you with an end-to-end cloud solution from one vendor. Oracle VM Server runs on any x86 machine and does not require an operating system to be installed on the server (this is known as bare-metal provisioning). Oracle VM Server is managed by Oracle VM Manager using a Web browser-based console. Oracle provides Oracle VM Server templates which are preinstalled and preconfigured software images that are designed to make configuring your virtualized operating system, database, middleware, or application software stack a fast and easy process.

Operating System Migration

In sticking with an as-is migration, the best option is not to move operating systems. If you decide to move directly to the Oracle cloud for the database or application tiers, you will have to move to Linux for the database and Linux or Solaris for the application. If your source operating system is UNIX, moving to Linux is not that difficult. A migration to Windows from Linux or UNIX is far more difficult.

SYSTEM, CUSTOMER ACCEPTANCE, AND PERFORMANCE TESTING

System testing performed by the IT staff or a third party typically comprises 10 percent to 20 percent of the overall migration effort. Customer acceptance testing involves more effort, since the complexity of the system being migrated impacts the magnitude of the effort, as shown in Table 2.6.

Table 2.6 System and Customer Acceptance Testing Level of Effort Based upon Migration Complexity

Complexity	Time Estimate
Simple	5–10 percent
Medium and complex	10–15 percent
Very complex	15–20 percent

Table 2.7 Performance and Tuning Level of Effort Based upon Migration Complexity

Complexity	Time Estimate
Simple	10–15 days
Medium	15–20 days
Complex	20–30 days
Very complex	30–40 days

Performance testing can take anywhere from 10 to 40 days depending on the complexity of the system, as illustrated in Table 2.7.

WARNING

Since testing typically comprises 30 percent of the overall effort to migrate, it is imperative that you include individuals from the Quality Assurance (QA) and IT staff that are familiar with any system testing tools the company may use. Perhaps your company has well-documented system test cases or tools that can expedite system and user acceptance testing. Determining how these tools can be used, or perhaps enhanced or modified, in the testing phase could have a significant positive impact on the length of the migration project.

MOVING TO PRODUCTION

The move to production is all about the size of the database, and the complexity (SQL complexity) and size (lines of code) of the applications accessing the database. These three components are mutually exclusive; you can have a very large database in which the application code is fewer than 500,000 lines (small in size) but contains very complex application business rules.

What constitutes a "large" database is a moving target. Five years ago a 500 GB database was considered large, and 10 years ago a 100 GB database was considered large. As disk speeds increase, high-speed disk interconnects are introduced, and the database engines themselves become more scalable and performant, the definition of a large database will change. Today, a database that is 500 GB or less can be migrated over the course of a weekend. Databases larger than 500 GB will take longer than a weekend to migrate and will require use of data replication technology which increases the time it takes to "unplug" the old system. Therefore, the old and new database systems will need to run in parallel for two to eight weeks while the new system is determined to be free of all issues. The same can be said for applications. Any application that contains more than 1 million lines of code will require an extra week or two to debug.

Large databases, complex applications, and applications with a sizable code base add time, cost, and risk to a migration project. With any production rollout, large or small, the new system will have some bugs. Resources will be required to test and implement the bug fixes.

OTHER THINGS TO CONSIDER

We do not cover IT training, user and technical documentation, and automated deployment tools in detail in this chapter as they vary greatly from customer to customer. Instead, we will provide a very high-level estimate of effort for these items. IT training will typically consume about two to three weeks for each key database developer and database administrator involved in the project. User and technical documentation can be a nonevent as in many cases they don't exist to begin with, or they can consume a considerable amount of time if they are extensive. Typically, user documentation does not need to change that much as we are not changing the user interface. Automated deployment tools that use a lot of database-specific calls will take days or weeks to migrate.

PROJECT MANAGEMENT AND ENTERPRISE ARCHITECT

A part-time enterprise architect and project manager will be required for a typically staffed migration project of four to six people. According to the IT project management "bible" *The Mythical Man-Month* [2], four to six people is used as a rule of thumb for projects that typically take 200 person days to complete. The idea is that adding more resources to a project will not reduce the length of the project, but rather will extend it. If the project exceeds 10 members, you will probably want to break the team into a database administration staff and a development staff and have a project manager for each team. In this case, the enterprise architect would become a full-time person. Companies migrating tens or hundreds of systems to the Oracle cloud have project managers and enterprise architects for a defined set of systems. These complex, multiyear migrations are usually managed by a large system integrator such as Tata Consultancy Services (TCS), Wipro Technologies, or Infosys that has experience in specialized migration practices. It is highly recommended that you involve a system integrator with experience in database and application migration projects. Some customers choose a system integrator because the system integrator is already working on an enterprise resource planning (ERP) system or because they already have a relationship with the system integrator. This approach can prove to be very costly and time-consuming as the system integrator needs migration expertise which is different from the expertise involved in implementing an ERP system.

MIGRATION EFFORT EXAMPLES

You can have the most complete estimating process and metric available, but the best indicator of project duration is past experience. Toward that end, we chose the following three projects to use as real-world example cases as they involve a variety of databases (SQL Server, Sybase, and DB2) across multiple languages (Visual Basic, PowerBuilder, and Java).

SQL Server Visual Basic Migration Estimate

This application was migrated for an ISV from SQL Server 2000 to Oracle 10g. The ISV was planning to integrate its shipping management solution with the Oracle Warehouse Management System that is part of the Oracle eBusiness Suite. The ISV wanted to have one database management and support technology for both its product and the Oracle eBusiness Suite. The database and application components were as follows:

- Application languages: Visual Basic and Visual C++
- Database connectivity: ODBC
- Tables: 150
- Database size: 2 GB
- Stored objects: 100 stored procedures, 50 triggers, and 5 views
- Application SQL: 1,500 SQL calls embedded in the application

Estimate

The project was scoped and completed by a niche system integrator, based in India, which performed 95 percent of the work offshore. The estimate called for a total of 56 days, with the following breakdown:

- Perform analysis/design, knowledge transfer, migration platform installation and configuration, and Oracle Workbench data and schema analysis: 5 days (2 people)
- Swap out ODBC drivers and test with application: 1 day
- Fix nonstandard SQL: 30 days (2 people)
- Fix very complex stored procedures and triggers: 10 days (1 person)
- Perform integration/system testing: 15 days (2 people)
- Conduct performance testing: 10 days (1 person)

The ISV performed a customer acceptance test. The fixed-price cost of the migration was $20,000.

Results

The project took one month longer to complete than first anticipated, due primarily to installation, configuration, and environment setup of the Visual Basic and Visual C++ development and ISV application code at the off-site India development center. As is typical in many migrations, all application components were not delivered, and many iterations occurred before all components were in place. Also, it took longer than expected for the system integrator to understand the functionality of the application so that it could be tested properly. The system integrator that performed the project did not make any money on this project because of time overruns that had nothing to do with scope changes or expansion of the work effort.

Sybase C++, PowerBuilder, Java, and Business Object Migration Estimate

This application concerned investment management, asset and fund administration, and fiduciary and banking solutions for corporations, institutions, and affluent individuals worldwide. The application was migrated from Sybase 12.5 to Oracle 11g. The customer was moving a data warehouse with data gathered from two separate Sybase servers. The database and application components were as follows:

- Application languages: 65 PowerBuilder objects, 25,000 lines of C++ code (Sybase Open Server), 3,500 lines of Java code, and business objects
- Database connectivity: ODBC and JDBC
- Tables: 46
- Database size: 500 GB
- Stored objects: 70 stored procedures with a total of 46,000 lines of code
- Middle Tier Application Server: Sybase Open Server with 16 registered stored procedures
- Application SQL: PowerBuilder with 173 data window components, 108 of which required changes
- Additional migration component: Sybase Direct Connect, as the second Sybase server was not being migrated off Sybase, so the migrated Oracle stored procedures needed to call these Sybase stored procedures, and Sybase Direct Connect provides this functionality

Estimate

The project was scoped and completed by a major system integrator, based in India, which completed 80 percent of the work offshore. The fixed-price cost of the migration was $140,000 for an elapsed time of 14 weeks. This included a two-week discovery period and a proof of concept for Sybase Direct Connect to call Oracle stored procedures from Sybase. The migration of Sybase Open Server registered procedures to Oracle and the use of Sybase Direct Connect added to the complexity of this project.

Results

This project had some cost and time overruns, which is typical of 80 percent of software IT projects. However, the project completion time was only extended by two weeks; this extension was to accommodate Sybase Open Server migration and performance testing of stored procedures, and installation and configuration of Sybase Direct Connect. This project resulted in a 10 times better performance on queries when comparing average query time between Sybase and Oracle.

DB2 PowerBuilder and Java Migration Estimate

This application was migrated for a provider of medical claims processing from a mainframe z/OS DB2 database to Oracle 11g. The application and database were migrated by two niche migration companies based in the United States. One company had deep expertise in PowerBuilder, Java, and Java EE and handled the application SQL and database migration connectivity changes. The other company had more than 30 years of experience performing DB2 mainframe migrations and therefore handled this portion of the project. The application architecture of this project may seem unique in that it is PowerBuilder with a mainframe z/OS DB2 database backend. However, a client/server application such as PowerBuilder talking to DB2 on a mainframe is fairly common. The database and application components were as follows:

- Application languages: PowerBuilder, Java, and Java EE
- Database connectivity: ODBC and JDBC
- Tables: 71
- Database size: 200 GB
- Stored objects: 35 stored procedures
- PowerBuilder source objects: 103
- Java source objects: 414
- Java EE source objects: 90
- Common Java utility source objects: 68

Estimate
The database migration (including DDL and data) and testing were estimated at 80 hours. This was a straightforward DDL and data migration using the migration vendors' internal tools.

The estimate to migrate the PowerBuilder application to run with an Oracle 11g database was four weeks. This included setting up PowerBuilder, identifying and changing the application SQL, supporting customer acceptance testing, and handling production rollout.

This application is a Web-based application written in Java and implementing Struts, Tiles, and some Web services based on Apache Axis. The Java portion was estimated to take approximately three weeks, not including two weeks of support during QA and two weeks following deployment to production.

The Java EE-based Web portal estimate was four weeks, not including two weeks of support during QA and two weeks following deployment to production. This included setting up PowerBuilder, identifying and changing the application SQL, conducting QA tests, supporting customer acceptance testing, deploying to the application server, and handling production rollout. It also included modifying and verifying at least six individual SQL calls, and modifying and verifying at least 35 individual stored procedure calls. The stored procedures were migrated by the customer.

Results
The cost of the migration increased from $160,000 to $420,000. This was largely due to significant scope creep; the number of application objects to be migrated more than doubled. Unit and system testing took months longer than expected because there was no access to the mainframe and any changes that needed to be

made to the Oracle database during testing needed to have a change order—even simple changes such as adding a database user or changing a column type on a migrated table. The move to production was delayed six months because of all the changes and delays.

However, the customer was very pleased with the results of the migration and is planning other migrations with these two partners. The customer was so confident in the lead system integrator's project management capabilities that the customer gave the system integrator overall project management responsibility after phasing out an independent consultant.

SUMMARY

Initial migration costs are just one component, and typically not the most expensive component, of the overall cost to migrate to the cloud. The three- to five-year hardware and software total cost of ownership, testing cost, and IT resource costs are the major costs inherent in a migration project.

The initial costs in terms of money and time are largely consumed by unit, system, and performance testing. The cost of the database migration effort is driven higher by the number of database stored objects and the volume of data involved. Application and integration infrastructure migrations are simplified if you choose to keep the same application languages and integration solutions. Hardware and software migrations to the cloud are simplified and reduced by using Oracle Exadata and Exalogic.

Migrating to the cloud is no different from migrating databases, applications, hardware, software, and other IT architecture components. Many niche and global system integrators have years of experience handling these types of migrations, as well as the tools, best practices, and methodologies required to quickly estimate a migration. This same expertise can be used to estimate your cloud migration effort.

Each migration project is unique. Custom-built ETL or integration solutions add two to three months to a project. Stored procedure generation tools add another two to three months. Extensive database administration monitoring and management tools can add one to two months. You may also choose to service-enable your client/server application which can provide Web accessibility, adaptable delivery, and business benefits with a limited time investment.

This chapter provided you with a solid framework, best practices, and precise percentages regarding where you will be spending your time in your migration effort. The real-world examples gave you empirical data. Both the Object Management Group[A] and Comsys-TIM[B] are working to collate empirical data from projects across

---

[A]OMG Software Metrics Meta-Model (SMM) [Internet]. Available from www.comsysprojects.com/SystemTransformation/tmmetricguide.htm.
[B]Comsys-TIM System Metric [Internet]. Available from www.comsysprojects.com/SystemTransformation/tmmetricguide.htm.

industries to come up with better estimating models for modernization and migration software projects.

In the next chapter, we will cover the overall migration phases and activities in detail. This is the next step in your cloud migration project.

Endnotes

[1]   McConnell S. Software Estimation: Demystifying the Black Art. Microsoft Press; 2006.

[2]   Frederick P. Brooks, Jr. The Mythical Man-Month, Anniversary Edition. Addison-Wesley Professional; 1995.

Methodology and Design

INFORMATION IN THIS CHAPTER:

- Migration Options
- Methodology and Design
- Migration Services

Like any software development project, migration projects require careful planning and good methodology to ensure successful execution. When migrating from one database platform to another a good portion of the database design can be carried forward, especially the schema design for relational database migrations. It may be necessary to make some changes to the existing design and architecture if you want to leverage new features in the Oracle database in favor of older mechanisms, such as using database table partitioning and Oracle Real Application Clusters (RAC) to support multiple workloads instead of maintaining different databases in sync with database replication technologies. Therefore, a certain amount of rationalization is possible when migrating to Oracle from other databases, resulting in consolidation of many databases and schemas from the source database into a few schemas in Oracle. To enable such rationalizations and other optimizations in database design, it is essential to understand a typical migration project life cycle and the importance of each phase in it. Many factors affect the success of a migration project, such as availability of a skilled IT staff, tools, and technologies for migration, an understanding of the source and target database architectures, and realistic project planning. Identifying these factors before embarking on a new migration project can speed up execution and help you to craft efficient solutions for challenges encountered along the way.

MIGRATION OPTIONS

Of all the options for client/server application migrations compared in Table 1.4 in Chapter 1, database migration is the most common because it allows users to migrate to new database platforms, yet leave applications intact, with no changes to existing functionality and business rules, including the languages in which the applications were originally developed. This approach provides the easiest migration path to a new platform, and ensures business continuity in the new environment, along with fewer upheavals. In cases where applications have become very difficult to maintain and update with new features to support business requirements, they are rewritten in new languages that leverage the latest technologies and standards. Such migrations turn into completely new software design and development projects instead of just platform migration efforts. In cases where the business functionality provided by an application is critical for the business and the goal is to make the application accessible from various channels (browser, mobile devices, etc.), the application is typically retooled to run in an environment which emulates a server to allow multiclient, multichannel access.

Legacy applications deployed on IBM mainframes and other proprietary and legacy platforms are usually retooled to run on open and distributed platforms using software that can mimic IBM mainframe environments or that can effectively provide the same capabilities on their own (e.g., Oracle Tuxedo).

Which migration option you choose will depend on your business requirements and constraints (e.g., time, cost, and feasibility). The easiest migration option is to Web service-enable an existing application so that it can interact with other applications on the Web or with applications deployed in a cloud environment. Of course, this approach also requires that these applications be modified to incorporate Web service capabilities by using either third-party solutions or native features, without requiring significant modification. Even if an application written in a language such as Visual Basic or PowerBuilder is not able to access other applications over the network, it can be modified to do so. It is also not necessary for every program comprising an application to be modified. Only programs that provide important reusable business services need to be identified and modified to Web service-enable them. Migration options such as database platform migrations and replatforming applications developed on legacy platforms are very popular because they are easier to execute and realize the benefits of such migrations quickly. On the other hand, migration options involving a complete rewrite/rearchitecture of an application or development of a completely new piece of software are less likely to be chosen due to the cost and time involved in executing such projects.

Lately, new technologies have emerged that aim to provide database transparency to applications. These technologies basically allow you to capture database calls issued by an application and then translate them on the fly to execute them against the target database. The goal of this approach is to significantly reduce application changes as a result of database migrations. However, organizations need to thoroughly test these technologies for performance and for accuracy of the converted SQL statements before deploying them in mission-critical environments. Some database vendors are making big claims that, using these technologies, database migrations can be completed within weeks. However, from the authors' experience, testing alone requires significant effort. These emerging technologies definitely have a role in reducing the overall migration effort in large migration projects by reducing changes to the application due to database migrations.

METHODOLOGY AND DESIGN

Regardless of the migration option chosen for implementation, a sound migration methodology and design needs to be in place before embarking on such a project.

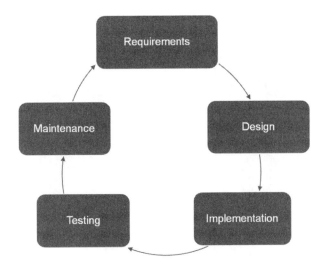

FIGURE 3.1

Waterfall Software Development Methodology

Traditional software development methodologies such as Waterfall consist of the distinct phases of requirements gathering, design, implementation, testing, and maintenance, as illustrated in Figure 3.1.

The Waterfall methodology can be applied to migration projects, but sometimes the requirements gathering phase is replaced with an assessment phase. For instance, for migrations involving a full rewrite or significant transformation to existing applications, the requirements gathering phase is applicable. In projects in which only the database platforms are being considered for migration, there is no need to gather business requirements again, since existing applications already have all the business rules and requirements taken care of. So, instead of requirements gathering, an assessment phase is used to understand the existing environment and determine the best way to migrate it to a new environment. Unlike Waterfall methodology, phases in a migration life cycle can be carried out in parallel (e.g., unit/functional testing of application and database components as and when they are migrated). Similarly, performance testing of some components can be performed before the application/database migration is complete.

Migration of one database platform to another requires some changes to existing applications due to the technical differences between various databases. Figure 3.2 illustrates a typical migration life cycle.

Let's take an in-depth look at each phase in the life cycle of a migration project.

Assessment

The assessment phase is akin to the requirements gathering phase of the Waterfall method for software development. Instead of gathering business requirements

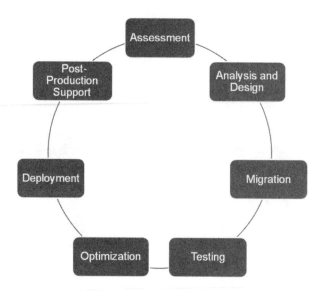

FIGURE 3.2

A Typical Migration Project Life Cycle

from a software development perspective, however, you collect information pertaining to project management (who will manage the project, and how), the potential cost of the migration, migration approaches, tools to use, and so on. In this phase, a detailed inventory of the application portfolio is created to assess the impact of database platform migration on the IT ecosystem, including other applications, integration services, reporting, and backup and recovery processes. For a thorough assessment, the following topics are typically of interest in this phase:

- **Drivers for migration (challenges, requirements)** It is very important to understand the drivers behind a migration effort. For example, if the customer's licenses for legacy technologies are expiring soon, their need to migrate to a newer platform is urgent. The expiry of official support and the extension of support for an existing database platform may be very expensive for such customers, so they must migrate quickly, but they may not need to transform their applications, so they would prefer very few changes to their applications as a result of the migration.
- **Inventory of current environment** Creating a detailed inventory of the current application portfolio really helps in terms of understanding the scope of a migration effort. This includes capturing information regarding the number of programs, scripts, and external interfaces involved. It also includes hardware and software configuration information, including operating system versions, database versions, features/functionalities in use, and similar information.

- **Migration tools/options**   It is not uncommon to test different migration tools and technologies to assess their efficiency and accuracy. A high level of automation along with accuracy in migration can result in less time spent in migration and testing. Many customers conduct small-scale proof-of-concept projects to try different migration options, such as emulation or wrapper technologies, which allow applications to communicate with a different database without requiring code changes in the application. This can reduce the overall migration effort in cases where the application is simple and does not have demanding performance requirements.

WARNING

Always choose a migration tool or vendor that has been proven, and does not claim to support migration of any programming language or database on the fly. In almost all cases, when vendors spend a significant amount of time enhancing their tools instead of actually performing migrations, some modification to the tools is essential to address fringe cases of programming language or database feature usage that cannot be automatically converted. Establish verifiable success criteria for these migration tools and/or vendors so that the chances of failure are reduced during migration project execution.

- **Migration service provider**   Businesses typically evaluate at least a couple of migration service providers if they do not have migration skills and staff in-house. In many cases, migration service providers utilize their own tools to perform detailed assessment and migration.
- **Migration effort estimate**   This is usually provided by the migration service provider or database vendor and is the most common information businesses request when considering a migration project. We discussed how to estimate a migration effort in detail in Chapter 2. As we noted, the estimate depends on factors such as database and application size, components, and database complexity factors, among others.
- **Training requirements**   Training requirements for existing IT staff on the new database platform need to be assessed to ensure that they can support the new environment effectively and can participate in the migration process if required. Therefore, it is important to identify appropriate training programs for the IT staff based on their roles in the organization. The most common training programs recommended for database administrators and developers who are new to Oracle database are:
  - Introduction to the Oracle Database
  - SQL, PL/SQL Application Development in Oracle
  - Oracle Database Administration
  - Oracle Database Performance Tuning

Knowledge transfer can also take place from the migration project team to the administration and development teams that will be responsible for maintaining the new system in the future.

- **IT resource requirement for the target database**   Requirements for deploying the new database environment also need to be assessed. This assessment should include critical database features and functions as well as additional software that may be required to support the migration process and maintain the migration after it has been deployed. These resources typically include hardware, storage, and Oracle software, including the Oracle database and Oracle SQL Developer, and optionally, Oracle GoldenGate. For virtualization in a cloud environment, Oracle VM software can also be used.
- **IT resource requirement for the migration project**   Resources such as the hardware and software required for performing migration tasks also need to be identified. Organizations may need to acquire new hardware and software to support the migration project, or they can provision these resources from a cloud service provider (Infrastructure as a Service [IaaS] and Platform as a Service [PaaS]).

Sufficient time needs to be allocated for this phase to have a complete and meaningful assessment of the migration process. It is not uncommon to see large IT organizations with tens of databases to migrate spending eight to 12 weeks performing a full assessment. When performing in-depth assessments to assist in migration projects, system integrators use an array of tools that capture exhaustive amounts of information from the source systems; this information helps them analyze the dependencies between an application's various components and the database, as well as the complexity of the migration effort. These tools analyze every application program and every line of code in these programs to paint a detailed picture. The following information helps a system integrator assess the impact of a database migration on an organization's applications:

- **Programs interacting directly with the database**   This helps the system integrator to identify the number of programs that may require changes to SQL statements or changes to database-specific APIs.
- **Programs or other applications that execute transactions directly**   This helps the system integrator to identify programs that may be impacted if there are any changes to transactional behavior in the target database (Oracle), such as:
  - Programs that have explicit transaction control statements in them (e.g., `COMMIT/ROLLBACK`). Typically, these programs maintain control over a transaction they initiate.
  - Programs that invoke a stored procedure to initiate a transaction, but have no control over the transaction. In this case, the stored procedure maintains control over a transaction.
  - Programs that issue explicit Data Manipulation Language (DML) statements (e.g., `INSERT/UPDATE/DELETE`), but do not control the full transaction. In many cases, a master program initiates these programs to execute database transactions and return results.
- **Programs or scripts that offload data from or load data into the source database**   These programs will need to eventually be modified to include

changes such as use of Oracle database-specific utilities, associated commands, and parameters, as well as changes to any embedded SQL.

- **The number of management or database administration scripts**   Identifying such scripts helps the system integrator estimate the effort involved in migrating these scripts by either rewriting them or discarding them completely to use Oracle-specific tools such as Oracle Enterprise Manager (OEM) for routine administration and monitoring tasks.

- **The type and number of external interfaces**   All of these interfaces need to be further analyzed to estimate the migration effort.

It is best to capture as much information as possible in the assessment phase and to analyze it to thwart any technical challenges that may emerge during migration. This also has the benefit of building comprehensive documentation in the long run.

> **NOTE**
> The assessment phase tends to consist of an intense exercise during which crucial decisions affecting the migration project are made. Sometimes organizations spend months instead of weeks finalizing their choice of migration strategy, tools, and service provider. Many service providers offer in-depth assessment as a paid service for performing an inventory of the current environment and reporting on the dependencies among various applications, impact analysis, and feature/functionality usage. During the assessment phase, it is quite common for organizations to conduct pilot projects to prove that the choices that have been made will help the organization achieve its goal.

Analysis and Design

The analysis and design phase usually consists of determining the implementation details on the target (Oracle) database. Because of the differences in implementation of data types, security roles and privileges, transaction management, and SQL code, it is important to develop a plan that leverages appropriate features and functionalities in the Oracle database. Care must also be taken to ensure that the chosen features do not result in an increase in application code changes or a decrease in data quality in terms of truncation of data elements such as digits or milliseconds from timestamp data. The following are the most important issues that need to be addressed during this phase:

- **Database schema layout**   It is very important to consider how to map the source database schema in Oracle as this can impact the applications and SQL statements embedded within it. Databases differ in how their database schemas, users, and objects are organized. Many databases support multiple databases under one database engine (governing processes). Under each database, objects can be organized in terms of schemas and users. Oracle, on the other hand, supports only one database per instance (or engine) and allows creation of multiple schemas within a database. This difference in database schema layout between Oracle and other databases can result in a collision of objects in the target database schema as other databases allow objects with the same name but with different structures to exist under different databases. As a result, new schemas may need to be created in Oracle and suitable modifications may need to be carried out in the applications to reflect the new database schema layout in Oracle.

- **Database object naming convention**   Three major issues usually come up during database migrations to the Oracle database with respect to database object naming convention:

  - **Use of reserved words**   Databases differ significantly in what they consider *reserved* words (i.e., words that cannot be used as object names or column names in database tables). This is because databases use these words internally in their software for data processing. During migration, it is possible that some database tables and their column names might run into this restriction on the target database (Oracle). Many migration tools, including Oracle's SQL Developer, provide information on such a possibility. These tools can also convert object names, using a predetermined convention, to an acceptable name in Oracle.

  - **Object name length restrictions**   Oracle also imposes an additional restriction of 30 characters in terms of length of database object names. Some databases, such as Microsoft SQL Server, allow object names up to 128 characters in length. So, during migration to an Oracle database, object names that violate this restriction need to be dealt with. The Oracle SQL Developer tool can identify such cases and generate a report that can help developers keep track of areas where this issue will impact the application.

  - **Use of special characters in object names**   Use of special characters such as # as the first character for object names in an Oracle database is not allowed; this is not an issue in other databases. As a result, such objects have to be renamed in the Oracle database during conversion, which may result in changes in the applications accessing those objects.

- **Data type mapping**   All databases support a variety of data types to handle numeric, character, large object, XML, and timestamp data. Data types available for handling numeric, character, and timestamp data are mostly standard, but they differ significantly in terms of limits on data length and precision allowed. The most common issues encountered during database migration to Oracle are:

  - **Lack of a Boolean data type or BIT data type**   The Oracle database does not have support for Boolean data types and BIT data types. So, while migrating to Oracle, these data types have to be converted to either a single-digit numeric or a single-character data type.

  - **Lack of proprietary data types such as** TIMESTAMP **in Sybase**   Some databases allow creation of special columns in tables (e.g., TIMESTAMP) that the database updates as and when a record in the table is accessed. The Oracle database does not support any such data types similar to what the Sybase database offers in the form of its TIMESTAMP data type.

- **Locking behavior**   Most relational databases require temporary locking of rows in tables when a user accesses the rows as a result of database query execution (e.g., `SELECT` statements). Because of this behavior, these databases may suffer from periodic lock escalations when under heavy load. Oracle, however, does not require row locking when simply reading rows. Instead, it supports true row-level locking and provides a read-consistent view of data. Along the same lines, other databases also allow reading of uncommitted data (a.k.a. dirty reads). This feature is typically implemented with the help of an isolation level in the database, which is traditionally used for reading data from tables without locking them. Oracle does not support this feature. Therefore, applications that use this feature need to be evaluated thoroughly to implement an efficient solution in Oracle.

- **Use of `COMMIT`/`ROLLBACK` in triggers**   Oracle does not allow use of any transaction control statements such as `COMMIT`/`ROLLBACK` in triggers. Some databases, such as Sybase, allow partial control (commit/rollback) of SQL statements that are also executed within a trigger. As such, migrating from a database that supports this behavior to the Oracle database requires changes in the trigger code. SQL Developer automatically converts these statements to autonomous transactions where applicable, but this may also have an impact on the overall transaction flow in the application, and therefore appropriate measures must be taken for remediation.

- **Use of zero-length strings (empty strings)**   Unlike Oracle, most databases support the notion of empty strings that have zero length but are not considered `NULL` (i.e., unknown). Oracle, on the other hand, does not support zero-length strings. In Oracle, if a column does not have any value, it is considered to have a `NULL` value. So, when migrating applications to Oracle from another database, it is necessary to convert any predicates that evaluate a table's column to a zero-length string to a comparison with a `NULL`. In Oracle, there is a difference between comparing a column to a `NULL` value and to an empty string and how the database engine resolves such a comparison. For example, the following query will not evaluate to `TRUE` in Oracle and will not return any rows, even if there is a row in the `EMP` table where the `MGR` column has no value (i.e., a zero-length string). Notice the use of the predicate involving a zero-length string.

```
SELECT * FROM EMP WHERE mgr = ' ';
```

However, the following SQL statement will evaluate to a `TRUE` condition in Oracle and return rows. Notice the predicate involving an evaluation for the `NULL` value.

```
SELECT * FROM EMP WHERE MGR IS NULL;
```

- **Case insensitivity**   This feature in a database allows data to be retrieved regardless of whether the search criteria match the data in the database (e.g., the data in the database may be in uppercase letters and the search criteria may be in lowercase or mixed-case letters). Obviously, this feature is implemented to enhance the user experience. Databases differ in terms of how they facilitate this feature in a database. Microsoft SQL Server allows enabling of case sensitivity by setting the COLLATE parameter at the database level or at the column level in a table. When you set this parameter at the database level, all tables support case-insensitive searches on them. In Oracle, this can be achieved in three ways.

1. Set up parameters pertaining to sorting and computational evaluations at the instance level (in the configuration file spfile.ora). The two parameters that control this behavior in Oracle are:
   * NLS_SORT=BINARY_CI (Default: BINARY)
   * NLS_COMP=LINGUISTIC (Default: ANSI)

2. To enable this feature in Oracle at the session level, the two parameters mentioned in the instance level configuration (i.e., the NLS_SORT and NLS_COMP parameters) can be set at the session level by issuing the following commands in the Oracle database using a tool such as SQL*Plus or some other database development tool:

```
alter session set NLS_SORT = 'BINARY_CI';
alter session set NLS_COMP = 'LINGUISTIC';
```

> **NOTE**
>
> To execute these commands the database user needs the ALTER SESSION privilege.

3. At the SQL Query level, this feature can be enabled by adding appropriate clauses in the SQL statement. For example:

```
Select * from scott.emp where NLSSORT (''ENAME'','nls_sort='
'BINARY_CI') =(NLSSORT('Miller','nls_sort=''BINARY_CI'''))
```

> **TIP**
>
> To ensure optimal performance for case-insensitive queries involving tables with large volumes of data, it is recommended that indexes also be created on the columns used for these queries, using the NLS_SORT clause as illustrated in option 3 (i.e., enablement at the query level). An index can be created as follows:
> CREATE INDEX ENAME_IDX ON SCOTT.EMP (NLSSORT
>   (''ENAME'', 'nls_sort=''BINARY_CI'''));

It is also possible to use the UPPER() function or the NLS_UPPER() function in SQL statements to convert the data fetched from tables as well as input identifiers into UPPERCASE. As discussed in option 3, this will require creating a functional index on the columns used for case-insensitive searches and modifying SQL statements to incorporate these functions. There may be other design issues specific to the source database in terms of how a particular feature or functionality has been exploited to facilitate a specific business requirement. Careful consideration and resolution to these design issues is essential to ward off any potential roadblocks during migration and post-migration efforts.

Migration

The amount of time it takes to complete the actual migration of objects and data from one database is relatively less than the amount of time it takes to complete an overall migration from assessment to production rollout. Migrations of one relational database to another are comparatively easier than migrations of a non-relational database to a relational database, because the organization of objects in a relational database is quite similar compared to non-relational databases such as hierarchical and network databases. All major relational database vendors also offer tools that provide robust migration capabilities in an automated fashion. Regardless of the level of automation and success factor of any migration tool, however, sometimes manual intervention will be required when migrating from one database to another. Database migration tasks can be divided into the following categories:

- Database schema migration
- Data migration
- Database stored program migration
- Application migration
- Database administration script migration

Of all the migration tasks listed, the application migration task requires the most manual effort, although new tools and technologies are being developed to facilitate this task. We will cover database schema migration and data migration tasks in more detail in Chapter 5, and we will discuss application migration in detail in Chapter 8. In this chapter, we will focus on best practices for executing these tasks.

Database Schema Migration

Database schema migration essentially involves migration tables, indexes, and views in a database. Relational databases are similar in terms of how their data is organized in tables and indexes, but they are different in terms of additional extensions to these tables and indexes that are designed to improve performance and facilitate development. Most migration tools can convert the database schema relatively quickly and accurately. Target-specific database schemas can also be generated from modelling tools such as Erwin. These are the most important things to consider during database schema migration:

- **Ensuring completeness of the schema**   It is necessary to ensure that all objects from the source database have been migrated over to the target database. It is very common to have multiple schemas and databases to support an application. Having circular dependencies among multiple schemas and databases may result in errors during schema creation on the target database, as some of these dependencies may not exist when a particular schema is being migrated. After creating all the schemas in Oracle, all the objects that are marked as invalid need to be recompiled and verified to ensure that they are migrated successfully.

- **Tables with system functions as** `DEFAULT` **value clauses on columns** Many databases support having system functions as the `DEFAULT` value clauses on table columns. In almost all cases, these system functions do not exist in the Oracle database. As a result, some tables may not be created in Oracle, making other dependent objects invalid. It is recommended that you analyze the log resulting from the schema creation task, and isolate and rectify such errors.

- **Using clustered indexes** Clustered indexes in databases such as Sybase allow data storage in a physically sorted fashion to match the logical order (index). As data is added, it is sorted and stored in the order defined by the clustered index. This helps to reduce the time it takes to return the sorted data and to retrieve data by co-locating the index as well as the actual data in the same object. The Oracle database provides similar functionality with index-organized tables (IOTs). In IOTs, the primary key columns and the non-key data are stored in the same object. This helps users avoid having to look up data in tables separately, after index lookups, while executing a query in Oracle.

- **Creating database users and role assignment** Proper database roles and privileges on objects must be assigned to users. Schema and object-level privileges can be grouped into roles and assigned to users as needed. Creating roles and granting them to users can help in managing many object-level privileges.

- **Changing object names** Any changes to the database object names due to restrictions in the database, as discussed in the "Analysis and Design" section of this chapter, need to be identified and shared with all team members so that they can make suitable changes in their applications or other database components.

- **Partitioning database tables** Oracle allows large tables to be partitioned into smaller segments for management ease and for better performance due to the database query optimizer's ability to prune partitions during query execution, resulting in a reduction in the overall amount of data scanned. Based on data volume, performance, and manageability requirements, some tables may be chosen for partitioning. Although many relational databases support table partitioning, they implement this feature differently in terms of the methods allowed for partitioning, such as range, hash, and composite partitioning. Migration tools generally do not migrate partitioning-related information when migrating database schemas. Therefore, it is important to consider an appropriate partitioning strategy in Oracle after schema migration and before data migration.

Data Migration

After database schema migration, some representative data from the source database is migrated to the target database to enable testing and to ensure that the data migration scripts or tools chosen for the task are configured properly. The most common approach for data migration is undoubtedly the use of scripts that execute database utilities to export data from the source database and import it into the target database (Oracle), because they are easy to use and are free.

Regardless of the tools and scripts used to perform data migration, migrations of very large databases require planning. When migrating very large databases (those with at least a few terabytes of data) it is important to have the right data migration strategy, have the appropriate tools, and, most importantly, use appropriate database features such as partitioning and compression. Migration of large databases is fraught with challenges, among them a narrow window of time and lack of system resources (e.g., staging areas for data files). The following data extraction and loading strategies can optimize the data extraction, transfer, and loading processes:

- Parallel extraction of data from the source database
- Loading of data into the target database in parallel
- Using multithreaded processes for data loading
- Avoidance of index maintenance during the data loading process
- Reduction of I/O operations and use of staging areas via named pipes for data transfer between source and target databases

The data migration task is less time-consuming than migration and testing of database stored programs and application migration. Data migration tasks can be categorized into the following three modes:

- **Offline data migration**   As the name implies, data in this mode is migrated in a disconnected or offline mode (i.e., data from the source database is extracted into flat files and then loaded into the target database using native tools and scripts). Because the extraction and the loading processes are disconnected from one another, users can load data whenever they have some downtime in the database, or during off-peak hours. This is typically accomplished using native tools and scripts provided by the database vendors (e.g., Oracle SQL*Loader from Oracle, and LOAD/UNLOAD utilities provided by the IBM DB2 database).
- **Online data migration**   Data migration in this mode involves connecting to the source and target databases using Java Database Connectivity (JDBC) or Open Database Connectivity (ODBC) drivers, or database gateways, and then migrating between them. As the name suggests, during the data migration, both databases have to be available for connections, and network connectivity between the two is required. Usually, this mode is used for smaller databases with workloads that aren't very heavy. Since data migration in this mode can generate additional load on the source system (CPU, memory, I/O operations), thereby impacting application performance, it is usually not recommended for large databases or heavily used databases.
- **Changed data capture (CDC)**   CDC involves tracking changes occurring on the source database and then periodically replicating those changes to the target database. This is a very useful method for migrating very large databases with little or no downtime availability. CDC can be implemented in two ways:
  - **Using log mining**   This is the most commonly used technique for implementing CDC. Log mining involves reading the online or archived transaction logs from databases and extracting transactions from them as they are

executed. After the changes are captured from the source, they are either stored in an intermediate file to be transmitted later to the target database, or immediately transferred and applied to the target database. This method is very popular because it introduces less overhead on the source system in terms of performance impact on existing databases and applications, and it is easy to set up and perform.

- **Using triggers**   With this method, triggers are implemented in the source database to capture changes and write them to a staging table; the changes are then replicated to the target database. Creating new triggers on source database tables is a cumbersome process that is fraught with challenges. In addition, this method significantly impacts the performance of the source system, and as such, it is not the most popular method for capturing changed data.

Oracle offers a variety of tools that support all the data migration tasks we've discussed. It also offers rich features and products that can optimize the loading, organization, and retrieval of data from the database. Table 3.1 illustrates various Oracle products and technologies that can be used for data migration tasks as appropriate.

Chapter 4 digs deeper into each product mentioned in the table. In large migration projects, a combination of the products mentioned in Table 3.1 can be leveraged.

Database Stored Program Migration

The task of migrating database stored programs includes migration of stored procedures, triggers, and views which, in many relational databases, are used for implementing critical business logic. In databases such as Microsoft SQL Server and Sybase, stored procedures and triggers are used extensively by developers to support simple functions (e.g., the CRUD operations CREATE, READ, UPDATE, and DELETE). However, using stored procedures exclusively for CRUD operations can result in

Table 3.1 Oracle Offerings for Various Data Migration Tasks

Data Migration Method	Oracle Offerings
Offline data migration	Oracle SQL*Loader utility, Oracle External Table database feature Oracle SQL Developer and Oracle Data Integrator can generate the scripts for performing offline data extraction and loading.
Online data migration	Oracle SQL Developer, Oracle Data Integrator, Oracle Database gateways
Changed data capture (using log mining)	Oracle GoldenGate and Oracle Data Integrator (for DB2/400, Oracle)
Changed data capture (using triggers)	Oracle Data Integrator (for most databases)

inflexibility because the type of operation executed against a table is limited by the functionality implemented in the stored procedure.

Major tasks associated with stored program migration are:

- **Cleaning and optimizing code**   Oracle SQL Developer and other migration tools support migration of stored programs very well. However, it is recommended that you test these converted stored procedures and triggers for accuracy and efficiency of the converted code. Developers can implement a simple business requirement in many ways, making it harder for tools to optimize all such coding techniques in the converted code. Stored procedures and functions with hundreds of lines of code or more should be verified and tested for efficiency in terms of database feature usage as well as optimized coding practices.
- **Handling errors in stored procedures and triggers**   For applications that depend heavily on stored procedures and triggers, it is very common to see nested stored procedure calls. Automated migrations may not be able to handle error handling for nested stored procedure invocation. Therefore, it is necessary to pay close attention to error handling, especially for nested stored procedure invocations.
- **Using temporary tables extensively**   Some database developers use temporary tables extensively to simplify queries and avoid writing a complex query involving several tables. Early versions of some databases also had restrictions on the number of tables that could be joined in a query efficiently. Therefore, migrating stored procedures with lots of temporary tables warrants a closer look so that they can be avoided and can result in simplified code that leverages the native features of an Oracle database. Typically, migration tools maintain a one-to-one mapping of temporary tables during migration from one database to another. But important stored procedures which are executed very often and have demanding performance requirements should be examined thoroughly to eliminate unnecessary temporary tables in the new environment.
- **Converting stored procedures into functions**   The Oracle database does not support returning results to callers using the RETURN verb in stored procedures. This verb is only allowed in Oracle stored functions and not in stored procedures. However, it is very common to find Sybase and Microsoft SQL Server stored procedures using the OUT parameter as well as the RETURN verb to pass values and data to the caller. Converting these stored procedures into functions in Oracle also results in a different call signature (i.e., the syntax for executing a stored procedure versus executing a stored function is different because stored functions in Oracle *must* return a value).
- **Determining the impact of stored procedures returning result sets on Java applications (JDBC)**   The Oracle database returns result sets to caller programs via explicitly defined OUT variables in stored procedures. However, other databases return multiple result sets implicitly, without having to declare variables to do so. This results in additional changes to Java programs when migrating to

Oracle, such as declaring additional variables, binding, and explicit access of these variables for result set data. We will discuss this issue in more detail in Chapter 7.

Application Migration

Application migration or porting can result from either migrating an application from one environment to another due to a complete rewrite, or simply from an underlying database platform that is being migrated to a new platform such as Oracle. Typically, application development falls into two categories:

- **Customized application development** In this category, applications are generally developed in-house, by IT organizations, to support business functions. These applications almost always try to leverage all the native features of the database platform, as well as other IT systems in the organization, to drive maximum performance and tighter integration. As a result, applications tend to be heavily dependent on the database platform in which they were initially developed. As a result, any change to the database platform may result in changes to the applications. Features and functionalities leveraged by these applications also depend on the developer's skill set. Developers try to use the features they are most comfortable with. Once an application becomes obsolete due to a lack of the skills required to maintain its features, or due to the application becoming too brittle to add new features, the application is migrated to a new environment.
- **Generic application development (or packaged applications)** Typically, this category applies to independent software vendors (ISVs). ISVs develop generic application software that caters to a particular industry or a vertical market. They also tend to develop applications that do not depend heavily on the database. In fact, major ISVs offer versions of applications based on a particular database platform. Migration of a packaged application from one database to another involves installing and configuring the new version of the packaged application and importing the data and all the customizations from the original application. This is by no means a trivial task, because thorough testing needs to be done after the migration. From time to time, ISVs are forced to add support for new databases to their application software due to customer demand. They are also under pressure to maintain a single or as few codebases as possible to reduce the effort involved in managing multiple codebases, each catering to a different database, because this means that if they have to implement a new feature, they will have to modify all the application codebases in a similar fashion and ensure consistency across them.

From a migration perspective, customized applications are always migrated to new database platforms fully, because there is no need for them to support both the old and new database platforms in the long run. These applications can be changed to take full advantage of the new database platform. But ISVs need to support all existing database platforms, even as they add support for new databases. So, for them, it becomes a porting effort because they are simply adding more code to an existing application so that it will also work with the new database. ISVs try to reduce the application software codebase by using conditional coding practices such as conditional branches to a different piece of code, depending on the database platform on which it is deployed. Very large enterprise resource planning (ERP) software packages usually have separate codebases for each database.

As we mentioned when we were discussing the migration assessment phase, understanding the impact of database platform migration on applications is very important. Applications depend on the database platform in many ways:

- **Database-specific connection information** Every database requires certain information to establish a connection with it. In the event of a database change, this information has to be updated in the applications that connect to a specific database. If every single program in an application connects to the database directly, instead of relying on a central database access layer, this otherwise trivial task becomes a challenge. This task can be automated through the use of scripts from the operating system to search and replace appropriate connection strings in application programs.

- **Use of database-specific parameters** ODBC/JDBC drivers for database vendors have different parameters to support different requirements, such as transaction control, date/timestamp formats, and so forth. The Oracle JDBC driver, by default, enables AUTO COMMIT on a connection. This might create problems, especially when calling a database stored procedure in Oracle which leverages global temporary tables. Having set the AUTO COMMIT by default, the data in temporary tables will be deleted after any data manipulation statement (INSERT, DELETE, or UPDATE). To avoid this scenario, AUTO COMMIT for a JDBC connection should be explicitly disabled. For example:

```
Conn.setAutoCommit(false);
```

- **Use of database-specific SQL statements** Using database-specific SQL statements with proprietary extensions requires changes when the database platform changes. It is a big challenge to identify how many application programs need to be changed because of their usage of SQL statements that do not conform to American National Standards Institute (ANSI) SQL standards or that are not supported by the Oracle database. In the assessment phase, there is a great deal of emphasis on identifying such programs and their database interactions in general (i.e., calling stored procedures, result set processing, embedded SQL usage, etc.).

- **Invoking database stored procedures and functions that return result sets** Applications using ODBC/OLEDB drivers generally do not need to be modified when the database is migrated to Oracle. However, as of the latest release of Oracle Database 11g R2 (11.2.0.1), Java applications using the Oracle JDBC driver invoking stored procedures returning result sets from the database need to be modified to accommodate Oracle-specific requirements in terms of including bind variables for result sets, processing of multiple result sets, and similar functionality. Hopefully, these changes will not be necessary in future releases of the Oracle database.

- **APIs for manipulation of large objects**   There are differences in JDBC APIs used for manipulating large objects in Oracle as compared to databases such as Informix.

Database Administration Script Migration

It is common to use scripts to automate general database administration tasks. Database administrators love to develop their own scripts to administer databases. However, using scripts to administer databases can complicate things because when script writers leave an organization, new administrators do not have full knowledge of how to use those scripts effectively. Scripts that are used for performance monitoring, and database administration tasks such as user mainte-nance, object maintenance, and database maintenance, need not be migrated to Oracle due to the availability of OEM, which can manage and monitor databases, application servers, and storage from a central console. Scripts that are used to extract or load data as part of batch processes executed from job schedulers may need to be migrated to make use of Oracle utilities (e.g., SQL*Loader, Data Pump, etc.) to perform similar functions. Oracle provides a rich set of tools to manage these processes—among them Oracle Data Integrator (ODI) and Oracle Warehouse Builder (OWB)—which don't require much coding. However, scripts leveraging native database utilities for data loading/unloading need to be ported to use Oracle database utilities instead.

Testing

Effort involved in testing the application and the database after migration usually is the largest contributor to the migration effort. Testing in a migration project usually comprises tasks such as data verification, testing of migrated business logic in stored procedures, functions, and triggers, testing of application interaction with the new database platforms, and testing of database maintenance scripts. Some of these tasks can be performed easily with the help of automated tools or relatively simple scripting. But some tasks, such as testing of database objects with business logic, can be cumbersome because of lack of automated testing tools. Also, any existing scripts that are currently in use in the source environment need to be ported to the new environment first, and they also need to be tested.

Let's take a look at the various tools and strategies that are used for each of these tasks:

- **Data verification**   The easiest way to ensure that the data migrated from a database to Oracle is accurate is to monitor the data migration process closely and ensure that no errors are reported during the process. Even if the migration tools do not report errors, issues such as truncation of decimal values and character data fields may result due to improper sizing of the columns in the target database. Migration of Unicode data also needs attention. Oracle's GoldenGate Veridata can be used for side-by-side comparisons of data between two databases; however, it supports only a few databases (SQL Server, Oracle, Teradata, HP Enscribe, and HP SQL/MP). More information about Oracle GoldenGate Veridata is available at www.oracle.com/us/products/middleware/data-integration/059246 .html. System integrators generally have their own toolsets that can assist with the data verification process.

- **Testing of database stored procedures and functions**   Usually these objects are unit-tested as they are migrated for syntactic and semantic accuracy. However, after migration of an entire database, it is necessary to test the interdependencies among different database objects. Oracle SQL Developer provides features for unit-testing a stored procedure and/or function. However, sometimes it is very difficult to come up with all the possible combinations of parameter values that stored procedures or functions can accept. Therefore, having all the test cases properly documented and scripted can assist significantly in testing efforts.

- **Application testing**   In most organizations, testing of custom applications developed in-house is performed by users who work their way through the user interfaces manually based on documented test cases. ISVs, on the other hand, usually have automated test suites available to test full applications. Testing tools such as the Oracle Application Testing Suite (OATS) can be used for functional and load testing of applications for scalability and performance, as it can assist in building test cases from scratch, especially for Web applications. OATS can record all interactions taking place via Web applications and replay them to test how the application interacts with the new database.

- **Database maintenance script testing**   It is very important to test any scripts associated with database backup and recovery tasks. Most backup and recovery tasks can be automated using OEM, and scripts and commands used by OEM for performing these tasks can also be reused. Testing of these scripts is a manual process that needs to be carried out in an isolated environment. The Oracle database also provides alternative ways to perform database backups, such as using disk-based backups to automatically perform incremental backups and recovery operations.

If a system integrator is chosen to perform the migration, testing usually becomes a part of the service offering because it requires significant effort.

Optimization

Migrating applications from one database to another database sometimes results in poor performance. This occurs because these applications are highly optimized for a particular database system over long periods of time. OEM can be used to help resolve any performance issues post-migration. It is very common for organizations to set aside at least two to three months for performance testing after migration of mission-critical applications. Some performance issues can also be caught during the functional/integration testing phase. But some issues may crop up only under certain amounts of load on the system. Therefore, it is essential to test the performance of the new platform thoroughly to identify potential bottlenecks in the system and address them before the new platform is rolled out into production. Performance issues can arise due to any of the following reasons:

- **Insufficient system resources**   Databases differ in their requirements for system resources such as memory, CPU, and I/O because they have been architected differently. Some databases use multithreaded processes, whereas Oracle is process-based on most platforms except Microsoft Windows. Oracle uses additional database structures such as UNDO segments that require additional I/O operations which other databases don't have. Hence, if the system on which the Oracle database is deployed is not sized properly, poor performance may result.

- **Bad SQL Query execution plans**   To optimize queries, Oracle's SQL Query Optimizer depends on statistics collected for database tables and indexes during the normal course of database operation. However, if these statistics are stale because of bulk data changes made in a short period of time, or are absent for some reason, the SQL statements will perform poorly. OEM proactively monitors the performance of SQL statements and will alert database administrators of issues. It also runs jobs to collect database object statistics periodically to avoid such issues. However, it is possible that during the migration, some complex SQL statements that were converted to Oracle require additional indexes.

- **Underestimated workload or concurrent user population**   Underestimating the peak workload or concurrent user population may result in under-sizing the system used for the Oracle database. This may also result in inadequate allocation of memory for the Oracle database engine in the form of a smaller shared global area (SGA).

- **Undersized Oracle database structures**   For optimal performance, it is necessary to size Oracle database structures such as the temporary tablespace and the UNDO segment tablespace (a.k.a. rollback segments) appropriately, since the Oracle database automatically allocates space in them as needed. If they are undersized, performance will be poor because of frequent allocations in these tablespaces resulting in increased waits by the database.

Many of these issues are identified proactively by OEM, including recommendations for addressing them. After the database migration and preliminary performance testing are done, Oracle Real Application Testing (RAT) can be used to test the impact of various optimization scenarios (e.g., the use of new indexes, the effect of partitioning, compression, and encryption, etc.) in the new Oracle environment. RAT allows capture and replay of the workload on an Oracle database, and it is much easier to set up and configure than other tools on the market.

Deployment

Many tasks to be executed in the deployment phase get their input from the assessment phase and from the analysis and design phase. During these phases, the target system architecture and all necessary software components to be used in the new system are evaluated. Based on the outcome of these phases, new software and hardware systems are acquired. Work on this phase may begin early in the migration project, as many organizations have to follow certain business practices regarding acquiring new hardware and software.

Because this phase may involve acquisition of new hardware in addition to installing Oracle database software in many cases, additional measures may have to be taken to configure system resources as per Oracle database deployment requirements, such as configuration of shared storage and configuration of inter-connected networking among the database server nodes that will be part of an Oracle RAC database. Common tasks executed in the deployment phase include the following:

- **Hardware configuration** This task includes configuring database servers, allocating storage, and configuring the network. Server configuration may also involve tasks pertaining to setting up a cluster to support the Oracle RAC database. In addition, the hardware configuration task involves setting up systems, networks, and storage at the disaster recovery site. Care must be taken when sizing the hardware and storage based on the workload profile of the application and the database. Policies and procedures need to be developed for deploying Oracle databases in a private cloud environment so that instances of Oracle databases can be provisioned as and when they are needed, and to consolidate Oracle databases onto the Oracle Exadata database machine platform.
- **Software installation and configuration** This task primarily consists of installing and configuring the Oracle software, and installing the migrated Oracle database schema on the systems deployed in the production environment to support the applications. After the database schema has been set up, database security roles and privileges need to be assigned to application users, along with access to the physical servers.
- **Initial data loading** After creating the database schemas in the production environment, the next task is to load the most current data from the source database. In cases where the source production database cannot be impacted with data extraction, the most recent backups are restored on a different server and the latest data is extracted from the backup. Then the data is loaded into the new Oracle database using tools and scripts that were chosen for the task during the analysis and design phase. It is also essential to ensure that desired indexes are created on all the tables in the database and that the latest table and index statistics are collected before the database is ready for users.
- **Testing of backup and recovery scripts and processes** It is very important to test all scripts and processes for database backup and restore operations. In many instances, administrators use a standard template to generate new scripts for the

new databases. However, these scripts need to be tested to ensure that they will perform as expected when it really matters; if they don't perform as expected, database recovery can be jeopardized. OEM allows configuration of backup and recovery tasks in an automated fashion which can help in avoiding any errors associated with manually scripting these tasks.

- **Capture of changes (from source) and switchover**   For databases that cannot afford downtime and are required to be available 24/7, it is essential that changes that took place during the initial data loading process or during the switchover phase be captured and applied to the new database to avoid missing any transactions affecting the integrity of the data in the new environment. Oracle GoldenGate can play a crucial role in this task of capturing changes in the source database and replicating them in the Oracle database after the initial data loading task is complete. It can continue to capture changes on the source database while the data loading operation is in progress on the Oracle database. The following steps are required in this process:
  1. Set up the changed data capture process on the source database.
  2. Extract the data from the source database.
  3. Load the data into the target database (Oracle).
  4. Apply the changed data captured from the source database to Oracle.
  5. Open the Oracle database for business use.

Post-Production Support

It is a common practice to support a newly deployed database environment with personnel who were involved in the migration process to troubleshoot any issues that may come up immediately after the new environment goes live. The following issues may arise during this time:

- Issues related to unfamiliarity with the new environment.
- Performance issues with SQL statements.
- Applications not performing as expected (missing functionality or incorrect behavior). This may happen if some components of the application were not migrated properly to the new environment and were not tested.
- Problems with data representation in the applications (formatting, Date/Time mask, etc.).
- Time required for database administrators and developers to become fully familiar with the new environment, including procedures for administering routine tasks.

MIGRATION SERVICES

Managing a large migration project requires careful planning, sufficient resources, and certain skill sets. Many system integrators have specialized practices focused on migrations, and have their own methodology, tools, and best practices.

For IT organizations that are planning to migrate many databases as part of a strategic move to consolidate database platforms, it makes sense to engage a system integrator to execute the project, because a system integrator can bring industrialized migration expertise to the table. It is also possible that the system integrator can simply augment his IT staff temporarily to enable him to perform migrations on his own. ISVs, on the other hand, can port their applications on their own because, for them, it is a matter of implementing new database functionality in existing applications as they have to support the other databases as well.

Migrating database platforms for packaged applications bought from ISVs, and installing additional software components of the application, such as the database access layer or, in some cases, new versions of the packaged application certified to run against an Oracle database, may be required. In such cases, it is best if either the ISV or an established system integrator with a dedicated practice focused on these applications is engaged to carry out the database platform migration. The application vendor may have a different codebase for each database that needs to be installed first. As such, migrating from one database to another without changing the application codebase will not work in those cases, and it may jeopardize the ISV's ability to support the application. For example, migrating a PeopleSoft human resources management system (HRMS) application deployed against an IBM DB2 database to a PeopleSoft HRMS application deployed against an Oracle database involves the following steps:

1. Install the PeopleSoft HRMS software and database schema for Oracle.
2. Migrate all the customizations in the PeopleSoft HRMS software from IBM DB2 to the Oracle database.
3. Migrate all the data from IBM DB2 to Oracle.
4. Test the new environment.

Migration of the database schema associated with a packaged application directly to Oracle using migration tools is not supported in most cases by the packaged application vendors. Many system integrators have practices dedicated to migrations and upgrades of a particular application package. Leveraging such system integrators can ensure seamless migration to the new environment.

SUMMARY

Migration projects of any size require careful planning. Assessing its current portfolio of applications can help an organization understand the challenges, complexity, and level of effort required to have its databases migrated to Oracle. Many tools facilitate database and application migrations. These tools differ in the level of automation they provide in migrations and in the accuracy of the migrated SQL statements. Performing proofs of concept with these tools to better understand their capabilities will be beneficial in the long run for large migration projects. Database migrations also have an impact on applications that are dependent on them.

Design-related issues in migrations will vary in complexity and nature within organizations depending upon feature/functionality usage. Some organizations set up policies to develop applications with the goal of being database-agnostic. In such cases, the impact of database changes will be minimal, as they would have avoided implementation of the proprietary features of a database. There is no substitute for comprehensive testing of the migrated/ported application along with the new database platform.

In this chapter, we discussed various migration approaches, tools, and the migration life cycle in depth. We also explored migration service options for different organizations (e.g., ISVs, IT organizations, etc.). The goal was to inform readers about potential choices in migration tools, and various design issues that should be considered. The next chapter will provide an overview of migration tools and technologies along with their strengths and weaknesses.

Relational Migration Tools

INFORMATION IN THIS CHAPTER:

- Initial Database Migration
- Initial Stored Object Migration
- Application SQL Migration
- Unit Testing
- Performance Testing
- System Testing
- Production Rollout
- Global and Niche Service Providers

This chapter covers the products and tools from Oracle and third-party partners that can help to accelerate the relational migration and associated application component of your cloud migration. The chapter is organized by project phase to keep the content consistent with the way we covered the migration process in Chapters 2 and 3. Some of the tools and products discussed in this chapter can be leveraged across the migration phases in different ways. However, we will make sure not to duplicate details of the products and tools where this occurs. You will most likely use the following products and tools in your database migration effort, shown here in order of most-heavily to least-heavily used:

- SQL Developer Migration Workbench
- SQL Developer Application Migration Assistant
- Oracle Enterprise Manager Performance Packs
- Oracle GoldenGate, Oracle Gateways, Oracle Warehouse Builder, and/or Oracle Data Integrator

Most customers use as many Oracle tools and products as possible. There are several reasons for this, but the most pertinent reason is that the tool you will use the most, SQL Developer, is both free and fully supported by Oracle. SQL Developer Migration Workbench is a feature of SQL Developer. Throughout this chapter, we will use the term *SQL Developer Migration Workbench* when the database migration features of SQL Developer are being used. Another reason is that customers prefer to use tools and products from the same vendor to which they are migrating their database. This makes it easier from a training and support perspective, but it also means there is only one vendor to go to if issues are encountered.

We will be covering third-party tools which offer support for source databases that Oracle does not support and, in some cases, offer capabilities not found in

Oracle tools or products. Global and niche system integrator tools—which can never be purchased without using the system integrator services—will also be discussed, as they often have complementary tools to the Oracle solutions, or tools with additional features. System integrators also offer migration expertise, as no tool or set of tools can possibly automate the entire process.

INITIAL DATABASE MIGRATION

The initial database migration is all about getting data and database schema from the source database to the Oracle database as quickly and inexpensively as possible. Oracle offers a number of tools and products, each with strengths and potential shortcomings (we say "potential," as each situation is different, and a shortcoming to one customer may not be a shortcoming to another customer). Some of these products are pull-based and some are push-based. *Pull-based* means the product is communicating directly with the source database and reading the source database tables to move the data across. Pull-based methods typically use ODBC, JDBC, or a native database protocol and SQL. The *push-based* method involves unloading the data from the source database and pushing the data across the network or to a shared disk so that it can be loaded into the Oracle database.

Another dimension to data migration is whether to stream the data or use the disk as temporary storage (e.g., disk to disk) on the source and target database servers. Streaming the data requires no disk storage space and is typically a fast way to move data. Data streaming does require a high-speed network interconnect. Using the disk-to-disk method can require significant disk storage space on both the source and the target. The disk I/O method is significantly slower than reading and writing to a data stream, and this slowdown can impact your approach to moving your new Oracle cloud environment into production. A stream-based solution will read the data from the source data and write it directly to Oracle using memory and processes to process communication. This can be achieved using JDBC, ODBC, and operating system named pipes. We will discuss named pipes in more detail in the next section.

Database API and Protocol Options

Before covering specific Oracle and third-party migration tools, it is important to cover the underlying database APIs and network protocols that are used across all the solutions in this section. The solutions discussed in this section all use one or more of the protocols shown in Figure 4.1. These options each have their strengths and weaknesses.

Figure 4.1 shows, at a high level, the architecture and configuration involved with each of the five options for database migration protocols and APIs. Along with the architecture, you need to understand the history, technology benefits, and technology drawbacks to help you decide which protocol or API is best for your unique migration situation. The following list of numbered options corresponds to the numbered options in Figure 4.1.

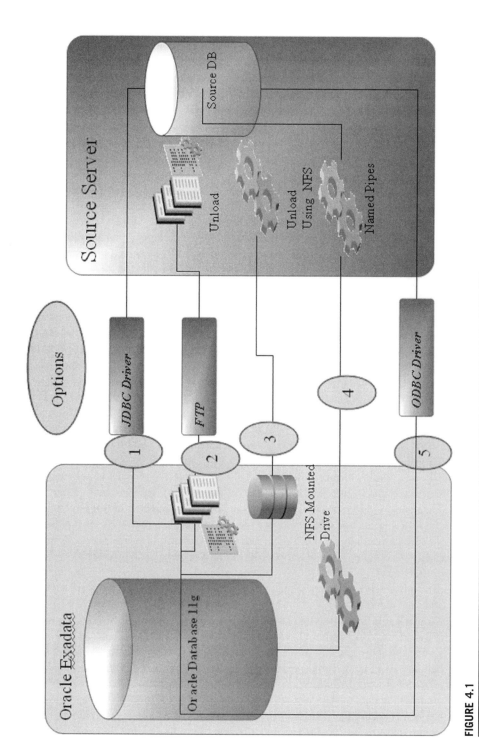

FIGURE 4.1

Protocol and API Data Migration Options Architecture

1. **ODBC**   ODBC has been around longer than most standards-based and proprietary database APIs. ODBC is supported by all the Oracle migration products except SQL Developer. You can use a JDBC–ODBC bridge driver to connect to SQL Server and other ODBC data sources when using SQL Developer. ODBC has had a history of being slower than other database access methods. This is still often the case, so it should be used with smaller data volumes or when performance is not a top priority.

2. **JDBC**   JDBC is faster and much more widely supported than ODBC. You should choose JDBC connectivity when you are pulling data from the source database instances, and you need a simplified setup and flexible connectivity with good performance across a wide range of non-Oracle data sources. JDBC is supported in all the Oracle data migration solutions.

3. **File Transfer Protocol (FTP)**   This is the classic, legacy "bulk unload and load" protocol for moving data between systems. FTP has been used for decades and is only preceded by *sneakernet* (moving data by copying it to tape or disk and physically walking or shipping it to the target location). FTP requires a lot of disk space on both the source and the target servers, and significant time is spent reading and writing data to and from the disk. Therefore, it is time-consuming and costly (in terms of storage) when moving large volumes of data. However, it is reliable, easy to use, and quick to get up and running. If your source and Oracle databases are in the same physical network within the confines of the same building, you do not need to worry about encrypting the data during the FTP transfer. If you are performing the FTP transfer over a public network or the source and Oracle database hardware platforms are physically in different locations, you can use secure FTP, known as FTPS. If a virtual private network (VPN) is available, VPN can be used to secure the FTP data transfer.

4. **Named pipe write and read**   Named pipes is an industry standard technology that uses process-to-process communication to move data from one computer to another. Named pipes is a cost-effective, easy-to-configure method of moving data using a process-to-process, in-memory push method of migration. All Oracle tools and products support the use of named pipes. Named pipes is frequently used along with SQL Loader (the scripts and control files automatically generated by SQL Developer Migration Workbench) to provide a fast, easy-to-implement, and cost-effective push migration solution. Because named pipes is a form of process-to-process communication, you would use this solution in a private cloud setting where both computers are in secured facilities.

5. **Network File System (NFS) mounted disks**   Like named pipes, NFS mounted disks are easy to configure, quick to implement, inexpensive, and an effective way to speed up data migration. NFS still requires disk space and incurs disk I/O, but the performance and cost are cut in half when compared to traditional FTP's unload and load method. When migrating data in a private cloud environment, securing the data during transfer should not be an issue as all the disk storage is physically secured in your facilities. The NFS disk that you are moving the data to may have to be encrypted. Migrating data in a public cloud or hybrid cloud

will require encryption for the data while it is being transferred and for the data while it is at rest. For data at rest, all major disk vendors offer disk encryption options for their storage products. Also available are open source software-based solutions such as TrueCrypt and GNU Privacy Guard. NFS data transfer encryption can be performed using something as simple as Secure Shell (SSH) or Kerberos.

SQL Loader and External Tables

SQL Loader is a great place to start when discussing Oracle database migration tools and products as it is utilized by Oracle SQL Developer Migration Workbench. SQL Loader is the primary method for quickly populating Oracle tables with data from external files. It has a powerful data parsing engine that puts little limitation on the format of the data in the data file. The tool is invoked when you specify the `sqlldr` command or use the Enterprise Manager interface. SQL Loader is the default push method that is used by SQL Developer Migration Workbench for data migration.

SQL Loader has been around as long as the Oracle Database log-on scott/tiger (scott/tiger has been the default development database user and schema name for the last 20 years or more) and is an integral feature of Oracle Database. It works the same on any hardware or software platform that Oracle supports. Therefore, it has become the de facto data migration and information integration tool for most Oracle partners and customers.

The Oracle database external tables feature is a complementary solution to existing SQL Loader functionality. It enables you to access data in external sources as though the data were in a table in the database. Therefore, standard SQL or Oracle PL/SQL can be used to load the external file (defined as an external table) into an Oracle database table. It also means that data unloaded from the source database using SQL Developer Migration Workbench can be loaded using external tables with no changes to the source database unload scripts generated by SQL Developer Migration Workbench.

Customer benchmarks and performance tests have determined that, in some cases, external tables are faster than the SQL Loader direct path load. In addition, if you know SQL well, external table loaded SQL is easier to code than SQL Loader control files and load scripts. However, in cases where you use SQL Developer Migration Workbench the control files and scripts are automatically generated for you.

Oracle SQL Developer Migration Workbench Database Migration

SQL Developer is a free SQL, PL/SQL, data-based modeling, unit testing, and database migration tool that can be used to create and manage database objects in Oracle, DB2, Sybase, SQL Server, MySQL, and Access databases. In this chapter, we will focus on the database migration features of SQL Developer. (More detailed information on SQL Developer usage is available in other books, including *Oracle SQL Developer 2.1* [Packt Publishing].)

SQL Developer Migration Workbench can use either a push or a pull method for data migration. You can push the database Data Definition Language (DDL), data objects, and stored objects from the source to the target Oracle database using an online or offline capture method. The online method uses a JDBC connection to connect the source database and read the database's system tables to gather all the metadata for the database being migrated. The offline method reads the source database tables using the source database's command-line interface (CLI) tool. In the case of Sybase and SQL Server, the CLI tool used is the Bulk Copy Program (BCP) utility. When using either the online or the offline capture method the actual data migration can occur using in-memory, streams-based functionality (a.k.a. streams-based data migration using JDBC), or the more traditional file unload from the source database in which the FTP flat file is output to the target database file system and then the data is loaded into Oracle using SQL Loader or Oracle external tables.

SQL Developer Migration Workbench 3.0 was released in early 2011 and includes support for C application code migration from Sybase and SQL Server DB-Library and CT-Library. Additional features include a CLI tool, a host of reports that can be used to fix items that did not migrate, estimating and scoping tools, database analysis capability, and a pluggable framework to support identification and changes to SQL in Java, PowerBuilder, and Visual Basic-based applications.

SQL Developer Migration Workbench actually started off as a set of UNIX scripts and a crude database procedural language parser based on SED and AWK. This solution was first made an official Oracle product in 1996. Since then, the parser has been totally rewritten in Java and the user interface has been integrated with SQL Developer.

Oracle Gateways

The core of Oracle's Gateway solutions is the Oracle database Heterogeneous Services (HS) feature. Heterogeneous Services provides transparent and generic gateway technology to connect to non-Oracle systems. Heterogeneous Services is an integrated component of the database; therefore, it can exploit all the capabilities of the Oracle database including PL/SQL and Oracle SQL extensions. The two methods of connecting to non-Oracle databases through Oracle HS are:

- Oracle Transparent Gateways, which are tailored specifically for non-Oracle systems and provide an end-to-end (Oracle to non-Oracle) certified solution.
- Oracle Generic Connectivity, which is based on ODBC and OLEDB standards, so it allows connectivity to any non-Oracle system which is ODBC- or OLEDB-compliant. This solution is free and available with the database. It is recommended for non-Oracle systems for which Oracle does not provide a gateway solution.

Both Generic Connectivity and Transparent Gateways are based on Oracle Heterogeneous Services. Both solutions are SQL-based federated legacy integration and data migration solutions and have existed since version 8.0 of Oracle Database. They are not that well known in the IT community, but they are very powerful and capable solutions.

The Oracle Gateways use a pull method to migrate any ODBC database to Oracle. They are often used in cases where SQL Developer Migration Workbench does not have support and using an ODBC driver does not provide data type mapping support, data transformation support, or the performance required. Often, Oracle Gateways are used to migrate data from DB2 on z/OS or iSeries platforms.

Oracle ETL and ELT Tools

Oracle has an extract-transform-load (ETL) product called Oracle Warehouse Builder (OWB) and an extract-load-transform (ELT) tool called Oracle Data Integrator (ODI). Both products can be used to migrate any JDBC or ODBC data source to Oracle. The key differences between these two products are as follows:

- OWB is a database-based solution and ODI is a Java-based solution.
- The base version of OWB is free with Oracle Database; ODI must be purchased and is part of the Oracle Fusion Middleware.
- An Oracle database is required for the OWB metadata repository and to hold the OWB transformations which are PL/SQL-based. ODI can use Oracle, SQL Server, or DB2 as a metadata repository and all transformations are performed using the SQL language of the target database.

Oracle Warehouse Builder

OWB allows users to extract data from both Oracle and non-Oracle data sources, as well as transform/load data into a data warehouse or operational data store (ODS) or simply use it to migrate data to an Oracle database. It is part of the Oracle Business Intelligence suite and is the embedded Oracle ETL tool in the BI Suite. With the usage of platform/product-specific adapters, it can extract data from mainframe/legacy data sources as well.

Starting with Oracle Database 11g, the core OWB product is a free feature of the database. In a way, this as an attempt to address the free Microsoft entry-level ETL tools such as Data Transformation Services (DTS) and SQL Server Integration Services (SSIS) from becoming de facto ETL standards because of their ease of use and cheap price (free).

OWB has always supported ODBC, and in 11g, JDBC connectivity is supported as well. It also works with the Oracle Gateways to pull both the database definitions and data from the source databases. In addition, it supports flat file migration for a push method of data migration.

Oracle Data Integrator

ODI is a product that Oracle acquired from Sunopsis SA in 2006. This acquisition may have seemed unnecessary at the time, as Oracle already had OWB for data migration and integration. However, the complaint from customers was that OWB required an Oracle database, was based on PL/SQL and therefore was very database-centric, and did not support target databases other than Oracle.

ODI is a data migration and integration software product, providing a declarative design approach to defining data transformation and integration processes, resulting in faster and simpler development and maintenance. Based on ELT architecture, ODI, unlike traditional ETL products, loads the data into the target database and then does the transformation processing. This is important for a number of reasons: The underlying target database SQL and database languages (such as PL/SQL, T-SQL, and DB2 SQL PL) are used to perform the transformations and not a proprietary ETL language; the RASP (reliability, availability, scalability, performance) of the underlying database can be used instead of a proprietary engine that is external to where the data resides; and, in most cases, getting the data into the database and then transforming it is a faster process.

ODI can migrate data using either the push or the pull method along with memory- or disk-based migration. The ODI pull method can utilize JDBC, ODBC, or ODI Knowledge Modules. Knowledge Modules (KMs) are code templates and prebuilt database connectivity modules. Database connectivity KMs exist for a number of source databases, including Sybase, SQL Server, DB2, Informix, and many more. You can also develop your own KM to move data from any data source to Oracle. Like any ETL or ELT tool, ODI can read flat files, or files from a named pipe, to support the push method of data migration. Like OWB, ODI can also work with Oracle Gateways to pull data from the source database and write it to Oracle.

Oracle Tuxedo Workbench for DB2 z/OS

Oracle Tuxedo Application Rehosting Workbench (ART Workbench) helps to simplify and accelerate mainframe rehosting by automating the code and data migration for a COBOL DB2-based mainframe application. This tool is specifically focused on DB2 mainframe z/OS database migrations and doesn't support Sybase, SQL Server, or other Linux/UNIX/Windows relational database management system (RDBMS) migrations. It will begin to support other mainframe data stores such as IMS in the next couple of years. For data migration, the ART Workbench performs complete analysis of all data definitions and access patterns to generate data schemas and logical access modules on the target. The ART Workbench also produces data unload, reload, and validate tools for automated migration of files and DB2 tables off the mainframe.

The database conversion process using the Oracle ART Workbench is as follows:

1. Run the ART Workbench catalog process to generate the database schema object inventory.
2. Run the ART Workbench DB2 to Oracle converter program which will generate the Oracle database schema object creation DDL files, a set of DB2 data unload mainframe Job Control Language (JCL) modules, Oracle SQL Loader control files, and UNIX shell scripts to load DB2 data into Oracle using Oracle SQL Loader.

3. Unload the DB2 data by running DB2 unload JCL modules and transferring unloaded data files to the ART Workbench platform.
4. Load the DB2 data into the Oracle database by running the data loading shell scripts generated by ART Workbench (in parallel, if possible).

As you can see, this is a push method of data migration that will use disk space and is not an in-memory, streams-based data migration process.

Oracle GoldenGate

Oracle acquired the GoldenGate software from the software company GoldenGate in 2009. Prior to GoldenGate, Oracle did not offer a heterogeneous bidirectional data replication solution. GoldenGate was clearly the leader in the marketplace for heterogeneous replication, so the acquisition moved Oracle to the forefront in the software space of log-based heterogeneous data replication solutions. Although the strength of GoldenGate is bidirectional heterogeneous replication, it can also be used to perform the initial migration from the source database to Oracle.

GoldenGate works in an initial batch Oracle database load by pushing the data to the target Oracle database using TPC/IP. This is an in-memory, script-based approach that requires no disk space on the source or Oracle database servers. The first part of the script creates an Extract and Replicate Task Group (ELOAD, RLOAD) that will be used to instantiate the target Oracle database. A task is a special process that, once started, reads from each source table, row by row. This data is transmitted to the Replicate group on the target that inserts each row of data into the empty database tables. The task will automatically shut down once all rows are read, transmitted, and inserted.

Third-Party Tools

There are two main players in the database migration space: Ispirer and SwisSQL. Both vendors have been in business for more than 10 years and offer support for major database vendors as well as support for some vendors that Oracle does not support. Ispirer and SwisSQL have trial licenses which are limited in nature and can make it difficult to use their products in a Proof of Value (POV) analysis without buying them. However, each product has a very attractive price point. In the case of Teradata, PostgreSQL, Progress, MaxDB, and Interbase/Firebird, Ispirer or SwisSQL will need to be used as Oracle SQL Developer Migration Workbench does not offer support for these databases. The alternative is to use ODI, OWB, Oracle Gateways, SQL Loader, or external tables.

Ispirer

Ispirer is a U.S.-based company that is focused on offering automated database and application migration tools. It will also perform fixed-price database migration using a combination of its database migration tool and professional services.

Its migration product, SQLWays, provides high-end conversion capabilities for automated migration to Oracle from all major databases, including IBM DB2 UDB, Sybase, Informix, Interbase/Firebird, MySQL, PostgreSQL, Progress, SQL Server, Sybase, and Teradata. The database migration can be performed using the SQLWays Studio GUI tool, or the SQLWays Command Line CLI solution. Both SQLWays Studio and SQLWays Command Line can use JDBC, or basic unload source utilities, and load into Oracle using SQL Loader scripts created by the tool.

SwisSQL

SwisSQL is an India-based company that offers not just database migration tools, but a number of database, network, desktop, application, and server management tools. Therefore, it is not just a database and application migration company like Ispirer. However, similar to Ispirer, SwisSQL will perform fixed-price database migration using a combination of its database migration tool and professional services.

The SwisSQL Data Migration tool offers migration from IBM DB2 UDB, MS SQL Server, Sybase ASE, MySQL, PostgreSQL, MaxDB, Teradata, MS Access, Excel, and CSV. These data sources are accessed via JDBC or can be unloaded using the native database unload utilities and generated Oracle SQL Loader scripts. The tool is a GUI-based solution.

Reducing Data Migration Time and Disk Requirements

In the "Database API and Protocol Options" section earlier in this chapter, we introduced three methods that you can use to speed data migration and reduce or eliminate the need for disk space. Here we will go into detail regarding why and how these methods speed up the migration effort. The three methods are mutually exclusive and each is used in specific situations:

- **Named pipes**   Named pipes eliminates the need for temporary disk data storage mechanisms to store the source and target flat files used to load the Oracle database; instead, data is moved in-memory. Named pipes is used in a push data situation where disk-to-disk is often used. Since disk I/O is a very time-intensive activity, named pipes can decrease the time it takes to move data from the source to the target by five to 10 times. Named pipes can be used with any of the initial database migration products and tools from Oracle mentioned in this chapter.
- **NFS mounted disks**   NFS disks can also be used to speed up data movement in a push data situation. In a typical disk-to-disk scenario, data is exported from the source database to the local disk and then pushed to the local disk where the Oracle database resides. By unloading the source database data to an NFS disk mounted on the Oracle database server, you eliminate an entire write to disk of potentially terabytes of data. When NFS is used as the network/remote disk, no special hardware or storage software needs to be purchased and installed. However, with the advent of inexpensive network attached storage (NAS) devices, there is no reason a NAS product could not be used instead of NFS. In fact, there is

no reason that NFS cannot be used with any of the initial database migration solutions.

- **JDBC and ODBC connection pooling and parallelism**   When using a pull method of data migration any product that uses JDBC or ODBC to connect to the source database to retrieve the data can utilize connection pooling and/or parallelism of extract and load processes. SQL Developer, ODI, and OWB all support process parallelism and connection pooling.

Matrix of Oracle and Third-Party Database Migration Tools

Table 4.1 highlights all the initial database migration options. It should help you quickly decide what option to use based on your source database, speed requirements, disk space availability, and how you want to interact with the process during development and implementation (through a GUI, CLI, or SQL).

Table 4.1 should make it much easier to decide which tool is best for your migration project. The most important factor is in the "Database Sources" column. If a tool does not support your source database, you should not even consider the tool. However, keep in mind that these products and tools are continually being enhanced with new source database support, so always check the vendors' Web sites first. Push and/or pull support, stream-based support, and interfaces supported are all very situation-specific. They probably even vary within your company depending on the migration project database source, database size, and type of tool interface your developers and database administrators are most comfortable with.

TIP

There are several benefits to using SQL Developer Migration Workbench, SwisSQL Data Migration, or Ispirer SQLWays to migrate database data. The first set of benefits are that these tools migrate not only the data, but also the DDL, indexes, constraints, and identity columns, and they resolve reserved word conflicts as well as make any changes to object names if they don't conform to Oracle's limitations on object name characters or length. More importantly, they store the table and data migration information in a metadata repository which is used by tools from Oracle (SQL Developer), Ispirer, and SwisSQL to migrate database stored objects and application SQL. This cross-reference between data, DDL, stored objects, and SQL application migration makes the entire migration process much faster and reduces the amount of manual effort required. Oracle Gateways, ODI, OWB, SQL Loader, GoldenGate, and external tables are all very effective ways of migrating data but are not comprehensive cloud migration tools.

INITIAL STORED OBJECT MIGRATION

Procedural database languages used in stored procedures and triggers are the most challenging aspect of database migration. This is because the procedural database languages have all the constructs of a 3GL language: if-then-else, while loops, for loops, case statements, error handling, and other logical constructs. These database

Table 4.1 Database Migration Products and Tools Summary

Product	Database Sources	Pull or Push	Stream-based Support	Interface
SQL Developer	Access, DB2 UDB, Informix, Sybase, SQL Server, MySQL	Pull and push	Yes, JDBC	GUI, CLI
Oracle Gateway	DB2 Linux/UNIX/ Windows, mainframe, iSeries, SQL Server, Sybase, or any ODBC data source	Pull	Yes, SQL	GUI, CLI, SQL
OWB	Flat files, ODBC	Pull and push	Yes	GUI, CLI, SQL
ODI	Flat files, JDBC, ODBC, XML	Pull and push	Yes	GUI, SQL
GoldenGate	Oracle, DB2 z/OS, JMS-based systems, DB2 Linux/UNIX/ Windows, Sybase, SQL Server, Enscribe, SQL/MX, MySQL	Pull	Yes	CLI, SQL
SQL Loader	Flat files	Push	No	CLI
External tables	Flat files	Push	No	SQL
Ispirer	Access, DB2 UDB, Excel, Informix, Interbase/Firebird, MySQL, PostgreSQL, Progress, Sybase, SQL Server, Teradata	Pull and push	Yes, JDBC	GUI, CLI
SwisSQL	Access, DB2 UDB, Excel, Informix, MaxDB, PostgreSQL, Sybase, SQL Server, Teradata	Pull and push	Yes, JDBC	GUI

procedural languages are not as robust as application development languages such as C, .NET, Java, or C#, but the parser to migrate the database procedural language needs to be very intelligent. Many tools are available from Oracle and third parties for migrating data in the source database, but only three options are available to migrate stored objects in the database.

The solutions are from Oracle, Ispirer, and SwisSQL. All three tools offer database data migration capabilities (as we discussed earlier in the "Initial Database

Migration" section), and the stored object migration tools from each vendor will have insight into any changes made to the database schema that will affect the migration of the stored objects. This makes these tools a great choice for migrating all database objects and the data itself.

Oracle SQL Developer Migration Workbench, the same tool used for data migration, will migrate all source stored procedures, triggers, and views. Like the database DDL and data migration functionality in SQL Developer Migration Workbench, the stored objects can be captured from the source database either online or offline. Individual stored objects can be migrated using the Scratch Pad editor feature. There is extensive reporting of the database objects that were captured, translated, and compiled in the Oracle database. The detailed migration reports show all the errors and warnings and a hyperlink will take you directly to the line in the stored object where the error or warning was issued. In Chapter 6, a technical deep dive and example migration of stored objects will provide you with in-depth knowledge of SQL Developer Migration Workbench stored object migration.

Ispirer SQLWays Studio can be used to convert objects by connecting directly to the source database using ODBC, or SQLWays Command Line can be used to convert stored object operating system files that contain all the stored procedures, views, or triggers. SQLWays can also be used to convert stand-alone SQL statements, functions, scripts, and various code fragments. Ispirer guarantees a 99 percent conversion rate [1]. However, you should test the tool on your stored object migration to see what sort of conversion success rate you get, as 99 percent success is very difficult to achieve. (Are you capturing, converting, or generating data into the Oracle database? Any of these tools can capture 99 percent of stored objects, as this requires simply reading the source objects from the source database system tables.)

The SwisSQL GUI tool (which is separate from the database data migration GUI tool) lets you migrate online, stored object scripts or individual stored objects. Online migration can be accomplished using ODBC or JDBC. SwisSQL claims up to 90 percent automated conversion [2] across stored procedures. Like the Ispirer claims for stored object migration, this is hard to believe for complex migration projects, and could also be impacted by the definition of success for the automated conversion; captured, converted, and generated in Oracle, or producing the same results in Oracle as the source database. Of course, "one-click" automated migration with 90 percent of stored procedures producing correct results in Oracle would, in most cases, be impossible to achieve.

Matrix of Oracle and Third-Party Stored Object Migration Tools

Table 4.2 lists the three vendor tools for stored object migration. Stored object support can change from year to year, so it is best to consult each vendor's Web site directly.

The core to each of these products is not its ability to capture the source database objects or generate the Oracle target schema. The key to how automated the migration is and the number of stored objects that produce the correct results in Oracle is how well the parser and translators function. Migrating any language from

Table 4.2 Stored Object Migration Products and Tools Summary

Product	Source Database Procedural Dialects	Integrated with Database Migration Tool	Unit Testing and Debugging Built In	DDL and Stored Procedure Script File Support	Interface
SQL Developer	MS SQL Server T-SQL, Informix Stored Procedure Language, MySQL Stored Procedure Language, and Sybase ASE T-SQL	Yes	Yes	No	GUI, CLI
Ispirer	MS SQL Server T-SQL, IBM DB2 UDB SQL, Informix Stored Procedure Language, MySQL Stored Procedure Language, PostgreSQL, Progress 4GL procedures, and Sybase ASE T-SQL	No	No	Yes	GUI, CLI
SwisSQL	MS SQL Server T-SQL, IBM DB2 UDB SQL, and Sybase ASE T-SQL	No	No	Yes	GUI

one syntax to another is a function of the parser and translator. Not all parsers and translators function in the same way, and each has its strengths and weaknesses.

NOTE

One of the main decision points in choosing a tool is the tool's source stored object support. When there is support from more than one vendor, it is not necessarily the best choice to select one vendor for all of your database migrations, or even a single database migration. Based on customer experience, some vendor tools do a better job with some constructs and others do a better job with other constructs in the same database. Therefore, it is not uncommon to use more than one tool for the same set of database stored objects.

APPLICATION SQL MIGRATION

Application SQL migration can be a very tedious and time-consuming task when you consider that even a moderately complex application can easily have 1 million or more lines of application code. Embedded in this application code are thousands of database SQL statements, calls to database stored procedures, and database connection strings. There are two basic approaches to making sure your current application will work against an Oracle database:

- **Static or compile-time SQL analysis and translation**   These types of tools will scan through the code before it is compiled and deployed to production. They will not only scan the code, but also make the appropriate SQL changes to the application that run against Oracle.
- **Runtime-based SQL translation**   The application is not changed at all, but is compiled and generated using the same compilers that are used for the source database. At runtime, a server or process traps the SQL statements and makes the appropriate change to the SQL, so it successfully runs against the Oracle database.

The biggest issue with static analysis and compile-time SQL changes is that many applications contain dynamic SQL. Dynamic SQL comes in two flavors, and both are equally difficult to identify and change. Classic database dynamic SQL is a SQL statement that has placeholders for the table names and/or columns. These place-holders are resolved when the SQL statement is prepared, at runtime, in the application code. SQL may also be dynamically built in the application code using a large text variable that holds the SQL as it is being built in the application code. For either type of dynamic SQL, it is difficult or impossible for the static tool to find the SQL and then determine what the SQL will resolve to or look like at runtime.

Runtime SQL translators can handle static and dynamic SQL statements. However, the problems they have are associated with overhead, cost, manageability, and ability to handle complex applications. The overhead relates to the translation of the SQL statement as it is being executed. Perhaps a translated SQL cache or a translation mapping table that is maintained by the translation's process instead of having to translate the same SQL each time it is executed can help. However, there is still overhead associated with a runtime cache or table lookup. The cost concerns the cost of an additional translation software engine and, potentially, a hardware component on which the translation engine or processes can run. Manageability involves the new middle-tier translation engine, as well as the expertise required to support and upgrade the software. Lastly, it is very unlikely that a runtime engine can anticipate all the different SQL statements, vendor-specific error messages, and return codes that are possible. Therefore, this solution is probably only suitable for very simple applications.

Oracle SQL Developer Migration Workbench Application Migration

Oracle SQL Developer Application Migration Assistant (AMA) is a tool that helps you migrate an application. You use AMA to identify and automatically convert source code SQL statements that require modification to run on the Oracle platform. Oracle AMA is a tool that helps convert applications at design/compile time.

AMA helps you reduce the time, risk, and financial barriers associated with migrating application layers to the Oracle platform. You use AMA to identify, analyze, and track the status of application migration issues, and make the necessary SQL changes automatically in the source code. You can customize AMA to suit your requirements and development environment. You do this by adding your own language (e.g., if you are using Ruby code development and Oracle AMA does not have an "out of the box" Rudy parser) rules XML file. This will tell the AMA tool to look for Ruby database calls.

For those languages where an AMA parser does not exist, the SQL Developer Migration Workbench scratch pad editor can be used to migrate application SQL from the source database dialect to the Oracle dialect. This is somewhat of a manual process, as the application SQL from the application or script is cut and pasted into the scratch pad editor and converted to the Oracle SQL dialect. The Oracle SQL is then cut and pasted back into the application code or script.

Oracle AMA also migrates C CT-library and DB-Library code to OCI. This is important, as migrating proprietary database API code can be a time-intensive, manual process. Many financial services companies have millions of lines of this code, and CT-Library and DB-Library are faster than JDBC and ODBC database access. Financial stock trading applications, manufacturing, and airport flight tracking systems where milliseconds can make a big difference often utilize C CT-library and DB-Library.

Ispirer

Ispirer SQLWays has capabilities for migrating SQL scripts (Perl, UNIX shell scripts) and database access code in C/C++, C#, Java, Visual Basic, ASP, VB.NET, and ASP.NET applications. This tool does a static analysis of the code at compile time and converts any SQL that will not work against an Oracle database. SQLWays also has the capability to migrate C/C++ applications that use the Sybase

CT-Library database API to access Sybase databases to other database APIs including ODBC, Oracle OCI, and Oracle Pro*C.

SwisSQL

The SwisSQL Console tool has a GUI that helps in SQL query conversion, including DDL, SQL, views, and indexes across database SQL dialects. Database administrators and developers working with multiple databases can type/load SQL queries in one database dialect and view equivalent queries in other database SQL dialects. This works much like the SQL Developer Migration Workbench scratch pad editor.

SwisSQL offers a JDBC driver that calls the SQL parser to translate the SQL from other database syntaxes to Oracle. This means Java applications can run unchanged against an Oracle database. The application only needs to be relinked with the SwisSQL JDBC driver. A company may not want to run this JDBC driver in production, so one option is to use the driver during migration and testing to determine the SQL that will need to change, and then to use the SQL Developer Migration Workbench scratch pad editor or SwisSQL Console to translate the SQL and make the change in the application code.

SwisSQL also offers the SwisSQL API. This API is used to make your Java application SQL calls database-independent, and therefore your Java applications portable across multiple databases. The SwisSQL JDBC driver uses the SwisSQL API. The SwisSQL API offers options to migrate all your queries on the fly through SwisSQL APIs that invoke the SwisSQL JDBC driver, or selected queries through direct API invocation. This option may be attractive to customers, or especially independent software vendors (ISVs), that will continue to run their applications against the source database and Oracle.

WARNING

Be careful of tools, products, middle-tier engines, and other solutions that claim they can translate all SQL syntax at runtime. There are far too many vendor-specific SQL extensions, differences in error handling, and vendor-specific database languages (such as Sybase and Microsoft SQL Server T-SQL) to make handling all these situations at runtime possible. Runtime translation handles both static and dynamic SQL, so runtime translation tools can cover more SQL statements than static/compile-time tools. This is because static/compile-time code analysis tools such as Oracle AMA and Ispirer SQLWays will not be able to translate dynamic SQL. This being the case, it is recommended that you use a combination of static/compile and runtime tools to migrate the application SQL. Initially, the static/compile approach takes longer, as changes to code will need to be made, but it does not require running all the application use cases. Running all system test use cases in many environments is not possible because they may not exist at all, they may need to be refined or updated, or the test team may require months to run all the use cases. The static/compile-time approach also does not require any special driver or third-party server to be run in your production environment, which is a huge benefit in terms of overall cost (including lower support and maintenance costs) and less complicated infrastructure. Compile-time SQL identification and change tools are also great since they don't have runtime performance implications, so you can tune the SQL before it is deployed in production. You also don't have to run the entire application to determine what SQL may not work at runtime.

UNIT TESTING

SQL Developer can be used to run queries of the tables in the source and Oracle databases side by side to compare the contents of the data and ensure that query results return the same data. The SQL Developer Migration Workbench scratch pad editor can be used to test stored procedure, view, and trigger results side by side in the source and Oracle databases. These capabilities provide very good database administrator and SQL developer tools for unit-testing the data, SQL, and stored object migration. Application developers can also use SQL Developer but may be more comfortable using an application development tool. Java application developers can use Oracle JDeveloper to create connections to DB2, Sybase, and SQL Server, and, of course, Oracle. This allows Java developers to unit-test SQL and stored object results as well as to view the data in both source and Oracle databases.

PERFORMANCE TESTING

Oracle Enterprise Manager (OEM) 11g provides a single, integrated solution for testing, deploying, operating, monitoring, diagnosing, and resolving performance problems. It delivers manageability and automation for your grid across both Oracle and non-Oracle technologies. This means OEM can be used to diagnose data migration issues across Oracle databases, non-Oracle databases, and the application tiers.

OEM was, at one point, a thick-client-based solution that had both slow response time and limited graphical capabilities. It also lacked support for other databases or even the Oracle Application Server. In the past few years, OEM has been upgraded to support other databases (Sybase, SQL Server, DB2, and others), Oracle Application Server and other application servers including IBM WebSphere, and Web-to-database-application and database-level tracing and diagnostics.

Oracle OEM also features add-on Diagnostic and Tuning Packs. The Diagnostic Pack enables users to detect performance issues across the infrastructure, and the Tuning Pack enables users to determine how to alleviate and fix performance issues detected with the Diagnostic Pack. These packs can be used in place of Oracle UTLBSTAT/UTLESTAT, and what is now called Oracle Statspack, which was introduced in Oracle 8i. Oracle Statspack has been the typical method of diagnosing Oracle performance concerns. It is a great tool, but it's a lot like coding in UNIX VI and really requires an expert to determine the root cause of issues. The OEM Tuning and Diagnostic Packs make the process more of a science than an art.

SYSTEM TESTING

System testing is a time-consuming piece of the migration process, as discussed in Chapter 2. However, because each customer's applications, hardware and software infrastructure, and databases are so unique, creating automated system testing products is very challenging. Oracle Real Application Testing is a product used in Oracle-to-Oracle database upgrades and migrations and can also be used for migrating to Oracle. During the performance and system testing phases, Oracle Real Application Testing is used to replay daily workloads against a test Oracle database and make changes to the application and database to see how they would impact the production system. You first run the full test on your customer acceptance testing use cases and capture the results using Oracle Real Application Testing. You can then replay this identical workload on your migrated development Oracle database, making changes to the application and database to see how these changes will impact the operation and performance of your production workload. This allows you to fully test your application and be confident that Oracle will perform well and produce the same results when you move to production.

> **WARNING**
>
> When a migration tools vendor states that a tool can "automate 90 percent of your database conversion," you need to ask the vendor what the claim means. First, does it mean 90 percent of the entire migration? This would be impossible, since we have already determined that unit, system, and performance testing are difficult and, in some cases, impossible to automate. Is the 90 percent for the database data, schema, stored objects, and application SQL? This would also be impossible to automate to 90 percent. If it is for the database stored objects, you can get 90 percent automation for the source capture. If you do not, you should not use the tool. You may even get close to 90 percent on the translation to Oracle PL/SQL. However, getting 90 percent automation for the generated stored objects with successful compilation in Oracle that actually produces correct results is not possible today. A 90 percent automation rate for application SQL, whether you are using static/compile-time technology or a runtime solution, is only possible for the simplest databases and applications. Be ready to ask detailed and tough questions before you start using any migration tool.

PRODUCTION ROLLOUT

If your database is small enough (typically less than 500 MB), the database data migration can occur without having to keep both systems running, or being concerned about failing over to the old database system. The size of the database is not the only issue, as complex or mission-critical systems may need a longer-term rollout to production than a "big bang" switch to the Oracle system overnight or on a weekend. This section covers the Oracle product GoldenGate, which is well suited for running both new and Oracle databases in parallel, supporting a data migration that may take days or even a week, or failing back to the old database system.

Oracle GoldenGate

GoldenGate, Oracle's zero-downtime solution, allows new systems to be continuously updated with the changes committed in the migrated database system so that applications and/or users can switch to the new system without any downtime. To support this approach, GoldenGate's core software platform captures, transforms, routes, and delivers transactional data in real time across heterogeneous databases and operating systems. This makes GoldenGate a perfect solution for the following production rollout situations:

- **Running both applications in parallel** GoldenGate supports bidirectional replication, so both the migrated database and the Oracle database can have GoldenGate log capture turned on and changes in both systems can be applied to the other database. This allows the Oracle migrated application to be tested for an extended period and any post-migration fixes to be made while both systems are in production.
- **Large database migration projects** When migrating terabytes of data, the data migration may take days. If your system is on 24/7 or the migration will take longer than a weekend (or the amount of time you can be offline), GoldenGate can be used to capture changes in the source database while the data is being migrated to Oracle. Then, once all the data is migrated to Oracle, the changes can be applied to the Oracle database and the application can start running against Oracle in production.
- **Fallback** Often with such projects, there is a concern about what will happen once you switch over to the new environment. GoldenGate alleviates many of those risks with fallback capabilities. After the switchover, GoldenGate captures the changes that occur in the Oracle database so that the source system is kept up-to-date in case there is a need to fallback to the old environment.

The bidirectional capabilities of GoldenGate provide a critical, database-level fallback contingency: A GoldenGate Capture module resides on the Oracle database, and a GoldenGate Delivery module resides on the migrated database. Upon switchover, these additional GoldenGate processes are turned on and continue to run so that the old system stays current with the new system, in case fallback to the old system is necessary. Even before turning on the new Oracle system, the GoldenGate Veridata product can be used to verify that the data is consistent in both systems, and can be run after switchover.

Oracle CDC

Oracle CDC offers log-based, nonintrusive change capture capabilities. The product offers change record filtering by operation, column, and content. It also offers flexible delivery models including batch, micro-batch, and events, and it includes reliable delivery and recovery as well as seamless integration with SOA Suite and ODI. The Oracle CDC JCA-based adapters are configured using Oracle JDeveloper. The Oracle CDC adapters are OEMed from Attunity Software. Oracle CDC is mostly focused on mainframe data stores (VSAM, IMS, Adabas, and DB2), but offers support for Microsoft SQL Server.

Table 4.3 Database Migration Production Rollout Product Summary

Product	Database Sources	Write Back to Source Database	Bidirectional Replication	Interface
GoldenGate	Oracle, DB2 z/OS, JMS-based systems, DB2 Linux/UNIX/ Windows, Sybase, SQL Server, Enscribe, SQL/MX, MySQL	Yes	Yes	CLI, SQL
Oracle CDC	SQL Server	No	No	GUI, CLI
ODI	Oracle, DB2 z/OS, DB2 iSeries, JMS-based systems, Informix, DB2 Linux/ UNIX/Windows, Sybase, Sybase IQ, SQL Server, Microsoft Access, Netezza, Teradata, SAS, and Salesforce.com	Yes	No	GUI, SQL

ODI CDC Knowledge Modules

ODI is used for initial data migration, but it can also be used for production rollout, as ODI offers both bulk load and CDC capabilities. Therefore, you could use ODI to load your Oracle database initially, and then to keep the Oracle database in sync with the migrated database. ODI CDC capabilities are provided through Knowledge Modules, as we discussed earlier in this chapter.

Matrix of Production Rollout Tools

ODI and GoldenGate provide overlapping and different source database support. In situations where ODI and GoldenGate provide the same support, GoldenGate would be the optimal choice because GoldenGate offers high-speed, log-based replication. ODI's strength is in bulk data movement that requires sophisticated data transformations, data quality and cleansing, and complex workflows. Table 4.3 provides details on the source databases supported, bidirectional capabilities, and interfaces.

GLOBAL AND NICHE SERVICE PROVIDERS

Why are we talking about service providers in a chapter on automated database migration tools? Well, no tool is completely automated; manual work always needs to be done, and someone needs to decide how to map data types, how database-specific features such as identity columns and constraints will be migrated, and how to handle differences in stored procedures, triggers, and views. Also, a group or company must own the migration effort. Ownership ensures accountability and increases the chances for success. Many companies can perform a database migration on their own using the tools in this chapter, but database migration is only one small aspect of moving to the Oracle cloud infrastructure.

Many global system integrators have Oracle practices dedicated to making companies successful using Oracle products and tools. Infosys and Tata Consultancy Services (TCS) are two of the few that offer dedicated divisions to perform database migrations to Oracle. These practices perform a majority of the work offshore in India, and in other countries such as Brazil and Romania where the labor force is inexpensive. Infosys and TCS will also perform all the work on-site if required by the customer. Additionally, Oracle partners with service providers that specifically focus on cloud migrations to Oracle. These providers include mLogica, Practical Transitions, J2SA, and rMantra. More information on these providers is available at www.oracle.com/technetwork/database/migration/third-party-093040.html.

All the service providers utilize SQL Developer Migration Workbench. In addition, they have their own set of tools, which they don't sell, that complement the SQL Developer solution. These tools provide support for data migration validation and verification, unit-test harnessing, production rollout, and other aspects of database migration not supported by SQL Developer Migration Workbench or other Oracle products.

NOTE

In the late 1990s, relational database migration tools did a great job with database schema and data migration. However, they did not support database object migration very effectively and they completely ignored any changes that would need to take place in the application SQL. Today, relational migration tools have matured and become more sophisticated when it comes to migrating database stored procedures, views, and triggers. The focus in the past couple of years has been on addressing changes to the application SQL when keeping the application language the same, and on developing tools to automatically migrate applications to Java EE. We have also seen a focus on not just converted database objects, but also making changes to the code to ensure that it will perform better in Oracle. As migration tools become more sophisticated and support more application, database, and infrastructure components, customers will continue to have higher expectations for support in tools for unit, system, and performance testing.

SUMMARY

The best option for migrating your database and application SQL to Oracle is Oracle SQL Developer Migration Workbench. If this tool does not support your source database, your next best option is SwisSQL or Ispirer SQLWays. If neither one of these supports your database, you should look at more generic database migration tools such as ODI, OWB, Gateways, SQL Loader, and external tables. However, using Oracle SQL Developer Migration Workbench, Ispirer SQLWays, or SwisSQL is your best option, as these tools move the database as well as other database objects such as stored procedures, constraints, views, triggers, and indexes. SwisSQL and Ispirer, along with SQL Developer, also migrate the SQL in the application and, in some cases, migrate proprietary database APIs such as CT-Library and DB-Library. Oracle SQL Developer also aids in the unit-testing phase.

Tools for migrating the database DDL and data are, by far, the most mature, and have the highest rate of success as this migration phase is the least complex. Migration of database stored objects is highly automated, and tools from Oracle, Ispirer, and SwisSQL have been around for at least a decade and provide high levels of automation. Manual intervention is still required to make small fixes, and each database object will need to be unit-tested. Production rollout is a far less risky proposition when you use Oracle GoldenGate. In the past several years, significant progress has been made in the areas of application SQL and proprietary database API migration. The migration phase which lacks a significant form of automation is in system and user acceptance testing. This is largely due to the fact that system and user acceptance testing does not have a consistent set of use cases and design patterns across customers. Data and DDL migration can be highly automated, as a small set of function points are involved. Stored object migration may have more function points and use of the stored object dialect may vary among customers, but there are still enough consistent use cases and design patterns to make automation possible.

This chapter covered, at a high level, the capabilities of the Oracle SQL Developer tool. The next two chapters will go into technical detail on how you can use this tool to quickly move your database to an Oracle cloud environment. A step-by-step example will be used with Oracle SQL Developer Migration Workbench so that you can use the tool on your own to do a database migration. Chapter 5 will cover stored procedure, view, and trigger migration using Oracle SQL Developer Migration Workbench and the SQL Server sample Northwind database which contains stored procedures, views, and triggers.

Endnotes

[1]   Ispirer. SQLWays Stored Procedures, Triggers, Schema, and Data Conversion: For all major databases. Available from www.ispirer.com/doc/sqlways_db_migration_brochure.pdf.

[2]   SwisSQL data sheet. Available from www.swissql.com/dbmigration-tool-ds.pdf.

Database Schema and Data Migration

INFORMATION IN THIS CHAPTER:

- Database Migration Tools from Oracle
- Database Schema Migration Tasks
- Data Migration
- Data Validation
- Sample Sybase Database Migration to Oracle Using Oracle SQL Developer

Database schema and data migration tasks typically comprise the first steps in a migration project. Migrating the schema and data allows organizations to continue migrating and testing other database and application components. Keeping the original database design intact during database migration makes it easier to perform data migration, verification, and application testing. In some cases, the database design is altered to improve performance by denormalizing certain tables or normalizing the denormalized tables to improve the flexibility of the resultant schema. This can result in changes to the applications and programs stored in the target database. Relational databases also have many differences, as we discussed in Chapter 3, which sometimes presents challenges during a migration from one database to another. However, most database migration tools available today offer functionality that facilitates the migration process while taking into consideration the differences in relational databases and appropriately handling these differences. Using these tools can greatly reduce the effort involved in schema and data migration tasks. Organizations that use modeling tools such as Erwin can generate database-specific schemas because these tools are capable of mapping the objects in the model to the chosen database. Modeling tools, however, cannot assist in migrating stored programs from one database to another, which is discussed in detail in Chapter 6, nor can they assist with data migration tasks.

DATABASE MIGRATION TOOLS FROM ORACLE

In addition to Oracle SQL Developer, a couple of other Oracle products can facilitate schema migration from other databases to Oracle. Although these tools are not primarily designed for schema migration, they can assist in schema migration along with data migration and integration. One big restriction with these tools is that they cannot migrate other database objects such as stored procedures and triggers. Using tools to perform migrations can reduce the chance of errors and shorten the migration time. In addition to Oracle SQL Developer, the following Oracle tools can facilitate schema migration:

- **Oracle Data Integrator (ODI)**   ODI can reverse-engineer table/index definitions from a variety of databases, and generate these objects in Oracle. ODI includes Knowledge Modules (KMs) for reverse-engineering different databases, and it provides a GUI to allow such operations. KMs in ODI are reusable code templates that can facilitate specific tasks in the data integration process, such as reverse-engineering objects from the source database, unloading data from the source, and loading data into the target database. ODI also supports data migration by leveraging native database utilities in offline mode, as well as using Java Database Connectivity (JDBC) drivers to migrate data in online mode. Online mode is also a generic way to migrate data from one database to another by using JDBC drivers. In addition, it is possible to use other extract-transform-load (ETL) tools to reverse-engineer non-Oracle database tables.

- **Oracle Database Gateways**   Database Gateways facilitate transparent access to a non-Oracle database from within an Oracle database via SQL and PL/SQL programs. A Database Gateway consists of two components: Heterogeneous Services (HS) and the HS agent/driver. The HS component is installed as part of the Oracle database software, and the database-specific HS agent/driver needs to be installed either on the same server as the Oracle database or on a separate server as a central gateway for accessing non-Oracle databases from Oracle. There is also an ODBC Gateway that functions in a similar manner, except that it requires a database-specific Open Database Connectivity (ODBC) driver. Some of the advantages of Database Gateways are that they facilitate transparent access to non-Oracle database tables, offer transparent data-type mapping, shield users from SQL semantics of the source database, and provide session and transaction management capabilities. Also, Oracle SQL statements can be used to access remote database objects as though they are residing in an Oracle database, and you can use database links to connect to non-Oracle databases as though you are accessing tables between two distinct Oracle databases. When you use Database Gateways, objects from non-Oracle databases can be created in Oracle with or without the data they contain. A table from a non-Oracle database can be created in Oracle as follows:

```
CREATE TABLE [TABLE_NAME] AS SELECT * FROM [TABLE_NAME]@[DATABASE_LINK];
```

Database Gateways also allow you to reverse-engineer database tables, as well as migrate data, as they can map data types automatically.

On its own, database schema migration is an important task because it lays the foundation for the target database. As such, it is crucial that database schema migration is performed carefully, and that all the technical aspects of the source database are handled appropriately in the Oracle database, to ensure a smooth and successful migration. In the following sections, we will discuss database schema and data migration tasks in depth.

DATABASE SCHEMA MIGRATION TASKS

The first step in the schema migration process is to map the logical and physical grouping of objects in the source database to the target database. To support an application, all database objects, including tables, indexes, views, and stored procedures, are *physically* grouped together by placing them in a database, or *logically* grouped together in a schema within a database. Sybase, SQL Server, DB2, and Informix are among those databases that support physical grouping of database objects; therefore, in these databases, it is possible to have schemas and objects with the same names existing under different databases with different structures. Oracle, however, allows only logical grouping of database objects via the use of *schemas*. In each Oracle database instance, only one database is allowed, and each database user created in Oracle is associated with a schema of the same name as the user. This difference results in a flattening of the schema organization in Oracle as compared to most other databases. Therefore, when migrating to Oracle it is essential that database objects in different schemas are mapped out and that corresponding schemas are set up for migration.

Another challenge that arises during schema migration is that when dependencies exist among different databases and schemas at the source, the target schema objects in Oracle will not be able to refer to these objects in other databases as they are being migrated. Therefore, having circular dependencies among objects in databases and schemas at the source complicates database migration. In such situations, it is best to create the schemas in Oracle before creating the objects in them, and to grant them privileges such as SELECT ANY TABLE or EXECUTE ANY PROCEDURE. Alternatively, the database administrator (DBA) role can be given to the Oracle database user(s) created exclusively for migration tasks. This will ensure that objects created in the target schema can access objects in other schemas, thereby avoiding compilation errors post-migration. Note that it may be necessary to recompile database objects a few times to make sure all the objects can resolve database/ schema dependencies post-migration. However, after the migration process is complete, these privileges can be revoked from the databases users in the Oracle database to meet the security standards of the organization.

> **WARNING**
>
> Since many databases allow multiple physical databases to reside under one database engine, a *database* in non-Oracle databases generally maps into a *schema* in Oracle. However, sometimes a particular database at the source may need to be split into multiple schemas in Oracle based on how the objects are organized within that database. If database names are hard-coded along with the object name (e.g., pubs2.aix in the application) changes to object layout in Oracle in terms of new schemas may result in application changes.

The next task in the database schema migration process is to map the data types in the source database to the target database. Although tools such as SQL Developer do a good job of mapping data types automatically, sometimes some of the default mappings may have to be altered. Mapping of numeric and character data types is fairly easy, since most databases have similar characteristics, with the exception of the following in Oracle:

- **Numeric data types**   Oracle has a single numeric data type, NUMBER, for managing all numeric data, including integers and doubles. It is possible to create database tables with data types such as INT and INTEGER in Oracle, but they are converted to the NUMBER data type implicitly (i.e., the data types are converted to NUMBER when they are created in the database). Oracle also supports the IEEE data types BINARY_DOUBLE and BINARY_FLOAT natively. These data types are more performant because they are managed natively in Oracle instead of being converted to the NUMBER data type. Table 5.1 lists the mappings of the most commonly used numeric data types in relational databases.

- **Character data types**   Oracle has the CHAR data type to support fixed-length character data with a maximum length of 4,000 bytes. It also has the VARCHAR2 data type to support character data of varying lengths with a maximum length of 4,000 bytes. To support Unicode data in table columns Oracle provides NCHAR and NVARCHAR2 for fixed-length and varying-length data fields. Table 5.2 lists the mappings of character data types in relational databases. In cases where the CHAR data type is used with the NULLABLE attribute in the source database (e.g., in

Table 5.1 Common Numeric Data Types in Relational Databases

Data Type	Non-Oracle Databases	Oracle
Integer	Integer	Number(10)
SmallInt	SmallInt	Number(5)
Decimal	Decimal(p,[q]), Money(p,[q])	Number(p,[q])
Real	Real	Number
Float	Float	Float, Binary_Float
Double	Double	Number (p,[q]), Binary_double

Table 5.2 Common Character Data Types in Relational Databases

Data Type	Non-Oracle Databases	Oracle
Fixed-length character data	CHAR(n)	CHAR(n) (<= 4000 bytes)
Varying-length character data	VARCHAR(n) (n<32767)	VARCHAR2(n) (n<=4000)
Unicode fixed-length character data	NCHAR(n)	NCHAR (n) (n<=1000)
Unicode varying-length character data	NVARCHAR(n)	NVARCHAR2(n) (n<=1000)

Sybase, `CHAR` data-type columns with the `NULLABLE` attribute are treated as the `VARCHAR` data type), it is better to map them into the `VARCHAR2` data type in Oracle. This is because, in Oracle, `CHAR` data types always have to be padded with spaces up to their maximum length in predicates to ensure correct evaluation regardless of how they are defined (e.g., `NULLABLE` or `NOT NULL`).

- **Character and binary large object data types**   These data types are primarily used for storing large amounts of data in a single column, whether it is character data or binary data in a record of data in a table. These data types are provided for optimal storage management, and they improve overall database performance by separating the storage of large data chunks from frequently accessed, smaller chunks of character data of the `CHAR`/`VARCHAR2` data types. Oracle mandates that data chunks larger than 4,000 bytes (1,000 bytes of Unicode data) be stored in the `CLOB`/`BLOB` data types. Typically, the `CLOB` data type is used for storing data in plain-text format, such as text/XML files, whereas the `BLOB` data type is used for storing binary data such as images, audio/video data, and Microsoft Office documents. Additionally, columns of these data types can be indexed to enable faster searches. For manipulating data in columns defined with these data types, special APIs are made available to developers, because in most deployments, data is inserted into these columns from files of different types, and data retrieval and presentation to users is accomplished via special interfaces such as Microsoft Office, browsers, and PDF readers. Oracle supports up to 4 terabytes (TB) of data in a single column of these data types. Databases have different naming conventions for these data types. Table 5.3 lists the data-type mapping between Oracle and other databases.

NOTE

The data-type mappings listed in Table 5.3 and those that are performed by migration tools by default need to be evaluated carefully. For example, if a source database has a table with a column containing the `VARCHAR(Max)`, `Text`, or `CHARACTER` data type, it need not be converted to a `CLOB` data type in Oracle if the maximum data length (real versus the limit) in the column is less than 4,000 bytes. In such cases, the data type for the column in Oracle can be set to `VARCHAR2`. Any changes to data types between the source and target databases not including simple numeric/character data types may result in changes to the APIs used to manipulate data in the columns of these data types.

Table 5.3 `CLOB`/`BLOB` Data-Type Mapping between Oracle and Other Databases

Data Type	Non-Oracle Databases	Oracle
Large character data type	`CHARACTER`(n), `VARCHAR(MAX)`, `TEXT`, `LONGVARCHAR`, `CLOB`	`CLOB`
Large binary data type	`VARBINARY(MAX)`, `VARBINARY`(n), `IMAGE`, `BLOB`	`BLOB`, `RAW (1-2000)`
Unicode large object data type	`NVARCHAR(MAX)`,	`NCLOB`

- **XML data types** XML data in Oracle can be managed in a couple of ways. XML data can be stored in columns of the VARCHAR2 data type (< 4,000 bytes) or in the CLOB/BLOB data types (< 4 TB). When using VARCHAR2 data types to store XML data, Oracle treats the data as though it were regular character data, and does not preserve whitespace and formatting in the XML document. Storing and retrieving XML data natively in Oracle can be accomplished by using the abstract data type XMLType. Using the XMLType data type allows Oracle to perform XML-related operations such as validations and searches. XMLType has built-in methods to manage XML data, and it provides SQL access to XML data in Oracle. This data type also allows XML data to be stored in Oracle in BLOBs as well as decomposing the XML data into relational format (nested tables) depending on how the table/columns are defined. For example, specifying a table as XMLType instructs Oracle to store the XML data in BLOBs, whereas specifying a column data type as XMLType in a table definition allows users to specify a BLOB or relational format (nested tables) as part of the table definition. Databases differ in how they support XML data in terms of data-type naming as well as functionality offered. Databases such as SQL Server and DB2 provide similar functionality with the use of the XML data type as well as using the NVARCHAR and VARCHAR(MAX) data types, just as Oracle does.

TIP

It is better to store XML documents that are frequently updated in small chunks relative to the overall XML document size, such as purchase order documents, as relational tables in Oracle. This can result in better performance, because relational databases are very good at performing online transaction processing (OLTP)-type transactions. But in cases where the formatting and whitespace in the XML document is important, and changes to the XML document are made in large chunks, it is better to persist them as BLOBs.

- **Date/timestamp data types** Oracle supports the DATE data type with precision of up to one second, and the TIMESTAMP data type with precision of up to one millisecond and support for time zones. Databases vary in terms of support for granularity of date/timestamp data, as highlighted in Table 5.4.

Table 5.4 Comparison of DATE/TIMESTAMP Granularity in Relational Databases

Data Type	Non-Oracle Databases	Oracle
Date	SMALLDATETIME, DATETIME	DATE (precision up to one second)
Timestamp	DATETIME, TIMESTAMP	TIMESTAMP
Time	Time(DB2)	NUMBER or VARCHAR2 (no equivalent data type)

- `BIT`/`BOOLEAN` **data types**   As mentioned in Chapter 3, since these data types are not supported in Oracle, typically they are mapped into the numeric/character data type in Oracle and implemented database-wide.
- **Special data types**   Most databases have special data types, such as `SERIAL` and `IDENTITY`, to generate unique numbers for use as primary/unique keys in tables. When a new record is inserted into tables with columns of `SERIAL`/`IDENTITY` data types, databases automatically increment the value of the column from the highest value used before to maintain uniqueness. Users do not need to implement logic via triggers or stored procedures to maintain unique values in these columns. Oracle does not support this feature, but it can be implemented in Oracle using a `SEQUENCE` object from which unique numbers can be generated in a series that can then be used as a unique/primary key value in a table. The `SEQUENCE` object in Oracle can be shared across many tables, but in almost all cases it is created separately for each table to maintain the uniqueness and serial order of the unique/primary key values. To implement this feature in Oracle, SQL Developer and other migration tools create `SEQUENCE`s and `TRIGGER`s for each table that has a `SERIAL`/`IDENTITY` column. This ensures that no changes to applications are required due to lack of this functionality in the database. If bulk data-loading activities are occurring on a regular basis on large tables, it is advisable that the `SEQUENCE` object be directly used in the `INSERT` statement instead of using `TRIGGER`s to avoid performance overhead. For example:

```
INSERT INTO [TABLE_NAME] ([COLUMN_LIST]) VALUES (SEQUENCE.NEXTVAL,.......);
```

> **TIP**
>
> When migrating data from other relational databases, it is best to disable `TRIGGER`s associated with the `IDENTITY` columns in Oracle, as there is no need to generate new numbers in Oracle because the data exists at the source and may conflict with existing data in columns used for foreign key constraints in other tables. This also speeds up the data-loading process because execution of the trigger can be avoided.

Databases such as Sybase and SQL Server also have a special column called `TIMESTAMP` (not the same as the `TIMESTAMP` or `DATETIME` data type) that can be included in a table definition. Only one column of this type is allowed per table. This column contains information in binary form regarding the order in which the database engine updates the table rows. The main reason to have this column in a table is to determine whether a row in a table has been updated by another user since the last time it was modified by the current user. As such, this column helps when implementing optimistic locking so that users need not lock rows while reading them, which is the default behavior in these databases. Since Oracle does not need locks when reading data, users do not need to implement special mechanisms for avoiding locks in the database. The only time it makes sense to have this column in Oracle is when the application depends heavily on this column and application changes need to be deferred until later due to time constraints. In such cases, it is better to write a trigger to update this column automatically whenever any row in a table is updated.

The next step is to actually migrate the source database(s)/schema to Oracle using a tool such as Oracle SQL Developer or a tool from another vendor. Almost all such tools do a very good job of migrating database schema objects such as tables, indexes, and views to Oracle. They also assist in producing a Data Definition Language (DDL) script to facilitate target schema creation in Oracle.

Schema migration in SQL Developer essentially consists of four main steps:

1. **Capture metadata from the source database.**   SQL Developer can capture the metadata pertaining to the source database in a couple of ways. It can connect to the source database using a JDBC connection and extract the metadata, or it can provide scripts that can be executed on the source database server to extract the metadata which can later be uploaded into the migration repository.

2. **Convert the captured database model to Oracle.**   SQL Developer converts the source database schema objects to Oracle and stores their definition in Oracle's migration repository. At this stage, the conversion simply takes place in the migration repository and the actual Oracle schema is not generated. SQL Developer also presents the user with the default data-type mappings that can be customized.

3. **Generate the Oracle schema.**   The Oracle schema is generated from the converted model that was created in step 2. You can have SQL Developer create the Oracle schema directly, or you can have SQL Developer generate a DDL script to create the Oracle schema which can then be customized to meet individual requirements. SQL Developer can create index-organized tables (IOTs) in Oracle from clustered indexes in the source database. However, SQL Developer does not create partitioned objects in Oracle, even if the source database objects were partitioned. Therefore, developers need to take additional steps to implement these features as per the guidelines developed in the design and analysis phase.

4. **Verify the Oracle schema.**   It is important to compare the objects created in the Oracle schema with the source schema to identify any missing objects that didn't get converted. SQL Developer assists in this phase by producing a variety of reports on the entire migration process, identifying issues such as which objects were converted successfully, which objects weren't converted, and so on. It also produces reports that compare the number of objects in the source and Oracle databases and their status (i.e., valid or invalid). If the Oracle schema was created with the DDL script in an offline fashion, the output from the script execution also provides information about objects that didn't convert successfully and didn't get created in Oracle. It is essential that all logs generated by SQL Developer or scripts be reviewed for any errors.

As with any tool, SQL Developer also has some limitations in terms of which databases it can migrate and what features and functionality from the source database it cannot migrate to Oracle. SQL Developer Version 3.0 and later support migration of SQL Server, Sybase, DB2 LUW, MySQL, and Teradata databases; SQL Developer does not support migration of Informix databases. The following limitations also apply to this release of SQL Developer with respect to database schema object migration:

- **Conversion of user-defined types**   SQL Developer only supports conversion of simple user-defined types that are created using only a base data type such as CHAR, VARCHAR2, or NUMBER. It does not support conversion of complex user-defined types. It converts simple user-defined data types to their base data types when converting tables to Oracle.
  Solution   To retain the original user-defined types in Oracle, you need to create the types manually, before the schema is generated in Oracle, and you must alter the DDL scripts for schema generation to reflect the user-defined types in Oracle.
- **Table columns with system functions as the** DEFAULT **clause**   Since Oracle does not offer built-in system functions like other databases do, SQL Developer does not convert these functions. As a result, some tables may not get converted to Oracle and may error out during schema creation. Moreover, these types of errors are not reported during the conversion phase in SQL Developer.
  Solution   It is common for developers to use the SUSER_NAME() function as DEFAULT on some columns in Sybase and SQL Server database tables for populating the current database user name in these columns. In Oracle, a majority of the information regarding the current database environment, such as user IDs, session information, and server information, can be extracted from the SYS_CONTEXT function with the USERENV namespace, and can be used as part of the DEFAULT clause value in Oracle database table definitions as follows:

```
Log on to Oracle Database as SCOTT user using the SQL*Plus
  utility.
SQL> create table TEST_DEFAULT (curr_date date,
  curr_user varchar2(30) DEFAULT SYS_CONTEXT('USERENV',
  'CURRENT_USER'));
Table created.
  SQL> insert into TEST_DEFAULT(curr_date) values (sysdate);
1 row created.
SQL> commit;
Commit complete.
SQL> select * from TEST_DEFAULT;
CURR_DATE CURR_USER
--------- ------------------------------
04-APR-11 SCOTT
SQL>
```

> **NOTE**
>
> The default value clause will be effective only if the columns on which it is declared are not part of an INSERT/UPDATE statement. If a user specifies any value for the column with a DEFAULT value including NULL, the default clause will not be executed.

- **Object naming issues and reserved word conflicts**   Some objects may fail to get migrated to Oracle because of restrictions imposed by the Oracle database in terms of the length of the object name and composition of the object name (i.e., use of special characters in the beginning of the object name) and sometimes object names conflict with the reserved words used by the Oracle database.

  Solution   SQL Developer simply appends an underscore (_) to the table or column name that has a conflict with the Oracle database reserved words. If an object name is longer than 30 characters, then SQL Developer will truncate the name so that it is less than 30 characters and will append an underscore, _, as a suffix. The Oracle database also prohibits use of special characters such as # and $ as the first character in object names. In databases such as SQL Server, Sybase temporary table names begin with a #. SQL Developer renames temporary tables with a prefix of TT_ as a workaround. It also generates a report identifying objects that have been affected by these issues. Based on the report, the DDL script for the Oracle database schema can be customized to change the object names/definitions appropriately.

After the Oracle database schema is created and verified with the source database, it is time to start the data migration task, which we will cover in the following sections.

DATA MIGRATION

Data migration, along with schema migration, is often the easiest task in any database migration project. Migration projects typically start with data migration to verify the schema migration tasks as well as to assist in other migration tasks, such as stored program migrations. For large database migrations, often a small subset of data from a test database is migrated to assist with testing efforts as well as to validate the data migration options and tools to be used. Organizations have many options and tools to choose from for data migration, as we discussed in Chapter 3. Each data migration option we discussed in Chapter 3 can be optimized to improve data load performance and reduce overall data migration time. Newer platforms with enhanced software and hardware technologies, such as Oracle Exadata Database Machine, can load data at a rate of 12 TB per hour. Data load rates can vary based on factors such as system configuration, number of indexes on the tables, and data types used. Not all systems can deliver the same performance as Oracle Exadata Database Machine, but in general, the time it takes to load data into Oracle from the source is not significant compared to the time involved in the overall data migration process.

Table 5.5 Level of Time Required for Different Activities Using Various Migration Options

Data Migration Task	Offline Method Using Scripts and/or Command-Line Interfaces (CLIs)	Using ETL Tools	Using Custom Data Migration Tools
Setup/configuration	High	Medium	Low
Runtime monitoring	High	Low	Low
Ability to be restarted	High	Low	Low
Performance	High	High	High
Learning curve	Low	Medium/high	Low

A majority of the time is spent preparing to extract data from the source system, transporting it to the target system, and validating the data-loading options and tools before loading the data into the Oracle database and verifying the data for accuracy after the data migration process is complete. The effort required to verify the data depends on the tools used. Most tools available for data verification post-migration require some manual effort in the form of creating verification policies which may consist of identifying the columns and tables that need to be verified, the data sampling size, and success and failure criteria. Table 5.5 summarizes the level of time required for different data migration options.

The data migration life cycle consists of four distinct and important phases. You should carefully consider each phase, as extracting data from a large and complex database and loading it into an Oracle database can be a resource-intensive task.

Data Extraction

There are three main considerations when extracting data from a source database. The first concerns the tools used to extract the data from the source database (whether it is the most recently backed up version of the database or a production version). In most data migration efforts, data is extracted from the source database into ASCII delimited files (flat files) using native utilities provided by the source database. To unload data from a large number of tables, SQL scripting or tools such as Oracle SQL Developer can be used to generate data unloading scripts which use the native database utilities. You should not use some of these tools to extract data when the database is in use, as they may cause table-level locks, which can further escalate into deadlocks in the database during peak hours. So, for large and heavily accessed databases, it is better to extract data from the source database during off-peak hours or to restore the most recent copy of the database on a separate server. Depending on the size of the database, data files can be very large and may require a large staging area. For very large tables that are partitioned in the source database, it is useful to extract the data from each partition into a separate file so that the data extraction process can be staggered and so that you do not have to allocate huge staging areas before transferring the files to the target system. Extracting data partitions from very large tables into files and then compressing them can also reduce the need for large staging areas as well as significantly improve the speed of the data file transfer process. Another advantage of this method is that using a separate file for each partition will allow the data-loading process on Oracle to be run in parallel, which can speed up the overall data migration process.

The second consideration for data extraction is the allocation of temporary storage for staging the data files. Sometimes it is difficult for organizations to allocate large amounts of storage space within their own IT infrastructure. In such cases, temporary storage can be allocated from cloud service providers. Cloud providers can meet temporary storage requirements at a very short notice, so they can be of great help in completing data migration tasks on time. However, depending on the sensitivity of the data and on regulatory/compliance requirements, the data files may need to be encrypted before they are transferred to servers in the cloud. The encryption and decryption process certainly can add additional overhead to the data migration task.

However, data privacy/security concerns and compliance requirements with mandatory government regulations such as HIPAA, Sarbanes-Oxley, etc., as well as corporate governance policies, may restrict organizations, especially those in the financial, health, and insurance industries, from sharing/storing data outside their own data centers. Governance, Regulations, and Compliance (GRC) reasons may force organizations to come up with plans to allocate staging areas within their own data centers as opposed to leveraging a cloud provider.

The third consideration during the data extraction process concerns formatting the data extracted from the source file into flat files. If data files have records of varying lengths with no distinct record separator, it will be difficult to load records from the data file later. Therefore, the data should be formatted either as a fixed-length record or as a varying-length record with a record separator. Having special characters embedded in character field values in varying-length records, such as \ or *, can cause problems during data loading in Oracle using SQL*Loader, because these characters can confuse SQL*Loader into considering them to be special instructions such as End of Line (EOL) or EOF (End of Field). Similarly, data records that have 00/00/0000 for date fields can be rejected later when they are loaded into Oracle. If possible, before you load the data into Oracle, you should clean it by executing scripts that can remove special characters from the data file.

Data Staging and Transfer

For small databases (10 GB or less in size), the data transfer process is not a big task. This is not the case when dealing with very large databases, however. To reduce the time required to transfer very large data files from the source to the target system, organizations have to consider compressing and decompressing their data files before and after the data transfer process, and they should determine the potential impact of performing this task on data migration timelines. File Transfer Protocol (FTP) utilities are available that can compress data on the fly during transmission. These utilities can be of great help in transferring large data files from the source to the target system. However, one major disadvantage with using this approach to transfer data files from one server to another is that large staging areas may be required on both servers until the data is loaded into the Oracle database. This approach will also delay the data-loading process on the target server until the file transfer operation is complete. To work around this issue, you should unload the data from the source database, transfer the data, and then load it into the Oracle database in stages so that there is no need to set up huge staging areas in both the source and target systems and then wait for the data transfer process to be complete before the data-loading process can begin.

Depending on the platforms used for the source and target databases and the availability of network connections between them and their physical locations, Network File System (NFS) can be used to share the data files between the source and target systems. Using this method, you can avoid the use of utilities such as FTP to transfer data files between systems, and therefore save a significant amount of time. If, for security reasons, physical network connectivity between the source system and the target system is not available within the same data center, portable drives such as Universal Serial Bus (USB)-based drives can be used to transfer the data. Again, this is feasible only if both the source and the target servers support USB drives. In newer systems this may not be a problem, but older systems used for the source database may not support USB devices.

When utilizing Oracle Exadata Database Machine as the target system, a database file system (DBFS) based on Oracle database technologies such as SecureFile LOBs can be used as a staging area for the data files that can be loaded into the Oracle database later. The Oracle DBFS is a feature that allows you to access files and directories stored in an Oracle database via a standard file system interface. Similar to NFS, it provides a shared network file system that looks like a local file system. It also has two components: a server and a client. The Oracle database acts as a server in this case, storing all the files in the DBFS as a SecureFile LOB. File system operation APIs are implemented in PL/SQL procedures. The DBFS allows you to create many file systems in one database installation, and store each file system's content in its own set of tables. DBFS is configured out of the box on Exadata Database Machine and is available for immediate use as a staging area for ETL tasks, file storage, and so forth. This removes the need to allocate separate staging areas on the Exadata Database Machine; the Oracle database backs up the files in this file system automatically as part of regular database backups. Using DBFS also allows faster loading of data from flat files into Oracle, since the files are accessed by the database using the high-performance InfiniBand network available in the system.

The process of staging data files on the source system and then transferring them to the target Oracle system for loading can also be avoided using named pipes. Named pipes are a mechanism for interprocess communication between processes on a server using First In, First Out (FIFO) buffers. Data transfer using named pipes can be extremely fast because it does not involve disk I/O, as the data transfer takes place via buffers. Named pipes also do not occupy space on the servers' local file system, thereby avoiding the need for a dedicated staging area on the server for data transfers. Named pipes are supported by almost all operating systems (as long as they are POSIX-compliant) and can be created as follows:

Named pipes can be created using either the *mkfifo* or *mknod* command on UNIX/Linux systems.

```
    mkfifo /tmp/mypipe
    OR
    mknod /tmp/mypipe p
```

Extracting data from a Sybase table to the named pipe created earlier:

```
    bcp testdb.dbo.employee out /tmp/mypipe -n -Usa -SLOCALDB -Pmypassword &
```

Loading data into Oracle using the same named pipe as input:

```
    Sqlldr userid=scott/tiger control=employee.ctl data=/tmp/mypipe &
```

Using "&" makes the data extraction and loading processes run in the background so that they can be launched from the same UNIX/Linux sessions.

NOTE

In this sample, it is assumed that both the Sybase server and at least the Oracle client server are installed on the same server. Generally, named pipes are only accessible locally on any server; however, access to a named pipe on a remote server is possible via tunnelling between the source and target servers using utilities such as Secure Shell (SSH).

Another advantage of using named pipes for data exchange is that the data-loading process does not have to wait for the data extraction and transfer process to complete, like it does in the traditional method of using files. Data loading can begin as soon as the data is fed into named pipes on the source system. This can dramatically reduce the overall data extraction and loading time.

Data Loading

You can load data into an Oracle database in many ways, using a variety of tools from Oracle as well as third-party providers. The Oracle SQL*Loader utility is the most commonly used tool for this purpose, as it is very efficient, easy to use, and free of charge. Oracle Database also offers a feature called external tables that provides functionality similar to the SQL*Loader utility (i.e., reading data from flat files), but in addition, it facilitates row-level data processing if required. External tables allow you to process data in flat files as though it were residing in a regular database table, and perform other SQL operations such as joins with other tables, cursor operations in stored procedures, and so on. ETL tools such as ODI, Oracle Warehouse Builder (OWB), SQL Developer, and Oracle Database Gateways can also be used for data migration and loading. Of these four tools, SQL

Developer and Database Gateways are the easiest to configure and migrate data. ODI and OWB can also be used for data migration, but there is a learning curve involved in mastering these tools as they are ETL tools that are rich in features and functionality, and they require some time to install and configure as compared to SQL Developer and Database Gateways. However, using sample code, tutorials available on the Web can shorten this learning curve to a great extent. In addition, these tools offer great features for monitoring and error handling as well as restart capabilities for data migration tasks required in large database migration projects. Moreover, they can connect to a variety of databases using standard APIs such as JDBC and ODBC in addition to leveraging the native utilities of the source and target databases, which may turn out to be a better solution for migrating data from smaller tables in the source database.

Let's take a look at how to optimize various Oracle tools to further reduce the time required for data migration.

Data Loading Using Oracle SQL*Loader

Loading data using Oracle SQL*Loader is the most popular method because database administrators are familiar with this tool since they use it every day. This method is also preferred when migrating tables with large amounts of data because it provides flexibility and convenience in terms of customizing the data-loading process.

Creating scripts to unload data from the source and load it into target database tables, especially when migrating data from many databases and schemas, requires a lot of effort. Additional scripts may be required for tasks such as disabling and enabling triggers and disabling referential integrity constraints during the data-loading process. Even if SQL*Loader is chosen for performing data-loading tasks, tools such as SQL Developer can aid in this process in the following ways:

- It can generate scripts to unload data from the source database and load data into Oracle using SQL*Loader.
- It can generate scripts to disable referential integrity constraints so that data can be loaded into tables in any order, and then reenable referential integrity constraints post-migration.
- It can generate scripts to disable and enable triggers on tables such as those for generating unique values for the primary and unique keys in the target database.
- It can add support for migrating CLOB/BLOB data-related constructs in the SQL*Loader scripts as well as pre- and post-loading scripts.
- It can provide configurable parameters such as default DATE/TIMESTAMP formats as well as NLS parameters for handling Unicode data as required by the Oracle database.

SQL*Loader provides many features, such as direct-path loading, parallel loading, and skipping of index maintenance, to speed up the data-loading process.

Using the Direct-Path Load Option in SQL*Loader

The direct-path load option in SQL*Loader enables faster data-loading operations because it bypasses SQL command processing in the Oracle database engine, as well as formats buffers with data and writes to database files directly. The conventional load option, on the other hand, formats buffers with data and prepares an INSERT statement before passing it to the database for execution. Hence, the direct-path load option is significantly faster than the conventional load option and generates less of a load on the database. When using the direct-path load option on multi-CPU systems, SQL*Loader uses multithreading by default, which enables conversion of column arrays to stream buffers and the loading of stream buffers in parallel. The following are key features of the direct-path load option in SQL*Loader that aid in the data-loading process:

- It always uses new blocks to write data into the database. As a result, it spends less time scanning partially filled data blocks for space.
- It uses multi-block asynchronous I/O for database writes.
- During the data load operation, the load process writes its own I/O, so it does not stress the database server and causes less contention with other users.
- Loading presorted data into empty tables is very efficient, as it eliminates the sort and merge phase of index building.

There are some restrictions in terms of when this option can be used in SQL*Loader because of its ability to bypass the SQL command option in the database. The main restrictions when using the direct-path load option with SQL*Loader are as follows:

- Referential integrity and check constraints should not be enabled on a table or a partition of a table.
- Triggers should not be enabled on a table.
- Loading data into a table with the BFILE column is not allowed. BFILE columns (data type) allow you to store the reference to a file on the operating system in the database.
- Use of SEQUENCE objects to generate unique numbers for primary and unique keys is not allowed since this option does not generate a SQL INSERT statement for the operation.
- Loading data into a parent and child table together is not allowed because referential integrity constraints must be disabled when using this option.
- The default clause on field values is not enforced with this option.

This option is enabled by passing the parameter DIRECT=TRUE to the SQL*Loader command line. For example:

```
sqlldr userid=scott/tiger control=emp.ctl direct=true
```

Using the PARALLEL Option in SQL*Loader

By default, only a single session of SQL*Loader is allowed to load data into one table. So, when loading data into large tables (partitioned or otherwise), it is desirable to be able to load data in parallel. Using the `PARALLEL` option, multiple sessions of SQL*Loader can be run to load data into a table with each session reading data from a separate input file. Note that, in this case, it is necessary to create multiple input files from the large data file. This option can also be used with the direct-path load option.

Multiple SQL*Loader sessions can be launched to load data in parallel into a table, as shown in the following code:

```
sqlldr userid=scott/tiger control=emp1.ctl direct=true parallel=true
sqlldr userid=scott/tiger control=emp2.ctl direct=true parallel=true
```

Bypassing Index Maintenance

Normally when data is loaded into tables in a relational database, associated indexes are updated to reflect the newly added data. Having many indexes on such tables can slow the data-loading process to a great extent. For this reason, when loading large amounts of data into tables it is recommended that you avoid index maintenance either by dropping the indexes before the data is loaded or by marking the indexes as unusable.

SQL*Loader provides two options for skipping index maintenance. Once again, this can improve performance for tables with a large number of indexes on them. To enable skipping of index maintenance in SQL*Loader use the `SKIP_INDEX_ MAINTENANCE` parameter (the default is `FALSE`) or the `SKIP_UNUSABLE_INDEXES` parameter (the default is `FALSE`), as illustrated in the following code:

```
    sqlldr userid=scott/tiger control=emp.ctl direct=true
skip_index_maintenance = true
    OR
    sqlldr userid=scott/tiger control=emp.ctl direct=true
skip_unusable_maintenance = true
```

The main difference between these two parameters is that the `SKIP_INDEX_ MAINTENANCE` parameter instructs SQL*Loader to avoid index maintenance altogether. When this parameter is used in SQL*Loader, it marks all the indexes on the table as unusable. As a result, after the data is loaded into a table, all the indexes on the table need to be rebuilt. The `SKIP_UNUSABLE_INDEXES` parameter, on the other hand, instructs SQL*Loader to not report errors when it encounters unusable indexes on a table during the data load operation. This means the indexes have been marked as unusable due to a previous operation on the table.

TIP

To rebuild indexes on large tables after a data load operation is complete you use the `PARALLEL` clause on the index so that all available resources (CPU, memory, I/O bandwidth, etc.) can be utilized fully. Using the `PARALLEL` clause for the index rebuild operation can speed up this process significantly. The `PARALLEL` clause can be altered as desired after the index rebuild process with a simple `ALTER INDEX` command.

Besides the aforementioned options in SQL*Loader, additional parameters available for further optimizing the direct-path load option include the ROWS parameter which controls the frequency of data saves (by the number of rows), the STREAMSIZE parameter (the default is 256000), and the COLUMNARRAYROWS parameter (the default is 500).

Data Loading Using the External Table Feature

Like SQL*Loader, external tables also aid in loading data from flat files into an Oracle database. As we discussed in the "Data Loading Using Oracle SQL*Loader" section, external tables allow users to create a table in the database where the data is stored in a file on the operating system (not in the database itself). Essentially, this feature provides a relational table-like interface to flat files for performing read and write operations seamlessly via SQL statements. Cursors can be opened on these tables and row-by-row processing can be performed if desired in a stored procedure or function in the database, just like in regular tables. An external table is created just like a regular table, with a few additional parameters to indicate where the flat file resides and some additional optional parameters such as file preprocessing parameters, as follows:

1. Create a DIRECTORY object in Oracle where the data file is located and give permissions to the desired user or to PUBLIC:

```
create OR replace directory EMP_DIR AS '/tmp/empdata';
grant read,write on directory EMP_DIR to public;
```

2. Create the external table with the name of the data file as part of the LOCATION clause and pass the DIRECTORY created earlier as the parameter for the DEFAULT DIRECTORY:

```
create table EMP_EXT
    (emp_number        CHAR(5),
    emp_last_name      CHAR(20),
    emp_first_name     CHAR(15),
    emp_middle_name    CHAR(15),
    emp_hire_date      CHAR(10))
    organization external
    (type oracle_loader
    default directory EMP_DIR
    access parameters
    (records delimited by newline
    fields (emp_number  char(5),
       emp_last_name       char(20),
       emp_first_name      char(15),
       emp_middle_name     char(15),
       emp_hire_date       char(10) date_format DATE mask ''mm/dd/yyyy''
       )
) location ('emp.dat')
);
```

```
    sqlldr userid=scott/tiger control=emp.ctl direct=true
skip_index_maintenance = true
```

or

```
    sqlldr userid=scott/tiger control=emp.ctl direct=true
skip_unusable_maintenance = true
```

With external tables, there are no parameters to instruct it to use a direct-path option to load the data into the table. To achieve similar performance benefits as direct-path loading in SQL*Loader, the INSERT statement used in conjunction with a SELECT statement on an external table should include the APPEND hint. Also, external tables do not have parameters that are similar to ROWS or COLUMNARRAYSIZE that are available for SQL*Loader, as SQL*Loader allows programmatic access to the data in the underlying flat file, giving users more control.

> **TIP**
>
> For best performance with external tables, use the PARALLEL clause on the external table and the APPEND hint on the target table. When using the PARALLEL clause on the external table in an Oracle Database Real Application Clusters (RAC) environment, make sure the input data file is available on all the nodes in the cluster so that any node that participates in the parallel operation can read data from the input file. For this purpose, DBFS can be used to stage the data file for use by external tables.

External tables also have a couple of advantages over the SQL*Loader utility in terms of how they read data from flat files and write it to database tables. As we discussed previously in the "Data Loading Using Oracle SQL*Loader" section, when you are using SQL*Loader and you want to speed up performance by loading data in parallel into a table, you must split the input file into many files. With external tables, however, users can specify the parallel read option just as they specify it on regular database tables without needing to split the data files—for example, by using the PARALLEL hint in the SQL SELECT statement, as illustrated in the following code:

```
    insert /*+ APPEND */ into EMP as select * /*+ PARALLEL(EMP_EXT, 4) */ from
EMP_EXT;
```

With this INSERT statement, the input data file will be read in parallel by multiple processes and loaded into the database table.

SQL*Loader and the external table feature perform in a similar manner. External tables do have more restrictions in terms of the data types they support (e.g., they do not support LONG data types), but they can read and write dump files that are compatible with the Oracle Data Pump utility. External tables are especially useful when data from a flat file needs to be joined with other tables in the database for transformation in a data warehouse (DW) environment.

Data Loading Using SQL Developer

A major challenge when using a purely script-based approach is the monitoring and management of numerous scripts to complete the data migration task, because for each table, there will be a SQL*Loader control file and a corresponding script or entry in a batch file for extracting data from the source database. It is a tedious task to ensure that all scripts have executed successfully and data has been loaded correctly without any rejections or errors. With numerous scripts to execute, it is important to be able to execute some of the scripts in parallel to speed up the data-loading process. Customizing the scripts, executing them in parallel, and then monitoring their progress requires additional effort.

Oracle SQL Developer can facilitate data migration from a source database to Oracle by directly connecting the databases using a JDBC driver, or by generating scripts to facilitate the data migration in an offline manner, as we discussed earlier in the "Data Loading Using Oracle SQL*Loader" section of this chapter. The main advantage of using SQL Developer in any migration project is that it enables users to migrate data in schema objects from the source database to Oracle with a click of a button. As part of the migration exercise using SQL Developer, users are required to set up source and target database connections; however, the same connections can be leveraged to perform data migration. This feature is very helpful, especially when there are hundreds or thousands of little tables that need to be migrated to Oracle. Regardless of the number of tables to migrate data from, SQL Developer can open many connections (configurable) to the source database, and transfer data in parallel from multiple tables, as well as reuse the connections to migrate data from the next set of tables. SQL Developer also reports the number of rows processed, errors, and similar information during the data migration, making it easier to monitor progress.

Performance of any data migration effort is very important, especially for large databases. SQL Developer's online data move option eases the effort required to move many small tables from the source database. However, it may also cause locking and lock escalations on the source database during peak hours due to heavy load, because many of these databases require locking of rows in tables when reading from them. In SQL Developer Version 3.0, there is no facility for setting appropriate isolation levels to support reading of uncommitted data to avoid lock generation. Therefore, it is important that users take appropriate precautions to deal with locking scenarios when using SQL Developer. Normally, SQL Developer is installed on a desktop or a laptop in the organization, and using that configuration for data movement will involve more than one network trip for the data (i.e., source database | SQL Developer | target database). To improve performance of the data move operation, it is best to install SQL Developer on either the source or the target system to avoid the additional network trip. Also note that you can deploy SQL Developer on all platforms, including Windows, Linux, and UNIX, as it is a Java-based tool.

When using scripts to unload data from the source and load data into Oracle, SQL Developer also generates a launch script for starting the individual table-loading operations in serial mode. This launch script can be split into multiple scripts so that multiple load operations can be started in parallel.

Data Migration Using ETL Tools Such as ODI

ETL tools such as ODI facilitate data migration in addition to offering robust features for data transformation, quality, and profiling. Data migration is an inherent capability of these tools. Unlike tools used exclusively for data migration from Oracle and other vendors, ETL tools such as ODI support a range of data sources as both source and target. They also support many connectivity options, such as ODBC, JDBC, file-based, and messaging, among others. ODI has the capability to reverse-engineer tables from many databases, and provides interfaces to migrate data from the source database to the target using native utilities as well as a generic JDBC driver-based interface. ODI can also schedule and monitor data migration tasks and automatically alert users regarding the status of task execution. Drag-and-drop functionality in ODI makes it easier to perform data migration tasks with error handling as well as restart and resume capabilities.

As with any ETL tool, using ODI for data migration involves a small learning curve, especially for organizations that are not familiar with it. However, ODI, with its flexible deployment capabilities in terms of both ETL and extract-load-transform (ELT), can assist organizations in building a leaner and more performant enterprise data integration and migration platform. ODI's capability to run data-loading and transformation capabilities without using an intermediary staging server makes it an excellent choice in many environments that are interested in avoiding building separate staging infrastructure as well as improving performance by directly loading and transforming data at the target database.

WARNING

Using the target database for loading and transformation activities may increase the load on the database. It is essential that the target system/database is configured and sized appropriately, keeping in mind the need for loading and transformation tasks.

DATA VALIDATION

It is important that the data in the new environment is exactly the same as the data in the old environment. Failure to verify the data post-migration may result in financial and legal trouble for businesses. Data verification for smaller databases is easy and can be performed visually in an ad hoc manner. However, verifying data in a large database environment can be challenging because of the amount and type of data that needs to be identified for verification and scanned for accuracy. Even with the existence of tools for data validation, some manual effort in terms of defining policies is required. Predefined policies for data validation in a complex environment are difficult to set up and maintain. Typical data elements that are considered for validation after a complex migration process include the following:

- **Accuracy of numeric data elements with decimal places**   Typically, columns that contain numeric data with decimals representing financial data, such as the cost or value of an item or stock, need to be verified so that they are accurate up to the last decimal place. During migration, any errors in the data-type mapping between Oracle and other databases can result in the decimal places getting truncated or even general truncation of the data element. As a result, the financial data will not be accurate in the new environment. Therefore, it is necessary to identify such data elements in the target database and verify them with the source database.
- **Accuracy of** DATE/TIMESTAMP **data**   Due to the difference in DATE/TIMESTAMP data element granularity, it is important to verify the accuracy of such data. DATE/TIMESTAMP data plays a very important role in all sorts of calculations, but particularly those in the financial industry. Validating columns with these data elements by checking the maximum and minimum values in the columns as well as completing a random and ad hoc visual verification of the data with a focus on granularity is very important.
- **Unprintable characters in character data**   Sometimes errors in data-loading scripts may result in the loading of field delimiters and other unprintable characters into character data elements. Although this may not cause major data integrity issues, it may not be acceptable to the business to have unprintable data in the customer-facing side of the business, especially in regard to customer names, addresses, and similar information. A common technique employed to detect data quality issues in such cases is to scan for unprintable characters separately from alphanumeric data that is usually present in such data elements.
- CLOB/BLOB **data elements**   Usually, CLOB/BLOB data is unloaded into separate files using scripts. However, any errors in referring to the size of the CLOB/BLOB data in the loading scripts may result in corrupt data being loaded into the database. Databases generally do not report errors during the loading process because they do not validate the content. The only way to verify the accuracy of such data elements is via ad hoc visual validation.

SQL Developer Version 3.0 has some basic data comparison capabilities in terms of scanning the source and target databases and ensuring that the record counts match. However, this may not be the most effective way to perform data validation because scanning all objects in a very large database will take a long time to complete. Oracle GoldenGate Veridata offers visual data comparison capabilities, but it supports only a few databases, such as Oracle, SQL Server, and Teradata. Migration service providers typically use home-grown solutions to perform data validation in migration projects (examples include TCS DCT, Infosys Clearware, and PracTrans Audit). Moreover, data validation tasks are usually part of a larger migration project, rather than an individual project; hence, the migration services offered by many system integrators and migration service providers often include data validation. Many service providers also use custom scripts as a way to automate data validation tasks. To validate data in environments with very large databases, it is essential that data elements for validation be identified, and that appropriate data validation criteria, such as random block sampling and the average/sum of certain data elements, be defined.

SAMPLE SYBASE DATABASE MIGRATION TO ORACLE USING ORACLE SQL DEVELOPER

Oracle SQL Developer facilitates database migration in a phased approach. Each phase of the migration task can be executed individually or in a wizard-driven manner. SQL Developer provides CLIs to migrate multiple source databases in batch mode, as well as a GUI interface to migrate databases in interactive mode. In this section, we will describe the schema migration process in depth using SQL Developer as the migration tool. As with any tool, there are some prerequisites for using SQL Developer for database migration, which we will discuss in the next section.

Prerequisites for Schema Migration Using SQL Developer

Having some basic knowledge about SQL Developer can go a long way toward jumpstarting a migration project using this tool. For the purposes of this chapter, the following are the prerequisites for performing migrations using SQL Developer:

- **Familiarity with SQL Developer**   This includes familiarity with tasks such as creating connections for databases, changing preferences to register third-party JDBC drivers, and managing database preferences in SQL Developer.
- **Familiarity with the Oracle Database**   This includes familiarity with Oracle database operations such as creating users and tablespaces, granting roles and privileges, and creating database objects.
- **Availability of an Oracle database**   An Oracle database is required to create a user/schema for the migration repository. This user/schema can be different from the user/schema that will be used to create the migrated schema objects in Oracle. Any cloud-based Oracle database service (Platform-as-a-Service or PaaS) can be used for this purpose to reduce the effort involved in acquiring new hardware and/or software for migrations, as well as installation and configuration of the Oracle database. Another advantage of using a cloud service is that user groups performing migrations can bypass security restrictions regarding software and database installations, as well as role and privilege restrictions for performing tasks such as migration repository setup, without violating established security

policies. After the migration is complete, they can get the migrated Oracle schema back into their own environment for further testing. GRC can force organizations to avoid using a cloud service provider because sensitive business information contained in stored procedures, triggers, and views may be stored in the migration repository from the source database.

- **Migration repository user and connection creation**   SQL Developer uses the migration repository to store information it captures and generates during the migration process. This requires a database user, which will be the repository user, and establishing the repository from SQL Developer in this user's schema. If no user exists for use as a repository, a database user/schema needs to be created. The Oracle Database version required for creating a migration repository is Oracle Database 10g or Oracle Database 11g (any edition, whether XE, Standard, or Enterprise). The database user created for the migration repository requires the following roles/privileges at a minimum:
  i. RESOURCE
  ii. CREATE SESSION and CREATE VIEW
    In order to migrate multiple databases simultaneously, additional roles/privileges are required:
  i. The RESOURCE role must be granted with the ADMIN option.
  ii. The CREATE ROLE, CREATE USER, and ALTER ANY TRIGGER roles must be granted with the ADMIN option.
    After creating the database user for the migration repository, a connection for the repository user needs to be created in SQL Developer. Multiple database users may be created depending on the number of migration repositories required, and connections for those users need to be created in SQL Developer before proceeding further.
- **Target user/schema creation**   A database user/schema where the migrated objects will be created in Oracle can also be considered a prerequisite. However, this step is optional, as SQL Developer can create an Oracle database user leveraging a database connection for a privileged database user. At a minimum, the database user for creating all the migrated objects requires the CONNECT/ RESOURCE privilege. SQL Developer can also generate the scripts for creating the target user/schema after the migration process is complete in the form of a DDL script.
- **Migration repository creation**   After creating the migration repository user, the next step is to install the migration repository in the repository user schema. A migration repository is associated with a database user, and since SQL Developer allows creation of multiple migration repositories using a unique database user for each, it is necessary to associate a database user with a migration repository every time SQL Developer is started to perform migration tasks. This feature also allows concurrent migrations from different databases to Oracle by launching SQL Developer in a separate session for each migration project. The migration repository can be created using SQL Developer in two ways:

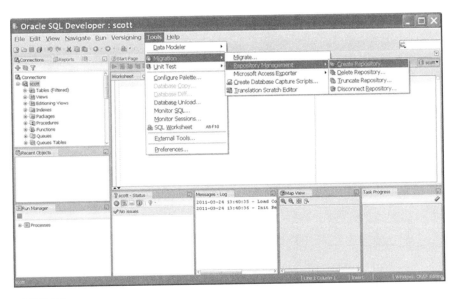

FIGURE 5.1

Migration Repository Creation from Main Toolbar in SQL Developer

   i. You can navigate from the main toolbar in SQL Developer to **Tools |
      Migrate | Repository Management | Create Repository**, as illustrated in
      Figure 5.1.
  ii. You can connect to the database as the repository user utilizing the connection
      previously created as part of the prerequisites, and then right-click on the
      connection and navigate to **Migration Repository | Associate Migration
      Repository**, as illustrated in Figure 5.2. The first time you do this the
      migration repository will be installed and associated with you as the user.
      However, subsequent invocations will simply associate the user/schema with
      the migration repository.

After ensuring that all the prerequisite steps are executed, the next step is to start the
schema migration process.

Database Schema Migration

Migration in SQL Developer is an easy, wizard-driven process. You can launch the
aptly named Migration Wizard directly from the main toolbar, or from the source
database connections and the Projects Explorer pane within SQL Developer. SQL
Developer uses the migration repository heavily for executing all these steps, and
output from each step is fed back into the repository to help generate relevant
reports. The first step SQL Developer executes is to capture metadata from the
source database, convert it to Oracle, and generate scripts for creating the target

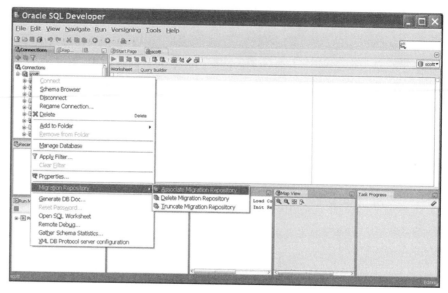

FIGURE 5.2

Creating Migration Repository from the Repository User Connection

Oracle database schema. Each step can be executed individually or in sequence by using the Migration Wizard in SQL Developer. It is also possible to execute only one step and skip the rest that come after it in the Migration Wizard. You can launch the Migration Wizard from the main toolbar by selecting **Tools | Migrate**, as shown in Figure 5.3.

You can also launch the Migration Wizard from the source database connection created in SQL Developer by right-clicking on it and choosing the **Migrate to Oracle** option.

The first step in the migration process in SQL Developer is to capture the metadata of schema objects from the source database. SQL Developer can capture this information in two ways:

1. **Offline capture**   With the offline capture option, SQL Developer can generate source database-specific scripts to unload the metadata files into flat files. After SQL Developer generates these scripts, they are shipped to the source database system and executed to extract the metadata from the database into flat files. The ASCII delimited files are then transferred to the system on which SQL Developer and the capture process in SQL Developer are run to load the metadata into the SQL Developer repository. The capture process simply uploads the data from the flat files into this repository without any transformation. The unload scripts typically use native utilities available in the source database, such as BCP for Sybase and SQL Server, and the UNLOAD command for DB2 for extracting the metadata. This operation does not stress the source system heavily, as it simply

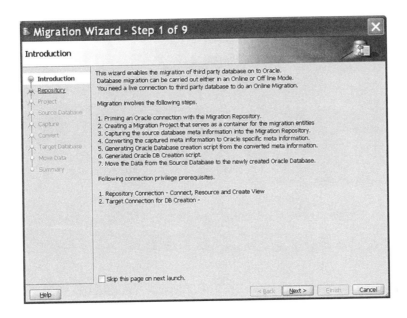

FIGURE 5.3

Migration Wizard in SQL Developer for Step-by-Step Migration

extracts the metadata (not the transaction data) and does not generate locks. This method is useful in cases where the administrative user passwords are not available to the user who is performing the migration, helping to maintain system security. It also helps in cases where a network connection is not available for the source system from SQL Developer due to the way network security is set up. Offline capture scripts cannot be generated from the Migration Wizard, so these scripts have to be generated from the **Tools | Migration | Create Database Capture Scripts** option, as illustrated in Figure 5.4. Clicking on the **Create Database Capture Scripts** option will present another screen, as shown in Figure 5.5, where you can select the database for which the scripts are required, the OS platform for which the scripts need to be created, and the directory where these scripts will be placed (usually the project directory specified in the wizard).

2. **Online capture**   With this method, SQL Developer can connect to the source database using a JDBC driver for the database, and extract the metadata for the schema objects as well as populate the repository. As mentioned in our discussion of the offline capture method, this process does not stress the source system heavily and does not trigger locking or lock escalations. Many open source JDBC drivers are available for different databases that can be leveraged for this purpose (e.g., Sybase and SQL JDBC drivers can be obtained from http://jtds.sourceforge.net). These drivers first need to be registered in SQL

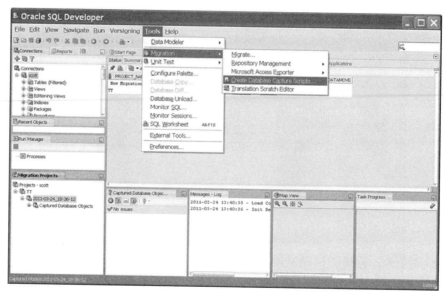

FIGURE 5.4

Accessing the Create Database Capture Scripts Option in SQL Developer

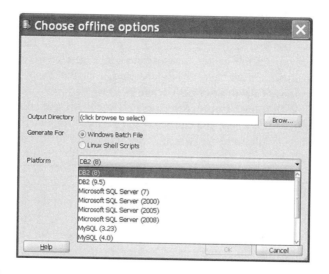

FIGURE 5.5

Options for Creating Database Capture Scripts

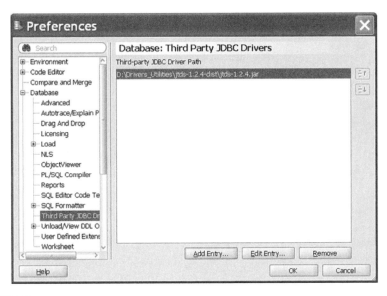

FIGURE 5.6

Registration of Third-Party Database Driver (JDBC) in SQL Developer

Developer so that SQL Developer can connect to the source database, as shown in Figure 5.6. After you register the drivers in SQL Developer, database-specific connection parameters appear in the Create Connection dialog window.

SQL Developer also allows implicit versioning of each capture process execution (i.e., every time a database is captured, it creates a new version of the capture and labels it with a new name in the repository). You can then browse all objects captured in each version available in the repository. Unwanted captures or failed captures can be purged from the repository as desired.

After completing the setup for the offline or online capture method, the next step is to launch the Migration Wizard either from the main toolbar or by right-clicking on the source database connection and choosing the **Migrate to Oracle** option. Each step in the Migration Wizard is explained in this section for better understanding of the process.

1. **Repository**   The first step is to select the database connection for the migration repository. As we discussed previously in the "Prerequisites for Schema Migration Using SQL Developer" section, it is possible to have many migration repositories in SQL Developer, so it is important to pick a database connection that is associated with the intended migration repository, as shown in Figure 5.7.

2. **Project**   In this step, you are asked to give a project name for the migration process and to specify a project directory, as shown in Figure 5.8. Any scripts and/or output from tasks that SQL Developer executes to perform a migration are

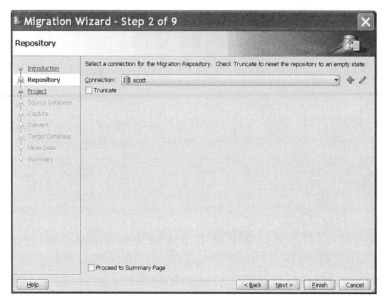

FIGURE 5.7

Selection of Database Connection for Migration Repository

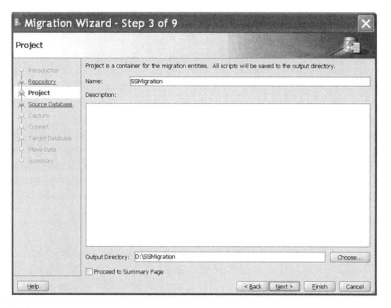

FIGURE 5.8

Specifying Project Properties for Migration

kept in this directory (e.g., DDL scripts for Oracle schema are also generated in this directory after the migration).

3. **Source database**   In this step, the Migration Wizard prompts you for the access mechanism to execute the capture process (i.e., online or offline). For online mode capture, it will prompt you to specify the source database connection created previously using JDBC drivers. For offline mode capture, it will prompt you to specify the directory where the metadata files extracted from the source system using the scripts generated by SQL Developer are kept, as shown in Figure 5.9. Navigate to the directory where the metadata files extracted from the source system are placed after clicking the **Choose** option, as shown in Figure 5.10.

4. **Capture**   Once the source database is made available to SQL Developer either via an online connection or by metadata files collected in offline mode, SQL Developer lists all the available databases from the source and lets you choose the database(s) that will be captured for migration later. In this step, it is possible for you to choose only a few from a list of databases available for migration; if only one database is available for migration, it is automatically chosen, as shown in Figure 5.11.

5. **Convert**   As part of the convert process, SQL Developer will map the data types from the source database into Oracle data types by default, as shown in Figure 5.12. It will then present a view of the mapping which can be edited

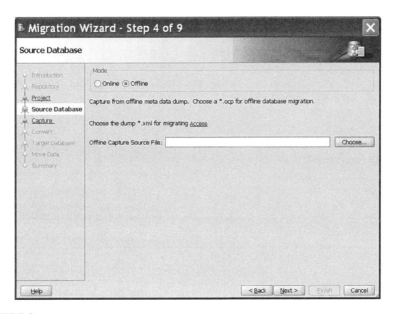

FIGURE 5.9

Selection of Database Capture Method

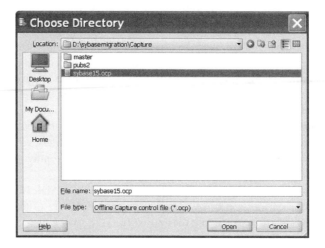

FIGURE 5.10

Selection of Metadata Files for Offline Capture

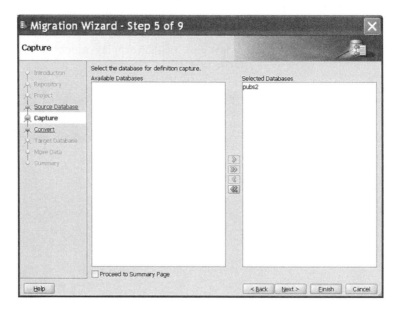

FIGURE 5.11

Selection of Available Database for Capture

as needed. More information on data-type mappings is provided in the "Database Schema Migration Tasks" section of this chapter. Clicking on the **Advanced Options** link at the bottom right-hand side of the screen will present another dialog window, as shown in Figure 5.13, which will allow

FIGURE 5.12

Default Data-Type Mapping for Sybase to Oracle Migration

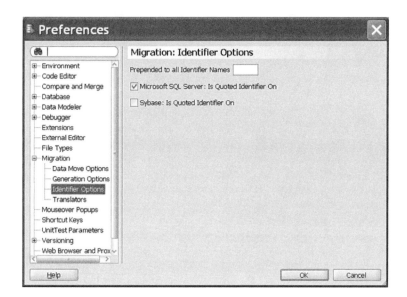

FIGURE 5.13

Setting Migration Preferences

you to decide on the naming conventions for all identifiers (e.g., all identifiers start with v_ or t_).

6. **Target database**   At this stage, you are prompted to specify how the target Oracle schema will be generated (i.e., online or offline). If you choose online mode, SQL Developer will prompt you for a database connection pointing to the target database schema which could reside either in the same database as the repository or in another database instance in a cloud environment. This database connection is then used to create the Oracle database schema objects in the target schema. If you choose offline mode, the scripts required to create the target database schema are generated and placed in the directory specified in step 2; these scripts can be executed later, with any modifications that may be necessary, as shown in Figure 5.14. Clicking on **Advanced Options** at the bottom of the screen presents the next screen, as shown in Figure 5.15, for configuring additional options for schema generation.

7. **Data move**   This step lets you decide how to migrate data from the source database to Oracle (i.e., online or offline), as shown in Figure 5.16. The online option allows you to migrate data from the source using JDBC connections to Oracle. SQL Developer can launch multiple connections to migrate more than one object at a time. This property can also be configured in SQL Developer by navigating to **Tools** | **Preferences** | **Migration** | **Data Move Options** and setting

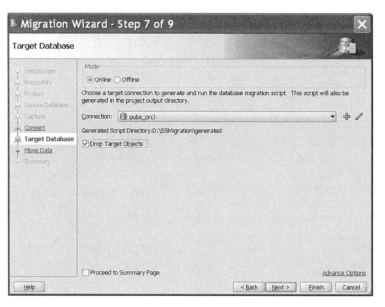

FIGURE 5.14

Target Schema Creation Options

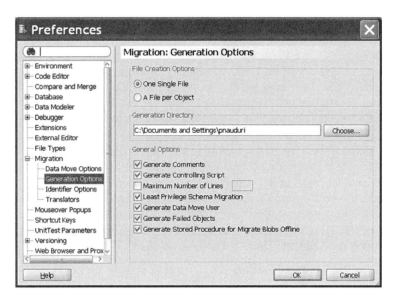

FIGURE 5.15

Advanced Options for Oracle Schema Generation

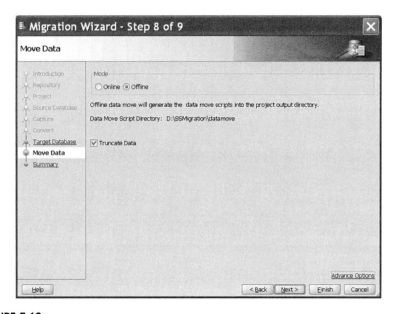

FIGURE 5.16

Data Migration Options Presented by the Migration Wizard

the number of connections based on available system resources (CPU, I/O bandwidth) and network bandwidth. This method is ideal for migrating many small objects from the source database to Oracle without having to manage scripts for data unload and load operations. For migrating tables with large data volumes, however, using special tools such as ODI or using a script-based approach (UNLOAD/LOAD scripts) is recommended. If offline mode is chosen, SQL Developer generates scripts for unloading data from the source database as well as SQL*Loader scripts for loading data into the Oracle database. These scripts are placed in the directory specified as the Project directory in step 1. You are responsible for executing these scripts on the source system and placing the extracted data files on the target system, as well as executing the SQL*Loader scripts to load data into Oracle. SQL Developer generates scripts to disable and enable integrity constraints in the Oracle database during the data-loading process. It can also generate and place commands to truncate data in the load scripts if the **Truncate Data** checkbox is checked.

Clicking on the **Advanced Options** link at the bottom of the screen presents the next dialog window, as shown in Figure 5.17, for configuring additional options for schema generation.

After clicking on the **Next** button and the **Finish** button on the Summary screen, the migration tasks will be executed as chosen. Only the tasks that were chosen will be executed. After the execution completes successfully, the project defined in step 1

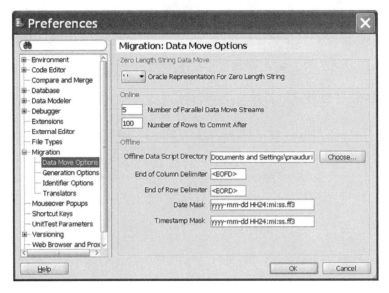

FIGURE 5.17

Data Migration Advanced Options

FIGURE 5.18

Project Explorer in SQL Developer after Successful Migration

appears in the Project Explorer at the bottom left-hand side of the screen in SQL Developer, as shown Figure 5.18.

Under the project tree, both *captured* and *converted* models are displayed so that you can compare how the source object was converted to Oracle.

As demonstrated in this section, you can perform database schema and data migration tasks efficiently using SQL Developer due to its easy-to-use interface and many reports on the migration tasks that can assist in verification and effort estimation.

SUMMARY

It is very important to pick the right set of tools to perform database schema and data migration tasks. All tools have strengths and weaknesses, and using only one tool or methodology for migration can be a limiting factor in any large and complex migration project involving a variety of database objects and large amounts of data to migrate. Tools and methodologies identified during the analysis and design phase can assist in the migration process tremendously. It is very common for organizations to use more than one tool in complex migration projects to reduce the overall effort required and to ensure successful execution of the project. Oracle tools such as SQL Developer and database utilities such as SQL*Loader and external tables can play a very useful role in any migration project. It is also important to understand the challenges that may arise during migration and to be prepared to address them in a timely manner, to help the migration project move forward.

In this chapter, we discussed the tasks involved in performing database schema and data migration, and we highlighted the data validation process via a step-by-step illustration of database migration using SQL Developer. More often than not, database schemas not only include tables, indexes, and views, but also a significant amount of business logic implemented in the form of stored procedures and functions. In the next chapter, we will discuss how to migrate those database components and their potential impact on applications.

Database Stored Object Migration

INFORMATION IN THIS CHAPTER:

- SQL Developer Environment for Sample Migrations
- Stored Procedure Migrations
- Triggers
- Views
- Unit Testing

Stored database objects are stored procedures, views, and triggers that reside in the database management system. Stored objects in the database are both a blessing and a curse. They are a blessing in that they offer object-oriented features such as encapsulation and reusability. Encapsulation is provided as all the business logic for your application can be placed in the database objects' stored procedures, which means the business logic is enclosed within the database objects and is not spread among a variety of application programming languages. They are reusable because they are centralized within the database and are accessible to any application programmer, database developer, business user, or partner that has access to your database. Often, business logic is repeated in different scripting languages, database access tools, extract-load-transform (ETL) tools, Java or .NET objects, and even end-user desktop tools like Microsoft Excel. And herein lies the curse of stored database objects: Because each database vendor has its own specific language in which stored procedures, triggers, and views are written, it is more challenging to migrate from one database to another, in which case you would probably be better off with SQL spread throughout your application and database scripts.

Migrating an application that has many stored objects is a more involved process than migrating an application that has all its database access in an object-to-relational tool such as Hibernate or TopLink. Migrating SQL in an application is easier than migrating stored procedures, but it is not as easy as migrating an application using Hibernate or TopLink. This is because Hibernate and TopLink generate the database SQL that is specific to the database you are using. Stored objects contain database-specific data types and database objects (such as system tables and global database variables), and they are written in a database-specific language syntax. The spectrum of difficulty in migrating database access and logic largely depends on the location of this logic, the degree to which the logic is centralized in the application or database, and, of course, the number of components that contain this logic. Figure 6.1 depicts the five most likely scenarios for database logic and the degree of difficulty.

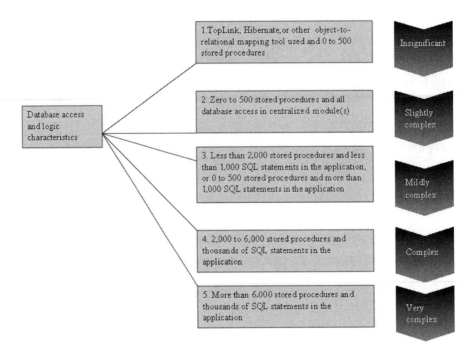

FIGURE 6.1

Five Most Likely Scenarios for Database Logic and Degree of Difficulty

As shown in Figure 6.1, a general rule of thumb is that SQL in the application is easier to migrate than thousands of stored procedures. However, with the use of the Oracle SQL Developer tool, stored procedures source stored object syntax is migrated to Oracle PL/SQL and SQL syntax. In addition, database features such as session and user temporary tables are migrated to their equivalent Oracle American National Standards Institute (ANSI) standard global temporary tables. It should also be noted that as SQL Developer becomes more adept at handling non-Oracle stored procedure syntax, the number of stored procedures impacting the complexity level will decline. Also, the number of stored procedures is not a scientific approach, as your organization may have thousands of simple stored procedures which can be easily migrated. The experience among migration specialists is that there is a direct correlation between the number of stored procedures and the high level of complexity in these stored procedures.

The process of migrating stored objects using Oracle SQL Developer is similar to the process of migrating your database schema and data:

1. Capture the source stored objects in offline or online mode. This process is very quick, as no language syntax parsing is performed. The stored object source syntax is stored in a set of tables in the migration repository.

2. Convert the stored objects in the migration repository from source syntax to Oracle SQL and PL/SQL syntax. Also, convert any user- and source-specific structures (such as temporary tables).

3. Generate the stored objects. SQL Developer will generate a script with all Oracle stored objects in it.

4. Fix any issues using the scratch pad editor. The SQL Developer scratch pad editor is used to compare the source and target stored objects side by side. Therefore, you can make any changes in the source or target stored objects. If you want to make changes to the source stored objects, you can translate them to Oracle and determine whether they will compile in Oracle.

5. Unit-test the stored objects using SQL Developer. You can use the SQL Developer SQL Worksheet tool to run the stored objects in the source and target Oracle databases. You can also create unit test cases in SQL Developer for Oracle stored objects using the Unit Testing feature. This feature does not yet support non-Oracle databases, but it reportedly will in a future release.

SQL Developer can capture, convert, and generate the Oracle database objects in less than 30 minutes for databases that contain thousands of stored objects. It is common for a single database with thousands of stored objects to have, at most, 10 common issues. Some stored procedures may report 20 or more warnings and/or error messages, but these are likely the same warning or error message repeated many times. The common issues will occur across the entire set of database objects as developers have usually used the "cut and paste" method of coding and the same syntax will be used. The benefits of a few common issues that repeat again and again are as follows:

- Resolving these common issues typically takes a few hours, and once a repeatable solution is found, it can be coded and implemented. A repeatable solution could be a Perl script that searches all stored procedures and does a search and replace in the Oracle database or in the generated Oracle stored object script. This automated script prevents developers from having to spend the time to make many small changes, thereby reducing the chance that they will make incorrect changes or introduce new issues.

- These issues can be reported to Oracle, which releases patches for the SQL Developer tool on a regular basis. Issues or constructs that cannot be converted can be logged into the standard Oracle support system to which all Oracle customers and partners have access. Once a number of issues have been resolved, a patch for SQL Developer is released and you are automatically notified that you can download this patch.

SQL DEVELOPER ENVIRONMENT FOR SAMPLE MIGRATIONS

This chapter is not intended to be a tutorial on SQL Developer or SQL Developer Migration Workbench. However, it will help to understand the connections and projects used for the stored procedure, trigger, and view being migrated in this

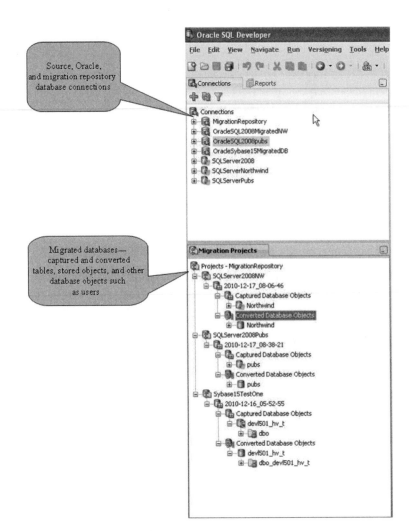

FIGURE 6.2

SQL Developer Connections and Migration Projects

chapter. This will help you to understand what you will need when you start your migration project. Figure 6.2 shows the connections you will need to perform in an online capture and the connections to the migrated Oracle databases.

The top window in Figure 6.2 contains the connections to all the source Sybase and SQL Server databases. It also contains the connection to the migration repository in Oracle and the Oracle target database schemas. The three migrated databases will be migrated to the same Oracle database containing three separate schemas. The bottom window in Figure 6.2 contains the three migration projects for the two SQL

Server databases and one Sybase database we will use as example migrations of a stored procedure, view, and trigger in this chapter. Each project contains the captured and converted database objects.

> **NOTE**
> To keep things simple, the SQL Server sample Northwind and Sybase/SQL Server PUBS databases were initially used for this chapter. However, only one trigger did not migrate correctly in the PUBS database of all the stored procedures, views, and triggers in the sample databases. Therefore, an anonymous Sybase 12.5 database was used to show a migration of a stored procedure and view.

Translation Scratch Editor

The SQL Developer Translation Scratch Editor is a feature you will find yourself using often to fix issues in the stored objects, translate application SQL, and fix stored procedures, views, triggers, and SQL in the source database. Objects and SQL modified using SQL Developer Translation Scratch Editor can then be retranslated into Oracle syntax and recompiled in the target Oracle database. The Translation Scratch Editor is in the Migration drop down under the Tools menu bar. The key benefits of this feature are:

- **SQL translation**   SQL Developer Migration Workbench migrates all stored objects in the source database. However, SQL can exist anywhere in your application, and the SQL Developer Application Migration Assistant (AMA) may not support the language in which your application was written. Any SQL statement can be translated using the Translation Scratch Editor.
- **Side-by-side view with recompile in source and Oracle databases**   The source and Oracle stored objects or SQL statements can be viewed side by side, edited, and recompiled without leaving the Translation Scratch Editor.
- **SQL block mapping**   By right-clicking in the source window pane, you can select the Translation Difference Editor. This will produce another window, shown in Figure 6.3. This will map each SQL statement and code block from the source to the Oracle translated version. For this small stored procedure this may not be an issue, but for large stored procedures this makes it much easier to debug and fix compile-time or runtime issues.

In Figure 6.3, you can see the mapping from the source stored procedure SQL blocks to the corresponding blocks in Oracle. You can also see the lines which lead you from the source SQL block to the Oracle SQL block. Clicking on the source or Oracle SQL block will draw a black box around the corresponding SQL blocks and turn the line from gray to *black*. The five shaded vertical boxes in Figure 6.3 on the far left of the source stored procedure can be used to navigate very large stored procedures. By clicking on these blocks, you are automatically

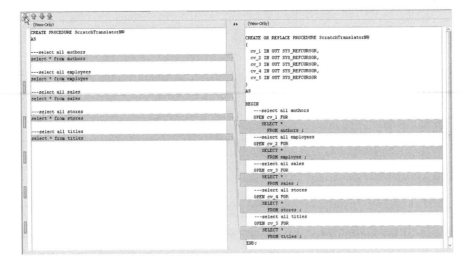

FIGURE 6.3

SQL Developer Translation Difference Editor

taken to the source and Oracle SQL statement and the statement and line are outlined in black.

WARNING

Your connection to the source database for Sybase and SQL Server needs to be "SA" or have "SA" privileges. This is because SQL Developer connects to and reads the database system tables to retrieve the Data Definition Language (DDL) for database tables and stored objects. If it is not possible to get SA privileges, you can run the scripts from the tool to perform an offline capture. A Sybase or SQL Server database administrator with SA privileges can run the scripts as "SA" and provide you with the output files. You can then import the output files into SQL Developer.

STORED PROCEDURE MIGRATIONS

Stored procedures will typically generate the most warnings and errors. As mentioned earlier, your stored object migration will typically have about 10 main issues. Of these, four to six will concern stored procedures. This is because stored procedures contain the most code and have the most complex business logic. In this section, we will cover the main structural and architectural differences between Sybase, SQL Server, DB2, Informix, and Oracle stored procedures, and the top syntax challenges and how to resolve them. We will also perform a migration of a complex stored procedure and fix any issues that arise.

Oracle Differences

Sybase was the first relational database management system (RDBMS) vendor to attempt to provide a tiered architecture in a relational database environment. Sybase introduced stored procedures and triggers as a way to move application logic away from the client and closer to the server. Stored procedures and triggers are now the most commonly used procedures for reducing network traffic in a SQL Server, Sybase, or DB2 environment.

Although Sybase was the first database vendor to implement the tiered architecture concept, Oracle has been the one to match and then expand on that concept. The additional features that Oracle offers include functions, packages, and binary-formatted PL/SQL.

Four key architectural differences exist between Oracle and Sybase stored procedures:

1. Returning result sets

   Sybase uses the Tabular Data Stream (TDS) protocol to return results to the client. Since Oracle has no concept of result sets or TDS type processing, results from an Oracle stored procedure must be returned through a reference cursor variable. Each `SELECT` statement in a stored procedure needs a corresponding reference cursor as an output parameter variable.

2. Error handling

   The Sybase stored procedure code needs to explicitly check for errors by performing a check of `@@ERROR` after each SQL statement. In Oracle, an exception routine is automatically called when an error occurs.

3. Return value

   The `return` command can be used in Sybase to return a value from a stored procedure. Oracle stored procedures cannot return a value, but Oracle functions can return a value. Therefore, SQL Developer will convert all stored procedures with a return value into functions. This may or may not be what works best in your environment.

4. Locking

   Oracle is the only relational database to have true row-level locking. Therefore, when migrating to Oracle you will experience far fewer locking contentions.

In Oracle, stored procedures are capable of returning all available server data types, not just a limited subset. Stored procedures can return an array or table of data. Stored procedures can also call a 3GL program. For example, stored procedures can update rows in the Employee table and then send an e-mail using a C program to the employee's manager confirming what changes were made.

Stored procedures also provide a method for supporting the object-oriented encapsulation feature within the database engine. Encapsulation means the name, data, and method are all stored within the same object. Encapsulation can be achieved by creating a stored procedure with the same name as the table and coding all table accesses within the stored procedure.

Top Challenges and Solutions

Stored procedures in a database are written using proprietary language supported by the database. These languages differ from one another significantly in terms of construct, syntax, features, and functionality. Migration tools convert the stored procedures line by line into Oracle.

The most common issues that come up during stored procedure migration are:

1. **Nested transactions** Some databases allow execution of transactions in a nested fashion. Basically, the idea is to allow nesting of explicit transactions. For example, if a program starts a transaction and then invokes another procedure that starts a new transaction, the transaction started by the procedure becomes nested within the context of the first transaction which was started by the caller program. If the procedure gets executed first, it will have its own transaction. However, this implementation is not available in other databases such as Oracle and DB2.

   Oracle allows transaction nesting in two ways. One way is to use the regular SAVE POINT feature in which a transaction can be marked with a SAVE POINT and then it can be either rolled back or committed by using the SAVEPOINT name in the ROLLBACK or COMMIT command. For example:

   ```
   INSERT INTO ... ;
   UPDATE .... ;
   SAVEPOINT  Savepoint1;
   INSERT ....;
   DELETE ....;
   ROLLBACK TO Savepoint1;
   ```

   In the preceding example, the ROLLBACK to Savepoint1 statement rolls back all changes made after the SAVEPOINT was created.

   The second option is to invoke transactions encapsulated from an existing transaction. This can be done using the AUTONOMOUS TRANSACTION feature. The AUTONOMOUS TRANSACTION feature allows a transaction to be executed and then either rolled back or committed independent of the global transaction under which it was executed. Some restrictions apply to the use of AUTONOMOUS TRANSACTIONs. First, a stored program such as a procedure, function, or trigger, once declared as an AUTONOMOUS TRANSACTION, can only execute autonomous transactions. Second, even though the transactions are executed in an independent manner, program control is not returned to the calling program until the transaction finishes.

2. **Temporary table usage** Unlike other databases, Oracle only supports global temporary tables. There is no support for dynamic temporary tables. So, when converting from other databases such as SQL Server or Sybase, all the temporary tables used in the stored programs need to be converted into global temporary

tables. This is not a big problem, but global temporary tables must be created before the objects using these tables are created in the database. SQL Developer converts the temporary tables properly and generates the DDL scripts to create these temporary tables.

Example Sybase Stored Procedure Migration

The stored procedure used for this example comes from a Sybase 12.5 database that contains 557 tables, 317 views, and 4,057 stored procedures. So, this is not a small database, but it is not a large one either; rather, it is indicative of a typical Sybase database. Of the 4,057 stored procedures, 269 did not convert to Oracle, 304 were converted to the Oracle model but were not generated into the target Oracle database, and 1,480 were converted into the Oracle database but were marked as "invalid." The stored procedures used in the example were selected for a couple of reasons:

1. A temporary table was used in the stored procedures. Temporary tables are very popular in Sybase and SQL Server stored procedures, and as we discussed earlier in this chapter, there is not a direct technical mapping of Sybase/SQL Server temporary tables to Oracle global temporary tables. This database application has 3,084 stored procedures that have one or more stored procedures in them, or a little more than 75 percent of the stored procedures.
2. The error that was generated is not a SQL Developer Migration Workbench flaw. This error would have occurred if you were migrating this stored procedure manually or if you were using SQL Developer Migration Workbench. Some errors or warnings using SQL Developer are caused by shortcomings in the parser, but this is not the case in this situation. This makes this a great example, as you will encounter it whether you are using SQL Developer, using a third-party tool, or performing the migration manually.

Here is the stored procedure in the Sybase 12.5 database as it is stored, after capture, in the Migration Workbench repository:

```
CREATE PROCEDURE t_party_details_dccy
AS
BEGIN
    /*-------------------------------------------------------*/
    /* Inserting Selected Currency into #rep_details table */
    /*-------------------------------------------------------*/
    /* The ORDER BY is used as there can be multiple depot currencies per depot
party */
        INSERT #rep_details
        SELECT group_order = 9,
                group_name_text = 'Depot Currencies',
                group_name_date = '',
                field_key_date = '',
```

```
                    field_key_text = '',
                    field_name = 'Selected Currency',
                    value = IE.ext_instr_ref_p2k
          FROM #instrparty IP,
              instr_ext_ref_p2k IE
          WHERE IE.instr_code_type_p2k = 'ISO'
          AND IE.p2000_instr_ref_p2k = IP.p2000_instr_ref_p2k
          AND IP.assoc_code_wil = 'DCCY'
          ORDER BY IE.ext_instr_ref_p2k

     IF @@error != 0
         RETURN
END
```

The `select` statement along with all selected columns is where we will focus our attention. Take a close look at the seven columns on the `select` statement.

Here is the converted code as it appears in the Oracle converted Migration Workbench repository and the generated Oracle 11g database:

```
create or replace
PROCEDURE t_party_details_dccy
AS
    v_sys_error NUMBER := 0;

BEGIN

    /*-------------------------------------------------------*/
    /* Inserting Selected Currency into #rep_details table */
    /*-------------------------------------------------------*/
    /* The ORDER BY is used as there can be multiple depot currencies per depot
party */
    BEGIN
      INSERT INTO tt_rep_details
        SELECT 9 group_order ,
          'Depot Currencies' group_name_text ,
          '' group_name_date ,
          '' field_key_date ,
          '' field_key_text ,
          'Selected Currency' field_name ,
          IE.ext_instr_ref_p2k VALUE
        FROM tt_instrparty IP,
          instr_ext_ref_p2k IE
        WHERE IE.instr_code_type_p2k = 'ISO'
          AND IE.p2000_instr_ref_p2k = IP.p2000_instr_ref_p2k
          AND IP.assoc_code_wil = 'DCCY'
        ORDER BY IE.ext_instr_ref_p2k;
    EXCEPTION
      WHEN OTHERS THEN
        v_sys_error := SQLCODE;
```

```
    END;
    IF v_sys_error != 0 THEN
       RETURN;
    END IF;
END;
```

The generated Oracle stored procedure also contains seven columns as this is exactly what the Sybase stored procedure contained. Everything appears to be fine, but the stored procedure does not compile in Oracle. Before we move on to the resolution and discuss what caused this compile error, let's take a look at the global temporary table that SQL Developer Migration Workbench created automatically. This Oracle global temporary table performs the same functionality, but has a different technical implementation, than the Sybase #rep_details temporary table.

```
CREATE GLOBAL TEMPORARY TABLE ''DBO_DEVL501_HV_T''.''TT_REP_DETAILS''
    (''GROUP_ORDER'' NUMBER(12,0) NOT NULL ENABLE,
       ''GROUP_NAME_TEXT'' VARCHAR2(30 BYTE) NOT NULL ENABLE,
       ''GROUP_NAME_DATE'' DATE NOT NULL ENABLE,
       ''FIELD_KEY_DATE'' DATE NOT NULL ENABLE,
       ''FIELD_KEY_TEXT'' VARCHAR2(30 BYTE) NOT NULL ENABLE,
       ''FIELD_ORDER'' NUMBER,
       ''FIELD_NAME'' VARCHAR2(50 BYTE) NOT NULL ENABLE,
       ''VALUE'' VARCHAR2(255 BYTE) NOT NULL ENABLE
    ) ON COMMIT DELETE ROWS ;
```

Note that this temporary table has eight columns.

Resolution of Issues

The following error is received when this stored procedure is compiled in Oracle:

```
Error(13,19): PL/SQL: ORA-00947: not enough values.
```

The error points out that there are eight columns in the Oracle global temporary table because the Sybase temporary table contained eight columns. However, the select statement for the insert into the temporary table only contains seven columns. This is because one of the columns in the temporary table allows NULLs, so it does not have to be present in the Sybase stored procedures. In Oracle, the insert with a select requires all columns to be present even if they are NULLABLE. Therefore, the missing column field_order (the sixth column in the global temporary table definition) is added to the select. The code change is as follows:

```
SELECT 9 group_order ,
    'Depot Currencies' group_name_text ,
    '' group_name_date ,
    '' field_key_date ,
    '' field_key_text ,
    '' field_order,
    'Selected Currency' field_name ,
    IE.ext_instr_ref_p2k VALUE
```

> **NOTE**
>
> Oracle stored procedures are often lengthier than their corresponding converted Sybase or SQL Server stored procedures. There are a number of reasons for this. The one reason that affects all stored procedures concerns error message handling. In Sybase and SQL Server, error numbers are placed in the @@error global variable. It is up to the database coder to then check the @@error after each SQL statement. In many cases, this is not done. The default in Oracle is to have an EXCEPTION section after each SQL statement. This extra code block plus additional code around the code block adds to the length of the stored procedure. The other major reason for lengthier Oracle stored procedures is that any select statement within an Oracle stored procedure requires a reference cursor to be added to point to the result sets. This adds to the length of the stored procedures' signature, adds the creation of a local variable, and adds to the select statement itself.

TRIGGERS

Triggers will typically generate the second highest number of warnings and errors when migrating a database to Oracle. As mentioned earlier, your stored object migration will typically have about 10 main issues. Of these, two to four will concern triggers (about 30 percent). This is because triggers contain DDL or commit transaction statements which do not port over to Oracle easily. In this section, we will cover the main structural and architectural differences between Sybase, SQL Server, DB2, Informix, and Oracle triggers and the top syntax challenges and how to resolve them. We will also perform a migration of a complex trigger and discuss how to deal with issues that crop up.

Oracle Differences

Triggers were first introduced by Sybase, and for many years they provided a strategic competitive advantage for the company. However, Oracle has since introduced triggers and has developed Sybase's core trigger functionality further. The additional features provided by Oracle include BEFORE and AFTER triggers, and the ability to fire triggers once per row or once per statement.

Triggers can be defined to execute before and/or after database events such as inserts and updates. For example, a BEFORE trigger can prevent an illegal million-row update from occurring. An AFTER trigger performs transaction auditing in distributed databases.

Sybase simulates a BEFORE trigger through the use of rules. Rules can be created and bound to table columns. The rules are checked prior to the data being inserted.

The ANSI declarative approach greatly simplifies the process of providing database-enforced integrity. It allows the programmer to define primary and foreign keys, default values, and unique keys when creating database tables. The database engine automatically enforces these rules to protect the system data. The declarative approach to referential integrity is superior to referential integrity that is enforced using programmatic checking with stored procedures and triggers. The declarative approach is more portable, is more standard, requires less maintenance, and offers better performance than other trigger approaches.

Top Challenges and Solutions

Like stored procedures, triggers also are written in the proprietary languages supported by the databases. Triggers are an essential part of application development and are written primarily to perform routine tasks that are to be executed when some changes occur in the database. The following are the main differences in trigger functionality between Oracle and other relational databases:

- **DDL statement support**   Oracle does not support any DDL commands in triggers, just like stored procedures. Other databases support certain DDL commands in the trigger (e.g., `COMMIT TRANSACTION`, `ROLLBACK TRANSACTION`, etc.). For example, SQL Server and Sybase databases allow users to use these DDL commands within a trigger. Using `ROLLBACK`/`COMMIT TRANSACTION` statements within a trigger can either roll back or commit the entire transaction, yet the trigger continues execution.

  Since Oracle does not support DDLs in triggers, the only way to handle this functionality is to designate the trigger as an `AUTONOMOUS TRANSACTION`. With this approach, all the transactions, commits, and rollback statements that are executed in the trigger become isolated from the rest of the transaction. The main problem with this approach is that by making the trigger an autonomous transaction, the original design of the application is altered. If the developer does not issue any commit or rollback statements anywhere in the process, the transaction will be affected. Also, by making the trigger an autonomous transaction, the transactions executed by it will not be governed by the main transaction. This may also have unintended consequences.

  The only other option is to revisit the database/application design and move the rollback/commit statements into the application as appropriate.

- **Use of** `INSERTED`/`DELETED` **virtual tables**   Databases such as SQL Server and Sybase support `INSERTED`/`DELETED` virtual tables which actually store the rows changed by a transaction. You can then use these virtual tables in a trigger by opening a cursor, reading from these tables as though they are regular tables, and so on.

  Since Oracle does not have this functionality natively, there are two ways to deal with this:

  - Convert the statement-level triggers in Sybase/SQL Server to row-level triggers. For a row-level trigger, Oracle supports capturing the old values and new values for table columns for each row that has been affected by the transaction. This is the current approach adopted by SQL Developer 3.0 Early Adopter Edition.

- Use a compound trigger in Oracle. This is a new feature introduced in Oracle Database 11g which basically encapsulates both BEFORE and AFTER statement execution actions in one trigger. This allows developers to capture the rows affected by transactions into either temporary tables or PL/SQL tables as part of the BEFORE STATEMENT option, and then process the resultant temporary table or PL/SQL table in the AFTER STATEMENT option.

Example SQL Server Trigger Migration

The trigger being migrated is the employee_insupd trigger in the SQL Server PUBS database. This is a great example, as it contains two rollback statements which are often found in Sybase or SQL Server triggers. Rollback or commit statements are not allowed in Oracle triggers, but there is a workaround which SQL Developer Migration Workbench will implement. This workaround may or may not work in your case, and we will discuss why this is true. In addition, SQL Developer Migration Workbench converted column names incorrectly in the select statement in the trigger.

The captured SQL Server trigger looks exactly like it does in the SQL Server database:

```
CREATE TRIGGER employee_insupd
ON employee
FOR insert, UPDATE
AS
--Get the range of level for this job type from the jobs table.
declare @min_lvl tinyint,
    @max_lvl tinyint,
    @emp_lvl tinyint,
    @job_id smallint
select @min_lvl = min_lvl,
    @max_lvl = max_lvl,
    @emp_lvl = i.job_lvl,
    @job_id = i.job_id
from employee e, jobs j, inserted i
where e.emp_id = i.emp_id AND i.job_id = j.job_id
IF (@job_id = 1) and (@emp_lvl <> 10)
begin
    raiserror ('Job id 1 expects the default level of 10.',16,1)
    ROLLBACK TRANSACTION
end
ELSE
IF NOT (@emp_lvl BETWEEN @min_lvl AND @max_lvl)
begin
    raiserror ('The level for job_id:%d should be between %d and %d.',
      16, 1, @job_id, @min_lvl, @max_lvl)
    ROLLBACK TRANSACTION
end
```

Pay close attention to the two ROLLBACK TRANSACTION statements and the
@min_lvl = min_lvl and @max_lvl = max_lvl **column names in the** select **statement.**

```
Oracle Trigger:
create or replace
TRIGGER employee_insupd
    BEFORE INSERT OR UPDATE
    ON employee
    FOR EACH ROW
DECLARE
    PRAGMA AUTONOMOUS_TRANSACTION;
    PRAGMA AUTONOMOUS_TRANSACTION;
    --Get the range of level for this job type from the jobs table.
    v_min_lvl NUMBER(3,0);
    v_max_lvl NUMBER(3,0);
    v_emp_lvl NUMBER(3,0);
    v_job_id NUMBER(5,0);
BEGIN
    SELECT :NEW.min_lvl ,
      :NEW.max_lvl ,
      :NEW.job_lvl ,
      :NEW.job_id
    INTO v_min_lvl,
      v_max_lvl,
      v_emp_lvl,
      v_job_id
    FROM employee e,
      jobs j
    WHERE e.emp_id = :NEW.emp_id
      AND :NEW.job_id = j.job_id;
    IF (v_job_id = 1)
      AND (v_emp_lvl <> 10) THEN
    BEGIN
      raise_application_error(-20002, 'Job id 1 expects the default level of
10.');
    ROLLBACK;
      sqlserver_utilities.resetTrancount;
    END;
    ELSE
      IF NOT (v_emp_lvl BETWEEN v_min_lvl AND v_max_lvl) THEN
      BEGIN
        raise_application_error(-20002, 'The level for job_id:%d should be
between %d and %d.');
        ROLLBACK;
        sqlserver_utilities.resetTrancount;
      END;
      END IF;
    END IF;
END;
```

Oracle SQL Developer changed two items of significance in the SQL Server trigger when it translated it:

1. **DDL rollback solution**   A rollback can be issued in the trigger if this trigger is an autonomous transaction. This is done by adding the statement PRAGMA AUTONOMOUS_TRANSACTION.

2. **Transaction count reset**   The trigger calls a stored procedure (resetTrancount) in the sqlserver_utilities package. This package and stored procedure are automatically generated by SQL Developer Migration Workbench. The package aids in the process of rolling back the transaction that caused the trigger to execute. The application code, whether it is in PL/SQL, Java, or some other programming language, can check the trancount variable to see if the transaction should be committed or rolled back. The code for resetTrancount is very simple:

```
PROCEDURE resetTrancount
IS
BEGIN
    trancount := 0;
END resetTrancount;
```

Resolution of Issues

We saw that SQL Developer Migration Workbench handles the ROLLBACK statement using an autonomous transaction. However, the translated trigger still has a couple of issues that need to be resolved.

1. The select statement columns MIN_LVL and MAX_LVL are assumed to be in the :NEW table within the Oracle table that contains the new values for the row for which the trigger was fired. Therefore, we get the following compile-time errors:

```
Error(11,11): PLS-00049: bad bind variable 'NEW.MIN_LVL'
Error(12,11): PLS-00049: bad bind variable 'NEW.MAX_LVL'
```

These columns are actually in the jobs table. The following change needs to be made:

```
SELECT min_lvl ,
       max_lvl ,
```

2. The statement to place the trigger in autonomous transaction mode (PRAGMA AUTONOMOUS_TRANSACTION) is in the trigger twice, so we get the following error:

```
Error(3,11): PLS-00711: PRAGMA AUTONOMOUS_TRANSACTION cannot be declared twice
```

The change is simple. Just comment out one of the PRAGMA AUTONOMOUS_ TRANSACTION statements:

```
PRAGMA AUTONOMOUS_TRANSACTION;
--PRAGMA AUTONOMOUS_TRANSACTION;
```

TIP

The script that SQL Developer generates to produce the new Oracle database schema is one long script that contains all the table definitions, index creations, stored procedures, views, and triggers. This script also "manufactures" a username, and uses "users" as the default tablespace and "temp" as the default temporary tablespace. For development and testing, this may work fine. For production, however, you will want to modify the script to contain the username you want to own the migrated schema, and place the data in the tablespaces you want for production. The other thing many customers do is to break the script into multiple scripts, as one big script is difficult to manage and probably not the way you maintain your DDL. Most customers break the one large script into multiple scripts: one for table definitions and indexes, one for triggers, one for views, one for stored procedures, and one for other database objects such as users, synonyms, and other database objects.

VIEWS

Views will typically generate the fewest warnings and errors when migrating a database to Oracle. Of the 10 main issues for stored objects, two to four will concern views (about 30 percent). Although the number of errors pertaining to views may be the same as the number pertaining to triggers, the amount of time spent to fix views will be significantly less. This is because views are much easier to fix than stored procedures and triggers, as they contain only SQL and no proprietary database language code. In this section, we will cover the main structural and architectural differences between Sybase, SQL Server, DB2, Informix, and Oracle views and the top syntax challenges and how to resolve them. We will also migrate a complex view and discuss how to resolve any issues that may arise.

Oracle Differences and Top Challenges and Solutions

Instead of discussing these topics separately, we combined them into this one section because no database programming language is involved, but there are differences in terms of SQL syntax. The differences between Oracle and other database languages concern SQL and function extensions. Top challenges for views are as follows:

1. **Common SQL differences** SQL Developer Migration Workbench has become quite sophisticated when it comes to handling common SQL differences between other databases and Oracle. Some examples of these are the use of `select` without a `from` clause, `select` with `@@spid`, and `FOR READ ONLY` on `select` statements. SQL Developer now handles these differences automatically.
2. **Null comparison** This is a big difference. In Sybase and SQL Server, a column that has `NULL` in it can be compared to an empty string. In these databases, `NULL` and "empty string" are synonymous. Oracle takes the mathematical definition of `NULL`; `NULL` means no value is present and `NULL` has no real value. In Sybase and SQL Server, the null comparison may be used in the condition statement or the

WHERE clause. In Oracle, this cannot be done since NULL values take many forms. The solution is to replace all Sybase's null comparison statements with Oracle's is null or is not null operators depending on the comparison being performed. Here is some sample code that demonstrates the differences in Sybase's NULL comparison operator and Oracle's is not null statement or Nvl function. Sybase and SQL Server will have the following SQL statement in a view:

```
SELECT *
FROM ScriptDefTemplate sdt
WHERE sdt.SetValue <> ''
```

The corresponding Oracle SQL statement looks as follows:

```
SELECT sdt.ScriptDefId, s.ScriptId, sdt.ScriptDefRelease
FROM WindowObject wo, ScriptDefTemplate sdt, Script s
WHERE sdt.SetValue IS NOT NULL
```

3. **Selecting from a table in another database** In Sybase and SQL Server, multiple databases can exist in the same database server. A select statement to access a table in database2 from database1 in Sybase or SQL Server would look as follows:

```
select * from database2..authors
```

In Oracle, databases map to Oracle schemas. So, in Oracle, this statement would become:

```
select * from schema2.authors
```

It is possible that you will move different Sybase databases to one Oracle schema. Therefore, you will not have the schema name qualification before the table name.

Example SQL Server View Migration

The view used for this example comes from the same Sybase 12.5 database that we used in the "Stored Procedure Migrations" section. Of the 317 views, 311 were converted to the Oracle model, 11 did not convert to Oracle, and 36 converted in the Oracle database but were marked as "invalid." This view was selected because the GROUP BY clause was a common reason that the 36 stored procedures were generated in Oracle but were marked as "invalid." The Sybase view looks like this:

```
CREATE VIEW t_frnf01_view
AS
    SELECT I.p2000_instr_ref_p2k,
      I.instr_short_name_p2k,
      convert (char (12), '') database_code
    FROM fixing_segment_wil F, instrument_p2k I
    WHERE I.p2000_instr_ref_p2k = F.fixing_instr_p2k
    AND I.instr_group_p2k != 'INDX' /* PAB gl021780 */
    GROUP BY
      I.p2000_instr_ref_p2k
```

Notice that the GROUP BY clause contains one field from the selected list of columns.

The converted and generated Oracle view looks like this:

```
CREATE OR REPLACE FORCE VIEW t_frnf01_view
AS
   SELECT I.p2000_instr_ref_p2k ,
     I.instr_short_name_p2k ,
     CAST('' AS CHAR(12)) database_code
   FROM fixing_segment_wil F,
     instrument_p2k I
   WHERE I.p2000_instr_ref_p2k = F.fixing_instr_p2k
     AND I.instr_group_p2k != 'INDX'/* PAB gl021780 */
   GROUP BY I.p2000_instr_ref_p2k;
```

The converted view looks like it converted properly as the GROUP BY clause is the same as it was in Sybase. However, Oracle has a stipulation that all columns in the select list must be present in the GROUP BY clause. This is actually a very suspicious GROUP BY clause as the select column list contains no sum, min, max, or count clause which is typical when you have a GROUP BY. So, it is likely that we can modify this select statement without changing the results.

Resolution of Issues

We receive the following error when attempting to compile the view in Oracle:

```
SQL Error: ORA-00979: not a GROUP BY expression
00979. 00000 - ''not a GROUP BY expression''
```

The workarounds and potential drawbacks to this Oracle error are as follows:

1. We could add the I.instr_short_name_p2k and database_code columns to the GROUP BY clause. However, the grouping of the results will be changed. This could produce different results.
2. We could remove columns that are not in GROUP BY from the select list. This will certainly produce different results, as the results coming back will be missing a column.
3. We could remove the GROUP BY clause. This may or may not produce different results depending on the combinations of I.p2000_instr_ref_p2k and I.instr_short_name_p2k in the result set.
4. We could remove the GROUP BY clause and add the DISTINCT keyword to the select list. This would ensure that no duplicates of the I.p2000_instr_ref_p2k column would appear in the results, but it will also have the side effect of limited results to unique I.p2000_instr_ref_p2k and I.instr_short_name_p2k combinations of columns.

In this type of situation, you have multiple options, each with side effects. Therefore, you have to do some trial-and-error testing. The testing we performed showed that the second solution (removing the GROUP BY clause) produced the correct results.

This testing also required collaboration with the database administrator and application subject matter expert (SME) to confirm that the change will work even if the data in the database changes. The database administrator was required to determine the constraints, indexes, column data types, and primary keys on the tables in the view, as well as provide some background on why the view was created. The SME provided details on the functionality of the application that used the view. It is not uncommon when debugging and fixing issues with stored procedures, views, and triggers that both a database administrator and an SME with extensive knowledge of the database, application, and system functionality play a very active role in the migration.

```
CREATE OR REPLACE FORCE VIEW t_frnf01_view
AS
SELECT I.p2000_instr_ref_p2k ,
    I.instr_short_name_p2k ,
    CAST('' AS CHAR(12)) database_code
  FROM fixing_segment_wil F,
    instrument_p2k I
  WHERE I.p2000_instr_ref_p2k = F.fixing_instr_p2k
    AND I.instr_group_p2k != 'INDX'/* PAB g1021780 */
```

> **WARNING**
>
> SQL Developer, by default, creates the views with SET FORCE ON, which causes the stored procedure to be placed into the database even though it has errors. The FORCE ON statement will cause you to believe a view has been created because it has no errors, when in reality it may have several errors. In addition, you don't see the errors and warnings in SQL Developer until you take this statement off the view signature. SQL Developer sets FORCE ON so that tables that are not created do not cause all views accessing these tables to fail. For debugging, you will need to take the SET FORCE ON statement off the view signature.

UNIT TESTING

Because you will spend most of your time migrating, debugging, and unit testing stored procedures, we will use a stored procedure test as an example for how to unit-test your stored objects. Views are simple to test, as you simply select from the view in both the source and the Oracle database using the SQL Developer SQL Worksheet tool. Triggers are a bit more difficult to test, as you will need to perform the database action (insert, update, or delete) which causes the trigger to execute. The insert, update, or delete, just like with the view, can be created and executed in SQL Developer SQL Worksheet. Making sure the trigger produced the correct results is a matter of viewing the table against which the trigger issued its action. Table data can be viewed in SQL Developer, so this is not an issue. Unit testing stored procedures is done using the SQL Developer unit test feature for the Oracle stored procedure. In this section, you will see how to use the unit testing capabilities in SQL Developer to test the migrated Oracle stored procedures. At the time of this writing, SQL Developer SQL Worksheet cannot be used to execute source stored procedures. This is a shortcoming that will hopefully be fixed as this would allow database developers to compare results from the source and Oracle database stored procedures in one tool.

Setting Up the Unit Testing Environment and Creating the Unit Test

Setting up the unit testing environment and actually creating the individual stored object unit test cases is well documented on the Oracle Web site (http://download .oracle.com/docs/cd/E15846_01/doc.21/e15222/unit_testing.htm). The unit test case feature requires a database repository that can be placed into any Oracle database, including the Oracle Migration Workbench repository database. Creating the individual unit test cases is a GUI wizard-driven process that takes a few seconds for each unit test case.

Unit Test of Oracle Stored Procedure

Once the stored procedure unit test case is created, it is very simple to execute the unit test case. This is done by executing the Oracle database object unit test case you created. Figure 6.4 shows the location from which to execute the unit test case SCRATCHTRANSLATORNW_1.

Right-click on the **SCRATCHTRANSLATORNW_1** unit test and you will see the option to **Run Test**. Selecting this option will immediately run the unit test case, and the execution path and results will be displayed as shown in Figure 6.5.

The top window in Figure 6.5 shows the results of the execution. Any errors and warning messages will be displayed here. The release of SQL Developer used for this book (Version 3.0.03) shows errors (see the circles with an X in them). However, in the bottom window in Figure 6.5, you can see that the unit test executed, and the five result sets can be viewed here. You can also see the five select result sets in the five reference cursors (CV_1 through CV_5). You can switch the result sets view in the bottom window by double-clicking on the **CV_1** through **CV_5** variables.

Unit Test of Sybase and SQL Server Stored Procedures

Unfortunately, SQL Developer does not have the capability to execute Sybase and SQL Server stored procedures in SQL Worksheet. In addition, you cannot create unit test cases for databases other than Oracle. You can, however, use Microsoft SQL Server Management Studio (SQL Server databases), Quest TOAD, Embarcadero Rapid SQL XE, and other database development tools from specific source database vendors.

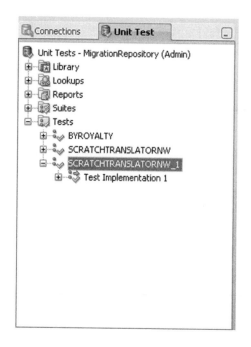

FIGURE 6.4

SQL Developer Unit Test Case Execution

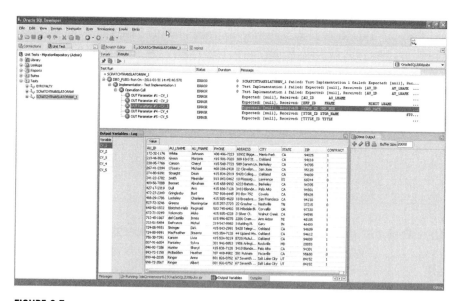

FIGURE 6.5

SQL Developer Oracle Convert Stored Procedure Unit Test Results

> **WARNING**
>
> Stored procedure reference cursors need to be OUTPUT parameters, not INPUT OUPUT parameters, as is the default migration with SQL Developer. Otherwise, unit tests of stored procedures will not show results. Therefore, all reference cursor stored procedure parameters need to be changed from INPUT OUTPUT to OUTPUT parameters. This will allow the unit test case to function properly.

SUMMARY

Many applications contain stored objects in the database, and these stored objects can be both a great benefit and a drawback when attempting to migrate databases. In this chapter, we discovered how SQL Developer can be used to greatly reduce the effort required to migrate stored procedures, views, and triggers from other RDBMSes to Oracle.

Stored procedure migration will typically be the most time-consuming aspect of database object migration. This is because stored procedures contain both vendor-specific SQL and procedural language code. Stored procedures also have complex business logic and typically contain thousands, if not hundreds of thousands, of lines of code.

Trigger migration is made more time-consuming when there are DDL statements or transactions. Oracle has workarounds for DDL statements and transactions in triggers, but some manual intervention is still required. Triggers do contain vendor-specific SQL and procedural code, but nowhere near the number that stored procedures contain. View migration is by far the easiest of the three migration types, as views contain no vendor-specific procedural language and the SQL in views is typically less complex.

This chapter demonstrated that migrating database stored objects is easy using Oracle SQL Developer. SQL Developer will capture, convert, and generate the source database stored objects. Not all objects will migrate over to Oracle without any errors, but as we saw in this chapter, most of the errors are easy to fix. You should now have the knowledge to start your migration of stored objects to an Oracle database using SQL Developer.

In the next two chapters, we will move from database migration to application migration. Chapter 7 discusses how to keep the application the same and change the SQL that will not work against Oracle. Chapter 8 goes into detail regarding migrating the application. As we will discuss in Chapter 8, you may need to migrate the client/server application language if you are moving your application to the cloud. This is either because the client/server language does not run in the cloud, or because you are moving to the Oracle Exadata private cloud platform and the application language you are using will not run on this platform.

WARNING

The Oracle DDL generated by SQL Developer is not fully optimized for performance and manageability of data objects (indexes, tablespaces), or for use of Oracle database features (free) and options (cost for the customer). Therefore, you will need to tune the table definitions, indexes, stored procedures, triggers, and views. The table DDL will need to be changed to get the optimal use of indexes. You may also want to modify the DDL to use Oracle options such as partitioning, compression, or encryption, or database features such as index-organized tables. The Oracle tablespace, by default, is USERS, and the temporary tablespace is TEMP, both of which you will probably want to change. The SQL in the triggers, views, and stored procedures can be tuned and optimized by using the Oracle Enterprise Manager Tuning and Diagnostic Packs, as discussed in Chapter 4.

Application Migration/Porting Due to Database Migration

7

INFORMATION IN THIS CHAPTER:

- Types of Application Changes
- Factors Influencing Application Changes
- Migration Options and Solutions
- Application Migration Tasks

Changes to an application as a result of a database migration are inevitable. The number and scope of these changes depend on the language in which the application was developed and how the application is implemented (e.g., two-tier, *n*-tier, etc.). Clear separation of various tiers within an application based on component function, such as user interfaces (UIs), business services, and data access components, can dramatically limit the number of required changes. In a two-tier or client/server environment, the lines between the UI, business service, and data access components are usually so blurred that they are implemented as one, thereby mimicking a monolithic architecture. Having a distinct database access layer can make it easier to identify and make changes to embedded SQL statements as well as database APIs. Generally in an *n*-tier architecture where server infrastructure is deployed (e.g., J2EE, Tuxedo), UI and business service functions are isolated to a greater degree from database functions, and tend to be database-agnostic. Therefore, these applications will potentially require fewer changes when underlying databases are migrated to a different vendor. Using a middleware (application server) product to communicate with a database also reduces the scope of the migration effort because any and all changes can be made once, at the middle tier.

A major challenge when porting applications to support a new database concerns identifying code segments that will require changes in order to function correctly in the new environment. In a client/server environment where the application logic is scattered in millions of lines of code, it is a big task to identify programs that require mandatory changes to SQL statements.

TYPES OF APPLICATION CHANGES

Changes to application programs can be categorized as follows based on their role within the application as well as their dependency on the underlying database platform:

- **Database connectivity** All actions taken in an application program with respect to database connectivity need to be modified as a result of changes in the underlying database platform, because every database requires parameters to be passed to the drivers in a slightly different order or sequence as well as the connection string format.

- **Embedded SQL statements**   Application programs can contain many types of embedded SQL statements, including plain SQL statements, dynamic SQL statements, and calls to stored procedures and functions in the database. SQL statements have proprietary extensions provided by the database vendors that need to be modified to conform to the requirements of the target database platform.
- **Application code changes**   In addition to embedded SQL changes in application programs, certain code segments may also need to be changed based on the type of driver used to access the Oracle database. Such code segments include those that handle result sets returned from the Oracle database, and those that make calls to an Oracle database stored function.
- **Database APIs**   Databases differ in how they implement APIs, thereby facilitating access to a host of database functions including data manipulation and transaction control. As a result of a database platform migration, these APIs need to be migrated to the new database platform.
- **Changes to external interfaces and replication solutions**   Typically, all relational database deployments have external interfaces that use native database tools as well as third-party tools to extract, transform, and ship data into other databases for reporting, data warehousing, or simply maintaining standby databases for load-balancing purposes. These interfaces and replication solutions will need to be changed depending on their type.
- **Error handling**   All databases differ in terms of the error codes and messages that are returned to application programs for different error conditions. These error codes and messages need to be modified to match those that are returned by the target database platform.
- **Performance optimization**   As a result of a database platform change, it may be necessary to optimize some driver settings and, potentially, the application code for better performance.

Out of these types of application changes, embedded SQL statement changes, error handling, and database API changes consume the most time in a migration project. Each of these changes will be discussed in-depth later in this chapter.

FACTORS INFLUENCING APPLICATION CHANGES

Application changes involving SQL statements or database APIs largely depend on how the application components interact with the database (e.g., database drivers used, type of database interaction, etc.). All relational databases provide standards-based drivers, such as Open Database Connectivity/Java Database Connectivity/ Object Linking and Embedding Database/ActiveX Data Objects (ODBC/JDBC/

OLE DB/ADO), to facilitate seamless database access from different interfaces. Database vendors differ somewhat in how they implement specific database APIs in these drivers. Using these standards-based drivers does not mean all database-specific functionality is completely transparent to applications. Therefore, applications have to be adapted to use appropriate database functionality in order to function correctly, even while using JDBC and ODBC drivers for database interaction. The following factors influence application code changes to support Oracle as the new database platform:

- **Type of database driver used**   Although the type of database driver the application uses should not influence the migration effort significantly, it does, especially in the case of Oracle database drivers. For example, Oracle's ODBC and OLE DB drivers are compatible with drivers from other vendors. Applications using ODBC drivers do not require any major changes as a result of a database change because Oracle ODBC drivers also provide similar capabilities when it comes to invoking stored procedures and functions in Oracle and returning result sets. However, Oracle JDBC drivers do differ from other JDBC drivers (from other vendors) in how they handle result sets returned from stored procedures and functions, as discussed in the "Application Migration" section in Chapter 3. Unlike Oracle, most databases return a result set implicitly when executing a stored procedure, without the need for special variables. Oracle, however, requires that variables of type SYS_REFCURSOR be declared as OUT parameters in stored procedures to return result sets. Drivers from database vendors such as Oracle and others are designed primarily to allow easier interaction with these vendors' databases, and they also contain performance enhancements to exploit native database features. Support for other databases (or their features) is not the primary goal of these drivers. Drivers from specialty vendors, such as the JDBC driver from DataDirect, provide uniform functionality across many databases. To support all databases with a common set of standard APIs, these vendors compensate for differences in functionality among databases by implementing additional functionality within the database drivers to retrieve appropriate metadata and wrapper functions based on the target database.
- **Type of database interaction**   Database interaction can be achieved in many ways (e.g., executing SQL statements directly, calling stored procedures and functions, dynamically generating SQL statements and their execution, etc.). Depending on the type of interaction, however, the types and complexity of application changes might vary. For example, applications that issue simple SQL statements to the database for execution might require changes if they have some proprietary extensions supported by the source database. However, if the SQL statements are mostly ANSI-standard SQL statements, fewer changes may be required. Similarly, applications that execute database stored procedures might require some changes, especially if they return result sets from the database.

- **Usage of built-in functions in SQL statements** Databases differ in regard to built-in function implementations for different data types such as character, date and timestamp, and numeric. For example, date arithmetic functions differ significantly among databases, as do character data manipulation functions. Embedded SQL statements with such database-specific functions will require changes when the database is migrated to Oracle.

- **Changes to database objects** Application changes also directly depend on changes to database objects in terms of name, data type, and so on. Any changes to the object names in the database due to restrictions on object naming in Oracle will most certainly require corresponding application changes.

- **Changes to transaction flow and coordination** Because other databases allow transaction control statements in triggers (e.g., COMMIT/ROLLBACK) and Oracle does not, changing them to autonomous transactions might be sufficient in most cases. However, in some cases, users may need to incorporate COMMIT/ROLLBACK transaction controls in the application instead of in the triggers.

- **Third Generation Language (3GL) programs (C and C++) with embedded SQL statements** All relational databases support 3GL programs executing SQL statements directly against the database. This is usually facilitated by running the source programs through a precompile and preprocessing phase in which the SQL statements are converted to native C and C++ functions and then the source programs are compiled and linked into binaries. Oracle also supports such programming facilities with Pro*C/C++ and Pro*COBOL precompilers for C/C++ and COBOL programs, respectively.

- **Conversion of 3GL programs based on call-level interfaces** In addition to supporting database access via standards-based drivers, most relational databases also allow programmers to write 3GL programs leveraging call-level interfaces exposed by the database (e.g., CT-lib and DB-lib programs in Sybase, DB2CLI in IBM DB2, etc.). Such programs need to be migrated to equivalent Oracle Call Interface (OCI) programs or to Pro*C programs in Oracle. These programs differ from traditional 3GL programs with embedded SQL statements, which require use of a preprocessor and/or compiler to convert the SQL statements into call-level interfaces supported by the database. When you are using 3GL programs leveraging native database call-level interfaces, there is no need to preprocess or precompile the programs. Instead, they are directly compiled and/or linked with appropriate libraries to generate the application binaries.

All 3GL programs with database-vendor-provided libraries that precompile source programs into an intermediary form to plug in to database access functions in client/server applications are typically coded into the programs as needed. In some cases, developers write special routines through which database access is performed in a centralized manner. All developers need to do to access the database is pass their SQL statements and database objects to these routines (or modules) in which database connections are established, and the SQL statements will be executed based upon user request.

MIGRATION OPTIONS AND SOLUTIONS

Application migration can be carried out in many ways, from scripts developed in popular languages such as Perl to identify code fragments that require changes, to technology that allows applications to interact with different databases with little effort. Each option has its advantages and disadvantages, and understanding them can help IT organizations select the best option to meet their business and technical requirements. Common factors such as number of code changes, type of code changes (i.e., extensive changes to embedded SQL statements, application code changes), and business requirements usually dictate the option chosen for application migration tasks.

Manually Identifying Changes and Modifying Applications

Manual effort is usually deployed when the number of changes required is small or only a few application programs need to be modified. Each affected application program needs to be analyzed for changes and then modified to make it work with the new database platform. This option is not ideal when hundreds or thousands of application programs need to be analyzed and modified. In terms of cost, this option involves manual effort, which may require hiring consultants to make the changes to the application; it does not require buying new tools or solutions. Risks associated with this option are manageable as there is not much code to modify.

Migrating Applications Using Scripts and Tools

Some organizations deploy script-based solutions to identify and, in some cases, modify application code in-place as part of the migration exercise. Usually, these scripts are developed based on languages such as Perl or tools and utilities provided by operating system vendors (e.g., AWK, SED, etc.). Although it is easier to develop these types of solutions, considerable time and effort goes into perfecting the scripts before they are actually used. Script-based solutions are typically the first step in developing a tool or product that can provide more automation and an easy-to-use interface.

A big difference between publicly available tools or products and script-based solutions is that IT organizations can buy tools or products and use them as they need them, whereas script-based solutions are typically used by service providers as part of their consultation offerings. Large system integrators tend to have their own tool sets (developed in-house or licensed from another vendor) as part of their migration service offerings. Script-based solutions are usually the steppingstone in development of a fully automated, complete tool set. Risks associated with script-based solutions are centered on potential inaccuracies as a result of insufficient testing against a variety of test cases. Generally, these solutions are specifically developed for applications based on a particular language or software development platform, at least initially, and their scope is then expanded to cover other languages and platforms. A major issue with all script-based solutions is that they lack critical documentation regarding how to use them effectively and understand how they function.

Oracle SQL Developer is an extensible and flexible solution for scanning application code for changes, and for modifying the identified code fragment within the application source. SQL Developer works on a rule-based approach wherein the rules for search expressions can be specified in an XML file that acts as a rules repository. Separate rules repositories can be created for different languages and platforms, such as Sybase CT-lib/DB-lib, Visual Basic, and PowerBuilder. SQL Developer can use only the rules repository to process programs written in one language at any one time. SQL Developer's approach in this area is very extensible because support for scanning new languages and constructs can be implemented as and when they are required, and it is not limited to any particular language.

SQL Developer's scanning functionality is a command-line option; hence, it can be scripted to process a large number of files and can be executed on many servers concurrently covering applications written and developed in different languages. The SQL Developer scan utility can be invoked as follows:

```
C:\sqldeveloper\sqldeveloper\bin>Migration -h=scan
SCAN:
Migration -actions=scan [-type=<db_type>] -dir=<input_directory>
    [-output=<directory>]
    [-analysis=<filename>]
    [-repo=true]
    [-log=<logFile>]
    [-help=]
where
    <db_type>          is the type of database your application is built for.
                       The default is Sybase where type is excluded. The type
                       is case insensitive.
    <input_directory>  is the directory which will be scanned for input files
    <output_directory> is the directory where all modified files will be put.
                       This can include Java wildcards
    <repo>             is the connection name for the migration repository
                       created in SQL Developer
    <log>              is the log file name that captures all the messages
                       generated by the utility
    <help>             is the option to generate more information on
                       a particular action such as scan and
                       associated options
Directory Example:
    Migration -actions=scan -dir=/code/application
     -log=/code/application/scan.log
     -analysis=/code/application/analysis.log
    Migration -actions=scan -dir=/code/application -repo=true
```

You can obtain the preceding example from the Migration.bat utility on Windows by executing the following command:

```
C:\sqldeveloper\sqldeveloper\bin>Migration -h=scan
```

A similar utility in a shell script format (Migration.sh) is also provided for Linux/UNIX environments.

The rules file for scanning applications in SQL Developer essentially consists of a search expression and the engine that will be used to translate the expression into Oracle. The main reason behind this approach is that users will be able to use Oracle's SQL parser or plug in any third-party parser to translate the source applications, providing Plug and Play capability. Here is a sample rules file for scanning Sybase SQL Data Manipulation Language (DML) statements in applications:

```
<?xml version="1.0" encoding="UTF-8"?>
<rulesfile version="1.0" name="Rules for SQL DML"
    description="Search rules to identify SQL in a file" xmlns:xsi="http://
www.w3.org/2001/XMLSchema-instance">
    >
    <ruleset name="DML" description="Find the DML in a file" type="SYBASE"
        target="ORACLE" enable="true" source="ANY">
        <required>
          <regex>

    <expression><![CDATA[bkpublic\.h|cspublic\.h|
mcconfig\.h|sqlca\.h|sybdbn\.h|sybfront\.h|sybhstmt\.h|
sybtesql\.h|cstypes\.h|mcpublic\.h|sqlda\.h|syberror\.h|syblogin\.h|
csconfig\.h|ctpublic\.h|mctypes\.h|sybdb\.h|sybesql.c|sybhesql\.h]]>
</expression>
          </regex>
        </required>
        <regex name="select statement">
            <example><![CDATA[select 1 from dual where 1=1;]]></example>
            <expression><![CDATA[select ?.+? ?from ?\w+]]></expression>
            <replacement translator="oracle.dbtools.migration.sybase.
translation"/>
        </regex>
        <regex name="delete statement">
            <example><![CDATA[delete from mytable where id = 3829;]]>
</example>

    <expression><![CDATA[([Dd][Ee][Ll][Ee][Tt][Ee](.+[Ff][Rr][Oo][Mm])?
+.+;)]]></expression>
    <replacement translator="oracle.dbtools.migration.sybase.
translation"/>
        </regex>
        <regex name="insert statement">
            <example><![CDATA[insert in mytable values (1,2,3);]]></example>

            <expression><![CDATA[([Ii][Nn][Ss][Ee][Rr][Tt](.+[Ii][Nn]
[Tt][Oo])? +.+;)]]></expression>
            <replacement translator="oracle.dbtools.migration.sybase.
translation"/>
```

```
    </regex>
    <regex name="update statement">
        <example><![CDATA[insert in mytable values (1,2,3);]]></example>
        <expression><![CDATA(([Uu][Pp][Dd][Aa][Tt][Ee] +.+ +[Ww][Hh]
[Ee][Rr][Ee].+;)]]></expression>
        <replacement translator="oracle.dbtools.migration.sybase.
translation"/>
    </regex>
    </ruleset>
</rulesfile>
```

> **NOTE**
>
> Scanning applications to identify SQL statements that require changes does have limitations, one of which is an inability to identify dynamic SQL statements. Many applications build SQL statements dynamically based on user input in the form of variables that may contain table names, a list of column names, and the predicate clause to be used in the SQL statements, and then they execute the SQL statements. Identifying SQL statements in such cases is difficult, as a fully formed SQL statement does not exist in the application source because it is generated just before execution.

Emulation Technology-based Solutions

Emulation technologies essentially capture the SQL statements issued by an application for a particular database, and convert them to meet the requirements of the target database platform. This conversion of SQL statements can take place at two layers in a software solution: namely the application client/database driver layer and the database layer. At the time of this writing, no commercial solutions are available that offer emulation at the database layer for an Oracle database. Instead, available solutions require that additional software components be deployed. Table 7.1 lists the currently available emulation/on-the-fly conversion technologies and their applicability in database migration.

Table 7.1 Emulation Technologies and Their Applicability in Database Migration

Emulation Technique/Tier	Database Driver Supported	At the Application (Driver)/On-the-Wire Layer?	At the Database Layer?
JDBC driver layer emulation	JDBC only	Yes	No
Database layer emulation	All drivers/all types of application clients	No	Yes

Emulation or conversion of SQL statements written for one database on-the-fly to another database on-the-fly has risks, such as the introduction of an additional layer of software as well as potential inefficient conversions. An emulation/on-the-fly conversion solution has the potential to significantly reduce the effort involved in application porting as a result of database migration. However, it does not reduce the effort required in application testing and the database migration itself.

JDBC Driver Layer Emulation

Most database access depends on standards-based drivers such as ODBC (for C/C++/Visual Basic/PowerBuilder) or JDBC (for Java applications). At the time of this writing, there are no commercially available solutions that provide emulation and conversion features for ODBC-based applications. For JDBC-based applications, SwisSQL offers a JDBC API wrapper that can be integrated with the target database JDBC driver. This wrapper captures the SQL statements executed by a Java application and converts them to the target database format before passing them to the vendor-supplied JDBC driver for execution. This type of technology is useful for all sorts of SQL statements, including static and dynamic statements, as it acts on the SQL statements that are ready for execution. This solution also does not require any application changes. Potential risks with this type of solution include inefficient translation/conversion of SQL statements and/or not being current with new features and built-in functions supported by the latest version of Oracle.

Database Layer Emulation

Similar to emulation at the database driver level, SQL statements issued from an application can also be captured and converted just before they are executed in the database. This solution may include deploying another layer of software between the application and the database, or installing such software as part of the database software on the same server. Risks associated with this type of solution are similar to those associated with emulation and conversion in the database driver layer. Also, this solution does not eliminate the need for migrating database schema and stored objects, or for data migration and testing of the application in the new environment. For databases with fewer and simpler stored procedures and triggers, this type of solution may work well, but for complex database deployments, additional effort will be needed, just as it is with the database migration, due to technical differences in databases.

APPLICATION MIGRATION TASKS

Regardless of the strategy used for application migration, changes to the applications are mandatory when a database migration is carried out. These changes may be simple, such as modifying the application programs to use Oracle-specific drivers, or complex, such as modifying the actual SQL statements. The effort involved in the application migration can be reduced significantly with the proper use of tools and scripts. In this section, we will discuss the most common application migration tasks in the order of their complexity.

Database Connectivity Changes

As we discussed in the section "Factors Influencing Application Changes" earlier in this chapter, you must change the driver, the connection formats, and the parameters and their order in applications involved in a database migration. In addition to changes in connection information, you may need to set additional parameters that can influence performance, transaction control, DATE/TIMESTAMP formats, and similar factors.

Oracle provides ODBC/OLE DB/JDBC and ADO.NET drivers for its database. Data source configuration for ODBC drivers is a standard procedure for any database.

ODBC-based Applications

It is very common for applications developed in PowerBuilder, Visual Basic, and C/C++ to use ODBC drivers for database access. Using ODBC for applications involves using a driver manager, database-specific drivers, and libraries. The ODBC driver manager is responsible for loading appropriate drivers and validations. It also provides portability in database access routines. Oracle Database provides ODBC drivers for Microsoft Windows as well as Linux/UNIX platforms. On the Windows platform, Oracle uses the Microsoft ODBC Driver Manager (ODBC Administrator). However, Linux/UNIX platforms require a separate ODBC driver manager which can be obtained from the open source project unixODBC.org (www.unixODBC.org) or from other vendors. Windows users can set up ODBC data sources using Oracle ODBC drivers by launching the Microsoft ODBC Data Source Administrator tool from **All Programs** | **Oracle** | **Configuration and Migration Tools** | **Microsoft ODBC Administrator**, as illustrated in Figure 7.1.

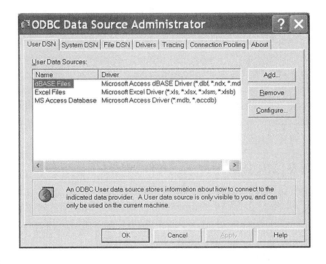

FIGURE 7.1

Launching Microsoft's ODBC Data Source Administrator

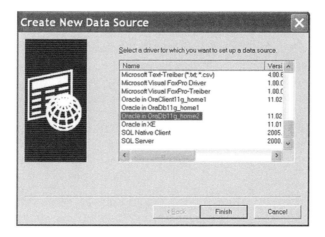

FIGURE 7.2

Selecting the Oracle ODBC Driver from the List of Available Drivers

To create a new Oracle data source using the Oracle ODBC driver, click the **Add** button under the **User DSN** tab. A new window will be presented in which you can select an ODBC driver from a list of drivers available on the machine, as illustrated in Figure 7.2.

Select the ODBC driver that is associated with Oracle from the list of drivers, and then click **Finish**. You will be prompted for connection information pertaining to an Oracle database, as shown in Figure 7.3.

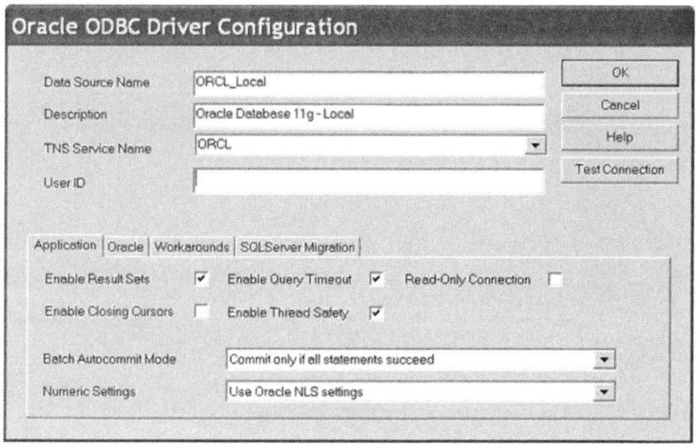

FIGURE 7.3

Creating the Oracle Data Source in the ODBC Data Source Administrator Tool

After filling in all the details related to an Oracle database connection, including the database TNS service name which is required for identifying the database service, click **OK** to finish creating the Oracle data source. You will need to repeat this process to create multiple Oracle data sources.

Oracle also provides an OLE DB data provider as part of its database software on Windows platforms. The OLE DB data provider is formally known as Oracle Provider for OLE DB and it supports Oracle database access via OLE DB and ADO. Support for .NET is available by allowing the OLE DB .NET data provider to interact with the Oracle OLE DB provider for accessing the Oracle database.

The Microsoft OLE DB provider (MSDASQL) can also connect to the Oracle database using an ODBC driver. Table 7.2 illustrates connection strings for the Oracle database using ODBC, OLE DB, and ADO in Visual C++, C#, and Visual Basic.

Table 7.2 Programming Methods and Associated Oracle Database Connection Strings

Database Driver	Programming Language/ 4GL	Sample Connection String

ODBC	Visual Basic	`SQL_ODBC_Connect(hodbc,`
		`DatabaseName,`
		`Len(DatabaseName),`
		`DBUserName,`
		`Len(DBUserName),`
		`DBUserPassword,`
		`Len(DBUserPassword))`

	C++	`Connect ( "DSN=ORCL;UID=scott;` `PWD=TIGER" );`

	PowerBuilder	`SQLCA.DBMS = "ODBC"`
		`SQLCA.DBParm =`
		`"ConnectString='DSN=ORCL;`
		`UID=dba;PWD=sql'"`

Oracle Provider for OLE DB (ADO)	Visual Basic	`conn.ConnectionString =`
		`"Provider=OraOLEDB.Oracle.1;User`
		`ID=user_name;"& _`
		`"Password=pwd;`
		`Data Source=ORCL;"`

Microsoft OLE DB provider (MSDASQL) +ODBC	C++	`'con.Open("Provider=msdasql;`
		`DSN=orcl;`
		`user id=scott;password=tiger;")`

Oracle OLE DB. NET	VB.NET	`con.ConnectionString =`
		`"Provider=OraOLEDB.Oracle;`
		`User Id=scott;" & _`
		`"Password=tiger;DataSource=Oracle;`
		`OLEDB.NET=True;`

Oracle offers two drivers for Java applications that interact with an Oracle database. The first one is a Type II JDBC driver, also known as a thick JDBC driver. The second one is a Type IV JDBC driver, also known as a thin JDBC driver. The Type II JDBC driver leverages an Oracle client (network APIs) to connect to an Oracle database, which is why it is known as a thick JDBC driver. The Type IV JDBC driver does not require any other software components and has a very small footprint, hence, the alternative name of thin JDBC driver. The Type II JDBC driver has some performance advantages as well, as it can take advantage of Oracle's high availability and failover capabilities for database sessions in an Oracle Real Application Cluster (RAC) environment. The Type IV JDBC driver is very popular because of portability reasons. Java applications connecting to other databases using the database vendor's Type II JDBC driver do not need any changes to Java APIs for database access. The connection strings for Type II JDBC drivers and Type IV JDBC drivers vary slightly, as listed in Table 7.3.

Since Oracle database client software is required on the server where the application is deployed for Type II JDBC drivers, configuration of the TNS alias for the remote Oracle database is the first step. As the name suggests, the TNS alias is usually created in a file named TNSNAMES.ORA located in the Oracle client software installation directory referred to by the `ORACLE_HOME` environment variable. In this case, the TNSNAMES.ORA file is located in the ORACLE_HOME\-network\admin directory and basically contains the Oracle database alias. Each database alias usually consists of such information as the Oracle database host name or IP address, the database listener port number, and the Oracle database identifier (the Security Identifier or SID) or service name for the database. The contents of the TNSNAMES.ORA file appear as follows:

```
ORCL =
   (DESCRIPTION =
      (ADDRESS = (PROTOCOL = TCP)(HOST = localhost)(PORT = 1521))
      (CONNECT_DATA =
         (SERVER = DEDICATED)
         (SERVICE_NAME = orcl)
      )
   )
```

Table 7.3 Oracle JDBC Driver Connection Strings for Oracle Database

Type of JDBC Driver	Connection String
Type IV JDBC driver (thin driver)	`jdbc:oracle:thin:@ [hostname]:[port_number]:[SID]`
Type II JDBC driver (thick)	`jdbc:oracle:oci8:@[Oracle DB TNS Alias]`

ORCL in the first line is the database alias for an Oracle database that is running locally on the same host, and the database listener port is 1521 (the default). The default service name for this database is set to ORCL during its creation.

Embedded SQL Changes

Embedded SQL statements appearing in application programs written in languages such as C/C++/COBOL are typically deployed for batch processing. It is also quite common for developers to execute SQL statements from application programs written in PowerBuilder, Visual Basic, and other languages as part of the user interaction with the database. As the database changes, the SQL statements may need to be modified to work properly against the new database. Here is a list of typical changes made to SQL statements in application programs due to database migration:

- **Object name changes**   During a database schema migration, if any objects have to be renamed in Oracle for any reason, including object naming restrictions or conflicts with reserved words in an Oracle database, these object names have to be updated in the application programs that make use of them. Having reports from the assessment and analysis and design phases can help users to identify programs which need to be updated to reflect new object names. Oracle SQL Developer generates a report listing all the object name changes during the database schema migration which can be used for identifying and modifying the application programs appropriately.
- **Built-in function changes**   It is very common for developers to use database-provided built-in functions in the areas of string, date/time, mathematical, and system functions to implement business logic. Although databases provide similar capabilities to a large extent, they differ in how they implement these functions. Table 7.4 lists the string functions in Microsoft SQL Server, Oracle, DB2, and Sybase.
- OUTER/INNER JOIN **syntax changes**   Prior to implementation of the ANSI standard on outer joins between tables in a SQL statement, databases differed in their implementation of these join features in terms of syntax used. However, when considering migration of legacy solutions with applications written years ago, it is quite possible that developers wrote the SQL statements leveraging the native syntaxes supported by the databases at that time. Table 7.5 illustrates the syntax differences among databases for outer joins between tables.

With the advent of the ANSI standard and its support among popular relational databases, this is no longer an issue. All major relational databases support the ANSI standard syntax of LEFT OUTER JOIN and RIGHT OUTER JOIN. Oracle Database 11g also supports these join operators.

- **Selecting the current date from the database**   Databases such as Microsoft SQL Server and Sybase allow users to write SELECT SQL statements that can retrieve the current date value from the database as follows:

```
Select getdate()
```

Table 7.4 System Functions in Sybase, Oracle, DB2, and SQL Server Databases

Function	Sybase/SQL Server	DB2	Oracle
Return a fixed value if the expression is NULL	ISNULL(expr1, expr2)	IFNULL(expr1, expr2)	NVL(expr1, expr2)
Length of a string	Len(expr1) or Char_length(expr1) in SQL Server	LENGTH(expr1)	Length(expr1)
Convert one data type to another for display or other tasks	Convert(data type, expression, format) or Cast (expr as data type)	Cast(expr1 as data type)	Cast(expr1 AS Datatype)
Add days, weeks, hours, and seconds to a date	Dateadd(datepart, number, date)	Direct addition of days and months to a year	Date arithmetic is possible in units of days (e.g., date+1 will return the next date). To get fractions such as hours/minutes/ seconds, divide one day into hours, minutes, etc.
Difference between two dates in years, months, days, etc.	Datediff(date1, date2)	Direct addition/ subtraction of dates possible	N/A
Extract day, month, year, etc. from a date	Datepart(datepart, date)	N/A	Extract(datepart FROM datetime)

Table 7.5 Syntax Differences for OUTER JOINs between Tables

Join Functionality	Sybase/SQL Server	IBM DB2	Oracle
Left outer join	Column1 *= Column2	FROM Table1 LEFT JOIN Table2 ON ...	Column1 (+) = Column2
Right outer join	Column1 =* Column2	FROM Table1 RIGHT JOIN Table2 ON ...	Column1 = Column2 (+)

Oracle provides similar functionality with the DUAL virtual table as follows:

```
Select sysdate from dual;
```

- UPDATE/DELETE **statements with multitable joins** Databases such as SQL Server, Sybase, and MySQL allow developers to write complex UPDATE/DELETE SQL statements that join multiple tables for updating or deleting rows from one or more tables. For example:

```
update employee

set employee.dept_code=department.dept_code

from employee,department

where employee.dept_code like '1%'

    and department.dept_name = ' Human Resources'
```

There are a couple of ways to write complex update statements in Oracle involving more than one table. One option is to use Oracle's MERGE SQL statement as illustrated here:

```
MERGE INTO employee
USING (SELECT * FROM department) department
ON (employee.dept_code like '1%' and department.dept_name = ' Human
Resources')
WHEN MATCHED THEN UPDATE SET dept_code = department.dept_code;
```

Another option is to use an inner query to fetch all the rows from the table to be updated and then joined with the desired table, as illustrated here:

```
UPDATE
(SELECT employee.dept_code as e_dept_code, department.dept_code as
d_dept_code
    FROM employee, department
    WHERE employee.dept_code like '1%' and department.dept_name = 'Human
Resources'
    )
SET e_dept_code = d_dept_code;
```

> **WARNING**
>
> In each of these SQL statements, the EMPLOYEE and DEPARTMENT tables should have a primary key constraint defined on the DEPT_CODE column. Failure to have a primary or unique constraint on the join column (DEPT_CODE) between these two tables will result in the following Oracle database error:
>
>   ORA-01779: cannot modify a column which maps to a non key-preserved table

Similarly, complex DELETE statements need to be converted to have subqueries instead of direct joins between tables in Oracle.

Application Code Changes

In addition to modifying embedded SQL statements, you may need to modify application programs (code) to meet certain requirements of the Oracle database and its drivers. Key factors that affect application code changes are as follows:

- Type of database driver (ODBC/OLE DB/ADO or JDBC)
- Calls to database stored procedures returning result sets
- Large Object (LOB) data manipulation

Applications that use ODBC/OLE DB/ADO drivers to interact with Oracle normally do not require any changes other than those made to the connection strings. In some cases, changes such as disabling the AUTO COMMIT feature in the driver may be required to prevent committing data after every DML statement executed by the application, such as when populating a temporary table in the database. Most importantly, Oracle ODBC/OLE DB drivers support the return of result sets from a stored procedure just as other drivers do. For example, the standard mechanism to invoke a stored procedure in an Oracle database using an Oracle ODBC driver is:

```
{CALL returnemprecs_proc(?)}
```

These calls are very standard and work across almost all relational databases, except for calls invoking an Oracle function. An Oracle function cannot be invoked in the same way as a stored procedure. The call to invoke a function in an Oracle database is:

```
{ ? = CALL returnemprecs_func(?) }
```

Calls to stored procedures in OLE DB/ADO are similar to calls used to invoke stored procedures in other databases. Just as in other databases, the REF CURSOR parameters in Oracle stored procedures and functions need not be bound explicitly in these applications. Oracle ODBC/OLE DB drivers also support the return of multiple result sets without the need for binding the REF CURSOR variables in application code.

Applications that use Oracle JDBC drivers may need to be modified to address the previously discussed issues of stored procedure executions which return result sets, LOB APIs, and return of auto-generated keys due to implementation differences with other JDBC driver vendors. It is very common for applications that access SQL Server and Sybase databases to execute stored procedures that return result sets. Let's look at a Java class that works with Sybase using DataDirect's JDBC driver which invokes a stored procedure returning a result set from the database:

```
try
    {
        // Initialize Variables
        dbConnection = ConnManager.getConnection();
        sbCallString = new StringBuffer();
        sbCallString.append("{call get_emp_names()}");
        cst = null;
        resultSet=null;
        empnames = null;
```

```
    // Execute Stored Procedure
    cst = dbConnection.prepareCall(sbCallString.toString());

    resultSet = cst.executeQuery();
    resultSet.next();

    empnames = resultSet.getString(1);
    resultSet.close();
    cst.close();

} // End of Try Block
```

Now let's look at how this piece of code needs to be modified to work with Oracle Database 11g using Oracle JDBC Driver 11g:

```
try
    {
    // Initialize Variables
    dbConnection = ConnManager.getConnection();
    sbCallString = new StringBuffer();
    sbCallString.append("{call get_emp_names(?)}");
    cst = null;
    resultSet=null;
    empnames = "";

    // Execute Stored Procedure
    cst = dbConnection.prepareCall(sbCallString.toString());

// resultSet = cst.executeQuery();
    cst.registerOutParameter(1, OracleTypes.CURSOR);
    cst.executeQuery();
    resultSet = (ResultSet)cst.getObject(1);
    resultSet.next();

    empnames = WebUtilities.stringNullTrim(resultSet.getString(1));

    resultSet.close();
    cst.close();
```

As the preceding code demonstrates, the modification involves binding the REF CURSOR variable in the Java code that is declared as an OUT variable in the get_emp_names() procedure in Oracle. So, if a procedure returns more than one result set, you must declare and bind all the output variables associated with the REF CURSOR variable in the stored procedure. These changes can become a major problem if many Java programs invoke stored procedures which return result sets from the database.

Oracle JDBC APIs for manipulating LOB, spatial, and other native data types are also different from drivers from other vendors. Therefore, you may need to modify the applications leveraging the Oracle JDBC driver and its APIs.

Database API Changes

You need to modify migrating application programs that leverage call-level interfaces provided by the database vendors to make them work with an Oracle database. Oracle offers OCI for this purpose. OCI provides rich functionality as well as robust performance in this regard, because with these interfaces, there is no additional layer of software to navigate through to interact with the database. Classic examples of applications based on call-level interfaces are the Sybase CT-Lib/DB-lib applications and DB2 CLI programs.

There are only a couple of options for migration of call-level interface programs:

- Rewrite the application programs in Oracle OCI. Oracle provides sample OCI programs and associated make files to compile and link the OCI programs into binaries.
- Use emulation solutions to capture the SQL statements executed by these programs and convert them to Oracle-compatible SQL statements at the database layer.

At the time of this writing, there are no publicly available solutions that can convert these programs automatically into Oracle OCI programs. Hence, a manual rewrite is the most likely option if these programs are deemed important in the new environment.

> **NOTE**
>
> The database-driver-level emulation option will not be applicable for migrating call-level interface programs because these programs do not use JDBC/ODBC drivers to connect to the database.

Changes to External Interfaces and Replication Solutions

Use of external interfaces to integrate with an upstream or downstream database is very common and is typically implemented via native database utilities to import and export data either into flat files or into a database-specific format. In cases of integration between heterogeneous databases, use of flat files is very common for data interchange. As a result of the database migration, these interfaces and the replication solutions used need to be changed. Table 7.6 lists the equivalent data interchange and replication solutions available in Oracle as compared to other popular databases.

Interfaces that leverage native database utilities and/or database commands to extract and load data need to be modified to use Oracle database utilities such as SQL*Loader. External interfaces that are implemented in tools and products such as Microsoft SSIS/DTS or IBM DataStage can be modified to access an Oracle database using Oracle database drivers such as ODBC and JDBC. There is no need to migrate these interfaces completely into an Oracle data integration solution such as Oracle Data Integrator (ODI). Usually, changes in data integration solutions such as

Table 7.6 Oracle Utilities, Replication Solutions, and Comparable Solutions from Other Vendors

Type of Utility or Solution	Oracle	DB2	Sybase	SQL Server	Informix
Data loader (flat files)	SQL*Loader, external tables in Oracle	LOAD utility	BCP/LOAD command	BCP/SELECT INTO.. [Text Driver] /iSQL	LOAD command in DB-Access
Data unloader (flat files)	None; data pump APIs (Oracle-specific)	UNLOAD	BCP	BCP/BULK LOAD and SSIS/DTS tools	UNLOAD command in DB-Access
Transaction replication	Oracle Golden Gate/Streams	Infosphere/DataStage	Replication server	Replication utility	Replication feature

Microsoft SSIS or IBM DataStage include changes to the drivers and metadata as the main data processing usually takes place in the tools themselves.

Any and all changes to the interfaces should be thoroughly tested for inaccuracies, syntactical errors, and performance issues.

Error Handling

Databases also differ in the error codes and messages they return when a database action results in an error condition, such as when an application tries to insert duplicate records in a table or when foreign key constraints are violated. When migrating databases to Oracle, it is essential that applications are modified to make sure they correctly return the error messages and codes returned from an Oracle database.

In some cases, users write code to take a special action on certain error conditions (e.g., update a table when the insert record action fails because the record exists in the table). In such cases, it is common to look for the duplicate record error message from the database and perform suitable operations, such as deleting the existing record in the row and inserting the new record, or simply updating the existing record in the database with the new values for all columns. Therefore, it is essential that the application programs have the correct error codes that are returned by an Oracle database for them to perform accurately. Table 7.7 describes common error codes that are returned by an Oracle database.

Databases return hundreds of error codes, but a majority of them are not handled within application programs because application programs typically do not perform many operations such as database maintenance (creation and deletion of objects), security grants, or space allocations in databases and tablespaces. It is always best to return the error codes and messages as returned by the database instead of processing them again in the application program. Doing so can help you to avoid hard-coding error codes and messages in the applications.

Performance Optimization

During the migration process and performance testing phase, it may be necessary to modify application programs that have high performance requirements in the new environment. You can optimize application programs to run efficiently in an Oracle environment by adjusting the following parameters and settings:

- FETCH **array size**   Applications that retrieve a large number of records from the database usually incur a performance overhead because they are retrieving one row at a time from the database due to network trips between the database and the application. Increasing the FETCH array size for drivers used in application programs in such cases can improve overall performance. ODBC/OLE DB/ADO.NET drivers allow users to set the array size programmatically. The FETCH array size (or buffer size) can be altered for an ODBC data source during data source definition in the Microsoft ODBC Data Source Administrator as illustrated in Figure 7.4.

Table 7.7 Common Error Conditions and Codes Returned by Oracle, DB2, and SQL Server/Sybase

Error Condition	Oracle Error Code	DB2 Error Code (SQL)	SQL Server/ Sybase Error Codes
Inserting duplicate records (unique constraint violated)	ORA-00001	SQL0803N	2601 (unique index), 2627 (unique constraint)
Inserting NULL values in a NOT NULL column	ORA-01400	SQL0407N	515
Foreign key constraint violation (no parent key found)	ORA-02291	SQL0530N	1776
Selecting more than one record when only one row is expected for the predicate evaluation (cardinality issues)	ORA-01427	SQL0811N	512
Table or view does not exist	ORA-00942	SQL0204N	2506
No data found (cursor exhausted)	ORA-01403	SQL0100W	100 (SQLSTATE CODE=02000)
NULL value fetched into host variables (C/C++/COBOL applications)	ORA-01405 (Pro*Cobol/C/ C++)	SQL0305N	02002 (DB-LIB)

In UNIX/Linux environments, the `FetchBufferSize` parameter can be set in the ODBC.INI file.

In the Oracle provider for OLE DB, the `FetchSize` attribute can be set on the connection as follows:

```
Set conn = NEW ADODB.Connection
conn.ConnectionString = "Provider=OraOLEDB.Oracle;User ID=scott;" & _
   "Password=tiger;Data Source=ORCL" & _
   "FetchSize=100;CacheType=File;"
```

In Java applications, the fetch size can be set with the method `setFetchSize()` on objects of type `Statement`, `PreparedStatement`, `ResultSet`, and `Callable Statement`. The fetch size in Oracle JDBC drivers is set to 10 by default. As a result, some Java applications may notice degradation in performance, especially those that retrieve a large number of records from the database.

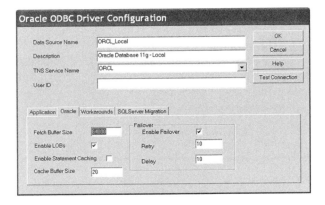

FIGURE 7.4

Adjusting FETCH Array Size for ODBC Data Source in Windows

Application programs written using Oracle precompilers (C/C++/COBOL) can enable array fetches in a FETCH statement by including the PREFETCH clause. However, the application needs to have the host variable arrays defined to fetch data from the tables successfully. The application code also needs to be written if and when the database returns an incomplete array of data.

- **Using statement caching**   Generally when a SQL statement is executed from an application program, it is first parsed and server-side cursor objects are created for the SQL statement. If a SQL statement gets executed repeatedly, it is advantageous to avoid parsing and creation of the server-side cursor object each time it is executed. Using the drivers' statement caching feature can help you to avoid expensive parsing operations. SQL statements that are repeated should also use parameterized variables instead of literals. Oracle drivers for ODBC, OLE DB/ADO, and JDBC all allow statement caching, and Oracle precompilers (Pro*C/Pro*COBOL) allow statement caching of dynamic SQL statements.

In the Microsoft ODBC Data Source Administrator tool (see Figure 7.4), you can enable statement caching by simply checking that option. For the OLE DB driver, you need to set the StmtCacheSize attribute just as the FetchSize attribute is set on the connection. You can also configure it in the Windows Registry by setting up the registry key \\HKEY_LOCAL_ MACHINE\SOFTWARE\ORACLE\KEY_*HOMENAME*\OLEDB\StmtCacheSize. The value of this key in the Registry should be set to greater than 0. The default value is 10 for this attribute.

TIP

In the Oracle provider for OLE DB the statement caching attribute is effective at a connection level (i.e., if same SQL statement is executed from more than one connection, this attribute needs to be configured).

For Java applications using the Oracle JDBC driver, statement caching is enabled implicitly for *prepared* or *callable* statements. Statement caching can be explicitly disabled by invoking the method `setDisableStmtCaching(true)` on *prepared* or *callable* statements. Explicit caching, on the other hand, allows users to create explicitly named statement caches from which any statement can be retrieved by providing a key. The major difference between implicit and explicit caching is that explicit caching stores both the metadata of the SQL statements as well as the state.

> **WARNING**
>
> Explicit caching of statements in Java applications stores data in addition to the SQL statements' metadata, and using that data for multiple executions may have unintended consequences. In addition, you must use a key to retrieve statements from the explicitly set up cache, so if a statement does not exist in the cache, the application will report an error. With implicit caching, if the statement does not exist in the cache, it will simply be cached.

Oracle precompiler-based application programs (C/C++/COBOL) can also benefit from this feature by setting the precompiler command-line directive `stmt_cache` to a nonzero value based on the distinct SQL statements as follows.

```
procob [opton_name=value]...[stmt_cache=20] ....
```

- **Reducing network roundtrips** In general, it is recommended that network roundtrips between applications and databases in a distributed environment be reduced to improve performance. Good coding practices, such as fetching data in arrays from the data for bulk data retrieval and using host variable arrays to execute `INSERT`/`UPDATE`/`DELETE` statements affecting bulk data, can help significantly in this regard. Oracle Database 11g also enables applications to cache data on the client tier with the client-side caching feature. Java applications using Oracle's Type II JDBC driver or applications based on ODBC/OLE DB drivers can all take advantage of this client-side caching feature in the Oracle database.

Application Build Process Changes

Applications that are written in C/C++/COBOL or that are based on call-level interfaces require database-specific build processes (i.e., compiling and linking programs with database-specific libraries, either static or dynamic) and may need Oracle database client software such as Oracle JDBC driver (Type II) or ODBC driver software. In such cases, it is essential that the existing make or build scripts be modified appropriately to include Oracle database client libraries. Oracle provides sample programs, as well as build scripts (make), for Windows/UNIX/Linux environments as part of its Examples distribution package, which is a separate distribution package from the Oracle database and client software packages.

Using the sample scripts to build demo programs provided by Oracle will ensure that the environment is set up correctly for such processes. Later, these sample build scripts can be incorporated into existing build scripts.

SUMMARY

In this chapter, we focused on application porting and migration issues encountered when migrating a database platform to Oracle. We covered various types of changes, factors influencing these changes, and various application migration tasks that need to be carried out. The amount of effort involved in making application changes can be minimized by choosing the right strategy (tools/emulation). Standards-based application development can also lead to fewer changes due to migrations. It is important to note that not all organizations interested in migrating their database platform to Oracle will run into all the issues discussed in this chapter. It is certainly plausible that some organizations may only need to perform a few of the modifications based on their application architecture, languages and drivers used, and coding practices. Moreover, some of the restrictions highlighted in this chapter regarding database drivers and functionality may not be an issue in future versions of the Oracle database. If a third-party JDBC driver such as the DataDirect JDBC driver is being used currently, only minor changes to the application may be required, such as modifying the connection strings. The next chapter focuses on application migrations independent of database migrations—that is, conversion of application programs from one language to another, or rewriting an application leveraging a new architecture and development framework.

Migrating Applications to the Cloud

8

Migrating applications to the cloud adds another level of complexity compared to simply changing the application SQL, database connections, stored procedure calls, and error message handling so that your application runs on an Oracle database, as we covered in Chapter 7. In some cases, the application language is no longer supported, the application language is not strategic to your organization, or your company is moving to a service-based architecture and your client/server application does not fit well into this environment. Perhaps you are running such an old version of the application language or product that upgrading, and all the testing involved, will cost just as much as migrating the language.

Because client/server-based systems require a client machine with large amounts of disk space and memory, and they lack peer-to peer capabilities, they do not easily fit into a cloud computing environment. Existing client/server applications need to be placed on a centralized server that is accessible over the Web in order to be "cloud-ready." This will typically require a migration of the application language. Application cloud migrations can also involve less intrusive methods such as Web service enablement, rehosting, or virtualization to quickly get your applications running on the cloud in weeks or months instead of potentially a year or more.

The most common target Oracle application migration languages, technologies, and products are Java EE, Application Express (APEX), commercial off-the-shelf (COTS), and Oracle Fusion Middleware products. The target software environment is categorized into languages, technologies, and products, as each of these categories has specific attributes that may make one target option more attractive in your environment than another. We will discuss the benefits and drawbacks of each target choice in the "Target Languages and Environments" section in this chapter.

Moving to the cloud is not just about migrating the application language. It is also about considering security, application provisioning, multitenancy, and other technologies that support the application. Client/server applications are inherently secure because the application resides on a computer inside the company's buildings. In order to use the system, the user has to be physically using the computer that hosts the application. In a cloud environment, the application can be run from any location, on any device, and the user is unknown to the system until he provides a username and password or other form of authentication. Therefore, the cloud server hardware, database, and network need to be highly secure. Application provisioning and multitenancy are also considerations that are unique to cloud computing. Application provisioning involves deploying applications to your cloud infrastructure with a few mouse clicks. So, when moving to the cloud, application provisioning will be made easier since there are not hundreds or thousands of client machines to deploy too. Multitenancy, or running multiple customers or departments on the same central hardware and software infrastructure, is not an issue for client/server applications since each user has her own instance of the application, and most likely each department or customer has its own dedicated database server. In cloud environments, the application, database, and hardware infrastructure are shared among departments or even companies. This chapter will address how multitenancy in the cloud can be achieved.

The last consideration discussed in this chapter is the target hardware and software environment for your cloud applications. Four options for the target hardware and software are explored in detail.

APPLICATION MIGRATION OPTIONS

In the "Migration Strategies" section of Chapter 1, we discussed the pros and cons of the four common strategies: rewrite/rearchitecture, replatform, automated migration, and emulation/Web service enablement. In this chapter, we will discuss these four strategies in more detail, along with two additional strategies: replacing the application with a COTS application, or replacing it with an Oracle Fusion Middleware product.

No single approach will apply to your entire application portfolio. Your corporate migration strategy will involve portfolio rationalization, as well as analysis of each application to determine the approach and target language or product for each application. One application may move to a COTS product, another may be automatically migrated to Java EE, and yet another replaced with Oracle Data Integrator (ODI). The proliferation of products that handle business processing and provide messaging infrastructure, data integration, business rule engines, user interface (UI) frameworks, and portals has moved developers from being pure coders to becoming application component builders.

> **TIP**
>
> If your goal is to move quickly from one application language to another with functional equivalence, automated migration is a great solution. If your goal is to make major changes to the architecture and take full advantage of the target language and service-oriented architecture (SOA), this type of method usually does not work. A more suitable approach would be to rearchitect your application, or to replace it with a COTS product or an Oracle Fusion Middleware product.

Emulation/Web Service Enablement

Emulation/Web service enablement should not be confused with SOA. SOA is an architectural blueprint, a way to develop applications, and a set of best practices for developing service-based applications and the infrastructure to support them. The Open Group defines SOA as "an architectural style that supports service orientation. Service orientation is a way of thinking in terms of services and services-based development and the outcome of services." [1] With this definition in mind, SOA can best be viewed as a journey to a better way of doing business and the technology architecture to support this better way of doing business. Web services, on the other hand, imply the use of standards such as Java/Java API for XML-based RPC (JAX-RPC), Microsoft .NET, or Representational State Transfer (REST). Web services also imply the use of Web Services Description Language (WSDL), Simple Object Access Protocol (SOAP), and/or J2EE Connector Architecture (J2EE CA) and Hypertext Transfer Protocol (HTTP). In other words, Web services are a very specific set of technologies. Web services will probably be a part of your SOA but are not mandatory. SOA is also a broader set of technologies including more than just Web services. Technologies such as Enterprise Service Bus (ESB), Business Process Execution Language (BPEL), message queues, and Business Activity Monitoring (BAM) are all part of SOA.

Web service enablement can bring your client/server environment into the world of the World Wide Web, Web 2.0, and all the other latest Internet and cloud-based technologies. Within days, a client/server system can be accessed via a Web browser. This is one of the biggest advantages Web service enablement has over other types of application migration options. Your time to market is weeks instead of months or years. The downside is that you now have an emulation and services layer to manage, upgrade, patch, and support in addition to your legacy client/server application, which the vendor may soon stop supporting.

Web service enablement is typically the first step in any application migration project. This is because it can be accomplished in days or weeks instead of months or years, like other application migration options. More modern languages such as Java EE and .NET have Web service capabilities built into them. 4GLs such as Visual Basic .NET, Oracle Forms, and PowerBuilder will need to upgrade to products released in the past five years in order to benefit from built-in Web service capabilities. 3GLs such as C, Basic, and Perl are more difficult to Web-service-enable.

In Chapter 9, a technical deep dive and case study using a product from Seagull Software will explain how any 3GL or 4GL, regardless of its native Web service support, can be Web-service-enabled.

Rearchitecture/Rewrite

Rearchitecting is also known as rewriting, reengineering, legacy renewal, forward engineering, and rip and replace. Rip and replace is a bit harsh, though. As the term implies (rip: to tear or split apart or open [2] and replace: to restore to a former place or position [3]), it is often used to belittle rearchitecture as a viable alternative. However, rearchitecting does not just create an equivalent application, but rather something much better: a new and improved application that takes advantage of new technologies such as Web services and SOA products.

Rearchitecture of client/server systems is significantly different from Web service enablement in a number of ways. First, you are changing not only the database and application components of your system, but also the entire supporting infrastructure. The infrastructure includes hardware, software, management tools, printing and reporting, archiving, disaster recovery, backup and recovery, the languages, security, database, transaction management, process flows, reporting, debuggers, development tools, database utilities, information integration, application integration, and more. Compared to Web service enablement, rearchitecture has a much more open spectrum of possible target architectures and implementation options. Rearchitecture also provides the opportunity to build a platform that is cloud-ready, supports virtualization, uses industry-standard cloud APIs, utilizes modern caching products, and can integrate with other cloud-based applications without having to use old methods of integration such as File Transfer Protocol (FTP) and flat files.

Chapter 12 includes a technical deep dive using a rearchitecture and forward engineering product to move a legacy client/server Oracle Forms application to a modern Java EE-based application, along with a customer case study. Chapter 13 also covers rearchitecture, but in this case moving from the 4GL client/server product called PowerBuilder to the free Oracle database product called APEX.

Automated Migration

Automated migration is a technique in which software tools are used to translate one language or database technology to another. The approach is typically used to protect an organization's investment in business logic and data in cases where the production source code cannot be found, the original developers have long ago left the company, or a solution that is quicker than rearchitecture is desired. Language translations are only considered automated if the scope of conversion handled by the tools is at least 60 percent. Sixty percent is recommended by the authors, as once you achieve less than 60 percent automation, it is better to rewrite, rearchitect, or replace the application. Automated migration is very fast and provides a one-to-one, functionally equivalent application. However, the quality of the target code is heavily dependent upon the source language, the language you are moving to, and the quality of the tool you use.

Two primary factors determine the quality of the target application. The first is the source paradigm. If you are coming from a procedure-based programming model such as C, the resultant Java will not be well-structured object-oriented code. Many vendors will claim pure object orientation (OO), or 100 percent-compliant Java EE. But, in reality, OO languages and programs can still be used in a procedural fashion. When the source is a step-by-step C application, that is what you will end up with after your migration to Java EE. This solution works quite well when the paradigm shift is not large. For example, going from C to C++ is much more attainable than converting from C to Java. This strategy is often used to migrate from 4GLs, such as PowerBuilder or Visual Basic, to the Java-based Java EE server-side software platform. The second factor is the quality of the tool and how well you are trained in using it. If you don't understand all the features and capabilities of the tool, you will most likely generate unusable code. The quality of the tool, unfortunately, will largely depend upon the specific constructs used in your 3GL or 4GL application. Vendor tools that work great at one customer site may not be as successful at another. The best advice is to either get a trial copy of the tool and try it yourself, or get the vendor to perform a Proof of Concept (POC) on a portion of the application you believe will be the most challenging to migrate.

WARNING

Some automated migration tool vendors will support a larger number of both source and target languages. The authors' experience is that you should avoid vendors that claim they support a long list of both source and target languages. Our recommendation is to use a vendor that supports one or two source languages and one or two target languages. This is because languages have so many different programming constructs that it is difficult, but not impossible, to support more than a few source and target languages.

COTS

COTS products are not frequently considered when a client/server migration project is undertaken. Companies can suffer from the "not invented here" syndrome (i.e., if it is not custom-written in-house, it will not be satisfactory), or they feel their applications are so unique that a packaged solution could not possibly exist. If the target package exists, COTS replacement can be a highly cost-effective strategy with a significant reduction in risk. This approach works very well with traditional applications such as billing, human resources (HR), and payroll, but you can also find many cloud-based applications for less traditional functions such as content management, electronic billing and payment, and mass marketing campaigns.

The implementation of a COTS solution assumes that the organization is willing to adapt to the new system paradigm. The new system paradigm involves conforming to the human and machine business processes of the COTS system, and the underlying application and database models. Therefore, core business processes must be altered and adapted. Another aspect of a COTS replacement is that it is often built on an SOA framework that you can leverage across your enterprise. For example, the latest release of Oracle Applications is built upon Fusion Middleware, which can enable an entire organization to more quickly integrate heterogeneous applications and data. Application and data integration can be done faster with Oracle Fusion Applications because it has a common data model for all modules and is Web-service-enabled.

Moving to Noncoding Fusion Products

Client/server applications contain mostly business rules and business logic. However, some of your applications may exist to support more infrastructure-related functions such as workflow, data warehouses, data marts or operational data stores (ODSes), business intelligence, reporting, Web portals, data or application integration, database replication, and messaging. Oracle offers products in the Fusion Middleware stack that can take you out of the business of writing custom infrastructure code and move you into a product-based noncoding environment. These Fusion products are noncoding because they contain all the application code in an out-of-the-box solution. The Fusion products have a GUI development environment, a command-line interface (CLI), APIs, or Web service interfaces so that you can customize or extend them to meet your unique requirements.

Moving your application to an Oracle Fusion Middleware product will exclusively depend on the functionality of the application. If your application has a lot of custom, industry-specific business logic, it is likely that moving to a Fusion product will not work. If your application code has infrastructure code, you may be able to move to an Oracle Fusion Middleware product.

Rehosting

Rehosting has become a well-known term when migration specialists discuss mainframe modernization alternatives. This is because rearchitecting, replacing, or automatically migrating 30- to 40-year-old applications that have been highly customized by many different developers can be very challenging. Rehosting, also known as "lift-and-shift," can be just as attractive an option in the client/server world, as it allows you to keep the application language the same but move the application to a hardware and software platform that can run in the cloud. It is a great way to leverage your current assets but not incur the risk of migrating languages. You can also leverage your current skill sets and your current business logic, and extend the life of your client/server applications that are working just fine—why fix that which is not broken?

The issue you face with moving client/server applications to the cloud via rehosting is "where will the applications run?" Currently, your applications are installed on client PC machines or other thick client devices; the Apple iPhone is in the thick client category as you actually download an application that runs on your iPhone; the application now needs to be hosted on a central server accessible through the Web. A handful of products from Oracle and third parties are available for hosting client/server applications in the cloud. Third-party solutions include Citrix XenApp (formerly Citrix WinFrame Server, Citrix MetaFrame Server, and Citrix Presentation Server) and VMware Server. Oracle solutions include Oracle Virtual Server, Oracle Tuxedo, and Oracle Exalogic.

Oracle Tuxedo is the leading open systems transaction processor (TP). It supports both COBOL and C/C++ applications, as well as Ruby and Python. Oracle Tuxedo can run on Oracle Exalogic to provide you both the application runtime environment (Tuxedo) and the cloud hardware infrastructure (Exalogic). Oracle Tuxedo can also be deployed on Oracle Virtual Server for a virtualized cloud environment. We will discuss Oracle Virtual Server and Oracle Exalogic in detail in the "Target Hardware and Software Stack Options" section later in this chapter.

WARNING

A client/server application cannot just be moved to a virtual server and be considered cloud-ready. The application is now accessible by many users, so it must be multiuser and multi-threaded. Oracle Tuxedo and Oracle WebLogic Server are both multiuser and multithreaded. A single-user C, C++, or Java application can be made multiuser by running this application in Oracle Tuxedo or Oracle WebLogic Server as these application server containers are multiuser and multithreaded. When using Oracle Virtual Server, it needs to be placed into a grid middle tier environment. This environment could consist of a cluster of commodity hardware components with a load balancer in front of the configuration for managing load balancing (multithreading) and multiuser connections. This virtual server grid can then run hundreds of images of the same application so that the application can service hundreds or thousands of users.

PORTFOLIO RATIONALIZATION

The first question companies must answer when moving client/server applications to the cloud is: "Where do I start?" From a business perspective, the department or organization that has the most influence, relationships with executives, or desire to migrate may often become the target of the application or applications to migration first. From an IT perspective, the application(s) that are the easiest to migrate or are at the end of their life in terms of hardware or software may be the first applications to migrate. The result of this treatment is that the cost, complexity, and overall effectiveness of the cloud migration program are exponentially higher and do not provide the highest possible ROI. A system, process, or methodology is needed that looks at the portfolio of applications without business or technical bias. This process is called *portfolio rationalization*. The output of the process is business data in order to make a practical and efficient recommendation of which, how, and when IT systems should be migrated to affect the highest business returns.

The methodology or process needs to be driven by business-specific drivers (business initiatives or priorities), reference metrics (real, factual, and objective data supporting the business), and weightings (methods to capture senior management's priorities and apply them to the collected facts). When analyzing your portfolio of applications, you need to address the following key dimensions in order to conduct a comprehensive business and technical rationalization:

- **Operational**   What effect does the effort have on the business and support processes?
- **Organizational**   How is the migration effort set up, and how does the project/program mix with existing organizational initiatives?
- **Infrastructure**   What is the impact of new or additional infrastructure components, ranging from computing platforms to network requirements?
- **Applications**   What application-level changes and/or impacts are influenced by the modernization effort?
- **Data**   What is the impact of the modernization or conversion effort on data architecture or data products?
- **People**   What is the current state of the people that support your applications? Are they ready to retire? What skills do they have?
- **New market opportunities**   Do current applications limit your ability to introduce new products to market, or limit your ability to beat or match the offerings of your competitors? Are you not able to enter new geographic locations because of inflexible client/server applications?

Because of the complexity and amount of information you need to gather, you must interview business and technology owners. This makes portfolio rationalization a highly manual process. No commercial products or tools are available to complete this phase of the migration effort. Large system integrators such as Infosys, TCS, Accenture, and CGI all offer portfolio rationalization services, or you can choose a niche modernization and migration company such as Vgo Software.

APPLICATION ANALYSIS

Once you have decided which application or applications to migrate first, you need to dive into the application(s) which you will be migrating. Most applications are not completely stand-alone; they interact with other applications or share data sources with other applications. Therefore, the first form of application analysis is a very high-level, abstract view of the application environment. This level of analysis looks at the application in the context of the overall IT organization. System information is collected at a very high level. The key here is to understand which applications exist, how they interact, and the identified value of the desired function. With this type of analysis, organizations can manage overall migration strategies and identify key applications that are good candidates for Web service enablement, rearchitecture, or replatforming versus replacing the applications with COTS applications or Oracle

Fusion Middleware products. Data structures, program code, and technical characteristics are not analyzed here. This type of tool can also help to redocument existing client/server assets.

The second type of application analysis is microanalysis. This examines applications at the program level. You can use this level of analysis to understand things such as program logic or candidate business rules for enablement, or business rule transformation. This process will also reveal things such as code complexity, data exchange schemas, and specific interaction within a screen flow.

A consideration when selecting a tool is whether you would prefer a dynamic (runtime) or static code analysis product. Dynamic code analysis has the benefit of tracking the application code path as it is happening (i.e., in real time). A dynamic tool will therefore capture interactions and integration points that may not be evident by scanning the code statically. The biggest issue with dynamic analysis is that the entire set of use cases for the application will need to be run in order to analyze all the code in the application. Therefore, most tools perform static code analysis.

Application analysis really took off during the Y2K (Year 2000) bug scare. Many of the companies that offer application migration analysis tools have their heritage in Y2K, and are therefore focused on mainframe languages such as COBOL. Micro Focus, Blue Phoenix, ASG (Allen Group), and Compuware are all companies that offer application analysis tools but may not support your client/server languages. Companies that offer products more aligned with client/server languages include:

- **Cast Software** The Cast Software Application Intelligence platform natively handles 26 unique languages including Java/J2EE, .NET, C, Pro C, C++, PowerBuilder, Visual Basic, ASP, Delphi, Oracle Forms, COBOL, JCL, and several scripting languages. Cast Software handles analysis of the database tiers for Sybase, DB2, Informix, SQL Server, and other open system relational databases. The valuable aspect of this product is that it not only scans the application code, but also ties application database access to the relational database to which it is persisting data.
- **Semantic Designs** The DMS Software Reengineering Toolkit supports custom analysis of C, C++, C#, Java, COBOL, PHP, Visual Basic, and many other languages.

It is interesting that many companies offer tools in the mainframe space, but few offer application analysis tools in the client/server arena. Perhaps this has to do with the limited number of languages on mainframes (mostly COBOL and Job Control Language or JCL), and the fact that mainframe systems have been around much longer.

The process of analyzing code and storing the resultant analysis is very common across both mainframe and client/server applications. In order to provide a common metamodel to enable product interoperability, the Object Management Group (OMG) created the ADM subcommittee several years ago. This subcommittee is focused on creating UML (with XML and XMI) standards in both the understanding/discovery and rearchitecting/forward engineering spaces. In the understanding/discovery space, the Knowledge Discovery Metamodel (KDM) has been ratified and has created a common Unified Modeling Language (UML)-based repository for all vendors to use. In the rearchitecting space, the Abstract Syntax Tree Metamodel (ASTM) will provide a standard for all forward reengineering services and tool vendors to use so that all language translation tools (that participate) use the same model and are UML-based.

3GL APPLICATIONS

The most common 3GL legacy client/server source application languages are C, Basic, Pascal, Fortran, Delphi, and Visual Basic. 3GLs such as Perl, Ruby, Python, C++, and Java are typically not considered legacy. What defines a 3GL as legacy is really up to the beholder, as a legacy application is considered to be anything that has been operational for a long time, no longer can be updated to meet the needs of the business, is expensive to maintain, and is difficult to integrate.

Most 3GLs cannot be placed in the cloud without using a third-party Web service enablement product or changing the application code, as they don't natively support Web services. Instead of Web service enablement or refactoring the application code, another approach is to move to a virtualization solution or software/hardware cloud solution such as Oracle Virtual Server or Oracle Exalogic running Oracle Tuxedo (in the case of C, C++, Python, and Ruby). Using a virtualization option allows you to move your application to the cloud without having to migrate languages or move to a new operating system. You can simply take the code as is and place it in a virtual machine (VM).

One company that has had great success in moving legacy C applications to Java EE is The Software Revolution, Inc. (TSRI). TSRI uses a software reengineering tool set called JANUS Studio. JANUS Studio provides automation for software assessment, documentation, transformation, refactoring, and Web enablement. A number of government agencies have used this automated migration approach to migrate C applications to Java EE and C++.

4GL APPLICATIONS

Fourth-generation languages (4GLs) became popular in the late 1980s. The lofty goal of 4GL was to move application development from the domain of IT coders to that of business users. By offering a graphical, drag-and-drop-based development environment, 4GL products became a way for companies to develop applications more quickly with less reliance on highly skilled 3GL developers. 4GLs did not succeed in moving development of applications to business users, but they were successful in reducing handcoding of applications. Products such as PowerBuilder, Visual Basic, Oracle Forms, and Informix 4GL became the standard method for developing client/server applications in the early 1990s. The biggest drawbacks to

4GL products are that the generated application is vendor-specific and the application could, until recently, run only on Windows PCs (Oracle Forms can be deployed on Many platforms). Just as you can move 3GL applications to the cloud by placing them in a virtualized environment, you can do the same thing with 4GL applications.

A number of companies offer solutions for moving 4GL applications to Java EE. These companies include Vgo Software, SoftSol, JSA[2] Solutions, ArtinSoft, and FreeSoft. These companies cannot support all the 4GLs that exist, so their offerings typically focus on one or two 4GL products.

TIP

An example of moving a 4GL to the cloud using virtualization was encountered at a leading Canadian company running old versions (7.0, 8.1, and 9.5) of PowerBuilder. The company was running a farm of 500 Intel boxes, each running the Citrix Server with a F5 BIG-IP machine for load balancing and connection pooling. The issue with moving this application and database to the Oracle cloud did not concern the application itself; rather, once the database was moved to Oracle, the old version of PowerBuilder could not be supported on the latest versions of the Oracle database. Therefore, the PowerBuilder application needed to be upgraded, which was such a lengthy process that the company decided to delay the project for a year. Of course, this only made the project more difficult the following year, as more changes to the existing PowerBuilder application and database were being made. Be aware that attempting to keep an application the same does not necessarily mean you will avoid a lengthy upgrade and testing process.

TARGET LANGUAGES AND ENVIRONMENTS

If you have decided to migrate by rearchitecting, using an automated migration approach, or replacing the application with an Oracle Fusion Middleware product, you need to decide which target language, framework, or Oracle product to use. Java using Java EE (Enterprise Edition) will probably be your choice runtime language when moving to an Oracle environment. We say "runtime language" here because you can generate a Java EE solution coding Java EE in a text editor, or using a development tool such as Oracle JDeveloper or Eclipse. Alternatively, you could use a Java EE framework or Oracle product like ADF that provide infrastructure services and visual/declarative design features to aid development of a Java EE application. One of the strongest attributes of 4GLs was the ability to use prebuilt components and create an application through a drag-and-drop interface. Java EE has matured so that Java EE frameworks and development tools provide this same type of drag-and-drop, component-based development solution, so you can avoid writing your Java EE solution from scratch.

In this section, we will discuss the Oracle APEX and Oracle Fusion products as potential target application deployment models. Oracle APEX is very different from Java EE as it runs completely inside Oracle Database. Oracle Fusion products will support Java EE applications that can run in the cloud.

Java and Java EE

Java is typically used for developing applications that are web based (n-tier architecture). The Java language used with Java EE is for server-based applications that lend themselves more to the cloud. Therefore, you will probably be using Java EE components such as Plain Old Java Objects (POJOs), Java servlets, and Java Server Pages (JSP) to develop your applications in the cloud. Enough Java EE books, Web sites, and publications exist that a deep discussion of Java EE is not required in this chapter.

Java EE Frameworks

Java EE frameworks take common design patterns used in Java EE development and put them into reusable class libraries. These class libraries implement the low-level database access, security, transaction processing, screen layout, data validation, business object construction, caching, and other development tasks so that the Java EE developer can focus on the business logic. The three most common Java EE design patterns focus on the presentation, business, and persistence layers:

- **Model-View-Controller (MVC) component**   One way to separate layers of a software application is to use an MVC architecture. The Model represents the business or database code, the View represents the page design code, and the Controller represents the navigational code.
- **Inversion-of-Control (IoC) container**   The business logic layer can be developed without coupling it to any other layers by using IoC. IoC lets the developer implement the business logic as POJOs and then connect them up so that they can be injected or called at runtime. This approach lets you avoid specifying the business objects as dependencies at compile time. It also decouples the business logic from the presentation, controller, and database access tiers.
- **Data Access Object (DAO) layer**   The DAO layer handles all the interaction with the backend relational database. When using a DAO framework, the Java EE developer does not have to write database SQL, handle database results, process error messages, or consider connection pooling or application data caching to improve performance and end-user response time.

The most common Java EE frameworks that implement these design patterns are Spring, Asynchronous JavaScript and XML (AJAX), Struts, Hibernate, and TopLink.

The Spring framework supports MVC, IoC containers, and DAO. The Spring framework is flexible in that you can use any MVC framework with it. However, it also provides its own framework, called Spring MVC. Spring MVC implements MVC-Model 2 for JSP. Spring has a very sophisticated IoC layer implemented using a JavaBeans factory container. This JavaBeans factory was implemented in part because of the complexity of Java EE Enterprise JavaBeans. Any DAO technology, including Java Database Connectivity (JDBC), Hibernate, and iBATIS, can be used with the Spring framework to persist data to a relational database and access persisted data.

Apache Struts is a free, open source framework for creating Java EE Web applications that are supported by the Apache Software Foundation. The Apache Software Foundation provides support for open source software projects. The objective of the Struts Framework is to separate the Model (database persistence) from the View and the Controller. Struts includes tag libraries that can be used in JSPs to separate the View from the Controller (which is implemented using a Java servlet). For the Model, Struts does not offer its own model implementation but can integrate with JDBC or DAO frameworks such as Hibernate, iBATIS, TopLink, and Object Relational Bridge.

The AJAX Framework is focused on the "V" (View or presentation) component of MVC. The AJAX Framework is a Web application framework that helps you to develop Web pages. AJAX is a collection of technologies (JavaScript and XML are at the core of these technologies) used to build dynamic Web pages on the client side. Data is read from the server or sent to the server via JavaScript requests. The data is transferred to and from the server using XML. The drawback to AJAX is that the developer needs to be proficient in JavaScript and XML (unless they use a framework like Oracle ADF). This makes it less like the other frameworks we discussed, as AJAX involves more manual coding.

Hibernate and TopLink are both DAO frameworks which provide an object-relational mapping (ORM) library. These frameworks persist (store) Java objects in a relational database transparently. DAO frameworks remove the arduous task of writing database Create, Read, Update, and Delete (CRUD) logic in an API such as JDBC.

Oracle Application Development Framework (ADF)

Oracle ADF is packaged with Jdeveloper and the ADF run-time requires a license that can be purchased with Oracle Fusion Middleware products or separately. ADF implements the MVC framework and makes developing Java EE applications for Oracle and many other Databases a much easier process than handcoding. Oracle JDeveloper is a free integrated development environment (IDE) that simplifies the development of Java-based SOA applications and user interfaces with support for the full development life cycle. Oracle JDeveloper enables you to develop Java enterprise applications as well as desktop applications. Oracle ADF is the framework that Oracle uses to develop Oracle Fusion Applications, the next generation of Oracle COTS applications. In Chapter 12, we will discuss migration to ADF in great detail.

Oracle Application Express (APEX)

The first thing to be aware of with APEX is that it is a database-centric product from Oracle. The second most important fact is that APEX is free when you purchase Oracle Database. APEX provides a Web-based GUI and drag-and-drop development environment. All Oracle APEX development is done in a Web browser, so you can look at it as being a 4GL development environment for the cloud.

Oracle APEX is a framework that uses the database and PL/SQL to produce Web pages. So, if your company has strong database skills and you have a large installation of Oracle Database, APEX may be a great fit for your migration to the cloud. If you can prototype the output to the browser as to what the screen will look like, you can create it in APEX. You can easily extend APEX using PL/SQL procedures or SQL, which you can expose to the built-in Web server while taking advantage of the security, logging, session state, and other application infrastructure the APEX system manages for you. You can also enhance the Web page layout and look and feel by developing code snippets in HTML, JavaScript, and CSS. The essence of Oracle APEX is approximately 425 tables and 230 PL/SQL packages containing 425,000+ lines of code.

Oracle Fusion Product Solutions

Using Oracle Fusion products can get your company out of the business of developing and deploying infrastructure software that does not add any business value to the organization. IT organizations are realizing they need to focus on the business logic, business rules, and business domain models that provide unique business benefits and make them more competitive. A few of the Oracle Fusion Middleware products that can replace custom-coded client/server application code are:

- **Oracle Data Integrator (ODI) for data migration and integration**   ODI is a data migration and integration product providing a declarative design approach to defining data loading, data transformation, and integration processes. Based on an extract-load-transform (ELT) architecture, ODI, unlike traditional extract-transform-load (ETL) products, loads the data into the target database and then does the transformation processing. This is a much different approach than traditional ETL products such as Informatica PowerCenter and IBM InfoSphere DataStage, which have specialized engines to perform the data transformations. ODI utilizes the underlying database engine scalability and performance attributes to perform the data transformations. ODI can read from and write to any data source that supports ODBC and JDBC, as well as natively supporting many messaging, database, and service-based source and target environments.
- **Oracle BPEL Process Manager for business processes and workflow**   Open system business automation processing is typically achieved through BPEL process manager products. The Oracle BPEL Process Managers let you orchestrate Web service implementations, human interaction, and system workflow quickly and easily using graphical, drag-and-drop techniques. The tools are end-user-focused, allowing users to orchestrate their own systems. The execution language for orchestration is BPEL, and the runtime engine is Java EE. BPEL supports human and automated orchestration.
- **Oracle Portal for the user interface and mash ups**   Oracle Portal provides an environment for creating a portal Web interface, publishing and managing information, accessing dynamic data, and customizing the portal experience, as well as an extensible framework for J2EE-based application access. The Oracle Portal solution is based on BEA AquaLogic User Interaction (Plumtree) and the

original Oracle Portal product. BEA had another portal-based offering called BEA WebLogic Portal. Features of this product are being merged into the combined Oracle Portal and BEA AquaLogic User Interaction. Oracle WebCenter is both a Portal solution and a Java-based UI framework that can be used to develop a complete Web 2.0, social networking, and information (including content management) management experience. Oracle WebCenter is developed using Java from the ground up (unlike Oracle Portal which was developed using PL/SQL) and is the strategic Portal product from Oracle.

- **Oracle Service Bus (OSB) for messaging and application integration**   OSB is a lightweight and scalable messaging platform that delivers standards-based integration for high-volume, mission-critical ESB deployments. It is designed to connect, mediate, and manage interactions among heterogeneous services, legacy applications, packaged applications, and multiple ESB instances across an enterprise-wide service network.

These are just a few of the Oracle Fusion Middleware products that you can use to replace custom-written infrastructure software.

NOTE

The authors of this book are surprised, and even shocked, by the number of companies that still have data integration and workflow systems built using UNIX shell scripts, database command-line utilities, and operating system commands. These applications support mission-critical business functions. However, they are built using old programming techniques such as FTP, database command-line file load and unload utilities, and UNIX Cron. These types of applications are prime candidates for moving to data integration software such as ODI and business workflow/process engines such as Oracle BPEL. The cost of maintaining, supporting, and enhancing a custom-built data integration stack for larger data integration platforms surpasses the initial expense and support costs for using a product such as ODI.

APPLICATION-SUPPORTING TOOLS AND CUSTOM SCRIPTS

Developers will most likely have many unit test scripts, performance validation scripts, or products such as HP LoadRunner, scripts to manage and monitor applications, development tools, debugging tools, application modeling tools, and source code control systems. Application documentation, both user and programmer, will need to be updated. These are all typically manual efforts that can be overlooked when migrating an application to the cloud.

APPLICATIONS IN THE CLOUD

Migrating the application is only one component of a migration to the cloud. Migrating, replacing, or upgrading the surrounding infrastructure can be just as big an effort. The application in the cloud has all the typical infrastructure components that a client/server application would have: security, provisioning, patching, upgrades, monitoring and management, network, hardware, operating system, and the application software itself. Chapter 10 covers in detail the infrastructure components and the impact that migrating to the cloud will have on your infrastructure, as well as the technology behind your cloud infrastructure. For now, let's use Table 8.1 to determine how your application deployed in the cloud will impact your infrastructure in either a negative or a positive manner.

Table 8.1 provides some of the reasons cloud computing from an application perspective is gaining so much traction with customers, independent software vendors (ISVs), and service providers. In most cases, the complexity, cost, required resources, and effort are decreased when your application is in the cloud.

Table 8.1 Impact of Infrastructure When Migrating Applications to the Cloud

Solution Area	Increase, Decrease, or Neutral for Sophistication, Resources, or Effort	Why
Security	Neutral	Security is considered neutral, as you get the benefit of centralized security when moving to the cloud. However, the disadvantage is that the risk of users outside the company increases significantly, as now users don't have to be inside the company's buildings to access the applications.
Provisioning (installation and configuration of application software)	Decrease	There is a substantial reduction in the effort required to provision application software, as now the application(s) reside in the central cloud infrastructure instead of in hundreds or thousands of client PCs.
Patching and upgrades	Decrease	Just like provisioning, it is much easier to apply patches and upgrade the application software when it is centralized.
Monitoring and management	Decrease	Monitoring and managing hundreds or thousands of PCs takes a lot of effort, as end users will place security, firewall, and unauthorized software on their PCs that can impact the operation of their PCs.
Network traffic	Increase	Network traffic will increase, as less processing takes place on the local desktop or laptop machine and more occurs on the centralized cloud server.

Table 8.1 Impact of Infrastructure When Migrating Applications to the Cloud *(Continued)*

Solution Area	Increase, Decrease, or Neutral for Sophistication, Resources, or Effort	Why
Hardware	Decrease	Hardware requirements for end users will decrease for the same reason network traffic increases: Now the end-user client/server machines can have significantly reduced processing power, memory, and storage space, as the processing is centralized.
Operating system	Decrease	The number of operating systems and operating system versions your company supports will decrease significantly, as the application interface will take the place of the browser, which is independent of the operating system, and your operating system choices will be narrowed to what you support in the data center. The device—in many enterprises, this will still be a PC—will still run an operating system. However, since the application is now running in the data center instead of on the PC, the PC operating system is less relevant.

TARGET HARDWARE AND SOFTWARE STACK OPTIONS

The hardware and operating system options for hosting your migrated application are varied and run the spectrum of "build your own" to "out of the box," as shown in Figure 8.1.

On the far left of Figure 8.1 is the option for choosing to build your own configuration without virtualization. In this configuration, each department or customer will have its own server without knowledge of other server configurations or reuse of hardware or software templates across the enterprise. The second option from the left in Figure 8.1 is where you will buy servers, data storage, networking equipment, and operating systems from a variety of vendors. However, the common piece of software across the enterprise is the virtualization software. This means you have to consider the hardware and software installed on other servers,

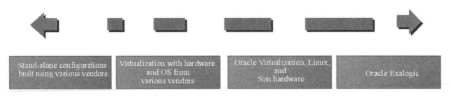

FIGURE 8.1

Range of Target Hardware and Software Options for Applications

as you will most likely need to migrate virtual servers from one hardware server to another because of out-of-memory conditions, failure of a hardware component, or upgrading hardware components. In these first two options, you build your cloud platform or hire a cloud service company to do it for you. The third option from the left in Figure 8.1 involves less effort to configure and implement, as all the hardware and operating system components are from one vendor: in this case, Oracle. The option on the far right in Figure 8.1 is an integrated hardware and software cloud offering from Oracle for running all your applications, called Exalogic.

Ironically, IT hardware and software vendors are moving the industry to consolidated hardware and software machines such as Exalogic. Exalogic, in a way, is analogous to mainframes that were introduced in the 1960s and are still running key systems at companies today. Exalogic, like a mainframe, has all the application server software, transaction processing engines, hardware, and software required to run your business on one integrated hardware/software product. The most significant difference is that Exalogic is built on open standards—operating systems, Java EE, Intel chips, Ethernet, InfiniBand and more—whereas the mainframe is all proprietary.

> **NOTE**
>
> The comparison of Exalogic to a mainframe is not entirely valid. This is because a mainframe also contains the database management software, as well as all supporting database software, on the same machine as the application server and application infrastructure software. Ironically, it is possible, but not recommended by Oracle, to run your Oracle database on the Exalogic machine. Exalogic does not have the hardware (Flash Cache) and storage software (Exadata storage cells) and other performance, scalability, and high-availability features that are present in the Exadata machine. Exalogic certainly has the memory and storage available to run your Oracle database, however.

Building Your Own Nonvirtualized Cloud

In the hosting and application service provider (ASP) world, the option to build your own nonvirtualized cloud is typically called *collocation*. Collocation is when one customer or department has a dedicated hardware server with dedicated networking

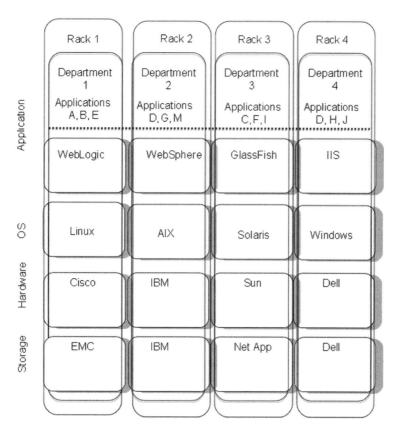

FIGURE 8.2

Building Your Own Nonvirtualized Cloud Architecture

that resides in its own "cage" (literally a caged-in area with a lock) within a data center. The advantage to the customer or department is that the hardware and network infrastructure is managed, maintained, secured, and monitored by a hosting provider or data center management team. Using this option, you are not only "rolling your own," as we will describe in the next section, but also building, supporting, and managing a custom hardware and software solution for each customer or department. Figure 8.2 depicts the wide variety of software and hardware options that are typically present in a cloud environment that is built without virtualization or Oracle Exalogic.

In order to build the configuration shown in Figure 8.2, you need to follow these high-level steps:

1. Assess your application requirements. This includes what operating systems, hardware, database drivers, network cables, power supplies, network devices, and storage are required.

2. Research available component technologies and vendor products. Review the products and technologies from vendors that span operating systems to storage to application servers.

3. Identify all software components and evaluate their compatibility, required drivers, and vendor certifications. Ensure that the application's middleware software will work with the hardware you have selected.

4. Obtain server, storage, network, and other components from vendor(s) for trial use. This includes negotiating with all the vendors to obtain the hardware and software required to perform a Proof of Value (POV) or POC.

5. Assemble the hardware components, including the network design.

6. Install the base software components sufficient for performing a network test.

7. Test the physical system, working with vendors to identify areas where they will need to supply changes or fixes.

8. Obtain and deploy patches and fixes from hardware vendors and deploy them to the test system.

9. Repeat steps 7 and 8 until the test environment is stable.

10. Deploy the application server and application software on the tested hardware platform.

11. Test the applications and application server software stack.

12. Obtain patches/fixes for identified defects from vendors and deploy them to the test system.

13. Obtain patches and fixes from software vendors and deploy them to the test system.

14. Repeat steps 12 and 13 until the application is stable and performance goals are met.

15. Finalize vendor price negotiations, support contracts, and vendor service-level agreements (SLAs).

16. Fully document the platform state and platform-specific operating/maintenance procedures, vendor support engagement practices, and internal triage protocols.

17. Move the system from testing/development to production.

18. Start over when someone changes the application requirements, when a key vendor product is discontinued or reaches end of life (EOL) prematurely, or when a key component vendor is no longer viable.

As you can see, this approach is much like building a car, airplane, or house on your own. You buy the components, first by negotiating with a number of individual companies with different pricing models, and then act as your own general contractor to get everything to work together.

Building Your Own Virtualized Cloud Platform

Virtualization is often immediately associated with VMware's vSphere. This is because VMware was the first open system vendor to have commercial success with virtualization technology. However, virtualization is an old technology, as IBM launched VM/370, now called z/VM, in 1972 for the IBM mainframe. Since 2001, VMware has offered server virtualization independent of hardware vendor certification. There is a program where hardware vendors can independently certify their components on VMware. Attempting to meet customer demand for preengineered solutions, VMware has partnered with Cisco and EMC to form a start-up company called The Virtual Computing Environment Company (VCE). VCE's Vblock solution is a combination of Cisco networking, EMC storage, and VMware virtualization and management. Department 1 in Figure 8.3 could be a Vblock solution or independent components acquired from Cisco, EMC, and VMware with Oracle WebLogic software for the application tier. Departments 2, 3, and 4 are running a combination of virtualization solutions using Microsoft VM, Citrix XenApp, or Oracle VM. All four solutions, for the four different company departments in Figure 8.3, do not offer an integrated hardware and application server software solution. The benefit of this is that you are free to choose any vendors to run your applications. The biggest limitation is that you now have to integrate the software stack with the hardware stack yourself.

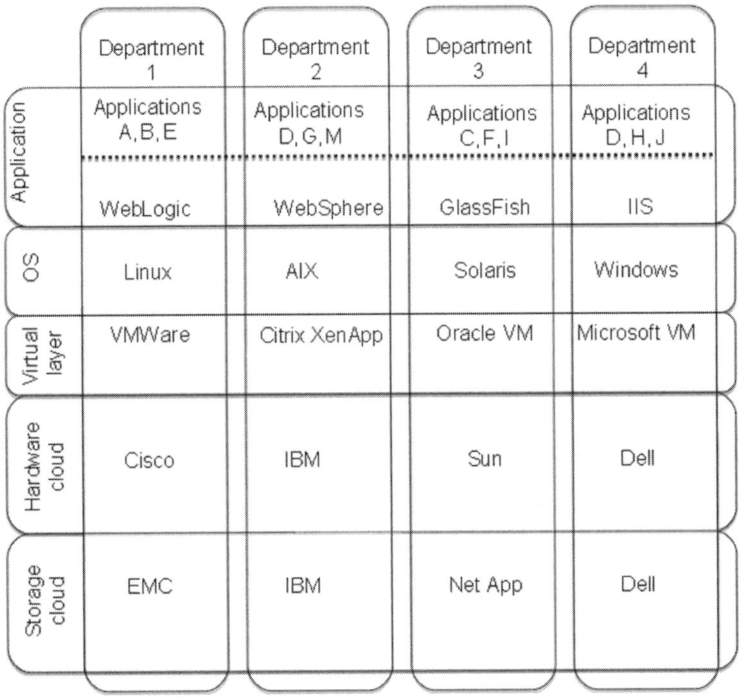

	Department 1	Department 2	Department 3	Department 4
Application	Applications A,B,E	Applications D,G,M	Applications C,F,I	Applications D,H,J
	WebLogic	WebSphere	GlassFish	IIS
OS	Linux	AIX	Solaris	Windows
Virtual layer	VMWare	Citrix XenApp	Oracle VM	Microsoft VM
Hardware cloud	Cisco	IBM	Sun	Dell
Storage cloud	EMC	IBM	Net App	Dell

FIGURE 8.3

Building Your Own Virtualized Cloud Architecture

You will need to complete the 18 steps listed in the preceding section in order to build the architecture in Figure 8.3. For this cloud option, you do get the added benefits of virtualization, which include:

- **Isolation**   Each VM is isolated from the others, so problems with one operating system or application won't necessarily affect the others.
- **Encapsulation**   A VM is a compact set of files which makes it highly portable. This means a VM can be backed up and recovered, migrated to a different data center, and/or automatically moved to a large server if the current server is running out of memory, processing power, or storage. It also means VMs can be used to "stand up" to a development, test, or user acceptance testing (UAT) environment rapidly, or a UAT environment can become the production system during a fix, patch, or application upgrade process.
- **Energy efficiency and reduction of server sprawl**   You now have better utilization of your hardware. According to press reports, most data-center servers are significantly underutilized:
  - As reported in *CIO Magazine* in May 2010, "For its own operations, the IT team analyzed the actual server load in its primary data center and found that, on the whole, each server had only about a 5 percent CPU utilization rate." [4]
  - In July 2009, Aberdeen Group reported that "midsize business server utilization rates on average are under 15 percent utilized." [5]

With only 5 to 15 percent utilization, consolidating applications to a server using virtualization can improve hardware utilization greatly.

- **Breaking the legacy "one application to one server" model with server consolidation**   With virtualization, one server can now run multiple applications, each within its own self-contained virtual environment.
- **Quick provisioning of VM gold images**   A gold image (a tested and validated VM image that has the application server and all configuration files) can easily be provisioned to an existing or new machine to support a new application or an existing application instance test or development image.

Oracle Virtualized Red Stack

The Oracle virtualized cloud platform takes the "build your own virtualized cloud platform" option one giant step forward. This is a giant step because all your hardware and software is from one vendor, and Oracle has precertified this hardware and software stack. This means you do not have to follow the 18 steps listed previously. As shown in Figure 8.4, you do have a choice in running Oracle Enterprise Linux or Oracle Solaris, as well as different versions of Oracle WebLogic, Oracle GlassFish, or any other application language your company utilizes.

The Oracle Virtualized Red Stack includes industry-standard processors based on Intel x86 and open source virtualization based on the Xen open source

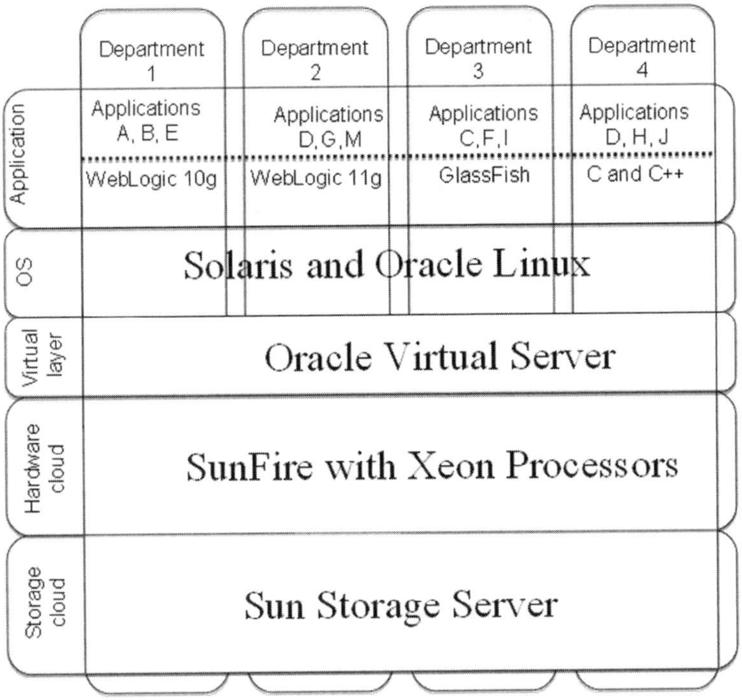

FIGURE 8.4

Oracle Virtualized Red Stack Cloud Architecture

virtualization software. Because the operating systems and virtualization software is from Oracle, these software components can be patched and upgraded at the same time, which keeps your software stack across your hardware platform in sync.

"Cloud in a Box": Exalogic

Exalogic is a preoptimized, preconfigured, and engineered hardware and software solution from Oracle. Oracle uses the term *cloud in a box*, as you can place the Exalogic solution in your data center and within a day be running applications on the environment. Like the Oracle virtualization solution, you have a choice of the Oracle Solaris or Oracle Enterprise Linux operating system.

The solution shown in Figure 8.5 is very similar, at first glance, to the Oracle virtualized architecture shown in Figure 8.4. The big differences are that this stack does not include a virtualization layer, and all departments are running on one physical server: Oracle Exalogic. Oracle Exalogic's integrated hardware and software stack offers many benefits, including Java EE performance and a reduction in deployments from months to days, optimized and tuned across the entire stack. Also, it is a standardized solution, making patching, upgrading, and management easier.

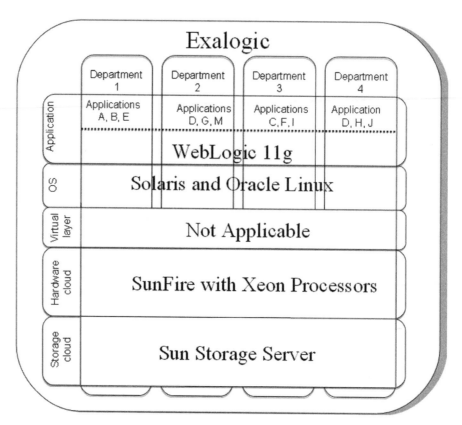

FIGURE 8.5

Exalogic Elastic "Cloud-in-a-Box" Architecture

Figure 8.5 does not show it, but non-Java applications can also be run on this platform. This includes any application that can run on Linux or Solaris using any application languages that can run on these operating systems. In addition, Oracle Tuxedo 11g can be used to run C, C++, Python, Ruby, and COBOL applications in a highly scalable transaction processing server.

Currently, Exalogic does not support Oracle Virtual Server, but there are options you can use to achieve the same result:

- **Oracle Solaris Zones** Oracle Solaris Zones are a form of operating-system-level virtualization. Different Oracle WebLogic Server instances and other Oracle Fusion Middleware components can be run on different OS virtual environments for optimal hardware utilization and to provide security so that one department or customer is protected from executing another department's or customer's applications. Oracle Solaris Zones also can be moved safely and easily between physical servers.

- **WebLogic domains** A WebLogic domain is an interrelated set of units to be managed as a WebLogic Server resource. For example, one customer or department can have its own domain consisting of all its applications. Each WebLogic domain has its own security credentials, is managed independently, and can be migrated from one physical server to another, assuming both are running WebLogic.

Pros and Cons of Each Hardware and Software Stack Option

We covered four options for the target hardware and software stack in this section. Table 8.2 lists the pros and cons of each option, so you can decide which option best fits your company's business and technical drivers.

Table 8.2 Hardware and Software Cloud Option Pros and Cons

Language, Technology, or Product	Pros	Cons
Build your own nonvirtualized cloud	• Optimize the stack for each application • Update and scale each application independently of others • Some can be cloud, some noncloud	• Heterogeneous environment, hard to manage • Low utilization and economies of scale • Cost of managing disparate configurations • Requires constructing your own hardware environment by integrating the disk storage, public and private networks, application software, operating system, processors, cooling, power unit and cabling, and rack or blade servers, management software, and more.
Build your own virtualized cloud platform	• Vendor neutrality • Hardware components can be refreshed as break-through technologies are offered for a specific layer of the hardware infrastructure • Database and application server software can be used from different vendors	• Need to build the hardware and software yourself • Need to make sure all the different hardware and software components work together • Patching and upgrading different vendor hardware and software products will happen at different times

(Continued)

Table 8.2 Hardware and Software Cloud Option Pros and Cons *(Continued)*

Language, Technology, or Product	Pros	Cons
	• Gain all the benefits of virtualization	and will potentially have a negative impact on other existing components • Managing and monitoring of software and hardware are done with a variety of vendor and third-party products • Virtualization sprawl can occur, as it is easy for a developer or administrator to copy a current VM to a test, development server, or even her own laptop or PC • Provisioning and scaling are not application-specific or application-aware
Oracle Virtualized Red Stack—OEL, OVM, SunFire, Sun Storage	• One vendor for software and hardware support and issues • Low cost for virtualization and operating system as they are both open source-based • Oracle-provided pre-packaged templates for software components including database, application server, and COTS applications • One management and provisioning tool	• Upgrade and patching of multiple (possibly hundreds or thousands) virtual servers
Exalogic	• Self-contained environment • One vendor for support and issues with the hardware and software • Upgrades and patches are predictable and will not impact hardware and software • Software stack is highly optimized for the hardware platform	• To gain immediate ROI you may need a large application or set of applications that will immediately use all the processing power of Exalogic • IT software and hardware are tightly coupled and provided by one vendor • No virtualization support

HOSTING OPTIONS

The "Target Hardware and Software Stack Options" section assumes you will be hosting your own application cloud environment. Your company owning the hardware and software for your applications was technically the only viable way to run your client/server application. This was because the applications ran on machines on users' desks. By running your applications in the cloud, other options are available to you besides owning the hardware and software to run the applications. You can even choose not to own the applications themselves. Using Oracle On Demand, a Software as a Service (SaaS) offering, to host your Oracle COTS applications, you can avoid the hassles of purchasing, supporting, maintaining, and upgrading not only the hardware and application server software, but also the applications themselves. Using an Oracle service provider partner such as Savvis or Terremark, you can not only avoid running Oracle COTS applications internally, but also run custom Oracle database and application server-based applications on their cloud platforms. Amazon only hosts Oracle Database as a Service (DaaS) at this time, so you can't host applications there as of today.

SUMMARY

You must take many technical and business considerations into account when migrating client/server application languages to the cloud. Technical considerations involve the source language, the skill sets of your organization, the need for a Web service-based system, and the target Oracle cloud infrastructure on which you plan to run the systems. Business considerations entail how quickly you want to achieve a migration ROI, the company's business strategy, and new markets you plan to enter in terms of both geography and products.

The target language, product, or technology will be driven by your company's strategic direction. For example, if your company has decided it is not in the business of building application software and has an off-the-shelf strategy, COTS will be your best choice. If your company feels the applications to support the business are too unique and provide a competitive advantage, migrating to web-based Oracle Forms, Oracle ADF, Oracle APEX, or Java EE makes the most sense.

Migrating to the cloud is not just about the application language. A major consideration concerns what your target architecture will look like. In this chapter, we covered four target hardware and software stack options and listed the pros and cons of each. If your business model is to build technology in-house and be completely vendor-neutral, rolling your own infrastructure may be the best choice for your company. On the other end of the spectrum, if you have decided that Oracle is your strategic IT vendor, moving to the Oracle Exalogic solution may be a better fit. You can also choose to outsource the management and operation of your cloud applications to a vendor such as Oracle, Savvis, or Terremark.

We have now covered all the fundamentals of moving your database and application to the cloud. You can take an evolutionary approach by Web-service-enabling your client/server applications, or rehosting your application to Oracle VM or Oracle Tuxedo. A more disruptive, revolutionary approach would be to rearchitect your application, move to a COTS product, or replace your application infrastructure with an Oracle Fusion Middleware product. Oracle Exalogic, one of the target hardware and software stack options, can support either an evolutionary or a revolutionary approach to cloud migrations. Starting with Chapter 9, we will provide real-world examples of database and application migration, as well as service enablement of current applications. Chapter 9 will go into depth on service enablement in particular, as it is the least intrusive method for moving your application to the cloud.

Endnotes

[1]   The Open Group [Web site on Internet]. Available from: www.opengroup.org/soa/soa/def.htm.

[2]   Merriam-Webster Dictionary [Web site on Internet]. Available from: www.merriam-webster.com/dictionary/rip.

[3]   Merriam-Webster Dictionary [Web site on Internet]. Available from: www.merriam-webster.com/dictionary/replace.

[4]   CIO Magazine [Article on Internet], May 18, 2010. Available from: www.cio.com/article/594091/Virtualization_Savings_in_the_House.

[5]   Aberdeen Group [Article on Internet], July 21, 2009. Available from: www.theinfoboom.com/articles/relieving-pressure/.

Service Enablement of Client/Server Applications

INFORMATION IN THIS CHAPTER:

- The Unique Client/Server Dilemma
- LegaSuite: Platform for SOA-Enabling Windows Client/Server Applications
- Step by Step for Creating an SOA Interface from a Legacy Windows Client/Server Application
- LegaSuite Runtime Considerations
- From Windows Client/Server Applications to SOA in the Real World

Year after year, surveys of IT leaders show that their goals are to improve business processes, control costs, improve employee efficiency, and align business and IT goals through legacy modernization. For example:

- According to a 2009 Forrester Research survey of more than 2,200 IT executives and technology decision makers in North America and Europe, "Modernizing key legacy applications is the top software initiative for businesses this year." [1]
- According to a *Computerworld* magazine blogspot, "Legacy modernization delivers much-sought ROEI. . . . Look for incremental enhancements to existing applications that leverage the possibilities for better user experiences without sacrificing operational integrity and without tossing away your past investments." [2]

Legacy systems are usually synonymous with mainframe and smaller mid-range (IBM i, DEC VAX) systems. And rightly so; with millions of lines of code and associated data and business logic, these traditional legacy systems are woven into the business fabric of the largest companies and governments around the world. In this chapter, we will refer to these mainframe and mid-range applications as "traditional legacy systems."

Traditional legacy systems may get the most attention (and complaints), but there are other systems that support business and government organizations that can be thought of as "new" legacy systems. These are the Windows client/server applications that multiplied with the proliferation of enterprise PC desktops in the 1980s and 1990s.

The irony is that the client/server application boom of 20 to 30 years ago was supposed to solve the challenges that traditional legacy applications presented. Client/server applications were less expensive to develop and maintain, were created with more modern languages, and were customizable to all sizes of organizations. Some were single-purpose applications, and some were multipurpose applications like customer relationship management (CRM) and enterprise resource planning (ERP) systems.

Yet, over time, they succumbed to the same problems that plague traditional legacy applications. The developers who created them left their places of employment, leaving behind little, if any, documentation. Vendors were bought or went out of business. New technologies became more popular, resulting in a dwindling pool of experts to maintain the systems. But in one way or another, millions of these client/server applications continue to be useful to the organizations they serve. And so they persist. They contain a lot of business knowledge and are an integral part of the way work is done. And like traditional legacy applications, enterprises have found it expensive and difficult to replace them.

The fact that client/server applications have become the new legacy shouldn't come as a surprise. Today IT leaders recognize that every application and system that existed last year will become legacy next year. The challenge is figuring out what to do with the client/server applications that continue to operate functionally in business and governments, but technically have become a burden to innovation and growth.

THE UNIQUE CLIENT/SERVER DILEMMA

Over the past 20 years, vendors and consultants small and large have come up with proven methods to improve, rewrite, or migrate off of traditional legacy applications. These methods have helped enterprises tackle the dilemma that legacy applications present: Pull the plug or start over.

This impossible choice no longer exists today. There are established practices and scores of successful projects in all areas of legacy modernization for traditional legacy systems. And importantly, the application modernization industry continues to evolve. Organizations now have a range of options to adapt their legacy applications to respond to marketplace demands.

For a short-term fix, organizations can rapidly enhance green-screen applications with a GUI. For a longer-term solution, organizations can use a service-oriented architecture (SOA) approach to assemble their application logic into modular services that can be reused across projects. The early-adopter customers are taking the strategic step of replacing older systems and applications with more innovative and responsive systems.

Now attention is turning to the aging stock of client/server applications. That's because IT leaders are finally waking up to the importance that entrenched client/server applications have to their organization and the unique challenges they present.

Like traditional legacy applications, client/server applications serve a functional purpose, and are challenging to innovate with and expensive and risky to move away from. Which means the same modernization application approaches can be considered:

- Replace the client/server system.
- Restructure the code underneath the client/server system with a newer language, such as Java or .NET (also referred to as lift-and-shift).
- Extend and reuse the client/server application using SOA interfaces.

Replacing Client/Server Systems with a Cloud-based Application

Replacing client/server systems is an option that is often used because the application seems lightweight compared to traditional legacy applications. Therefore, replacing a CRM with a Software as a Service (SaaS)-like system such as salesforce.com may seem like an easy solution. But doing so requires migrating customer data to the cloud and accepting the rules and logic of the new solution. A Gartner report identifies data and vendor lock-in as one of the main drawbacks to replacing in-house applications with SaaS: "Disadvantages can include inconsistent data semantics, data access issues, and vendor lock-in" [3].

Restructuring Client/Server Code

There are some challenges that IT shops encounter when restructuring client/server application code:

- The code was written using a programming language such as PowerBuilder, Visual Basic, FoxPro, Visual C++, or CA Gen (formerly AllFusion Gen, Coolgen, and COOL:Gen).
- The application has a GUI.
- The business logic is embedded in the application and often woven into the user interface.
- The source code is often not accessible.

These challenges complicate the options of restructuring code and starting from scratch. Creating new business logic by restructuring the source code is very risky since there's a high chance of disrupting the application. And it's time-consuming because of the undocumented nature of client/server applications. The languages client/server applications were developed in have evolved and their respective tooling now offers plenty of new functionality, such as Web service APIs, Web 2.0, and widget libraries. However, restructuring code means more than simply bringing source code to the new tools. If a project requires creating a new user interface or a set of callable Web services, the application will have to be carefully redesigned because the client/server application user interface and logic are typically intertwined. Implementing a restructure initiative whereby the application was developed following an object-oriented programming paradigm tends to have a higher success rate. That's because the business logic might be neatly encapsulated in a set of classes which can be reused for different purposes.

> **WARNING**
>
> The restructuring of applications will typically be a very long, complex, and risky business process. Service enablement, on the other hand, can be completed quickly, involves a significantly smaller investment, and is far less intrusive to the existing application code.

Complicating things further, few owners of commercial off-the-shelf (COTS) applications actually own the source code. And in the case of homegrown applications, the original designers and developers have left the organization and taken with them the knowledge that is vital to the source code. In some cases, the code is well documented, but it is so complicated that attempts to rehost, automatically migrate, or rewrite it would be too expensive to make the migration viable.

Reusing Client/Server Applications Using SOA

Accessing client/server application business logic using direct data access may offer an alternative method for integrating with the data of a client/server application. While data can be accessed directly using Open Database Connectivity/Java Database Connectivity (ODBC/JDBC) or SQL methods, this application approach requires two important considerations:

- The business rules that govern the use of data for input and output are completely embedded in the client/server application. When using integration directly through the data interface, the business logic is completely bypassed.
- Data is often available only through business logic which is not in a database. An example of this would be an invoice total calculated in the application based upon the order lines, instead of being stored as a total value in the database.

Because of these reasons, the direct data access application approach presents unreasonable risks that often involve substantial rewriting or duplication of business logic. However, if database stored procedures exist there is less risk of circumventing business logic while creating SOA interfaces. These database stored procedures, which contain business and database access logic, can be called directly.

Adding to this challenge is the fact that universal protocols, similar to those used with legacy applications running on mainframes (3270), IBM i (5250), OpenVMS, and DEC VAX (VT), are not available for client/server applications. In fact, each development environment in Windows can use different messaging protocols or customized Windows controls (also known as owner-drawn controls) to map the input and output of the data to the Windows user interface.

So, let's reiterate the problem here: How do you SOA-enable a Windows client/server application when the following is true?

- No APIs are available for an existing Windows application.
- A COTS application vendor doesn't support Web services.
- There is no access to or knowledge of application source code.

This is where using SOA for modernizing client/server applications at the user interface level has proved vital. SOA technology for client/server applications solves these challenges by facilitating the creation of services for Windows applications. As a result, traditional client/server applications that were once designed for human interaction can now be used in SOA and cloud deployments.

TIP

Creating Web services involves cataloging, through application analysis, your application functionality which also helps with its maintenance, code review, and future modernization projects. This is why it is often the first phase of your multiyear client/server migration effort.

LEGASUITE: PLATFORM FOR SOA-ENABLING WINDOWS CLIENT/SERVER APPLICATIONS

Rocket Software recognizes the challenges and the need to transition client/server applications to a more modular SOA and cloud-enabled state. LegaSuite is a technology platform from Rocket Software that enables developers and application experts to rapidly create standards-based interfaces to facilitate application integration and SOA initiatives.

With LegaSuite, Rocket Software takes a tools-based application approach to client/server application modernization which provides the following benefits:

- Enables standards-based access to key Windows client/server applications
- Automates repeatable, time-consuming development tasks
- Eliminates installing clients on every desktop by running a Windows application in "server" mode
- Improves productivity by making desktop and enterprise applications work more efficiently

All Windows 32-bit applications are supported, including applications written in languages such as PowerBuilder, Visual Basic, MFC/Visual C++, CA Gen, FoxPro, Delphi, and Smalltalk. LegaSuite even supports Java applets and Windows 16-bit applications.

To SOA-enable a Windows application, you simply launch a Windows application in the LegaSuite Workbench, which automatically generates scripts while you step through the application. The result of the navigation is encapsulated as microflow, a series of steps which contain the application navigation as well as input and output application mappings.

Developers can use the LegaSuite Workbench integrated development environment (IDE) to combine and redesign multiple actions, as well as the input required on multiple Windows UI panels, into one function. This provides a browser-based solution or a component-based interface to enable integration functions in other applications or to publish Web services for a Windows application.

The Workbench also facilitates the full cycle of development from deployment, testing, and debugging all the way to integrating with your existing change management infrastructure.

After development, developers publish the SOA interface to the LegaSuite runtime environment where it can be called by other applications such as Web applications, portals, and business process management (BPM) and Enterprise Service Bus (ESB) suites. LegaSuite's Windows Integration Engine executes multistage transactions through state flows. Because the LegaSuite runtime is a native Windows engine, it can run as a Windows service, and supports session pooling, load balancing, and queuing capabilities.

The LegaSuite Windows Integration Engine contains a microflow engine. Microflows simplify the process of performing navigational and data extraction functions, enabling multiple Windows dialogs to be combined as a single callable service or as part of a composite application, or simply refaced as a new Web-enabled application or Web service. The result is the functionality of a reengineered application by altering the application granularity without affecting the original target source.

The LegaSuite Windows Integration Engine relies on the Windows messaging layer, drives the Windows application through XML commands, and allows for session pooling and session maintenance of concurrent Windows application sessions.

The requesting program or user (client) can communicate with the LegaSuite Windows Integration Engine using Web services or XML via Hypertext Transfer Protocol/Simple Object Access Protocol (HTTP/SOAP) or sockets, using the XML User Interface Language (XUL) for thin client integration or directly via the COM/ .NET-based programmatic interface.

STEP BY STEP FOR CREATING AN SOA INTERFACE FROM A LEGACY WINDOWS CLIENT/SERVER APPLICATION

LegaSuite for Windows consists of the following components: the LegaSuite Workbench for development and the LegaSuite Windows Integration Engine for the runtime.

The LegaSuite Workbench is an Eclipse-based IDE which provides specialized LegaSuite views and perspectives. In Figure 9.1, the Resource Explorer on the left shows an itemized view of the project. The middle section in Figure 9.1 shows the custom editor known as the Microflow Diagram Editor. The LegaSuite Engines view on the right side of Figure 9.1 shows insight into the running of LegaSuite

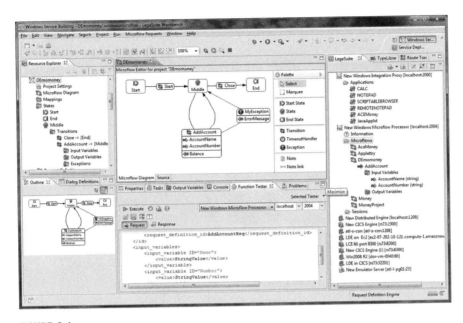

FIGURE 9.1

LegaSuite Workbench IDE Displaying Automated Services Development

integration engines. The Function Tester view on the bottom of Figure 9.1 facilitates the testing of Web services.

The LegaSuite Windows Integration Engine has two components:

- The LegaSuite Windows Integration Proxy is a component that exploits the Windows messaging model to intercept and interpret communications between the Windows operating system and a Windows client/server application.
- The LegaSuite Microflow Processor is a state engine that executes microflows.

Both engine components are stand-alone, native Windows applications written with performance in mind, and use technological innovations such as multithreading and nonblocking Windows sockets. The architecture diagram in Figure 9.2 shows all the components of LegaSuite and how they work together to enable SOA enablement of a Windows client/server application. The Windows Microflow Processor and Windows Integration Proxy boxes depict the runtime components, the Workbench box depicts the development environment, and the Transaction-based clients box depicts the Web services consumer, or client.

The Windows Integration Proxy executable works directly with the Windows client/server application. Its tasks encompass driving the application through a set of XML commands, retrieving and placing data into the application, serializing the GUI to XUL, and maintaining connectivity. The LegaSuite Windows Integration Proxy can use a few methods to talk to the application.

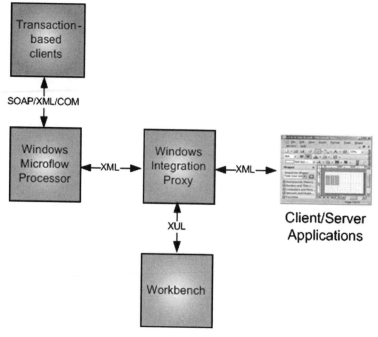

FIGURE 9.2

LegaSuite Client/Server Modernization Architecture

> **NOTE**
>
> You can retrieve data from the controls of a client/server application in three ways:
>
> - By accessing the Windows messaging loop
> - By intercepting a low-level API (e.g., the `draw text` procedure before it is posted on the message queue)
> - Via Windows Clipboard support
>
> One approach is not recommended over another. It is just a matter of which approach makes the most sense for you, and how your application currently works.

The Windows Integration Proxy has the ability to listen to messages sent by the operating system to the application. This is key, because Windows applications are event-based. This means they act on messages that the operating system posts to the main thread of the application. These messages are received from the client/server application's message queue by repeatedly calling the `GetMessage` function in a section of source code called the `event` loop. The LegaSuite Windows Integration Proxy can interpret those messages to retrieve the current state of the application. More modern graphical interface frameworks, such as Windows Forms, MFC, and

Delphi, do not typically require applications to directly access the Windows message loop, but instead automatically route events such as key presses and mouse clicks to their application-appropriate handlers as defined within the application framework. However, the message loop is used as the underlying method for these frameworks; it just is not exposed to the developer.

The LegaSuite Windows Integration Proxy can also hook directly to the application and intercept low-level APIs, such as the `draw text` procedure before it is posted on the message queue. The proxy also works with accessibility frameworks such as Microsoft Active Accessibility (MSAA) or the Java Access Bridge (JAB). Accessibility frameworks address the needs of assistive technology products and automated test frameworks by providing programmatic access to information about the user interface. Lastly, the LegaSuite Windows Integration Proxy can work with the Windows Clipboard function to retrieve data from controls.

Due to the close relationship between the LegaSuite Windows Integration Proxy and the application, the LegaSuite Windows Integration Proxy must reside on the same machine as the application.

On the left side of the architecture diagram in Figure 9.2 is the second executable known as the LegaSuite Windows Microflow Processor. This is a state engine responsible for executing transitions and managing states. The LegaSuite Windows Microflow Processor works with the application via the LegaSuite Windows Integration Proxy by issuing commands supported by internal LegaSuite libraries. This is how the LegaSuite Windows Microflow Processor offers more deployment flexibility, and provides the ability to load-balance multiple proxies and queue requests in cases where all proxies are too busy to process new requests.

Development Process

Developing an SOA interface from a Windows client/server application requires a series of steps. We will demonstrate this process by using the LegaSuite Development Workbench and the AceMoney application. (We are using AceMoney because it is a commonly available client/server application for managing personal finances.)

Setting Up Your Development Environment

First, you launch the LegaSuite Server which starts the LegaSuite Windows Integration Proxy and LegaSuite Windows Microflow Processor. Then you can start the development environment, the LegaSuite Workbench.

The next step is to create a Windows Service Building project. The LegaSuite Workbench is made up of multiple views and perspectives, optimally configured to allow developers to perform a specific task. Given that it's necessary to use the LegaSuite Windows Integration Proxy for development tasks related to client/server applications, the LegaSuite Engine's view will be present in the Windows Service Building perspective. Figure 9.3 shows a view of multiple applications configured in one runtime engine.

FIGURE 9.3

LegaSuite Engines View

In Figure 9.3, you can see several applications available through the LegaSuite Windows Integration Proxy. To add a new application you need to provide the application's information to the LegaSuite Windows Integration Proxy configuration, which includes the name of the executable, path, and any input parameters. Figure 9.4 shows where these configuration settings can be configured.

This is also the time to configure Microsoft Windows Terminal Services and provide the necessary credentials. Using Windows Terminal Services is not required, but it is recommended. When dealing with client/server applications, quite often you need to overcome the behavior of how Windows displays controls. In order to increase application performance, Windows might not paint controls which are not displayed in the forefront of the Windows desktop (e.g., they are hidden behind another window). Running each instance of an application in a separate Terminal Services session allows you to isolate each instance from accidental interactions with other applications. Also, using Terminal Services gives you another way to do session pooling and parking with multiple instances of the application running (license permitting).

Creating a New Project and State Diagram

Once the application is configured, you can start a new project where you specify which application you want to work with (from all the applications configured to the LegaSuite Windows Integration Proxy). Once the project is created, the Windows Service Building perspective is opened, with the microflow state diagram view in the center, as shown in Figure 9.5.

The state diagram consists of states and the transitions between them, describing the function or functions within the application. A state can be defined by the appearance of a particular dialog, or a particular value in the control. The transition describes the path required to get from one state to another. A transition may result in an error, and that's when the Exception Handler can be used to report the failure back to a user. In addition, in order to reach a particular state, some input values might be necessary. Using input and output variables allows developers to parameterize microflows.

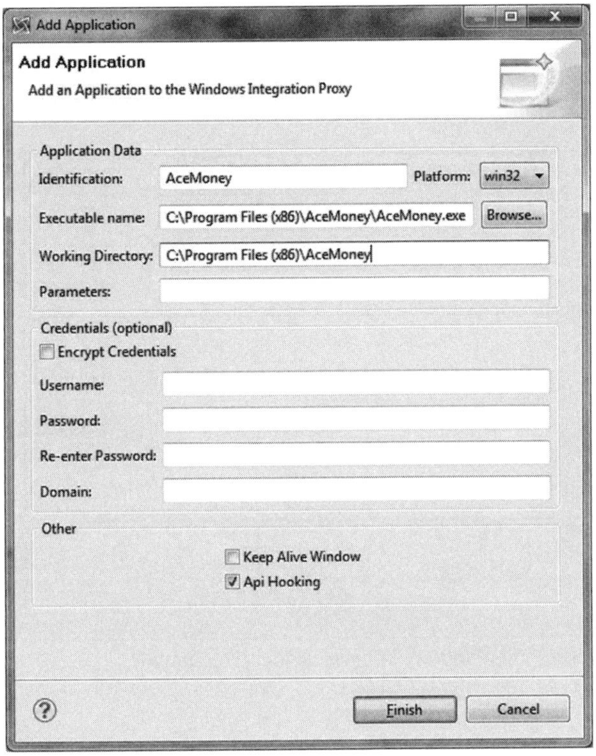

FIGURE 9.4

LegaSuite Application Configuration Settings

Let's look at a few screenshots from the AceMoney personal finance manager application and see how you create a state diagram. Figure 9.6 shows the main menu of the AceMoney application.

From the main dialog, a user can launch multiple functions, such as paying bills, or adding a new account as shown in Figure 9.7.

To represent a user setting up an account in AceMoney you would use the state diagram shown in Figure 9.8.

The state diagram in Figure 9.8 consists of three states (a Start, Middle, and End state) and three transitions (Startup, Close, and AddAccount). The Startup transition will traverse from the Start state to the Middle state by launching the application. In the Middle state, you can run the AddAccount transition which adds new account information (such as name and number) and returns a balance. Note that the instance of the application can remain open and you can execute the AddAccount transition multiple times on the same instance of the application. Then, for security reasons, you can close the application by executing the Close transition to the End state.

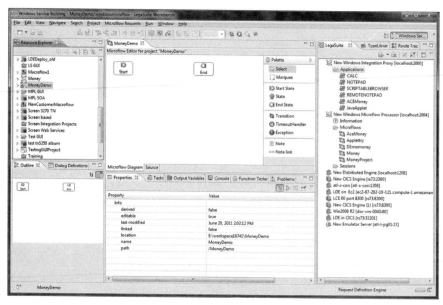

FIGURE 9.5

Workbench Showing the Windows Service Building Perspective

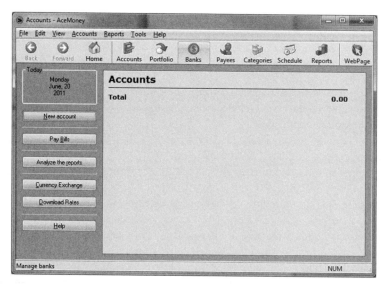

FIGURE 9.6

Main Menu of AceMoney

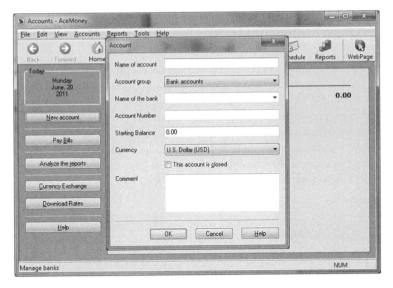

FIGURE 9.7

Adding a New Account

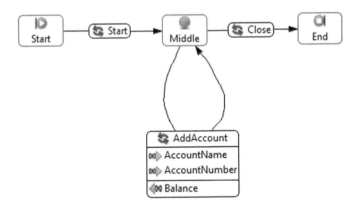

FIGURE 9.8

The State Diagram for a User Setting Up a New Account in AceMoney

From the LegaSuite Workbench, simply click the **Recording** button to launch the Transition Recording Wizard, which will map Windows dialogs and controls and record navigational steps through the application.

Let's have a look at the sample code that will be generated:

```
(Line 1) set Dlg=WaitForDialog(ServerSession, "Accounts -
AceMoney")
(Line 2) Dlg.UnknownControls(2).Buttons("&New account").Push
```

```
(Line 3) set Dlg = WaitForDialog(ServerSession, "Account")
(Line 4) Dlg.EditBoxes(0).Text = TScript.InputVariable("AccountName")
(Line 5) Dlg.EditBoxes(1).Text = TScript.InputVariable("AccountNumber")
```

In this particular piece of code, you can see the Accounts dialog (line 1) and the New Account button click (line 2). Then, after the Account application dialog screen executes (line 3), you automate data entry by setting two input variables: AccountName (line 4) and AccountNumber (line 5).

After a transition is recorded, you can create request definitions which correspond to Web service definitions. It is possible to define more than one request definition from a single flow. In this example, you have only one request definition which will translate to the following SOAP request:

```xml
<?xml version="1.0" encoding="utf-8"?>
<soap:Envelope xmlns:xsi="http://www.w3.org/2001/XMLSchema-instance"
xmlns:xsd="http://www.w3.org/2001/XMLSchema" xmlns:soap="http://
schemas.xmlsoap.org/soap/envelope/">
    <soap:Body>
        <AddAccount xmlns="http://money.com">
            <AccountName>Test</AccountName>
            <AccountNumber>10000600002</AccountNumber>
        </AddAccount>
    </soap:Body>
</soap:Envelope>
```

In the state diagram paradigm, a request definition has a direct impact on the path of execution undertaken by the engine. For example, Figure 9.9 highlights a route taken based on the preceding request. Without input variables, there would be no need to run an AddAccount transition.

```xml
<?xml version="1.0" encoding="utf-8"?>
<soap:Envelope xmlns:xsi="http://www.w3.org/2001/XMLSchema-instance"
xmlns:xsd="http://www.w3.org/2001/XMLSchema" xmlns:soap="http://
schemas.xmlsoap.org/soap/envelope/">
    <soap:Body>
        <PerformActionResponse xmlns="http://money.com">
            <PerformActionResult>
                <Balance>0.00</Balance>
            </PerformActionResult>
        </PerformActionResponse>
    </soap:Body>
</soap:Envelope>
```

The path shown in Figure 9.9 assumes that no errors will occur. In a test or Proof of Concept (POC) environment, you don't anticipate that any errors will occur, but in real life that is rarely the case. Therefore, let's have a look at how to deal with exception handling.

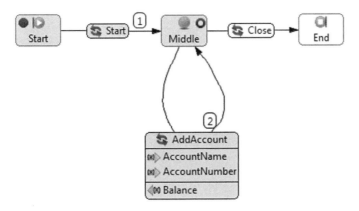

FIGURE 9.9

The State Diagram Path Taken for Adding a New Account

Handling Exceptions

Let's assume a user forgot to provide account name information or provided the wrong information. In a real-world scenario, the lack of an account name would be best verified by a schema validation of the SOAP request before LegaSuite starts the process. Let's show how this would work to get an idea of how exception handling works.

If a user clicks the OK button in the AceMoney application without filling in an account name field, the application displays a warning message, as shown in Figure 9.10.

In the Exception Handler, you will collect the message from the dialog, dismiss the dialog, and return to the Middle state. An exception is simply another form of transition, which you drag onto the state diagram from the palette. Figure 9.11 shows the resultant state diagram with exception handling added.

To record this transition you need to first reproduce the problem. You will launch the application and reproduce the warning dialog by clicking the OK button without filling in the account name. Once the application is in the required state, you can start the recording by double-clicking on the MyException transition in the state diagram.

During recording, you can capture the error message displayed on the dialog by right-clicking on an appropriate control and setting up an output variable. Figure 9.12 shows how this is done.

```
(Line 1)  Set Dlg=WaitForDialog(ServerSession, "AceMoney")
(Line 2)  TScript.OutputVariable("ErrorMessage") - Dlg.Statics(1).Text
(Line 3)  Dlg.Buttons("OK").Push
(Line 4)  Set Dlg=WaitForDialogServerSession, "Account")
(Line 5)  Dlg.Buttons("Cancel").Push
(Line 6)  Set Dlg=WaitForDialog(ServerSession, "Accounts - AceMoney")
```

FIGURE 9.10

Warning Message of AceMoney Application

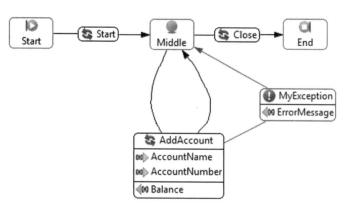

FIGURE 9.11

State Diagram with Exception Handling

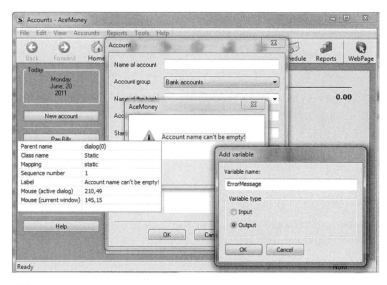

FIGURE 9.12

Collecting the Error Message through Recording

The preceding code snippet shows LegaSuite waiting for the warning dialog to occur (line 1). Then it collects the message from a Statistics control on the dialog (line 2) and presses the OK button (line 3). Next, it waits for the Account dialog (line 4) and automatically presses the Cancel button (line 5) to return to the main dialog of the application (line 6), which defines the Middle state in our diagram.

While testing the AddAccount Web service request with empty input variables, you can observe the path that the LegaSuite Windows Integration Engine will calculate for this scenario. Figure 9.13 shows that after executing steps 1 and 2, the Windows Integration Engine detected an error and runs the MyException transition.

The XML message to get this exception to occur looks as follows:

```
<?xml version="1.0" encoding="utf-8"?>
<soap:Envelope xmlns:xsi="http://www.w3.org/2001/XMLSchema-instance"
xmlns:xsd="http://www.w3.org/2001/XMLSchema" xmlns:soap="http://
schemas.xmlsoap.org/soap/envelope/">
    <soap:Body>
        <AddAccount xmlns="http://money.com">
            <AccountName></AccountName>
            <AccountNumber></AccountNumber>
        </AddAccount>
    </soap:Body>
</soap:Envelope>
```

The AddAccount SOAP response will be in the format of `soap:Fault` indicating that an exception has been raised. Not all scenarios will require such dramatic steps.

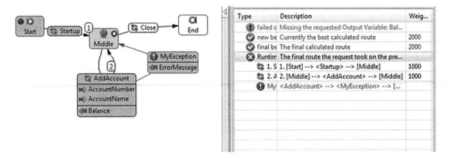

FIGURE 9.13

Execution Path with Exception

It might be enough to record a transition which returns an informational message to a Web service consumer. The XML message that is returned looks as follows:

```
<?xml version='1.0' encoding='UTF-8'?>

<soap:Envelope
xmlns:xsi="http://www.w3.org/2001/XMLSchema-instance"
xmlns:xsd="http://www.w3.org/2001/XMLSchema" xmlns:soap="http://
schemas.xmlsoap.org/soap/envelope/>
    <soap:Body>
        <soap:Fault>
        <faultcode xsi:type="xsd:string">soap:Server</faultcode>
        <faultstring xsi:type="xsd:string">
            Account name can't be empty!
        </faultstring>

        </soap:Fault>
    </soap:Body>
</soap:Envelope>
```

Testing and Debugging

A few times in the previous paragraphs you've seen the state diagram with paths highlighted in gray. This feature is called route tracking and it assists with testing various scenarios and demonstrating the state engine logic behind the execution. In addition, it is possible to place breakpoints, either directly in the source code of the transition or simply on the particular state. After placing a breakpoint, the request needs to be executed, and when the runtime arrives at the breakpoint, the LegaSuite Workbench will switch to the Debug perspective. The Debug perspective has all the common debugging facilities and views to allow for stepping through code lines and evaluating variables and expressions, as shown in Figure 9.14.

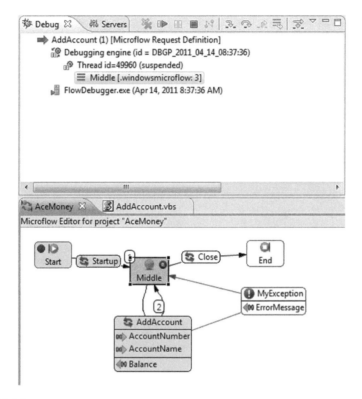

FIGURE 9.14

Debugging Perspective

Source Control

In a multideveloper environment, team development is a critical aspect of an efficient development process. But even if only one person is working on a project, establishing application life-cycle rules is beneficial for an organization. In addition, having source code preserved in a central location rather than on a personal computer decreases the risk of losing data. Therefore, it's a good practice to check completed work into a centralized repository. Being an Eclipse IDE, the LegaSuite Workbench will work by default with the open source Concurrent Versions System (CVS), and the eclipse.org Web site offers a plethora of plug-ins from a number of vendors. Once a plug-in is installed and configured to connect to a repository, checking in is as simple as right-clicking on the source file.

Services Registry

With the number of services growing in today's enterprise environment, meaningful cataloging is an absolute must. This is where a service registry, or Universal Description, Discovery, and Integration (UDDI), serving as a central repository comes in very handy. It might be an internal company UDDI where partners could be allowed to search for services as well. Such a catalog provides details about Web service functional areas (taxonomies) as well as binding details (location, contract, transport, etc.).

As UDDI has become a de facto standard for service registries in SOA solutions, there are many commercial and open source UDDI servers available. Oracle has a UDDI registry called the Oracle Service Registry. Using a registry will help companies to address two critical problems in the enterprise: communication and responsibility. The registry allows others in the company to see who is responsible for a given service, as well as how to work with Web services on a technical level.

TIP

The authors of this book do not recommend that you make a service registry a top priority. This is because you are mostly likely only going to have, at most, several dozen services deployed into production in the first year or two. It is the authors' feeling that a service registry only adds value when you have hundreds of services in your organization.

LEGASUITE RUNTIME CONSIDERATIONS

As we mentioned in the "Step by Step for Creating an SOA Interface from a Legacy Windows Client/Server Application" section, the LegaSuite Windows Integration Engine runtime consists of two native Windows executables (the LegaSuite Windows Integration Proxy and the LegaSuite Windows Microflow Processor), which, in a production environment, are run as Windows services. A key runtime question to ask is where will your client/server application run once it becomes a service provider?

Typically, the whole solution is hosted in one location. With the evolution of the cloud infrastructure, it sounds appealing to offload an organization's IT burden to an outsourced location (a.k.a. the public cloud). But not everybody feels confident about moving his client/server application entirely to a public cloud. There are security questions around the location of the data due to the fact that, together with the client/server application, an underlying database would need to be moved to a cloud data center as well. Not all organizations are comfortable hosting data outside their own data center, as it may actually violate some compliance regulations and offer no way to assure the organization in which country the data resides. Fortunately, you can consider a hybrid cloud deployment. Figure 9.15 depicts options for various deployment configurations ranging from private to public. If the

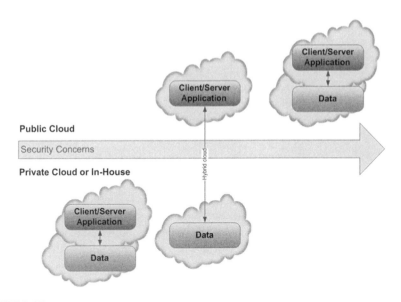

FIGURE 9.15

Cloud Deployment Options for Client/Server Applications

communication between the server and database can be secured, leaving the database in-house and hosting the client/server solution on a cloud server may make the most sense. Dividing components of an existing solution might not always be feasible, not only due to technical limitations, but also due to licensing.

With LegaSuite, your deployment options can be expanded further. The LegaSuite Windows Integration Proxy needs to reside on the same machine as the client side of the application due to our method of integrating with the application, which relies on the messaging and API rather than screenshots. But the state engine and Web server can securely run in the cloud environment.

Even if you choose to leave your applications in-house, by automating them and creating Web services you may alleviate quite an IT burden. If your client/server application becomes a Web service provider, there is no need to install and maintain it on every desktop. The client/server application may run on a dedicated server(s), which will be easier to maintain than a multitude of desktops.

One key advantage of utilizing this technology is that the actual client/server applications managed by the LegaSuite Windows Integration Engine are shared among multiple clients. A concrete host connection is required only when clients decide to commit their input. For this purpose, LegaSuite for Windows maintains a configurable session pool. LegaSuite can launch many instances of the application on the same server machine, allowing you to support the load required for a Web service provider application.

Pooling connections between the LegaSuite Windows Integration Engine and the host client/server applications results in much more efficient use of resources and greatly reduced idle time for the client/server applications. In addition, performance and user experience are not negatively impacted as a result of this application cloud deployment approach.

The LegaSuite Windows Integration Engine can internally load-balance connections to divide the work over multiple machines, or it can be load-balanced by any industry-standard solution. Terminal Services/Citrix is not required for session pooling. However, use of Terminal Services/Citrix may be required for applications with highly customized owner-drawn controls.

Sizing for Performance and Scalability

Fulfilling service-level agreement (SLA) requirements for an SOA solution requires careful consideration in the case of client/server integration. What matters most are the resources used by an instance of the Windows application and how many instances need to run concurrently to fulfill performance requirements.

Take the following scenario: A solution requires 50 unique users with an exclusive connection to a client/server application. To fulfill such a requirement, you will need 50 instances of an application running concurrently, possibly in a Windows Terminal Server environment. Let's assume the application uses 100,000 KB of memory while in use, but not a significant amount of CPU time, and the Windows Terminal Services session uses about 15,000 KB. Therefore, to run 50 instances concurrently, a machine with available memory of at least 50 times 115,000 KB is required. The LegaSuite Windows Integration Engine consumes a relatively small amount of resources, between 20,000 KB and 100,000 KB to run 50 instances. These sample numbers come from analyzing an application during regular use, but some applications "take a resource hit" during startup, which also has to be accommodated while planning hardware for the runtime environment.

It's not necessary to use Terminal Services to launch a number of application instances (e.g., you can launch n Windows Calculators on your desktop). However, from experience, it is a good practice to use Windows Terminal Services. Considering that you are usually dealing with older applications that have not been written with automation in mind, and some do not allow multiple instances, using Terminal Services to isolate each instance ensures the quality of the integration. In layman's terms, this lets each instance believe it is the one and only instance running on a given machine.

Another aspect of sizing is how to determine the number of concurrent instances when using session pooling. When turning a client/server application into a service provider, you can increase the performance of the solution by reusing the same instance of the application by multiple requests. In the first example mentioned earlier, it was not possible to use session pooling because, due to auditing requirements, each user needs to be logged in to the application.

First you need to evaluate the average execution time of the Web services created. Execution time will depend on the complexity of the Web service flow. Because the client/server applications were written for human interaction rather than for a high transaction volume, some of the services may execute at a slower pace as compared to other legacy transaction servers. Let's look at the following requirements: 4,000 Web service calls during a 10-hour window, each one taking about a minute to execute. This translates to approximately seven concurrent requests every minute. Therefore, seven concurrent instances of the application are needed to fulfill a requirement of this volume. Assuming that each request takes about a minute, those sessions will be busy for 10 hours. Consequently, the hardware requirements for the machine will have to satisfy, at a minimum, seven times the amount of resources consumed by the application.

All those estimates are based on careful observations of a unique application. As a result, it would be advisable to conduct performance testing before sizing a box for a production environment. This may cause quite a predicament, as hardware provisioning may take a while; this is why deploying SOA to the cloud makes perfect sense as provisioning in the cloud is much easier than hardware and software provisioning.

Load Balancing

As the volume demand increases on a client/server application, one machine may not be enough to fulfill the required SLAs. If you are running hardware in your own data center (a private or hybrid cloud) a load-balancing solution might be a good approach.

The LegaSuite Microflow Processor has built-in queuing and load-balancing capabilities; however, by no means do these capabilities replace the use of a standard load balancer in a high availability environment. The LegaSuite Microflow Processor can be used to load-balance multiple LegaSuite Windows Integration Proxies—for example, in cases when it's not possible to launch multiple instances of the application on the same machine. Figures 9.16a and 9.16b show some potential architecture diagrams using a load balancer. Figure 9.16a shows use of a third-party

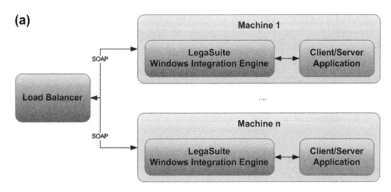

FIGURE 9.16a

Load-Balanced Architecture Options: Using a Third-Party Load Balancer

(b)

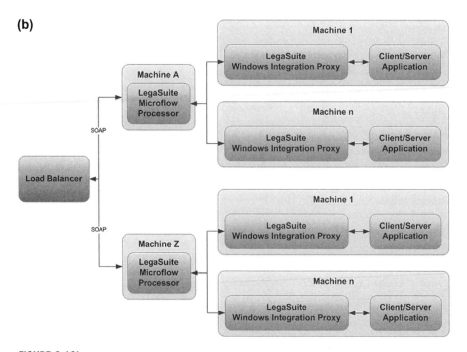

FIGURE 9.16b

Load-Balanced Architecture Options: Using a Third-Party Load Balancer with the LegaSuite Microflow Processor for Additional Load Balancing

load balancer, while Figure 9.16b shows a third-party load balancer with the LegaSuite Microflow Processor for additional load balancing.

From the LegaSuite perspective, both load-balanced architectures depicted in Figures 9.16a and 9.16b allow for fault tolerance. However, a single load balancer is a single point of failure. While these generic architectures might be applicable in many situations, it is recommended that you perform a detailed analysis of the environment, including performance, sizing, and failover requirements, before deciding on the load-balancing solution.

NOTE

Not all load balancers support sticky sessions (a client session is tied to a specific server) which are required if you intend to use the LegaSuite Windows Integration Engine with exclusive sessions (i.e., stateful sessions assigned to a specific end user). For example, Windows Network Load Balancing (NLB) supports limited forms of session stickiness and it's mostly used for stateless applications—that is, applications that do not build any state as a result of a request (Microsoft Internet Information Server [IIS], Microsoft Internet Security and Acceleration [ISA] Server, and others).

Infrastructure Changes

In an SOA solution, the client/server application becomes a service provider. That means you no longer need to deploy it on every desktop, and instead can deploy it in a centralized server location. As we discussed in the previous section, this may require provisioning new server hardware or cloud space to fulfill throughput requirements. A centralized location makes it easier for the IT department to maintain client/server applications, apply any necessary patches, and so on.

Another aspect of changing from desktop to server architecture is authentication. In a typical client/server scenario, each user is authenticated to the application. When switching to SOA, this may no longer be a requirement. Yes, a user has to be authenticated to a Web service, but not necessarily to the client/server application, which helps with implementing session pooling. Therefore, when designing an SOA solution, authentication and auditing requirements need to be considered. For example, let's say you need detailed logging for something like an audit trail that has to keep track of who has worked with and what has been done with an application. Detailed logging like this can be performed at the SOA level, but it may require each Web service consumer to be uniquely authenticated to the application. Therefore, auditing requirements need to be taken into consideration when devising a security architecture for the SOA solution.

Including Client/Server Application Logic with Oracle Middleware

IT organizations that look to integrate their existing business applications with new Web-ready applications or reuse them in new ways face a similar set of challenges. They need to find an SOA-based way to integrate existing business applications with new infrastructure in support of new business initiatives. Simply put, they need to rapidly connect old and new systems using easily maintainable, standards-based approaches.

To address this challenge, many organizations implement some form of integration middleware, such as an ESB or message-queuing middleware (MQM), or a BPM suite. These solutions are proven for connecting new applications—standardizing messages, improving process flows, and orchestrating interactions. But they fall short when they have to integrate with key legacy systems and business logic from traditional applications running on mainframe and mid-range (IBM i, OpenVMS) systems, as well as nontraditional legacy client/server applications. This is where LegaSuite fills the gap between integration middleware and existing applications. It allows you to provide SOA interfaces from key legacy applications which can then be used in complex infrastructures, such as Oracle SOA Suite. Since Oracle SOA Suite is based on Web services, any of the products in the suite (Oracle Server Bus, Oracle BPEL, Oracle Business Activity Monitoring, and others) can consume the services exposed by LegaSuite.

FROM WINDOWS CLIENT/SERVER APPLICATIONS TO SOA IN THE REAL WORLD

The application of SOA to enable client/server applications to respond to changing enterprise requirements is gaining momentum. Large corporations and state and federal governments look toward service-enabling Windows client/server applications that have become integral to their operations but offer limited options when moving to the Web and the cloud.

The following case study summaries are based on actual projects that were successfully deployed in the past two years. All three projects were conducted at larger organizations which had pain points that needed to be addressed in an aggressive time frame—usually within six months.

- UK government
    - **Solution** Liquidlogic specializes in social care software that lets UK health and social care agencies collaborate to deliver improved services to the public.
    - **Challenge** The government needed to integrate information from local agencies' Windows client/server applications with Liquidlogic's Integrated Children's Systems (ICS) solution to enhance case management for protection of vulnerable children.
    - **Results** LegaSuite enabled the Liquidlogic system to sit on top of existing local authority client/server applications to provide a unified view of all available information about a case, and share that across multiple back-end systems, irrespective of computer-operating infrastructure.
- Retail
    - **Company** This is the largest distributor and retailer of hardware, renovation, and gardening products in Canada.
    - **Challenge** As part of an enterprise-wide SOA initiative, this company needed to integrate Tibco's iProcess BPM solution, Oracle's E-Business Suite (Java applet), and BMC's Remedy Windows applications.
    - **Results** The company used LegaSuite to create SOA interfaces from its client/server applications to preserve the business logic and extend the life of its applications.
- Telecom
    - **Company** This company is a leader in US telecommunications services and one of the top 10 largest companies in the United States.
    - **Challenge** Through acquisitions, the company has an application portfolio of multiple mainframe, mid-range, and Windows systems and needed a single vendor that offers multiplatform enterprise SOA integration.
    - **Results** The company chose to implement multiple LegaSuite projects that integrate core applications with its SOA initiatives. It used LegaSuite to expose Windows client/server applications as SOA interfaces to automate the opening of wireless accounts.

In the following subsection, we will take a closer look at how LegaSuite helped a nonprofit organization in California to modernize its public assistance enrollment process.

Case Study In-Depth: Social Interest Solutions Modernizes Public Assistance Enrollment Process with LegaSuite

Social Interest Solutions (SIS) is a nonprofit organization dedicated to leveraging technology innovation to improve consumers' access to public and private health and social services. As an active influencer and promoter of policy reform, SIS has successfully developed and deployed pioneering technology solutions that have positively impacted the quality of life for more than 7 million of the nation's underserved population.

Challenges

SIS's One-e-App system is a Web-based screening and enrollment application that offers low- or no-income residents in California, Indiana, Arizona, and Maryland an expedited and simplified way to apply for a range of public and private benefit programs. One-e-App provides a one-stop solution for consumers by not only screening them for the available programs, but also delivering the applications and supporting documents electronically to the appropriate eligibility and enrollment systems. One-e-App does so by using a range of technologies which allow One-e-App to deliver data to a system in a nonintrusive way and without any changes to the other system.

In California, One-e-App has helped residents and case workers in 14 California counties move from an onerous, paper-based application process to one that's automated and modernized. By doing so, One-e-App has helped to eliminate barriers to public programs that make a difference in the lives of children and families in need.

After achieving early success with One-e-App, SIS wanted to enhance the system to electronically deliver applications to CalWIN, the eligibility system used by 18 counties to determine eligibility for key public assistance programs such as Food Stamps and Medi-Cal, California's Medicaid health care program. But since CalWIN is a Windows client/server application, SIS had to find a way to access and integrate with it using an innovative SOA interface.

Solution

After looking at several options, SIS selected LegaSuite from Rocket Software to provide an SOA interface between One-e-App and the key CalWIN client/server application. LegaSuite automates the screening process to determine eligibility for all the programs CalWIN administers.

The solution is best summarized by the customer:

> *"Our clients often have constraints such as limited resources and conflicting priorities,"* [4] *says Ashok Rout, deputy chief technology officer at SIS. "We*

knew that developing a traditional interface was not going to allow us to effectively and efficiently integrate One-e-App with CalWIN to streamline the eligibility and enrollment process. We used LegaSuite to build a nonintrusive interface to connect to CalWIN's front-end systems, allowing us to leverage existing legacy systems while at the same time modernizing the entire benefits application enrollment process. We have relied on LegaSuite for the last four years, and the technology has helped us address some pretty challenging integration issues." [5]

Results

Using One-e-App, a resident or a community assister completes a Web-based application process. Once the application is completed in One-e-App and the applicant is preliminarily eligible for any of the programs that CalWIN supports, the application gets electronically routed to a county worker. The county worker reviews the application and any documents submitted by the applicant, and decides whether to deliver the application to CalWIN. LegaSuite automatically navigates through 50 to 60 CalWIN screens to deliver the application data electronically. This drastically reduces manual processing time and improves accuracy, letting residents enroll in a program in a day or two instead of weeks.

This is what Rout has to say about the results of the project:

"LegaSuite allows us to deliver systems that enable people experiencing hardships to gain access to much-needed programs. The tool plays a critical role in helping us leverage One-e-App to mask data integration complexities in order to offer those in need access to Medicaid and food stamp programs in counties throughout California, Maryland, Arizona, and Indiana." [6]

NOTE

The implemented solution offers an SOA interface between customers' One-e-App Web interface and a key PowerBuilder client/server application. This once-manual process is now automated, which drastically reduces processing time and improves accuracy, and helps county agencies better assist their underserved residents.

SUMMARY

SOA enablement allows you to use today's technology to improve your ROI from yesterday's applications. SOA enablement is a great way to start the process of migrating your client/server applications, for the following reasons:

- Like other legacy apps, Windows client/server apps aren't going away. The business logic they contain is indispensable to organizations.

- Today, with cooperative technologies such as SOA and the cloud, there are more options than ever for organizations to quickly respond to the needs of users and tie into their client/server applications. You don't have to start over, and rarely do IT departments have the budget to do so.
- What matters today is that organizations realize that they can stay competitive with the client/server technology investments they have and position themselves strategically for the future.

Using SOA enablement, you can quickly and painlessly get your client/server application on the cloud.

This chapter went into detail regarding the LegaSuite solution to SOA-enable client/server applications. The LegaSuite Workbench is a GUI-based, coding-free solution driven by industry standards such as state diagrams, XML, and, of course, Web services. The LegaSuite Windows Integration Engine is a scalable, performant solution that can be deployed in a private or hybrid cloud. In this chapter, we discussed the following LegaSuite Workbench and LegaSuite Windows Integration Engine features and benefits:

- Retrieving data from application controls can be done in three ways:
  - By accessing the Windows messaging layer
  - By intercepting the low-level API (e.g., the `draw.text` procedure before it is posted on the message queue)
  - Via Windows Clipboard support
- The LegaSuite Windows Integration Engine drives a Windows application using a combination of:
  - Keystrokes
  - Mouse clicks
  - Specific control messages
- Recording is position-independent. Recording (e.g., mouse clicks) is done on an application control's relative position to a parent window. Therefore, moving the application fields around does not impact the runtime.
- The LegaSuite Windows Integration Engine does not use screen scraping. Because LegaSuite for Windows is accessing controls, there is no need to rely on using text recognition or other techniques that use a screenshot of an application as their starting point. For example, a Windows application can be minimized and still successfully driven by the LegaSuite Windows Integration Engine.
- The control reflection model allows for different methods of unique control and window identification. A complex decision tree can verify not only the application title, but also, for example, the presence of certain controls on a dialog, the state of a control, and so on.
- The LegaSuite Windows Integration Engine is extensible. For example, a third-party Component Object Model (COM) object can be used to access data/controls.
- Session pooling and transaction pooling further boost performance. By using multistage transactions and sharing sessions across different client requests, the

LegaSuite Windows Integration Engine can minimize usage of the host Windows application and increase performance.

- Session pooling and transaction pooling on the LegaSuite Windows Integration Engine, Terminal Services, or Citrix are optional.
- The LegaSuite Windows Integration Engine has the capability to queue requests and handle load balancing.

The case studies at the end of the chapter demonstrated how SOA enablement can allow you to integrate core client/server applications with your SOA initiatives, provide a unified view of all available information across different client/server applications, preserve the business logic and extend the life of applications, and consolidate numerous manual workflows into one automated workflow. The next chapter will continue with the discussion of cloud infrastructure that was covered at a high level in this chapter and in Chapter 8.

Endnotes

[1] Forrester Research, June 8, 2009. Forrester: top corporate software priority is modernizing legacy applications. Press release. Available from: www.forrester.com/ER/Press/Release/0,1769,1285,00.html.

[2] Regev Yativ, December 6, 2010. Ten IT trends to watch in 2011. From a blog post on Computerworld. Available from: http://blogs.computerworld.com/17473/ten_it_trends_to_watch_in_2011.

[3] Gartner, May 17, 2011. Available from: www.cbronline.com/blogs/cbr-rolling-blog/five-ways-to-migrate-applications-to-the-cloud-according-to-gartner-170511.

[4] Quote by Ashok Rout, deputy chief technology officer, Social Interest Solutions, regarding SIS modernizing its public assistance enrollment process with LegaSuite.

[5] Ibid.

[6] Ibid.

Oracle Database Cloud Infrastructure Planning and Implementation

10

INFORMATION IN THIS CHAPTER:

- Oracle Database Cloud Implementation Considerations
- Infrastructure Planning for Database Migrations to Oracle (DBaaS)

Deploying new Oracle databases as a result of a migration presents opportunities to rationalize database schemas and instances when compared with the source database. It also requires infrastructure planning for the Oracle platform that typically begins at an early stage in the migration life cycle, after the target architecture and requirements around high availability, performance and scalability, backup, and recovery are clearly defined. Most importantly, organizations always ask about the hardware and storage requirements for the new environment as compared to the source platform. In many cases, customers try to use their existing hardware to run Oracle software in an effort to maximize their ROI. However, this may not be possible in cases where the source platform (hardware, database, and/or application server software version) is earlier than the OS versions currently supported, or if the existing hardware infrastructure comprises slower CPUs and has less memory. When migrating to a new platform, it is common for organizations to choose the latest versions of databases and application server software, such as Oracle Database 11g and Oracle Fusion Middleware 11g. Newer versions of software typically require newer versions of operating systems, which may not be available on older hardware. Database migrations as a result of IT infrastructure consolidation efforts require planning for shared resource allocation among different applications, as some applications may be more critical to the organization's line of business than other applications. IT administrators must also plan to deal with sudden spikes in resource usage by certain applications in a shared and/or centralized environment. Finally, the impact on applications and software components needs to be assessed based on the hardware platform chosen. For example, when moving from a Windows to a Linux or UNIX platform, it is essential that appropriate drivers, such as Open Database Connectivity (ODBC) and Object Linking and Embedding Database (OLEDB), are available on the target platform.

ORACLE DATABASE CLOUD IMPLEMENTATION CONSIDERATIONS

As organizations implement virtualization to roll out Infrastructure as a Service (IaaS) and/or Platform as a Service (PaaS) offerings, as well as to drive server consolidation, facilitate server management, and take advantage of surplus processing capacity in idle servers, it is essential that they understand the impact of server virtualization. To derive maximum value out of IT infrastructure, reduce management costs, and potentially reduce software licensing costs as well as maximize resource utilization (i.e., reduce capital expenditures), organizations should consider consolidating databases and operating systems and not just limiting their consolidation efforts to servers and storage. To provide an Oracle Database as a Service (DBaaS), it is essential to consider workload consolidation, as the databases consume a significant amount of resources, including hardware, software, and management effort.

Server Consolidation and Virtualization (IaaS and PaaS)

Typically, IaaS providers provision all the resources associated with a service, such as operating systems, databases, and application servers, in the form of a virtual machine (VM) image. They simply deploy a VM image with the desired configuration parameters, such as the number of virtual CPUs, amount of memory, software version, and vendor, as requested by the consumer. Cloud providers build a library of images containing standard software configurations that can be deployed in minutes by customers via a self-service portal. The advantages, disadvantages, and best use cases for virtualization are as follows:

- **Advantages:**
  - Provides clear isolation between different environments
  - Easy to deploy and undeploy
  - Complete environment (OS + database and/or application server) can be migrated to another server easily
  - Standard configuration (OS/server) for all deployments
  - Full VM images can be backed up using storage replication
- **Disadvantages:**
  - Overhead of CPU/memory with each VM deployed
  - Redundant software deployment with multiple VM images on the same server
  - Sprawl of VMs in the environment (too many VMs in data centers and private clouds)
  - Vendor-specific VM software and the type of CPU partitioning (hard versus soft partitioning) can increase the license cost of Oracle software
  - Using storage replication does not guarantee zero data loss where databases are deployed; can also replicate corruptions from the primary site at the storage tier to remote/standby server
  - Does not help in standardization of operating systems and databases (this may matter only to some users)
- **Best Use Cases:**
  - Ideal for deployments where users request software of different versions from vendors (Microsoft, IBM, Oracle, etc.) in a shared environment

- Useful in private clouds and data centers to bring up test, development, and QA environments on short notice
- Ideal for deployment in cloud environments when users request complete isolation

Server consolidation using virtualization may be the only option in some cases when products from many vendors are deployed to widen the customer base. Even in private clouds, server virtualization will sometimes be the best option to deal with exceptions in standards and policies.

Workload Consolidation and Database Migrations to Oracle (PaaS or DBaaS)

Using virtualization as a way to offer PaaS provides excellent isolation between individual deployments as well as easier deployment, monitoring, and chargeback capabilities. But from the perspective of a cloud provider (public and private clouds), this method of offering PaaS does not help much in terms of reducing the cost and effort involved in capital and operational expenditures and efficiency, as the provider must manage and maintain a wide range of software products. For public cloud providers (both IaaS and PaaS), there is not much choice in terms of supporting a wide range of products as the service offerings are tied to customer demand. But when these providers consider PaaS offerings around an Oracle database (DBaaS) with fewer or no isolation concerns, or for a limited group of consumers (private clouds), there are opportunities to improve resource utilization and reduction of capital and operational expenditures by implementing workload consolidation involving operating systems and databases. In addition, this can improve resource sharing at all layers (I/O, memory, CPU, and network) in a centralized environment.

Database migration to Oracle presents a unique opportunity for workload consolidation as well as server consolidation and virtualization. As we discussed in Chapter 3, the Oracle database differs from other databases in terms of schema layouts as well as support for multiple databases under a single database engine. Furthermore, in many databases it is a common practice to deploy and maintain multiple database engines and databases for reporting and other requirements, to reduce the load on transactional systems by using replication technologies. Therefore, when creating Oracle databases and schemas, organizations have two choices:

- **Database/instance level consolidation**   Create an Oracle database instance for each database engine in the source environment, and then create schemas in Oracle to map each database and schema that exists under a database engine at the source. Using this approach can trigger the potential for a conflict as the same schema names might be in use under different databases at the source, which will result in a duplicate user/schema error in the Oracle database environment. In such cases, one option is to assign a new name to one of the conflicting schemas. Another option is to create another new Oracle database instance, and then to create the conflicting schemas in it and continue creating unique schemas under

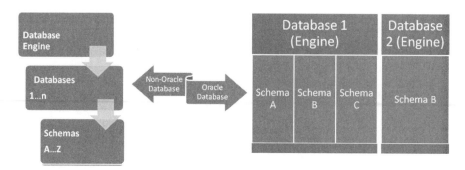

FIGURE 10.1

Database/Instance Mappings between Non-Oracle and Oracle Databases

one Oracle database instance. With this approach, the number of Oracle database instances can be reduced to just a few. Figure 10.1 illustrates a typical mapping between non-Oracle databases and schemas and Oracle database instances and schemas.

When migrating databases to Oracle in the manner shown in Figure 10.1, it is possible to create many database instances in Oracle for each source database engine.

WARNING

Creating too many Oracle database instances will result in increased consumption of such resources as CPU/memory and storage on the servers, because each database instance will have its own set of files, background processes, shared memory allocations, and so on.

Oracle database instances created as a result of migration (as illustrated in Figure 10.1) can be deployed on one large symmetric multiprocessing (SMP) server, or on separate servers and have database links created so that they can communicate seamlessly. All such instances can also be configured in one Oracle Real Application Clusters (RAC) environment which allows users to run multiple database instances. Figure 10.2 illustrates the deployment of migrated Oracle databases in an Oracle RAC environment.

- **Schema level consolidation**   Instead of running many databases and instances in Oracle for transactional, reporting, and backup purposes, it is best to map databases and schemas from the source database into schemas in an Oracle database. For workload separation and fine-grained management, an Oracle RAC database can be used so that different workloads can be isolated to different nodes based on their profiles, such as online transaction processing (OLTP), data

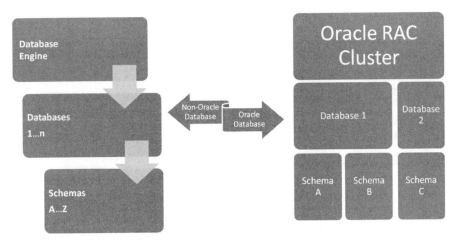

FIGURE 10.2

Oracle RAC Environment Supporting Multiple Oracle Databases

warehousing (DW), and so on. In addition, it can be configured in such a way that workloads with higher priorities can run on other nodes during peak hours or to handle unexpected spikes. For simple database migrations (i.e., where only the database is being migrated to Oracle), it is best to map each database and schema from the source database to a schema in Oracle. Figure 10.3 shows a simple mapping of multiple databases and schemas to an Oracle RAC database.

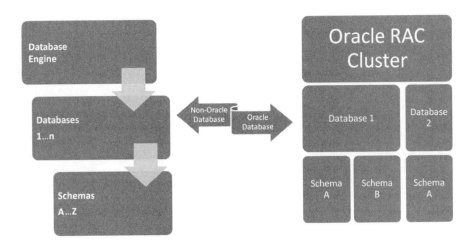

FIGURE 10.3

Mapping of Multiple Databases and Schemas to an Oracle RAC Database in a Consolidated Environment

Typically in an Oracle RAC environment, only one database is created which is then accessed from multiple instances running on nodes in the cluster. Consolidating all the schemas from the source into one RAC database can improve server resource utilization.

> **NOTE**
>
> In Figures 10.1, 10.2, and 10.3, the boxes denoting Schemas A, B, and C do not indicate that these schemas are accessible from only one node in an Oracle RAC cluster. All schemas created in an Oracle RAC database are accessible from all RAC cluster nodes.

Creating a couple of database instances under an Oracle RAC cluster can provide isolation and management flexibility (e.g., rolling patch upgrades for database instances). Having separate database instances for applications with different priorities—for example, a mission-critical instance and a non-mission-critical instance—can improve environment availability and manageability. However, when the Oracle RAC cluster needs a major upgrade (e.g., due to a major version change) the whole cluster, including the databases, will be unavailable. Major upgrades and changes to the database software or to the databases in general are treated as planned downtime, and to provide continuity in IT operations, end users are redirected to a standby database in a remote data center.

In addition to understanding the options for workload consolidation, it is also important to understand the process for implementing workload consolidation, outlined as follows:

1. Standardize on operating systems and databases that are deployed in the data center. Reducing the types of software (versions and vendors) to just a couple from half a dozen or more, which is very typical in large organizations, can result in substantial savings in capital and operation expenditures. It can also result in a reduction in the manpower required to maintain all the different databases, operating systems, and so on, as each requires different skill sets, even in the face of the cross-training that most large organizations impart to their IT staff.

2. Consolidate disparate database instances into a few, utilizing technologies such as an Oracle RAC. Reducing the number of deployed database instances can reduce management costs as well as improve the utilization of resources and reduce data duplication. It may also help you to avoid using costly replication technologies to maintain separate databases for reporting, data warehousing, and so on. Instead of creating a new database instance for every request that comes in from developers and testers for an Oracle database environment for development and testing purposes, a new schema can be created in an existing database that is deployed in a server pool in the development and testing environment. By following this practice, the organization can avoid installing many copies of the Oracle software on the same server and starting all the associated background processes. Of course, new database instances can be created if it is necessary to

ensure isolation from other users and workloads on the same server or to deploy the database instance on another server.

3. Use Oracle database features such as instance caging and the Oracle Database Resource Manager to restrict the amount of server resources used by multiple Oracle database instances, schemas, and users. This can allow multiple applications and workloads to exist on the same servers.

4. If it is important for the organization to reduce the manual effort involved in provisioning, it is recommended that the organization deploy a self-service portal (a Web application) so that users can provision it themselves based on the availability of resources, priorities, and configuration requirements.

5. Optionally, if the organization wants to employ a chargeback mechanism for usage of servers, storage, and databases from a central pool, sufficient data needs to be gathered from the IT infrastructure and processed for chargeback reports. The type of data that needs to be gathered (servers, OS, database, storage, etc.) depends on the level of service granularity required. Since we are talking about DBaaS here, it is important that all data pertaining to CPU, memory, I/O, and database space consumption be gathered for chargeback considerations.

As organizations move to consolidate various workloads into a centralized environment, concerns regarding security, availability, and reliability will sometimes come to the fore. In instances where a certain workload cannot tolerate downtime because databases and operating systems are being brought down for maintenance due to issues with other workloads, it is recommended that these important workloads be assigned to a separate environment where high availability and reliability measures such as Oracle Data Guard, Oracle GoldenGate, and the Oracle RAC have been implemented. Workloads can be grouped separately based on their priorities, type of usage, performance, and high-availability requirements. There certainly will be exceptions to the established policies.

Database Considerations for Multitenant Applications (Software as a Service or SaaS)

Using multitenant applications, an application provider can service many customers that are interested in executing the same business function. This model of service basically enables the SaaS model of cloud computing as customers can subscribe with an application provider for access to certain business functions without having to set up a data center to host the application and incur all the costs associated with that process. At the same time, customers typically pay for the number of users accessing the applications as opposed to bearing the total cost of installation and maintenance of the environment for supporting the application. It is also very easy for customers to bring new users on board when necessary. Some of the most popular multitenant applications in the market today are Salesforce.com and Oracle's Siebel CRM on Demand.

To implement support for multitenancy in applications, organizations have two choices:

- **Separate databases for each customer** With this option, the application provider needs to create a database (an instance in Oracle) for each customer, and when the customer logs on to the application their database information can be used to connect them to the target database. This task of identifying the database location and connection information is handled by the application. As we discussed earlier in this chapter, having too many database instances can consume a lot of resources on the servers. As a general practice, this method is typically used when some customers demand higher isolation levels for their data, stricter performance, and high availability numbers.

- **A single schema and database for multiple customers** With this option, which is the most popular method chosen by SaaS providers, data is stored for all customers in a single set of tables in one or more databases, as all the customers are using the same application (and thus are executing the same business function). This option requires careful design and planning in order to manage different workloads from different customers, to provide adequate security and isolation so that customers cannot see one another's data, and to handle different customers and set their unique identifiers when they log on. The task of providing each customer with a unique identifier (a sort of digital signature) that is carried along in all transactions executed by the customer is handled by the application. As a result, every row in every table that belongs to a customer carries the unique identifier associated with that customer. Some tables that store data that is common among all customers and is used specifically by the application may not carry the customer signature information.

SaaS providers may decide to use more than one database to host customers' data to conform to service-level agreements (SLAs) demanded by a customer with regard to performance levels, availability of databases in case of failure, and stringent uptime requirements with respect to the database and the application. The Oracle database offers rich features to enable application providers to develop SaaS offerings for their customers. Key Oracle database features that can enable SaaS services are:

- **Oracle Virtual Private Database (VPD)** The need to store data from multiple customers in the same set of tables, and then ensuring that customers cannot see data owned by other customers, is a very important task that needs to be enforced for each and every customer request. Any accidental slipups will result in exposure of a customer's data to unintended recipients, which can lead to legal challenges. With the help of the Oracle VPD feature in the database, however, this requirement can be implemented with very little coding and can be enforced on all requests from customers using any tools and APIs to connect to an Oracle database. This feature provides a set of database functions (APIs) that can ensure that when a customer executes a transaction in an Oracle database, an appropriate predicate indicating the customer's unique identifier is also appended to the SQL statement that the database executes to service customer requests. This automatic predicate injection to the SQL statement ensures that, regardless of the tool a customer uses to access data in a multitenant database environment, the customer will only see the data he owns. Typically, this feature is implemented by creating a database log-on trigger in the Oracle database so that anytime a customer logs on using his preferred tool or application, his VPD context policies are set properly, which builds the appropriate predicate that needs to be injected into the SQL statements to ensure accurate data retrieval and manipulation.

- **Oracle RAC database**   The Oracle RAC database provides scale-out capabilities so that whenever more processing power is needed, new servers can be added to the environment without taking down the system. Similarly, servers can be removed from an Oracle RAC database environment without impacting existing users. The Oracle RAC can also enable workload management, as we discussed in the "Workload Consolidation and Database Migrations to Oracle (PaaS or DBaaS)" section earlier in this chapter, by isolating workloads to different nodes in the cluster based on their priorities.
- **Oracle database partitioning**   Oracle database partitioning enables users to divide large tables into smaller segments so that they can be managed efficiently (at a partition level), and to improve query optimization by eliminating the need to scan unnecessary partitions. In a SaaS environment, when data from many customers is stored in the same set of tables, the tables can become very large and unmanageable. Using the partitioning feature of the Oracle database ensures that large tables can be administered easily (for backups, maintenance operations such as index rebuilds, etc.).
- **Oracle Database Resource Manager**   Controlling access to critical server resources such as the CPU and database resources such as storage space can be very helpful in terms of ensuring that groups of users who demand higher performance at all times can be satisfied easily.

Multitenancy in applications cannot be an afterthought, as it will require a major effort to introduce this capability in an existing application. It is very important for multitenant applications to meet workload requirements from small and large customers alike. Applications need to be designed to handle multitenancy from the beginning of the software development life cycle. Doing so can result in a multitenant application that handles a large number of customers with varied user populations, as well as a database that can perform as expected by all consumers.

INFRASTRUCTURE PLANNING FOR DATABASE MIGRATIONS TO ORACLE (DBaaS)

IT infrastructures consisting of a server platform, storage, and network need to be planned ahead of rolling out a DBaaS offering as well as deploying new Oracle databases as a result of database migration. IT organizations have many choices to make with respect to selecting appropriate components as part of an IT infrastructure for supporting Oracle databases. As a result, when different workloads are consolidated into fewer or just one Oracle database, the servers hosting the database need to be sized appropriately, because there will be more users as well as more transactions and queries on the new database as compared to the source database platform. Database memory allocation (cache) parameters also need to be configured appropriately based on the workload and the user population.

Platform Considerations

There are many choices for a target platform in terms of using new servers versus existing servers, clustered systems versus SMP servers, VMs versus direct deployment of software on servers, and public cloud versus private cloud deployment. Oracle databases can be deployed on small servers running Windows or Linux operating systems as well as on very large SMP servers. Oracle databases can also be deployed in a clustered environment using the Oracle RAC database (i.e., many small servers or nodes that are connected to act as one large database server). When it comes to deployment in the cloud, Oracle database instances are offered as services by many cloud providers as part of their PaaS or DBaaS offering. Similarly, deploying a new Oracle database instance in a private cloud environment is much simpler than setting up an environment from scratch. Each of these choices will dictate the requirement for additional hardware and software components and sizing, as well as additional impact on the applications.

Using Existing or New Servers for the Source Database Platform

IT organizations have shown interest in using the resources they already own. This can reduce the effort involved in acquiring, installing, and configuring new hardware (servers). Operating system version incompatibility, along with the amount of memory on the server and the number or speed of the CPUs or cores on the server, may render existing hardware unfit for a new database deployment because of a potential increase in the number of users and transactions. As of this writing, Oracle has announced that it will discontinue all software development on Intel Itanium processor-based servers. As a result, this might impact an organization's future plans for deploying Oracle software.

New servers, on the other hand, sport faster CPUs and more memory than those that are in use already. New servers can allow organizations to scale workloads and drive consolidation efforts. Oracle Database and Fusion Middleware software can be run on a variety of hardware platforms, such as Intel x86 (both 32- and 64-bit), SPARC, and POWER chip-based platforms. There may also be a need to acquire new storage systems to support Oracle databases if the installed capacity is not adequate, as the Oracle database can leverage any type of storage system, including network attached storage (NAS) and storage area network (SAN) systems. If there is already enough capacity in the existing storage systems, new partitions can be carved out for use by Oracle databases. Oracle also offers engineered systems such as Oracle Exadata and Exalogic, for running database and Java applications, respectively, which can significantly reduce the effort involved in installing and configuring new systems and managing them on a daily basis, thereby delivering extreme performance for all types of workloads and applications.

Using SMP Servers versus a Cluster of Servers

Deploying an Oracle database on an SMP server is very common in IT organizations as this has been the practice for a long time. However, over the past decade or so, IT organizations have increasingly been deploying Oracle RAC databases using many small servers to act as one large database server (i.e., grid computing). This type of configuration provides scale-out capabilities because administrators can add or remove nodes online as the situation demands. The Oracle RAC database also provides scalability and high availability within the data center.

Deployment of Oracle RAC databases requires the following additional hardware and software:

- **Interconnects between cluster nodes** To facilitate communications and the synchronization of the database cache across cluster nodes, an interconnect is necessary. Therefore, additional network switches may be required to deploy an Oracle RAC database. It is common to deploy at least GigE (Gigabit Ethernet) networks exclusively for cluster interconnects. It is recommended that public network traffic is not allowed on the private interconnects between the database nodes so as not to impact overall database performance. Hence, customers are discouraged from using public virtual local area networks (VLANs) shared by other users as cluster interconnects.

- **Cluster file system/volume manager** The Oracle RAC database is based on a shared disk architecture (i.e., all files that constitute the database must be available for read and write operations to all the nodes in the cluster at all times). To facilitate this, a shared file system (or raw devices) and a cluster-aware logical volume manager are required. Oracle Automatic Storage Management (ASM) software fulfills this role and is available on almost all the platforms on which the Oracle database is available. Customers can use ASM with regular (non-RAC) Oracle database deployments as well, to take advantage of such capabilities as online addition and removal of disks, automatic data redistribution to new disks, data mirroring, and easier interfaces to manage storage by database administrators.

- **Clusterware** To create and manage multiple servers, as well as managing heartbeats and quorums, special software is required. Oracle Clusterware is well suited to performing these functions and is available on all platforms starting with Oracle Database 11g.

> **NOTE**
>
> Both Oracle ASM and Oracle Clusterware are available with the Oracle database software for free. Oracle Clusterware can be used to provide active-passive high availability for applications running on a server, such as batch jobs and application servers (custom-developed), because of its ability to restart applications upon failure, as it can be configured and coded to detect application failures (abnormal shutdowns).

Because of the additional software components as well as communications between database nodes in an Oracle RAC database environment, it is essential to consider the overhead associated with this when sizing the environment. To deploy an Oracle database on an SMP server there is no need for interconnects or cluster file systems.

Virtualization

The primary reason for virtualization's increase in popularity is that new environments can be quickly deployed or taken down within a matter of minutes, and active environments can increase or reduce their resource requirements based on demand. Traditionally, installing and uninstalling software is a tedious process, as after software is installed, additional tasks such as database creation and configuration must be executed, which can take 30 minutes or more to complete. It is much easier and faster to create a VM image with the required database software and databases that can be deployed with a single mouse click.

Regardless of whether they decide to deploy their databases and applications in a public or a private cloud, many organizations are moving toward virtualized environments within their own data centers to reduce management costs and improve utilization of existing IT resources. In such cases, organizations must be aware of VM sprawl within the data center, as each VM that is deployed consumes additional resources in terms of memory, CPU cycles, and storage. This can also lead to data duplication within the data center. Virtualization also adds some performance overhead as a result of organizations that prefer to deploy mission-critical applications and databases directly on the servers, as they cannot afford to incur the performance overhead associated with virtualization. Implementing a virtualized deployment of Oracle Database/Fusion Middleware software includes the following steps:

1. Deploy the VM software (Hypervisor) on servers that are identified to be part of the server pool for virtualization.
2. Create a library of VM images with the desired version of the operating system, Oracle Database/Fusion Middleware software, and so on.
3. Use Oracle Enterprise Manager (OEM) or other provisioning tools to deploy VMs on demand.
4. Monitor resource usage by the VMs.
5. Gather metering/chargeback data (optional).

Creation of VM images for specific configurations of databases to support various workloads is generally a one-time effort, but it is important nonetheless so that these VM images can be deployed as and when needed. Prebuilt Oracle VM images containing Oracle database software can be downloaded from www.otn.oracle.com to speed up the deployment process.

> **WARNING**
>
> The Oracle database and application server can run on VM products from companies such as VMware. In such environments, if users run into any technical issues, they may be asked to reproduce the issue in an environment where the Oracle database or application server is deployed on a server directly (not in a VM). However, Oracle fully supports Oracle databases deployed on an Oracle VM.

Deploying Oracle Databases on a Public/Private Cloud

To deploy Oracle databases in a public cloud, organizations simply need to purchase or subscribe to services from public cloud providers such as Amazon and Savvis. Using the cloud provider's self-service provisioning and administration portal, customers can provision computing resources as necessary and pay for their usage. In large organizations with private cloud deployments, the deployment process is also very simple, as they do not have to worry about acquiring new hardware and software and installing, configuring, and optimizing it. The IT department charged with managing the private cloud environment takes care of these tasks. In the case of database migrations in a cloud environment, the following steps need to be taken:

1. Ensure access to IT resources in the cloud. To use a public cloud service, a subscription is necessary; for private clouds, internal processes have to be followed.
2. Deploy the migrated database schema and data. Deploying the new database schema in Oracle is a straightforward process which can be accomplished simply by executing a Data Definition Language (DDL) script or by connecting to the database instance using any supported tool, such as SQL Developer, and creating the database objects. Migrating data from a source database to an Oracle database deployed in the cloud is no different from migrating to an Oracle database within a data center. However, some cloud providers may restrict the options and tools that can be used to upload data into the database (e.g., high-performance solutions utilizing scripts taking advantage of named pipes may not be allowed due to security concerns). In such cases, using flat files as the means to transfer large amounts of data is a viable (and probably the only) solution.
3. Set up database security roles and user privileges. After creating the database schema and loading the data, it is very important to set up database user security and assign users the appropriate privileges. In a cloud environment, depending on the level of isolation provided for each consumer, certain restrictions may be enforced, such as access to database management views and system tables, and

whether authority should be granted on certain database privileges. When a database service is offered with a higher level of isolation, such as a VM with a database running inside it, these types of restrictions may not be placed on consumers.

TIP

The Oracle Database Vault can be used to restrict database administrators in an Oracle database from accessing other database administrators' data as well as restrict their administrative functions in the database. Oracle database administrators are aware that a database user with a DBA role has almost complete authority over the Oracle database.

---

4. Test that the application's connectivity to the database in the cloud is seamless to avoid any issues due to security restrictions or lack of privileges in the database.
5. Manage and monitor the database environments. Even in a cloud environment, consumers are given tools to monitor resource consumption and administer applications and database schemas via self-service portals by cloud service providers, or within an organization by using tools such as Oracle Enterprise Grid Control.

Platform Sizing

It is very important to size the platform for deploying databases and application servers that run critical business applications, to ensure that it meets all SLAs pertaining to response times, throughput levels, and so on. Optimal performance can also mean that important application modules complete their tasks within the allotted time (e.g., weekly or monthly overnight batch processing jobs). Platform sizing typically includes sizing of servers, storage systems, and databases. Different factors determine the sizing of each component.

Server Sizing

The most common question customers ask when embarking on a database migration project is how large the target server where the Oracle database will be deployed should be based on the server configuration in use for the source database. Customers also ask if the Oracle database can be deployed on the source server itself, as they plan to retire the database after the migration. This may be possible if the server hardware running an operating system is compatible with the latest version of the Oracle database software. But if the organization plans to acquire a new server as the source database is running on a very old and slow server, the following factors affecting the size of the target servers should be considered:

- Processor clock speeds (GHz/MHz)
- Number of CPUs/cores on the servers
- Total memory/bus speed
- Chip architecture (e.g., Intel x86 Xeon, Itanium, SPARC, POWER/RISC)

- Targeted workload consolidation (batch and OLTP workload on the same system)
- Deployment of VMs as opposed to direct deployment of database software
- Changes to the storage system (rare, but possible)

Rapid advances are being made in the areas of processor chip speeds, the number of cores on each chip, and the type of memory and amount of memory they can access for building faster and more energy-efficient computer processors and servers. As a result of these advances in computer servers, hardware systems become obsolete very quickly. It has become a norm to refresh IT hardware every three to five years in most organizations to keep up with the pace of advances in this area and to derive a maximum ROI. Most software technologies and products also have a shelf life of about three to five years. Therefore, it is also essential to refresh hardware to adopt new software technologies as they may not be available on older hardware platforms. For end users, this means it is difficult to obtain a server that is identical to an existing server in terms of CPU clock speed, number of cores on each CPU, and total memory on the system after a couple of years. That makes it difficult to size the new environment as there are many factors to consider for such an effort. Server sizing can also get a bit tricky if the IT organization decides to adopt servers with different chip architectures than the source server, such as from POWER/RISC to Intel x86, PA-RISC to Intel x86, or Intel Itanium to Intel x86—64-bit, as processors based on different chip architectures have different performance characteristics. Luckily, there is a nonprofit corporation called Standard Performance Evaluation Corporation (www.spec.org), of which Oracle and other major IT organizations are members, that publishes performance benchmarks for computer servers, Java application servers, messaging systems, Web servers, and service-oriented architecture (SOA) software stacks. Of all the performance benchmarks compiled by this organization, the SpecInt benchmark is the most important for raw server sizing. The SpecInt benchmark assigns a relative performance number to each make and model of hardware with a given chip configuration (e.g., Intel Xeon, 2.1 GHz, two cores per chip). By using the SpecInt benchmark results you can size a server by comparing the relative performance numbers between the old and new servers. Server sizing is not just based on CPU ratings, but on other factors as well, such as resource utilization, type of workload, peak user population, and database deployment options (e.g., Oracle RAC, Oracle Database [single instance], etc.).

   The amount of memory available on a server is also important when considering the deployment of Oracle databases, especially if it is expected that thousands of concurrent users will be connecting to the database. A big difference between Oracle and other relational databases is that the Oracle database is based on a process-based architecture—that is, all Oracle database background tasks are run as OS processes. Every single connection to an Oracle database will actually start a background process on the database server. Each process started on a server will consume a certain amount of memory as well as CPU resources based on the type of task it is executing. As a result, an Oracle database handling thousands of dedicated connections may require more memory because of each background process being spawned for each connection. You can avoid creating a large number of connections to an Oracle database by using connection pooling at the application/middleware tier, or by enabling the Universal Connection Pool (UCP) feature in Oracle Database 11g which can assist applications that don't have connection pools implemented. One other way to reduce the number of connections to the database is to use the multithreaded server (MTS) feature of an Oracle database. An MTS-enabled Oracle database starts a dispatcher process that starts a pool of background processes to manage connections to the database, and will distribute the database requests from applications to a background process in the pool that is not busy.

Storage System Sizing

Sizing of the storage system is important because most organizations have SAN/NAS systems from which they carve out storage space for new databases. Therefore, IT organizations need to know how much storage space must be allocated for a new Oracle database to be deployed. Sizing needs to be carried out for production as well as development and QA databases in a centralized environment. When acquiring new storage systems for use by an Oracle database, organizations generally can choose the type of disk drive (e.g., slower, high-capacity [terabytes] drives versus faster, low-capacity [hundreds of gigabytes] drives). For optimal database performance, it is recommended that you choose low-capacity, high-performance drives which provide the best I/O response times for OLTP and other mission-critical systems. Storage systems with high-capacity disks, on the other hand, can be used to archive data, maintain database backups, and perform other similar tasks. Therefore, an effective information life-cycle management policy can be set up whereby the most recent or most frequently used data is stored on high-performance systems and other data resides on a high-capacity, low-performance storage system. Optionally, the data on the high-capacity, low-performance system can be compressed to reduce storage costs.

Exadata System Sizing

The Oracle Exadata machine is a complete system; it contains database servers, storage cells, and network switches. As such, it removes the guesswork involved in storage, network, and server sizing with respect to Oracle databases from the perspective of overall available capacity. However, since this system comprises several database servers and provides a great deal of storage capacity, it is essential that you determine if a migrated database is a good candidate for deployment on Oracle Exadata. Key factors that influence a migrated database's suitability for deployment on Exadata are:

- Number of CPUs/cores currently deployed for supporting the database/application
- Size of the database in gigabytes/terabytes
- Performance requirements
- System resource utilization in the current environment

On an Exadata machine, each database server has 12 cores (two CPUs), with 96 GB of memory in the X2-2 model. Table 10.1 summarizes the configurations for the X2-2 version of an Exadata machine under different models.

As Table 10.1 shows, the Exadata machine packs a lot of compute power as well as storage. Therefore, any database that is being migrated to Oracle must at least be running on a server in the current environment with the configuration either matching or exceeding the configuration of an Exadata quarter-rack machine. If an organization is migrating many databases, both Oracle and non-Oracle, as part of a database consolidation drive, individual database processing/storage requirements need not be taken into consideration, but overall compute, storage, and network bandwidth requirements for all databases targeted to be deployed on the Exadata machine need to be considered.

Exadata Sizing Considerations for Cloud Services

The minimum allocation unit of compute power is one database node (i.e., 12 cores) in an Exadata machine. As the Exadata machine does not support the use of a Hypervisor (virtualization technology), it is not possible to deploy VMs leveraging only one or two CPUs. It can only be used for database instance/schema-level consolidation. As the Exadata machine supports only Oracle Enterprise Linux as the operating system or Solaris 11 Express (x86) and is meant for deploying an Oracle database, it is not an ideal platform for IaaS deployments (bare metal configurations with any OS). PaaS offerings that do not require OS-level isolation (i.e., the ability to run VMs with an operating system and an Oracle database for each customer) can take advantage of the full potential of the Exadata machine by creating many database instances or many schemas in one database instance as needed. Similarly, SaaS offerings can benefit significantly from an Exadata machine as the Exadata can handle large workloads easily since it can offload some of the query processing to the storage cells. In a SaaS environment, because data pertaining to many customers can be stored in the same schema, the databases can become really large.

The Exadata has great compression and encryption features for larger databases, making it an ideal platform for SaaS offerings. To run multiple instances of Oracle databases on each node and yet restrict CPU usage by database user processes, the instance caging feature of the Oracle database can be used. Instance caging allows database administrators to restrict the CPU usage for each database instance by setting the `CPU_COUNT` parameter in the database configuration file (spfile.ora or init.ora). One advantage of instance caging in the Oracle database is that CPU resources can be oversubscribed to multiple instances running in one server. With oversubscription, it is possible to ensure that idle CPUs can be used by any active database instances, but when contention occurs between instances for CPUs, instances with higher values for `CPU_COUNT` can grab more CPUs than others.

Database Sizing

Database sizing is another important task in any database migration project, and the most common question customers ask concerns how large the Oracle database

Table 10.1 Configuration Summary for X2-2 Exadata Machine

System Component/ Exadata Model	Quarter Rack (X2-2)	Half Rack (X2-2)	Full Rack (X2-2)
Database server*CPUs/cores	2*2*6 (2 servers, 2 CPUs each, 24 cores)	4*2*6 (4 servers, 2 CPUs each, 48 cores)	8*2*6 (8 servers, 2 CPUs each, 96 cores)
Database server memory	2*96 (192 GB)	4*96 (384 GB)	8*96 (768 GB)
Number of storage cells (12 cores each)	3	7	14
Number of disks in storage cells (high-capacity disks/high-performance disks)	3*12*600 GB (high-performance disks) or 3*12*2 TB (high-capacity disks)	7*12*600 GB (high-performance disks) or 7*12*2 TB (high-capacity disks)	14*12*600 GB (high-performance disks) or 14*12*2 TB (high-capacity disks)
Total raw storage capacity (approx.)	21 TB (high-performance disks) or 72 TB (high-capacity disks)	50 TB (high-performance disks) or 154 TB (high-capacity disks)	100 TB (high-performance disks) or 336 TB (high-capacity disks)
Total flash cache	1.1 TB (approx.) total on all 3 storage servers	2.7 TB (approx.) total on all 7 storage servers	5.3 TB (approx.) total on all 14 storage servers

should be if their Sybase database is 100 GB in size. To answer this type of question, the following architectural and implementation differences between Oracle and other databases have to be considered:

- **Database components**   An Oracle database consists of components such as UNDO segments, which sets it apart from most relational databases. It is very common for organizations to allocate tens of gigabytes of storage for UNDO segments. UNDO segments allow an Oracle database to capture changes taking place on database blocks and lets the database reconstruct an image of a table record that will point to the state before the modification occurred. This segment is heavily used when users are querying data at the same time other users are modifying it. Similarly, it is also possible to create multiplexed Redo logs in the Oracle database (multiple copies of Redo log files), also known as transaction logs. Multiplexed Redo logs force an Oracle database to write a transaction entry (when it is committed) to multiple copies of the Redo log file as an extra layer of protection from corruption of Redo log files. Redo log files are sized anywhere from 50 MB to a few gigabytes.

- **Database objects/type in use**   Database object sizes also vary among databases based on their type and on what data types they use. Relational databases differ in terms of how they manage data of certain types (e.g., CHAR columns in Sybase/ SQL Server, when set to *non-nullable*, behave as fixed-length columns, whereas in Oracle, CHAR columns always behave as fixed-length columns). Similarly, databases also differ in the number of bytes required to date/timestamp data elements. Oracle's NUMBER data type implementation is quite flexible in terms of data storage. It is a variable-length implementation of storage (i.e., it occupies the amount of storage required to store the actual data versus the storage bytes declared during table creation). Bitmap indexes in Oracle store only the significant bit of the repetitive data in a column that is indexed, making this an ideal choice for data warehouses. Bitmap indexes in Oracle occupy significantly less storage than a regular b*tree index.

- **Type of Oracle database deployment (RAC/non-RAC)**   Each instance of an Oracle RAC database requires its own set of TEMP tablespace files and Redo logs. As a result, in the case of a multinode RAC deployment, several of these files will exist for each database instance. Since the Oracle RAC database differs significantly from other databases, this type of storage may not exist in other databases.

- **Database features in use**   Implementation of many of the Oracle database's advanced features, such as advanced compression and Exadata Hybrid Columnar Compression (EHCC) in the Oracle Exadata Database Machine, can reduce the database size significantly. On the other hand, use of the Flash Recovery Area (FRA) to enable database recovery from on-disk backups can increase storage utilization as a copy of the database along with the archived Redo logs are stored on the disk for quick recovery. The impact of using FRA can be greatly reduced by using the compression feature of the Recovery Manager (RMAN) utility.

As you can see, the target Oracle database size depends on several factors which cannot be determined without knowing details regarding the implementation.

Backup and Recovery and Disaster Recovery Strategy

When migrating to Oracle, you need to conduct a thorough review of the organization's backup and recovery policies and mechanisms, as well as its disaster recovery strategy and any implementations in place for a source database, in order to design and implement an effective solution for backup/recovery and disaster recovery in the Oracle environment. Oracle's Data Pump database import/export utility helps users conduct a complete database import and export. Oracle database files can also be copied after shutting down the database and making sure all pending transactions are completed. This method is known as a cold backup of the database. To perform online incremental backups, RMAN is used. RMAN can efficiently back up large databases as it can back up only the changed data blocks in data files instead of backing up the full file, and it can detect block-level corruptions.

Backup and recovery solutions are implemented mainly for maintaining database backups such as daily incremental backups or daily full backups. They assist in recovery from database corruptions or loss of database files due to issues in storage systems. Restoring files from database backup sets and recovering the database to the desired point in time requires quite a bit of time depending on the size of the database, the size of the files to be restored/recovered from backup media such as tapes, and the recovery period. Most companies store older backup files off-site to ensure that in case of a total loss of the primary data center, there will be a fallback option to recover some of the data. Starting with Oracle Database 10g, a new method of taking backups and using them for quick recovery was introduced, leveraging the Flashback feature in the database. This feature allows database administrators to allocate additional storage to keep the most recent backup of the database (incrementally rolled forward to the previous day) on-disk and all the associated log files and archived Redo files required for recovery up to the current time. With this feature, an Oracle database can be recovered very quickly and does not require time-consuming operations such as restoring large files from tapes. To provide uninterrupted services to users in the face of complete data center outages due to power failures, network failures, and natural disasters, organizations can implement disaster recovery solutions that entail maintaining a standby data center that is typically miles away. With disaster recovery solutions, IT organizations can configure the database and application environment in such a way that upon losing services in the primary data center, end users will be able to connect to the databases and applications in the remote standby site and continue performing their tasks. There are three ways to maintain a standby site in sync with the primary database in Oracle:

- **Use Oracle Data Guard** This is the only solution that can ensure zero data loss in a disaster recovery scenario. Data Guard can be configured in Maximum Availability, Maximum Performance (Primary Site), Zero Data Loss, and Real-time Apply modes so that administrators can choose a mode that suits their business requirements. The main advantages of Oracle Data Guard are as follows:
  - With the Active Data Guard feature, the standby site can be used in read-only mode to run reports while it is being updated from the primary database.

- Oracle Data Guard can prevent logical and physical corruptions from being replicated to standby sites.
- Standby sites can be quickly converted into a development or QA database, and after completing their tasks can be reconverted into standby sites.
- **Oracle GoldenGate** A standby Oracle database can also be maintained by using Oracle GoldenGate. Oracle GoldenGate extracts online changes from the database transaction logs (both online and archived `Redo` logs) in the primary Oracle database and replicates them to a standby database. It can replicate transactions between different Oracle database versions on different hardware platforms as well as replicate to and from non-Oracle databases such as SQL Server, Sybase, DB2, and Teradata. It also provides near-real-time replication capabilities between databases in a bidirectional manner, setting it apart from Oracle Data Guard which can replicate data in only one direction (i.e., from a primary database to a standby database). Oracle GoldenGate plays a key role in deploying Oracle databases into production after migrating from another database by keeping the Oracle database in sync with the source database which is continuously being updated as the data migration is taking place.
- **Storage replication/mirroring** It is a common practice for organizations to deploy storage replication/remote mirroring technologies, such as the EMC SRDF family of software, as a disaster recovery solution. The primary driver for this type of deployment is that these organizations support many databases and applications and they all need some sort of disaster recovery solution. Since Oracle Data Guard only supports Oracle databases, it is not a good fit in that scenario. The major disadvantages of this option for deployment in a pure Oracle environment are as follows:
    - It is an expensive solution to implement, as opposed to Oracle Data Guard which is offered free of charge from Oracle. Only the Active Data Guard feature of Data Guard needs to be licensed.
    - Database corruptions in both the logical (unintended database updates) and physical (block corruptions in the storage tier) tiers are immediately replicated to the remote site in an undetected manner. This can put the reliability of the standby site in jeopardy.

Disaster Recovery for Oracle Exadata Database Machine

Oracle Exadata Database Machine only supports Oracle Data Guard and Oracle GoldenGate as the primary mechanism for maintaining standby sites. It does not support any storage replication or remote mirroring technology for disaster recovery. The reason behind this restriction is that the storage servers in Exadata are not regular SAN/NAS systems. These storage servers are composed of CPUs, flash memory, and Direct Attached Storage (DAS) devices and they are not connected to outside networks (out of the Exadata machine itself) directly.

As a result of a workload/database consolidation effort resulting in consolidating all Oracle databases onto Oracle Exadata or a separate pool of servers, Oracle Data Guard or Oracle GoldenGate can be used for disaster recovery.

There is no need for organizations to invest in expensive storage replication/ remote mirroring solutions for environments that have separate environments for Oracle databases. This can be a big reason for Oracle workload consolidation onto Exadata.

Monitoring and Management of the Oracle Database Cloud

Oracle provides comprehensive tools in the form of OEM Grid Control to manage virtually all layers in an Oracle Exadata Database Machine. OEM can also be used to manage and monitor Oracle databases residing outside an Exadata machine. Many organizations standardize on tools from other vendors to manage different systems and technologies in the data center. OEM is primarily used for managing an all-Oracle environment. But it can also monitor non-Oracle databases, application servers, operating systems, networks, and storage systems by using appropriate plug-ins. It can also provision a RAC database and enables proactive monitoring of the database's performance. For managing Exadata's storage cells and InfiniBand network infrastructure and other components of an Exadata machine, a separate plug-in is provided.

OEM is also tightly integrated with Oracle Enterprise Manager Ops Center (formerly Sun Ops Center) to manage the Sun servers in the Exadata machine.

SUMMARY

Deploying a new database in a data center involves many tasks. It involves planning for the deployment of databases for development, testing, and QA, in addition to deploying databases for production. IT departments also need to plan and implement solutions for information protection at various levels within the infrastructure, as well as backup and recovery and disaster recovery solutions to provide business continuity in light of data center outages. Due to the many options available to organizations in an Oracle database for consolidation, management, monitoring, and security when migrating from another database, careful consideration of all pros and cons associated with a specific database feature or functionality is required.

In this chapter, we discussed crucial aspects of deployment of an Oracle database as well as topics such as consolidation and virtualization, along with best practices, to highlight their importance in building a highly scalable, manageable, and agile database platform. As we discussed in this chapter, it is important to consider the impact of the operating system, database standardization, and consolidation when deploying PaaS and SaaS offerings in addition to server virtualization as a means to support IaaS and PaaS offerings today. Oracle offers a complete solution for development, deployment, management, and monitoring of cloud services. The next chapter provides a case study highlighting a Sybase database migration to Oracle performed by mLogica, a preferred partner of Oracle.

Sybase Migrations from a Systems Integrator Perspective, and Case Study

INFORMATION IN THIS CHAPTER:

- Why Consider Database Migration from Sybase to Oracle?
- Technical Challenges
- Key Architectural Differences between Sybase ASE and Oracle
- Keeping the Current Sybase Environment Running during the Migration
- Migration Tools
- Cost of Migration
- Sizing the Target Oracle Database Environment
- Infrastructure Migration Challenges
- Server Consolidation
- Oracle mLogica Case Study

mLogica is a specialized systems integrator with primary expertise in database performance management. mLogica consults on Sybase database performance challenges and database migration issues, and provides database products and solutions for customers globally, from premium New York City financial services firms, to leading California media and entertainment companies, to stock exchanges and banks from Bangladesh and the Maldive Islands.

Amit Okhandiar, the author of this chapter, is the CEO and founder of mLogica. This chapter deals primarily with mLogica's experience in working with clients who, over the years, have asked mLogica to help them evaluate and/or support them with their database migration initiatives from Sybase Adaptive Service Enterprise (ASE) to Oracle. mLogica provides assessments on the strategic pros and cons of Sybase-to-Oracle migrations from business and technology perspectives. mLogica analyzes existing trends in the database marketplace, what business users are telling us, what database trainers are reporting in regard to database cross-training (i.e., where the jobs are), what analysts are saying, and the investments that both Sybase and Oracle have made in terms of database innovation. Based on this information, mLogica prepares a business case and justification for migration from Sybase to Oracle for its customers.

The opinions in this chapter are those of mLogica and are based on the company's 10-plus years of experience and expertise in the database market. This chapter offers what mLogica considers to be best practices and lessons learned when migrating a Sybase database to Oracle, from the perspective of an Oracle systems integrator as well as a systems integrator that has been managing and improving the performance of Sybase installations worldwide. The chapter concludes with a case study that provides details regarding the experiences of a global telecommunications company that migrated from a Sybase and PowerBuilder environment to an Oracle and .NET environment.

WHY CONSIDER DATABASE MIGRATION FROM SYBASE TO ORACLE?

Sybase database migration projects are not always limited to database migrations. In fact, many projects entail operating system (OS) migrations (from Windows to UNIX or Linux, from an HP to a Sun platform), application migrations, interface rewrites, application redesign, server consolidations and virtualization, and platform standardization, to name a few. In many instances, these additional migrations make sense, since they add business value by providing an excellent return on investment (ROI) for executive management.

Every client with whom mLogica has spoken over the years has had their own reasons for considering a migration from Sybase to Oracle. Although their reasons were different, each customer had the same goal in mind: Achieve a strong ROI and an upgrade in performance, while mitigating business risk.

One of the major reasons that clients voiced to mLogica concerned what the future holds for the Sybase ASE data manager. Based on conversations with clients, it is mLogica's opinion that, whereas Oracle has a road map for continuing to release a database that is secure, performant, and innovative and that provides support for mission-critical systems, the current state of Sybase ASE poses business risk and uncertainty in terms of long-term viability. Furthermore, mLogica's clients have voiced concern about Sybase's database R&D investments, and they feel that Sybase may not be able to keep up with Oracle in terms of features, functionalities, and technological advances.

Another major reason that mLogica clients have considered a Sybase migration to Oracle is that they feel that, over the years, Sybase has sent mixed messages to the market regarding its commitment to the ASE product. For instance, the merger of SAP and Sybase in 2010 focused more on accelerating the reach of SAP solutions across mobile platforms than it did on highlighting SAP's commitment to Sybase ASE. In fact, the market's perception is that SAP acquired Sybase primarily for Sybase's expertise in mobile and in-memory technologies, since SAP is already investing heavily in these two areas, as noted in the following analyst quotes:

> *"They are investing in two areas they think will be important for them, namely mobile technology and in-memory databases, both areas where Sybase is*

strong."—Ray Wang, partner with Altimer Group, as reported in InfoWorld, *May 12, 2010* [1]

"While SAP management stated that it will continue to support other leading database vendors, our sense is that SAP will try to have customers use Sybase instead of the Oracle database. We do not expect them to be successful in this effort."—Laura Lederman, analyst with William Blair & Company, as reported on ZDNet.com in an article by Larry Dignan, May 13, 2010 [2]

Additional market analyses further reinforce what appears to be a confusing, and tenuous, future for Sybase ASE. For example, although the road map for the future of Sybase ASE is not clear, profits from Sybase database maintenance revenue are very high [3], indicating that Sybase continues to increase maintenance fees for existing customers. In addition, technology research firm Gartner Inc. recently published vendor share numbers for 2010 for relational database management systems (RDBMSes) [4], and Figure 11.1 shows the database market share numbers for each vendor in this space. As the figure shows, Oracle expanded its lead and owned 48.1 percent of the RDBMS market for 2010. Gartner also reported that Sybase's database market share declined by 49.7 percent and that now the company has a market share of less than 2 percent. mLogica feels this may represent a trend in the database market to move away from Sybase, even after the SAP acquisition of Sybase, as shown in Figure 11.2. Sybase's dramatic decline in revenue may also mean that SAP has not been able to reassure the market that Sybase's product line has a future in this space.

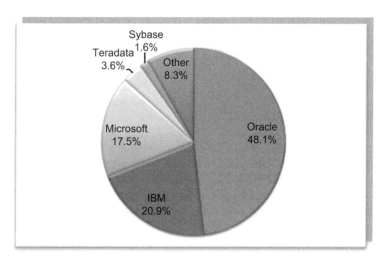

FIGURE 11.1

Database Market Share by Vendor

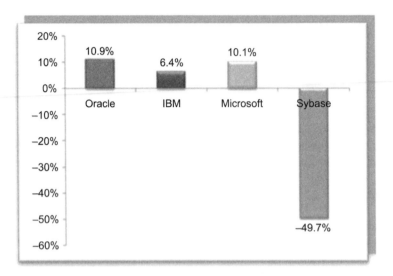

FIGURE 11.2

Database Market Share Increase or Decrease for 2010 by Vendor

Besides the aforementioned reasons, additional concerns that mLogica clients have voiced regarding their decisions to migrate from Sybase to Oracle include the following:

- **Dissatisfaction with Sybase**   Sybase customers are dissatisfied with Sybase's compliance and audit-led sales models over the past several years. Every database vendor (and every application vendor) wants to ensure (rightfully so) that their customers are paying their due as per their licensing agreements. However, numerous Sybase customers have reported to mLogica that they feel Sybase has pushed the boundaries in terms of its tactics and approach toward its customers regarding compliance. Loyal customers hope and expect that, post the SAP merger, Sybase will start to provide value-based solutions and not primarily depend on compliance (support revenue) for its gross profits.
- **Sybase's eroding market share**   As shown in Figure 11.1, market analysts have been quite vocal in expressing their concern regarding Sybase ASE's long-term viability. A decline in Sybase's new license revenue was a major concern for Sybase's customers. Some customers believe that SAP will turn this around and make Sybase ASE a leading database, increasing the company's market share.
- **Maintenance and upgrade costs for Sybase ASE on Sun/Oracle and HP environments**   The maintenance costs of Sybase and Sun/Oracle and HP are high. Server consolidation and virtualization are major initiatives for many customers. Customers are looking at their servers in a holistic way, from applications to databases to hardware. Software license upgrades are expensive as well. Many customers have found an attractive ROI in migrating their

applications to a virtualized and consolidated environment, while migrating Sybase to Oracle.

- **Lack of Sybase database administrators** Sybase database administrators are difficult to find, since most of them have retrained themselves in Oracle or other databases. In addition, the general pool of Sybase database administrators is diminishing every year. Forrester Research estimates that "globally, only about 5% of database administrators (DBAs) are trained on Sybase, and this number has not increased over the past three years." [5] This is a challenge for Sybase, as well as for Sybase customers. Most technologists considering a career in database administration are not looking at Sybase as their preferred database. Colleges and universities are not using Sybase in their student labs. PowerBuilder customers, partners, users, and programmers have experienced this firsthand when attempting to build PowerBuilder applications with a Sybase database as the backend.

- **Lack of standardization on Sybase ASE among the IT community** Many companies, especially large enterprise organizations, are keeping Sybase in containment mode, which means that no new applications will be implemented in the Sybase environment. Even though Sybase has maintained a high retention rate within its existing accounts, new accounts and new applications being deployed at existing accounts are hard to come by.

- **Difficulty in upgrading from Sybase 12.x to Sybase ASE 15** Many Sybase customers who have not yet upgraded to Sybase ASE 15 are considering migrating away from Sybase and toward Oracle. This is because the expense associated with a Sybase ASE 15 upgrade, in many cases, would cover the cost associated with migrating to an Oracle database.

- **Inability to run ASE on SAP** SAP is working aggressively to remediate this issue. SAP's recent announcement that Sybase ASE is certified on SAP [6] will help; however, there is still a major perception issue in the market. Analysts and major customers are waiting to see how many mainstream customers will actually consider migrating their SAP applications to an unproven Sybase database running under SAP. Many customers will also have to wait and see if SAP can address performance issues related to SAP application architecture and Sybase database architecture that did not allow SAP applications to run successfully on Sybase ASE in the past. Sybase needs to establish some mainstream reference customers to make the case in this regard. Being certified will not mean much if SAP can't bring in reference customers right away. On the contrary, mLogica is seeing Sybase customers migrating to Oracle without having much effort and marketing push from Oracle in this matter and this clearly shows in the database market share numbers mentioned earlier in this section.

- **The desire for additional options** The lack of database market share has driven independent software vendors (ISVs), original equipment manufacturers (OEMs), and Software as a Service (SaaS) cloud providers to migrate away from Sybase. In fact, the lack of independent software and application vendors that support Sybase ASE has had the ripple effect of driving more customers off of Sybase, which then causes more ISVs to stop supporting Sybase. This has been a major challenge for Sybase and the Sybase community. The market is hopeful that SAP's strong channel community will be attracted to an SAP-based database offering; however, mLogica has not seen any proposition that would stimulate SAP channel partners to look at Sybase ASE.

In summary, a decision to migrate from Sybase to Oracle should not be an emotional one. You should plan properly, evaluate automated tools, engage the Oracle Platform Migration Group (PMG) for their free advice to calculate the ROI that you should expect to gain three to five years after migrating, and, above all, set the right expectations with your executive management and end users.

TECHNICAL CHALLENGES

For most customers, database schema migrations and database migrations are comparatively easy to perform. The challenges crop up when migrating stored procedures, triggers, and views, as they will take longer than migrating the Data Definition Language (DDL) and data. mLogica actually had a customer that estimated their migration effort would take 80 hours, since the migration tool they were using indicated that; they were in for a big surprise when their stored procedures refused to work in the Oracle environment. Indeed, one of the key challenges in this type of migration concerns stored procedures. If the customer uses Sybase T-SQL extensions extensively, this will create additional work. If the customer is a heavy user of Sybase DB-Library, CT-Library, Open Client, and Open Server, migration of these code lines, applications, and interfaces could require a rewrite. However, Oracle is set to release a feature to its SQL Developer Migration Workbench that will automate the migration of Sybase DB-Library and CT-Library code. We have also seen Sybase users become confused with the migration options between Sybase ASE to Oracle and Sybase IQ to Oracle. Sybase IQ is a completely different database. The assumption that Sybase IQ is so different has killed migration projects for some of our customers as there are no tools to automatically migrate Sybase IQ databases. However, Sybase IQ-based systems' DDL and data can easily be migrated manually. Oftentimes Sybase IQ-based systems are easier to migrate to Oracle than Sybase ASE environments.

The most important challenge of all is to increase the performance of transactions and queries for end users. The Oracle RDBMS needs to be properly tuned to ensure success from a performance perspective. The user experience in the end will define the success or failure of the migration. These may be trivial points for experts, but mLogica can't count the number of times when these points have been missed completely on migration projects. Another point that is not unique to Sybase is the fact that Oracle migrations are executed the same as any IT project. They involve test and quality assurance (QA) environments, separate development and test environments, and above all, a plan that is executed for parallel runs, production migration, and support programs for performance and tuning in the post-migrated production environment. If you don't know where you are going, you might wind up someplace you don't want to be. Planning and execution per the plan is the key to success.

Keeping risk mitigation in mind, mLogica recommends the following migration planning process:

- Examine the existing platform (hardware and infrastructure) architecture and determine the equivalent capabilities in the target Oracle platform.
- Examine the Sybase database capabilities that have been utilized in your application and determine the equivalent capabilities in the Oracle product set.
- Examine third-party functional and business applications and determine the equivalent capabilities in the Oracle commercial off-the-shelf (COTS) or Oracle ISV solutions.
- Measure organizational readiness and overall migration risk.
- Develop a strategic database migration plan, including a detailed road map and cost estimate, and employ implementation support strategies.

KEY ARCHITECTURAL DIFFERENCES BETWEEN SYBASE ASE AND ORACLE

Oracle and Sybase are both relational databases that grew up during the era of client/server computing. Therefore, they have a lot in common:

- A multithreaded, multiuser relational database engine
- Support for American National Standards Institute (ANSI) standard SQL for performing Create, Read, Update, and Delete (CRUD) operations against the database engine
- A database programming language that is used to create stored procedures and triggers in the database to enable encapsulation of business logic and processing in the database engine
- Common database objects such as views, groups, users, and user-defined data types
- Support for database replication, online backup and recovery, and mechanisms to identify and tune SQL

There are also many differences that, in mLogica's experience, create challenges for companies migrating to Oracle in terms of which migration approach is best and which Oracle features and options are appropriate to use. These differences are covered in detail in the following sections.

Database Server

Sybase database servers consist of a data server and a backup server. There are two processes of the Sybase database server, whereas an Oracle instance has five mandatory processes: SMON (System Monitor), PMON (Process Monitor), LGWR (Log Writer), DBWR (Database Writer), and CKPT (Checkpoint). The optional ARCH archive process writes filled redo logs to the archive log location(s). In an Oracle Real

Application Cluster (RAC), the various `ARCH` processes can be utilized to ensure that copies of the archived `redo` logs for each instance are available to the other instances in the RAC setup should they be needed for recovery. Additional Oracle background processes include the CJQ job queue processor, CQJ0 job queue controller, FMON mapping libraries, LMON locking manager, and MMON collector for AWR (Automatic Workload Repository). It is good to understand the server architecture differences between these two databases; however, these differences will not have an adverse effect on your migration project and estimates.

A key difference is that the Sybase data engine can have multiple databases within one engine. Oracle, on the other hand, has one database for the entire data engine. This can cause customers to believe they need to create an Oracle database server for each Sybase database. This is not the case, as Oracle has the concept of schemas (i.e., a database user). Therefore, a Sybase database is mapped to an Oracle schema.

Memory Model

The operating system sees the Sybase database as one process to which multiple users connect. The operating system is allocated the total amount of memory allocated to the database; this doesn't increase or decrease as the number of users changes. The Sybase memory model has three main areas:

1. The program area where the data server executable resides
2. The area for the stored procedure cache for optimized SQL calls
3. The data cache area for recently fetched pages

Sybase manages memory internally that was allocated at the time the server was started. However, Oracle runs as multiple processes within the operating system. The operating system views each processor as one user of the database. This means the Oracle database will require more memory than the source Sybase engine. The Oracle database engine, however, can handle more concurrent users with less processing than the Sybase database engine. This is because the Sybase engine is busy handling user threading and task switching, while in Oracle, these operations are handled by the operating system. The Oracle shared global area (SGA) is the main storage area for the Oracle database engine. Five memory structures make up the SGA: the shared pool, buffer cache, redo buffer, large pool, and Java pool. The shared pool contains the Library cache and the Dictionary cache. The buffer cache holds copies of read data blocks in Least Recently Used (LRU) order. The `redo` log buffer contains changes made by `INSERT`, `UPDATE`, `DELETE`, `CREATE`, `ALTER`, and `DROP` commands. The large pool is an optional memory area providing large areas of memory for session memory, I/O server processes, and backup and restore processes. The Java pool is used by any Java objects running inside the Oracle database. Most applications will not have Java applications running inside the Oracle database unless Sybase T-SQL stored procedures are migrated to Oracle Java stored procedures instead of Oracle PL/SQL stored procedures.

Similar to the server architecture, it is important to understand the architecture differences in the memory model of these two databases; however, these differences will not have an adverse effect on migration projects and estimates.

NOTE

Sybase decided to not use the multithreading capabilities of the host OS. Therefore, in the Sybase database engine, there is a thread for each user that is managed by the database engine. Oracle, on the other hand, chose to utilize the multithreading capabilities of the host OS. The Oracle approach means you will have more OS processes, as user database processes are OS processes. The Sybase approach means there are not as many OS processes, but rather many threads within the Sybase engine which contain all user connection information. These different approaches can cause companies migrating from Sybase to Oracle to increase the amount of memory on their database engine hardware server.

Transaction Processing

Both Sybase and Oracle databases were initially designed for online transaction processing (OLTP) and they both do a great job in that regard. Sybase writes transactions to the data cache first; from there, they are written to transaction logs and the database device. If a Sybase Replication Server is set up, the transaction is then replicated from the log files to the warm standby or high availability (HA) server. Transaction log files are very important in the Sybase architecture. The Sybase Replication Server relies on log files for HA or data sharing. In the event of a hardware failure or database corruption, the data is restored from the log files. Except for Image fields (BLOB), logging of the transaction is a required feature for all Sybase database servers.

On the other hand, Oracle writes transactions to the redo log buffer first, then to the data file buffer, and then to the data files. This means Oracle transactions don't have to interface directly with OS data files or with the data file cache, which speeds up the processing of transactions. Once the transaction is committed, it moves to archived logs. These archived logs are used to restore the database in the event of a hardware failure or database corruption. Unlike Sybase, Oracle doesn't require you to perform transaction logging. Oracle transaction logging can be performed at the database level or even on a table-by-table basis. Typically, Sybase database administrators go through a learning curve when it comes to transaction logs when migrating from Sybase to Oracle.

Analytics

Oracle offers several built-in analytics functions for running averages (AVG), covariances (COVAR_COUNT, COVAR_SAMP), linear regressions (REGR_AVGX, REGR_COUNT, etc.), and variances (VARIANCE, VAR_SAMP), to name a few. A client can successfully utilize the Oracle database to build a data warehouse, operational database, or mixed-use data store using these functions. Oracle also offers Oracle Data Mining (ODM) and Oracle online analytical processing (OLAP) services (cubes) built into the Oracle database engine. Both ODM and Oracle OLAP are options (they have a cost associated with them) of the Oracle Database Enterprise Edition.

Sybase ASE does not have equivalent functions for most functions offered by Oracle, except for a few, such as ranking within a group (DENSE_RANK; supported by both Oracle and Sybase ASE) and popular variance-related functions (STDDEV_POP, VAR_POP, also supported by both Oracle and Sybase ASE).

Sybase offers another product called Sybase IQ that is specifically designed for data warehousing and that competes with Oracle Exadata in price and performance. Sybase IQ cannot be compared to Oracle Exadata because of architectural differences. Sybase IQ is a column-based database that is designed specifically for analytics and ad hoc queries. Also, because all columns are indexed by default and by design, ad hoc query performance, as required by analytics, is one of IQ's strong advantages over many "normal" databases. Single row inserts are also not great in vector-based (column-based) databases—bulk loading of data is the best way to go for these solutions. Sybase IQ, unlike Oracle Exadata, is also not for mixed use/mixed workload (both data warehousing and OLTP) environments.

Both Oracle and Sybase support leading business intelligence (BI) tools such as IBM Cognos, MicroStrategy Business Intelligence Platform, SAP Business Object, Actuate ActuateOne, and others. Oracle also offers Oracle Business Intelligence Enterprise Edition 11 g (OBIEE) for ad hoc BI Web-based dashboards.

Oracle supports materialized views, or database objects that contain the result set of a query. Oracle uses materialized views (previously known as snapshots) to replicate data to nonmaster sites in a replication environment and to cache expensive queries in a data warehouse environment. Sybase doesn't have an equivalent solution but can create a trigger, for example, to serve the same purpose. Sybase ASE does support both materialized and virtual computed columns.

Procedural Languages

T-SQL from Sybase and PL/SQL from Oracle are both easy-to-use and robust procedural languages for writing database stored procedures. Sybase database administrators love to write stored procedures and make the database do most of the work. You can see hundreds to thousands of stored procedures in a typical Sybase database.

Using tools such as SQL Developer to convert T-SQL stored procedures to PL/SQL has become much more prevalent in migrations over the past few years. The standard practice is to break down store procedures into simple, medium, complex, very complex, and custom complexity "buckets." SQL Developer will initially capture, convert, and generate most of the simple and medium stored procedures with a minimal (if any) amount of manual work. Complex and very complex stored procedures might need more manual work; however, there might be fewer of these in a migration. The percentage of automated conversions will therefore depend on the ratio of simple to very complex stored procedures.

Security

A simple way to look at security is that Sybase is considered open and vulnerable until it is secured. Oracle, on the other hand, is considered locked and secured until it is opened. Top Sybase database administrators should have all the tools in hand to have a secure and reliable database; however, sometimes this does not happen. Oracle keeps the security holes closed until the business requires that the database administrator makes the database more flexible. Both approaches have pros and cons. Some database administrators welcome preimplemented security measures; others prefer a more open system with security under their control.

Use of Sybase ASE starts with `sa` (for system administrator) as the initial login, and `sa_role`, which indicates a superuser. The database administrator is then expected to create various roles and user logins at the database administrator level, and then grant access to these new users. Use of Oracle starts with several prebuilt accounts including `system` and `sys`. As with Sybase ASE, the Oracle database administrator is required to create database administrator-level accounts and grant access to these new accounts.

Instead of storing database usernames and passwords in the database, both Sybase and Oracle support storing authentication in a Lightweight Directory Access Protocol (LDAP) server. Sybase's Active Directory Server for LDAP can be considered equivalent to the Oracle Internet Directory (OID) and Microsoft Active Directory (AD).

Backup and Recovery

In the Sybase world, many database administrators still simply use `dump database` and `dump transaction` to perform offline or online backups. Many also use `mined`, and a feature called `archive database` to dump single tables for single table restoration. Similarly, `load database` and `load transaction` are used for recovery. Sybase does support most leading third-party backup and recovery tools.

Oracle, on the other hand, provides a sophisticated tool called the Recovery Manager (RMAN), which allows database administrators to perform online backup and recovery through automated processes. Similar to Sybase, Oracle also supports most leading third-party backup and recovery tools. Oracle has also introduced Flashback Databases, Flashback Query, and Flashback Table to prevent database administrators from having to restore an entire database when an errant Data Manipulation Language (DML) command has been issued or a table has been dropped by accident.

High Availability

When estimating the effort to migrate from Sybase ASE to Oracle, looking beyond backup and recovery to HA is important. Does the current implementation of Sybase include the Sybase Replication Server? If so, what is the Replication Server's role? What is the topology? Warm stand-by implementation may be a simple challenge, as compared to peer-to-peer implementation of the Replication Server. Is the implementation global? Where are the servers located? Are the users accessing the servers across the equator? These and many more questions should be addressed to avoid performance and implementation issues, especially if the migration project is part of an overall server consolidation and virtualization project. These are not major issues; they simply need to be considered in the project plan and addressed during implementation.

Sybase ASE also offers a High Availability Option that provides support for failover.

Oracle GoldenGate provides database replication to keep Oracle databases in sync, and even keep Oracle and Sybase databases in sync for HA. Many of the features and options that are built into the Oracle database, such as TAF (Transparent Application Failover), DataGuard, Oracle Streams, and Standby Database, will help achieve similar or better options than the current Sybase HA implementation.

Partitioning and Storage

Semantic partitioning is used to reduce the contention on a single table. Parallel processing, augmented by a multifold increase in data, and the need among users to have access to data in an immediate fashion, have increased the contention on a single table. The semantic partitioning approach splits a single table into multiple partitions that can be accessed independently while maintaining the data integrity of a single table.

Both Oracle and Sybase support semantic partitioning. Sybase stores tables in segments and these segments are allocated for the database. The transaction logs are stored in their own segment, always on a separate device so that, in the event of a system crash, log files can be accessed to restore the data. This, however, is not mandatory; every once in a while mLogica finds a client who stores the transaction files on the same device.

Oracle stores its tables in tablespaces, which are one or more data files. Oracle RACs and the Oracle File System (OFS) give Oracle users better I/O performance over conventional file systems. Oracle offers Oracle Automatic Storage Manager (ASM) whereas Sybase integrates with IBM Tivoli Storage Manager.

TIP

Oracle ASM is the Oracle recommended approach to storing data in your Oracle database. ASM removes the need for database administrators and system administrators to spend days or weeks setting up a storage configuration. It also greatly reduces the day-to-day management of database storage.

Database Clustering

For database clustering, Oracle offers Oracle RAC, which uses a shared cache architecture to provide additional scalability and database availability. Oracle RAC has been widely implemented, especially in the private cloud architecture.

Sybase's answer to database clustering is Sybase ASE Cluster Edition (ASE CE), which uses shared-disk clustering technology. Sybase ASE CE is positioned to be used for HA, load balancing, management, and virtualization. ASE CE has still not been adopted by Sybase's mainstream customers.

Sybase Analytics Appliance versus Oracle Exadata

Sybase launched the Sybase Analytics Appliance in partnership with IBM, Micro-Strategy, and mLogica. This was Sybase's answer to the appliance market, offering a preintegrated, preconfigured, and pretuned BI appliance. Sybase has not been marketing this product actively in recent years.

On the contrary, Oracle's engineering and sales and marketing departments have been focusing on Exadata quite aggressively. Oracle Exadata is the database machine that is a preconfigured implementation of Oracle RAC data servers using InfiniBand networking. Oracle Exadata supports both BI/data warehousing and OLTP database-based applications within the same Exadata platform.

Performance

Performance management is critical prior to migration. You should set a performance benchmark on the source Sybase ASE database and then compare that benchmark on the migrated Oracle database. Many companies that have achieved successful migration projects revert back to their original database because a performance benchmark didn't exist and users become frustrated. Performance and tuning of the Oracle database should be an integral part of a migration plan and should be executed during each test run.

Development Tools

Sybase provides ISQL as its interactive SQL query tool. Many database administrators use Sybase Central to perform basic database administrative tasks. Sybase also provides Workspace for stored procedure debugging and a graphical interface for SQL queries. Many third-party management tools, including Bradmark, DB-Artisan, and mLogica Performance Manager (MPM), provide added functionality for advanced database management, monitoring, and administration.

Oracle's equivalent of Sybase ISQL is SQL*Plus. Oracle's equivalent of Sybase Central and Workspace is Oracle Enterprise Manager (OEM) and Oracle SQL Developer. The three key performance components of OEM are the Active Session History (ASH), Automatic Workload Repository (AWR), and Automatic Database Diagnostic Monitor (ADDM). These components help the database administrator to determine what resources are being used and what statements are consuming them (ASH), what health indicators are affected (AWR), and what changes might be helpful (ADDM).

Oracle databases are supported by many third-party tools, including DB-Artisan and MPM, to name a few. MPM shows where all the end-user wait time is being spent. In addition, MPM is a performance data warehouse capable of historical trend analysis.

KEEPING THE CURRENT SYBASE ENVIRONMENT RUNNING DURING THE MIGRATION

One of the biggest challenges in database migration is time management—in other words, how to manage an existing Sybase environment and the new Oracle development environment with your resources. Should your team work on the new Oracle environment, learn and train on Oracle, or maintain the legacy Sybase databases? This challenge is amplified as, given the condition of the economy at the time of this writing, many database environments are resource-challenged. Resources are just spread too thin in today's environment of cost-cutting and doing more with less. The answer to the time management question, however, is obvious. The legacy Sybase databases must be maintained in order to keep the business running, the users satisfied, and the service-level agreements (SLAs) compliant. Since the Oracle environment is the future, it is natural for database administrators to learn and train on Oracle. Even if you are outsourcing the migration work to another firm, your team still needs to be actively involved in Oracle training, since your team must have the domain knowledge. mLogica has found that the best approach is to let a third-party firm with expertise in Sybase databases manage the Sybase legacy environment while your team learns and trains in Oracle.

MIGRATION TOOLS

Migration tools, such as Oracle's SQL Developer Migration Workbench and Oracle JDeveloper Application Migration Assistant (AMA), are available from Oracle at no charge. There is no reason why everyone should not take advantage of these free resources.

SQL Developer can migrate schema and data with ease. It can help convert Sybase triggers to Oracle triggers and Sybase T-SQL stored procedures to Oracle PL-SQL stored procedures. It can also help capture, create, and migrate data models. SQL Developer supports migration of most database objects such as tables, indexes, views, functions, stored procedures, triggers, constraints, keys, identity columns, temporary objects, defaults, and user-defined types.

As mentioned in the "Procedural Languages" section earlier in this chapter, when using SQL Developer it is critical that you test the stored procedures that failed completely, or those that have limitations and require manual code changes. AMA provides support for this on the application migration side. It can help analyze and identify the parts of the code that would require modification to run on the Oracle platform.

mLogica's Data Performance Manager (DPM) is an excellent tool that helps identify wait time and looks at queries and stored procedures over time and identifies areas that need to be addressed, such as the 15 worst performing queries. MPM answers the questions: "How long did my user wait?" and "What was my user waiting for?" MPM's Performance Intelligence stores data in a performance data warehouse and uses standard BI techniques such as trending and slice/dice/drill. Vast amounts of performance data are presented in easy-to-understand formats.

During the first trial run, these tools will help you create a list of all the main objects you must consider in the project plan: tables, indexes, constraints, triggers, stored procedures, custom data types, and so on. You will also need to identify application data issues, impacted UNIX/Linux scripts, all the interface programs, infrastructure and management components with dependencies on the database, and target performance requirements.

WARNING

The focus in this section—and in the book in general—is that migrating the DDL and data from other databases to Oracle is one of the easiest aspects of a migration effort. However, as data volumes have grown, it is not uncommon to migrate from 1 terabyte (TB) to 40 TB of data from Sybase ASE or IQ to Oracle Exadata. In these cases, data migration can take from three to five weeks to complete. This is because, at a minimum, three data migration iterations will be required. The first iteration will be the first full test migration. The second will be a test run of the production migration, and the third will be the actual production ("go live") migration. Some customers may be more comfortable with one or two more test runs to work out any data quality issues, optimization of the data migration, or changes required to the DDL. Each data migration iteration can take from one to four days depending on the approach taken, the amount of parallelization that can be achieved, and the speed of the disks and network. Migration of "big data" should not be taken lightly.

COST OF MIGRATION

The blunt answer to the question "How much will a migration cost?" is, "It depends." mLogica has seen simple projects lasting three to four months with a staff of two or three developers and database administrators, to moderate projects lasting six to nine months with a staff of five to 10 developers and database administrators, to complex projects lasting 12 to 24 months with a team of 15 to 30 developers and database administrators. The implementation cost can also vary from less than $100,000 to several million dollars.

The best approach to creating a value proposition is to look at all the costs associated with your current environment, your Total Cost of Ownership (TCO), and all the other nonquantifiable issues associated with your existing infrastructures over a three- to five-year period. Some of the things you should look into when calculating your TCO are support fees for existing licenses, costs of upgrading to new hardware, licensing costs related to growth in terms of number of users and data, costs of database administrators for maintaining existing databases, and costs of third-party consultants if you can't find and retain in-house Sybase database administrators.

SIZING THE TARGET ORACLE DATABASE ENVIRONMENT

Typically, when clients migrate from Sybase ASE to Oracle, platform migration plays a large role in the decision due to the licensing fee associated with the change in platform. Most clients would also migrate from existing hardware to better and less expensive hardware. A proper analysis is needed since you need to look at both current and future requirements. In general, the following guidelines apply when sizing the Oracle database environment:

- **Disk space** Total size of Sybase devices (data and log) plus 50 percent is safe for both Dictionary Managed Tablespaces (DMTs) and Locally Managed Tablespaces (LMTs).
- **Memory** Plan to double the size of the Sybase server since the Oracle instance is a combination of background processes and the SGA.
- **CPU** Number of CPUs = "max online engines" gives you the parameter value in Sybase. New boxes will typically have more cores for the money. Plan to double the number of CPUs or cores as well.

INFRASTRUCTURE MIGRATION CHALLENGES

The typical challenges of a database migration include stored procedure migration, application SQL migration, and testing. mLogica finds that, beyond these challenges, other items such as performance, extract-transform-load (ETL) processing, management, and SQL development tools all pose unique challenges.

However, many clients also include infrastructure migrations (e.g., hardware platform migrations, such as HP to Sun/Oracle and/or operating system migrations such as Windows to Linux) in the project scope. The following are some key migration drivers:

- Reduction in TCO initiatives
- Architecture standardization
- Server consolidation and green IT initiatives
- Leveraging of new technologies such as virtualization or cloud deployment initiatives
- Issues related to capacity planning, performance, security, and stability

In most cases, a combination of several such drivers plays a role in initiating a migration project. Whereas no single driver may be sufficient to warrant the cost, the sum of the business objectives are needed to justify the migration.

SERVER CONSOLIDATION

To ensure an ROI for migration projects, most customers also evaluate and include server consolidation as part of the overall project. Server consolidation strategies help to reduce application and database licensing and support costs. Newer hardware devices are faster and less expensive than before, and are more reliable. They are also better in terms of power consumption and in promoting any corporate green IT initiatives.

Five main areas should be evaluated:

- Hardware server consolidation
- Storage and disk system consolidation
- Infrastructure consolidation including management system and backup systems
- Database instance consolidation
- Operational management consolidation (relocation of distributed operational and support personnel to a central location while maintaining the geographic distribution of the server state using automated tools and technologies)

However, server consolidation should not only look at reducing the number of servers, but also at simplifying and optimizing the overall existing IT infrastructure. In addition, centralization and physical consolidation of hardware devices, data integration, and application integration should be key components of an overall server consolidation strategy. The following are some areas for consideration:

- **Usage patterns for the application**   This includes OLTP, OLAP, mixed use, batch reporting, ad hoc reporting, data mining, advanced analytics, and so on. Can these workloads be combined on one database server?
- **Middle-tier application servers**   Application server consolidation may also be performed along with database consolidation.
- **CPU utilization**   Can CPU resources be combined/shared across the data server engines? How will performance be impacted? Will CPUs manage runaway queries?
- **Network and bandwidth requirements**   Will database and application server consolidation increase your network bandwidth requirements?

mLogica, in partnership with Oracle, has engineered the Data Consolidation Server (DCS) hardware and software appliance to address these very issues. DCS includes Oracle 11 g, Oracle's leading TimesTen In-Memory Database (IMDB), augmented by server management software from mLogica. Figure 11.3 shows how all the pieces of this engineered data consolidation server work together. The objective is to provide a preconfigured, pretested, fine-tuned and engineered hardware and software platform

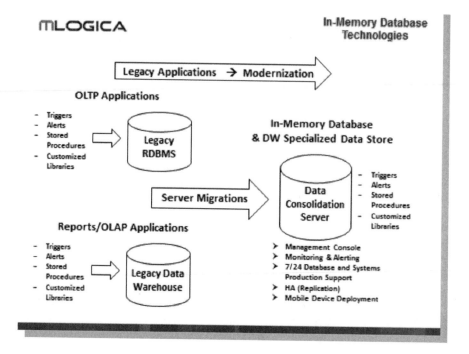

FIGURE 11.3

Database Consolidation Server with IMDB

for high performance. IMDB, as the primary data source or as a cache option to Oracle 11 g, can provide ultra-fast, subsecond responses for client applications.

This solution, along with Oracle Exadata, offers Sybase customers two great options when consolidating Sybase databases to an Oracle platform.

ORACLE mLogica CASE STUDY

As we mentioned at the beginning of this chapter, customers have their own reasons for migrating to Oracle. This case study discusses the experiences of a leading global telecommunications company. The company wanted to migrate its corporate accounts billing system from Sybase to Oracle on the database backend and from a Sybase/PowerBuilder client/server application software and ColdFusion Web site to a single Asynchronous JavaScript and XML (AJAX)-based Web interface on the frontend. The billing system is responsible for more than $1 billion in annual receivables for the company's Fortune 2000 accounts. The project took one year, with the main business driver being a reduction of operational and development costs through consolidation into a single database technology (Oracle is used extensively in other areas of the company) and a single Web-based frontend technology. Secondary benefits of better performance and higher scalability were realized by using Oracle Database 11 g. The system had about 20 upstream and downstream system interfaces that needed to remain the same so as not to interrupt processing and to meet billing SLAs with customers.

Business Drivers

The two main business drivers for this project were cost and performance. Oracle is the corporate database standard, but this billing system was written in the mid-1990s using the Sybase database and Sybase's PowerBuilder client/server tool. Combined with other Sybase applications in the company, the system was costing more than $1 million in support fees plus the cost of keeping a trained Sybase database administration staff. The migration to Oracle allowed for a reduction in overall support costs and a reduction in the database administration and development staff required to add new features and to maintain the application. In addition, the use of Sybase PowerBuilder as a frontend application required specialized programmers plus the overhead of building and deploying a Windows Microsoft Installer Package (MSI) kit when making even small bug fixes was hard to manage and costly to deploy. Consolidating to a single Web platform would reduce all of these costs.

The Sybase database on the company's older hardware was also running out of memory and CPU space and would have required new hardware to keep up with the increased workload. By moving to Oracle, the company dramatically decreased upstream interface file load times, thereby increasing the system's scalability which was needed to meet SLAs when adding more customers.

Situation Analysis

With large annual receivables of $1 billion, great financial risk was associated with the migration, including not meeting the company's Sarbanes-Oxley policies. What if the invoices were wrong? What if the SLAs weren't met? This had been a topic of conversation for several years, and previously the thought of migrating from Sybase to Oracle had been deemed too risky. But the mLogica team laid out an approach with the customer to mitigate that risk. The amount of money being spent on Sybase support fees could be used to fund a team to analyze the existing system and provide Proofs of Concept (POCs) for how the code and the data would be migrated safely to Oracle. The ROI would occur with two years of operation. And as long as the project plan didn't rush the development team and regression tests were run to ensure no changes, the customer would get a successful result.

The Challenge

With 1.5 TB of data and indexes in 500 tables, 1,000 stored procedures used to retrieve and manipulate the data, 100 shell scripts as backend drivers, hundreds of

Java and PowerBuilder classes, and 20 upstream and downstream interfaces, the migration to Oracle had to be executed with great technical care. While SQL is standardized, each vendor has its own dialect and proprietary extensions, not to mention its own development tools and utilities for interfacing with the client programs. In addition, there were known (and unknown) areas within the 15-year-old application that had fallen out of use, so identifying what data and code really needed to be migrated was challenging.

Implementing the Solution

The backend customer team converted the schema, handling the differences in data types, SQL and stored procedure languages, transaction management, and data migration. The differences in Sybase T-SQL versus Oracle PL/SQL were cataloged, and weekly cross-training among team members led to standardized templates and patterns for handling the differences. Some patterns were simple, such as function differences in handling date and time data types; some were harder, such as removing the use of Sybase #temp (temporary) tables as well as converting to reference cursors as output parameters in stored procedures. And, in some cases, code was rewritten and streamlined to take advantage of Oracle features such as pipelined functions.

ETL tools were built to stream the 1.5 TB of data in parallel from the Sybase tables to their Oracle equivalents and to allow the measured migration of data. In addition, custom tools were created to compare the result set output of selects and stored procedures from Sybase against their Oracle equivalents to ensure that there were no regressions for the downstream interfaces. Performance tuning was put into play during the six-week parallel production mode to allow for the creation of statistics and indexes as needed, as well as the insertion of plan hints into a handful of SQL statements.

Results

After one year of architecture, design, development, and testing, the system went into production in fall 2010, to great success. The system has been very stable, requiring only minor performance tweaks during its first month of operation. The user base has been thrilled to have an up-to-date system and the operational database administrators have been able to focus on only one technology. The customer is happy that the mLogica approach succeeded in removing the risk of changing out the Sybase technologies for such a large and important system. And the customer expects it will meet its investment goal in 2012.

SUMMARY

Database migrations from Sybase to Oracle, or any other database, for that matter, are not trivial. Planning is the key to success. Automated tools are available from

Oracle and other third-party vendors that can help reduce your overall migration cost and mitigate risks. If the migration is planned and executed correctly, you can exceed management's ROI expectations, and meet your SLAs and user satisfaction ratings, all while migrating to a modern platform powered by Oracle.

The project discussed in this chapter's case study took a year to complete. mLogica has seen simple projects completed within three months, and moderate projects completed within six to nine months. Complex projects that involve multiple databases and a variety of applications can take as long as one to two years to complete. mLogica recommends breaking one massive migration into several smaller projects; migrate all your simple databases first, and then target the complex databases. mLogica also recommends minimizing the addition of new projects during the migration; we prefer not to attempt hardware server consolidations and database migrations at the same time, though many times this becomes necessary since a new set of consolidated hardware is integral to a positive ROI.

Endnotes

[1] An article in InfoWorld Magazine, May 12, 2010.

[2] An article on ZDNet, written by Larry Dignan, May 13, 2010.

[3] SYBASE INC-FORM 10-K February 26, 2010.

[4] Gartner vendor share numbers for 2010 for RDBMSes. Available from: www.oracle.com/us/products/database/number-one-database-069037.html.

[5] Forrester Research press release. Top Corporate Software Priority Is Modernizing Legacy Applications. Available from: www.forrester.com/ER/Press/Release/0, 1769, 1285,00.html.

[6] Katherine Burger, May 17, 2011. News from 2011 SAPPHIRE NOW: SAP Announces Strategies to Leverage Relationships with Sybase and Accenture. UBM TechWeb. Available from: www.banktech.com/architecture-infrastructure/229500761.

Application Migration: Oracle Forms to Oracle Application Development Framework 11g

12

INFORMATION IN THIS CHAPTER:

- Oracle Application Development Framework Introduction
- Options: Rearchitect or Rewrite
- Migration/Rewrite: Common Implementation Steps
- Other Forms-to-ADF Mappings
- Case Study: Manufacturing and Logistics
- ADF in the Cloud

This chapter introduces you to the exercise of migrating an Oracle Forms application to Oracle Application Development Framework (ADF) v11. You will receive basic information introducing you to Oracle ADF and how legacy Oracle Forms components can be mapped to the functionality in ADF.

A case study outlining an engagement that Oracle migration partner Vgo Software completed with a large manufacturing and logistics company in the United States is also included. The project entailed the conversion of an Oracle Forms v9 application to Oracle ADF v11g. This chapter was written by Vgo Software, a division of NEOS Holdings, LLC, based in Hartford, CT, USA. Vgo is a modernization company with deep experience in Oracle Forms migration and conversion. Additionally, Vgo is an Oracle Safe Switch partner, helping clients on Sybase, Informix, DB2, and Microsoft adopt Oracle technologies.

This chapter is very useful even if you are not migrating from Oracle Forms. If your target environment is Java EE and you are migrating from Visual Basic, PowerBuilder, or any other 4GL language, you will learn about the components of Oracle ADF that you can use to build a Java EE application. So, if you are rearchitecting or rewriting any 4GL application to a Java EE cloud-based application, you will benefit from this chapter.

ORACLE APPLICATION DEVELOPMENT FRAMEWORK INTRODUCTION

For those new to the technology, Oracle ADF is a Java-based application framework with which you can build enterprise-class Web applications. ADF is based on many technologies such as JavaServer Faces framework and includes components for the development of feature-rich Web applications. ADF applications can be developed using Oracle's JDeveloper integrated development environment (IDE). JDeveloper provides many wizards, drag-and-drop features, and integration plug-ins for other components in the Oracle Fusion software stack. JDeveloper makes it easy to develop ADF applications by providing these features, though it still requires a good degree of education and experience for a developer to be an expert with JDeveloper and ADF.

> **NOTE**
>
> When thinking of where your Forms application is going, also think about the strategic direction of your application portfolio, and then the staff you have to get you there. It is imperative that you consider your team's ability to maintain, support, and grow the application to continue to meet business demands.

Oracle ADF Organizational Impact

When considering adopting ADF into an organization, one must consider the learning curve of adopting new technologies. In this case, it is a significant change in thought for developers. Typically, Forms developers have developed sophisticated client/server code where reuse was somewhat limited to the use of libraries or "cut and paste" as a pattern (although "cut and paste" is a common practice and as such it is not limited to Oracle Forms only). Code has been duplicated within Forms objects and within Forms applications. Some forward-thinking organizations in the late 1990s abstracted their databases by creating a Create, Read, Update, and Delete (CRUD) PL/SQL layer and moving substantial (in processing cost) code from their forms to a PL/SQL business rule layer that calls the PL/SQL CRUD layer.

However, in the world of Java and ADF, different architectural choices abound. The usage of these design choices can be considerable as it requires a change in mindset—instead reuse, consolidation, object design, process execution, and transaction state all have to be reconsidered when designing enterprise-class applications.

From a resource perspective, it is becoming increasingly difficult to find highly talented Oracle Forms development resources. Even off-shore staffing companies are having a hard time retaining Forms developers. In the near future, it will be extremely difficult to find people to support a decidedly legacy client/server development environment such as Oracle Forms (not web enabled Oracle Forms but Client/Server version). Where are all these Forms programmers going? They are going to learn ADF, JDeveloper/Java EE, and/or other languages. Customers should consider training and complete new development projects using JDeveloper and ADF in the near to mid-term to get their developers to begin the transition to the Web-based cloud computing world.

As paradigms continue to evolve, such as the adoption and maturation of cloud computing, greater requirements for flexibility and scalability will be demanded from the application development platform. Oracle ADF, in combination with Exalogic and Exadata, or Oracle Enterprise Linux and Oracle Virtual Server, provide such a platform.

> **TIP**
>
> JDeveloper and ADF 11g are a great combination as an end-state architecture for Oracle Forms customers looking to modernize their application to the cloud. Combined, they provide the best path for retraining your existing Oracle Forms developers to develop and deploy Java EE applications quickly.

OPTIONS: REARCHITECT OR REWRITE

Considering the maturation of ADF, the modernization of Oracle Forms is a very appealing option. Until ADF v11 was released in beta in 2008, Oracle Forms customers had few appealing alternatives. Options were limited to complete rewrites using other J2EE technologies, such as Java Server Faces (JSF), JavaBeans, Struts, or Java Swing applications, modernizing Oracle Forms by incorporating web services calls, use of Java components and using latest features in Oracle Forms. However, the Oracle Forms community needed more "Forms-like" architectural components and abilities, such as maintaining state through commit logic in a form (supported by ADF task flows in ADF v11) and tighter security enablement.

For Oracle Forms customers, ADF v11 has become a very viable alternative for modernization. The question then becomes, "How do I do adopt ADF?" Essentially, there are two alternatives: Modernize to ADF and attempt to reuse as much of your existing Forms business logic and flow as possible, or rewrite the application from scratch using JDeveloper and ADF v11.

Rearchitecting

The modernization approach discussed here assumes the use of tools to assist in the conversion of the Oracle Forms application to a new destination (ADF). Oracle does not provide a tool or utility to convert Oracle Forms to ADF as it does for upgrading Oracle Forms from one version to another. A good alternative is to partner with an experienced vendor, such as Vgo Software, that uses tools and solid processes to modernize Forms applications. This provides the consistency and efficiency of a tools-based approach, while also ensuring that everything is done to your speci-fications. There are few tools in this market, and they range from those that conduct valuable application portfolio assessment and discovery (such as Vgo's ART product) to actual code generation (Vgo's Evo product). But whether you are buying a tool or using a vendor with a tool, it is the output that matters; if you cannot live with the end state of the code, it is not worth the time. In many cases, the use of a tool to generate code on its own will not yield supportable, maintainable code.

The rearchitecture option has several distinct pros and cons:

Pros:

- Reuses your business logic effectively
- Results in increased efficiencies in creating the application architecture for your application
- Creates a true Java/Java EE/ADF application
- Is much faster than a rewrite
- Cleans up and consolidates objects in Forms applications
- Incorporates business process redesign into the effort
- Can support Forms/ADF coexistence points

Cons:

- Requires some manual rework, which may be considerable based on the structure/quality of the old forms.
- Is more expensive than an upgrade of Oracle forms to Web-based Oracle forms.
- May result in "blind" conversions, that is, simple generation of 1:1 Forms code automated migration, no understanding of existing application, or "black box" (a runtime emulation server or product) implementations. The past experience of Oracle and its Forms migration partners is that clients cannot maintain this kind of code base.

The act of modernizing an Oracle Forms application to ADF is a big undertaking. Underestimating the size, scope, and complexity is the leading cause of failure for these efforts. Readers considering converting their Forms applications should have extensive experience with both Forms and ADF prior to engaging in this type of project, or work with a partner with experience in both areas.

> **WARNING**
>
> Watch out for completely automated migration tools that perform blind conversions. In blind conversions, a tool is used to simply convert code to another programming language, without consideration for cleanup or reuse. This leaves you with an application that cannot be maintained or supported.

Rewriting from Scratch

Rewriting a Forms application isn't as simple as opening JDeveloper, mapping your business components, and generating a new application. When rewriting from scratch, the customer should be contemplating his or her business process from scratch as well. That being the case, this approach entails all the rigor of new application development: collecting business requirements, determining functional flows, creating business rules, creating design specifications (for infrastructure and database as well as the application itself), testing and QA methodology and criteria, user acceptance criteria, GUI specifications and usability, testing at all levels, security implications, end-user training, documentation, and rollout. Myriad technical functionalities that are specific to each environment and each organization are intermingled.

Like the rearchitecture option, the rewrite option has several distinct pros and cons as well:

Pros:

- Results in the exact application that was required
- Function and technology should be a match
- Architectural design optimized based on current technology
- Application supportable and maintainable to industry (or at least company) standards

Cons:

- Longest and most costly option
- Presents high risk to business operations
- Unlikely that existing components, or developed business rules, will be reused, as time spent analyzing and extracting logic is typically not invested when requirements and design are brand-new
- Low business tolerance ("Why are we doing this again when we already have a good system?")

The most compelling option in completely rewriting an application isn't based on technology; it's based on business needs. Alone, business needs don't seem touched upon in the countless blogs and papers. However, business needs ultimately drive all technology decisions. If your business has evolved in its processing or has major process changes in store that increase business value, you should rewrite. Even in a rewrite you may not need to throw everything out and start over. It is unlikely that a new application will create entirely new business rules if the process is still the same. For example, a Forms application that processes new applications for an insurance company is still going to process the same work, but perhaps in a different manner. Therefore, code segments that validate a policy ID, or ensure that the product chosen with the contract is a valid combination in a given state, are still likely to be valid business rules. The authors' recommendation is to assess the existing Forms application and extract rules that can be reused in a new application. Vgo Software has a product called ART (for "Application Reporting Technology"), an application portfolio assessment tool, that provides deep technical insight into what is in each form, as well as how all the forms, in one or multiple Forms applications, work together. ART will store this data in a repository which then can be mined and transported into the Oracle Fusion Business Rules repository, or for use with Oracle Exalogic WebLogic Application Server.

NOTE

In comparing whether to rearchitect or rewrite an application from scratch, consider the business benefits of each option. Looking for the "cheapest" way to get to ADF from Forms is not, on its own, a significant reason for leaving Forms. A business driver is called for to initiate this level of project.

MIGRATION/REWRITE: COMMON IMPLEMENTATION STEPS

This section provides a technical introduction to steps that are common when using ADF to rewrite an application. This knowledge is also applicable if you are rearchitecting an application. This section will introduce the following ADF concepts: data model, application module, task flows, View objects, and some UI components.

Forms-to-ADF Mapping

Table 12.1 reflects some of the common Forms and ADF object mappings, complexity associated with converting these Forms objects, and notes specific to their migration to ADF.

As Table 12.1 shows, many components of the ADF framework were really created with Forms developers in mind. Even if that isn't the case, the designers of ADF have taken some of the aspects of Forms that make it a great 4GL tool and implemented those same concepts in ADF.

No other Java frameworks have the concept of an LOV that is so tightly integrated with the framework itself. Other frameworks do not allow for drag-and-drop creation of everything from the data model to the UI as ADF provides. Other application frameworks also lack the concept of a task flow, a construct which figures very prominently in ADF applications when mapping to Forms functionality.

In a typical Forms modernization, a single form can be mapped to a single ADF task flow, especially if the application was well designed to start. The mapping is a sensible one because the ADF task flow will maintain the transaction boundaries in much the same way a typical Oracle form does. Also, task flows can be nested. Just as one form can call another form and become responsible for the transaction, so too can one task flow call another task flow and become responsible for its transaction. Task flows are similar in other ways because they will contain the flow of screens that were originally in the form. Normally one task flow will make use of one application module and that application module will contain the complex business logic that once resided in the original form.

Other mappings in Table 12.1 are similarly straightforward, particularly the mapping of View objects to blocks. In a Forms application, a block is responsible for defining a set of related attributes that are, 75 percent of the time, based on a query or a table in the database. Those attributes may be displayed or may be hidden from the UI and only used in calculations. A View object in ADF is much the same. Most

Table 12.1 Forms-to-ADF Mapping

Forms	ADF Mapping	Complexity	Notes
Forms	Task flows (for transaction management) Application modules	High/ medium	• Specific to application • Complexity depends on Forms state
List of values (LOV)	Read-only View objects	Medium/low	• Usually maps one for one
Query-based blocks	View objects	Low	• Always map this way
Tables (called from database in Data Manipulation Language [DML] statements)	Entity objects	Low	• Always map this way
Transactions	Task flows	High	• Usually maps one for one
Triggers	Java method (programmatic) or Groovy expression (declarative)	High/ medium	• Usually maps one for one
Windows and canvases	JSPX pages, Panel Groups, Page Fragments	Medium/low	• Always map this way
Libraries	Application modules	High/ medium	• Depends on complexity
SQL	View objects	Medium/low	• Requires good discovery and knowledge between a business rule and navigational rule

View objects are based on a table or a SQL query. View object attributes have properties that define what the defaults are for those attributes when displayed in the UI; this is very similar to Block Item properties within a form.

JSPX pages (XML-compliant Java Server Pages) are the natural and obvious mapping for windows and canvases from a form on the surface. The main difference is that in Forms, Block Item properties defined the visual representation of the attribute; in ADF, the View object attribute properties are defaults and hints for JDeveloper. Therefore, when you drag the components on the page, JDeveloper knows what type of component to place and what the properties are for that component. Once that is done, however, those properties can be modified on the JSPX page itself to differ from the default properties given in the View object. This allows the same View object to be used in more than one screen to reduce the number of View objects needed. View objects can also be further refined by defining a set of view criteria that may include only some of the attributes.

What Doesn't Map?

A number of items in Oracle Forms (especially in Oracle Forms Version 6 and earlier) do not "map" to the Web application world in general, or to ADF in particular. This is not to mean that there is not a direct path to implement the same functionality in the Web world as some of this functionality can be mapped into low level Java APIs. Examples of these are:

- `HOST`, `ORA_FFI`, User Exits
- Local client operations, which will change to operate on the application server such as `READ_IMAGE_FILE`, `TEXT_IO`, and other operating-system-based commands
- Other points to consider: tabbed canvases, `SYNCHRONIZE`, `TIMERS`, mouse events (`mouse_over`, `mouse_enter`, `mouse_leave`), icons (need to be converted to JPG or GIF), and Windows API (WinAPI) calls

Also, business functions often have to be reconsidered based on the stateless environment you are in when you create a Web application. Addressing these challenges ahead of time will save a lot of time later in the project. Again, proactive awareness of what is really in your Forms application will help tremendously at development time.

The ADF Data Model

This section is not meant as an introduction to ADF concepts. Many books have already been written on this topic. Instead, this section will cover the base concepts of ADF so that you can understand the migration process described in this chapter.

The ADF data model is the core of how ADF interacts with the database, presents data to applications, contains application business logic, binds database results to the presentation tier, controls application page flow, and displays results to the client. The data model in an ADF application consists of application modules, View objects, View object links, entities, and entity associations. Every table that needs to have write access will have an ADF entity and an associated updateable View object. Database views, SQL queries, and read-only table access require the use of read-only View objects which are based on SQL queries. Figure 12.1 depicts the ADF data model and how it looks as compared to the Forms architectural model.

The Model layer in ADF is the most important part of an ADF application. Not only does it provide the actual persistence, but it also provides data caching, transaction management, and hints for UI development. Validation can be done at the Entity level so that any view built on top of that entity will have the same validation enforced.

An application module is essentially an aggregate of Model layer Views and/or service methods needed to perform a task and any business logic that might be used. While creating the Model layer View objects, one can add these objects to an application module, or they can be added later.

Migrating Forms to ADF

While the process to migrate Forms to ADF can seem daunting, at the center of the effort is an understanding of the ADF Model layer and how it relates to the

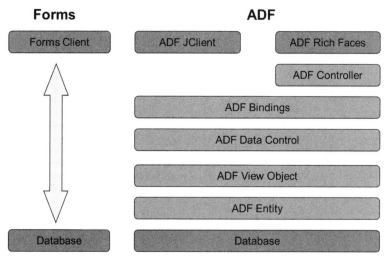

FIGURE 12.1

ADF Data Model

same concepts in Forms. Once you have that understanding, you can begin the process outlined next to create an ADF Model layer to support the necessary functionality.

The first step is to identify the blocks and relationships existing in the Oracle form. From those objects you will identify which Entity objects, updateable View objects, and read-only View objects will need to be created. In addition, some read-only View objects may be necessary to support LOVs.

A developer can use JDeveloper's New Business Components from Tables Wizard to create the initial entities and corresponding View objects. If the entities already exist from a previous effort, it is simple to create the View objects themselves through another wizard.

After the initial creation of the objects, the developer must tweak them a little. For each entity, take the time to assign any UI hints, such as length of field, field type, and labels. Assign LOVs to the View object attributes that need them. Finally, create view links for the relationships as outlined by the form.

At this point, if the aforementioned artifacts were added to an application module during code generation, they will be visible in the Data Controls panel in JDeveloper. In master-detail relationships, View objects may be referenced more than once. They are referenced first for their initial import into the application module and again separately for the relationship. When defining master-detail relationships several levels deep, it is a best practice to remove the duplicates and use only one View object reference. Doing so will result in a data control with a single and simple hierarchy rather than any one View object duplicated one or many times.

> **TIP**
>
> If you are using ADF to create a Web-based application, you need to set `jbo.locking.mode` to "optimistic" in the application module configuration properties. By default, it is set to "pessimistic," which is fine for Swing applications but not for Web-based applications that wish to take advantage of database pooling.

Application Module Client Exposed Methods

A developer can add methods to the application module that task flows or Web pages can use. To do so, create public methods and then use the Java tab for the application module to expose your methods to the UI. When methods have been made accessible, they will show up in the data control as shown in Figure 12.2.

Once the methods have been exposed via the application module client, they can be used in task flows by dragging and dropping the method into the task flow diagram from the data control. Alternatively, they can be dropped directly onto a JSP/JSF or Facelets page which will create a button that calls the appropriate method. A final option is to make the call to the exposed method inside a managed JavaBean. Using the task flow or the managed bean will allow you to add other interactions around the method call, such as displaying a confirmation message to the user that the method succeeded or failed. Users can also be directed to another page after calling one of these exposed methods.

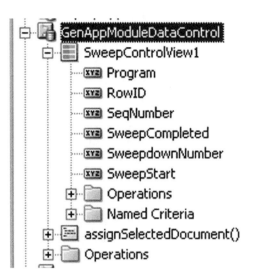

FIGURE 12.2

Application Module Methods

> **WARNING**
> It is important that developers take care to avoid any direct SQL calls within an application module method. If the business logic calls for a new row to be added to a table, for instance, that row should be added to a View object instance associated with the application module. This will allow ADF to manage the transaction. Since ADF provides a caching layer, any direct inserts or updates performed on the database will cause the ADF cache and the data actually in the database to be out of sync. It is a slight learning curve for developers, but it allows the application to take full advantage of the ADF Framework.

View Objects and Queries in the Application Module

By using View objects properly from within an application module's Java implementation, it is possible to completely avoid writing standard SQL and connection logic. While most developers enjoy that low level of control, using the tools provided by ADF does have benefits. The first and foremost of these is the ability to refactor queries and View objects without having to change the Java implementation at all.

A View object can be filtered simply by adjusting the `where` clause:

```
public void setFilter(ViewObjectImpl view) {
view.setWhereClause("SOME_FIELD='Some value'");
view.executeQuery();
    }
```

Second, by using a View object's `createRow` and `insertRow` methods, a developer can take advantage of any validators that have been defined in the View object at design time. Also, writing SQL statements can be avoided. Obviously, one would want to add whatever error handling seemed appropriate. Error handling should mirror messaging and format from the original form.

```
public void addToView(ViewObjectImpl view) {
    Row newRow = view.createRow();
newRow.setAttribute("SomeField", "a test value");
view.insertRow(newRow);
    }
```

ADF Task Flows

One of the strengths of Oracle Forms, and client/server applications in general, is a consistent method for persisting data to the database. In Web applications, transaction state and persistency, especially when converting from a client/server application, require extra design and attention.

ADF has the concept of a task flow, which aids in this transition. While the data model consisting of entities, View objects, and so on is responsible for the actual persistence, a task flow is used to provide the transaction context around that interaction. This concept, introduced in ADF 11g, provides an easy mechanism for implementing transactions that span multiple pages and are tightly integrated with the Entity caching layer. As mentioned previously in the section "The ADF Data Model," this is only advantageous when the ADF data model is actually used for persistence. Direct calls to the database for inserts or updates will cause inconsistency and bugs in the application.

ADF task flows are similar to Spring MVC Web flows or Business Process Execution Language (BPEL) diagrams. They define entry points and actions that can be taken by logic or by user decisions.

Bounded Task Flows

A bounded task flow represents a single transaction. This means a commit or rollback action from the data control (the data control is the visible component created by the definition of the application module) executes a commit or rollback for any changes made during the task flow. This is important because saving one screen will also commit changes on other screens, if those screens are part of the same task flow.

Existing forms map well to bounded task flows in ADF 11g. Each form will normally encapsulate a particular process in a system. If the original application was well designed, the mapping will be very close to that of "one form to one task flow." If the original Forms application is very complex, or poorly designed, and contains too many screens, it would make sense to design it into multiple task flows.

TIP

Use the Use Existing Transaction If Possible selection so that if you nest your task flows the transaction will be handled by the parent. This option is *not* selected by default.

At certain points in a task flow, the user is usually presented with a screen or view. It is not necessary to create the corresponding Web pages right away—one can do that after designing the task flow. Double-clicking on a View (this is not to be confused with the data model's View object) will start a wizard to help in the creation of a Web page.

In the example shown in Figure 12.3, there is actually only one Web page: the "entryPoint." The `Commit`, `Rollback`, `CreateInsert`, and `Delete` nodes were dragged from the data control which allows JDeveloper to create the necessary bindings. The `showSavedMessage`, `setCancelMessage`, and `clearMessage` nodes set values in a bean which the UI has access to. Upon execution of any of the data operations, a new message is prepared for the user to inform the user of how the data operation went. Since the data editing page has an output text field bound to the message property of the shared bean, the message is automatically shown. This happens without refreshing the entire page because a Partial Page Trigger is implemented on the output text component that directs the framework to only refresh that portion of the page. This is a standard task flow implementation for simple search, add, and edit pages that only require a table of data. The data can be edited directly in the table component itself, and the entire flow is very similar to how a simple Oracle form might work, but with the added benefit of an enhanced search component.

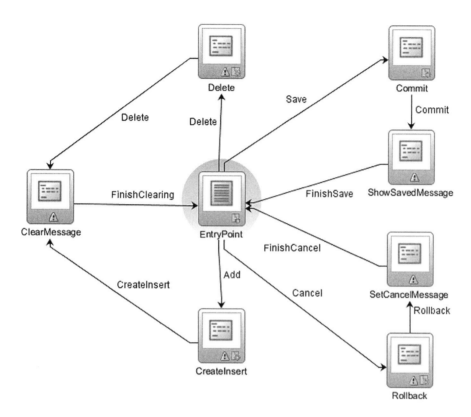

FIGURE 12.3

ADF Task Flows

UI Access to the Data Model

When designing the screens, it's usually straightforward to drag Model objects from the Data Controls panel onto the page. Methods defined in the application module (if exposed to clients) can also be used directly. For example, one might drag a view of products from the data control to the page in design mode. ADF will then prompt the developer with a list of possible ways to render the data. One commonly chosen way to render data is an ADF table. The ADF table is an editable or read-only grid of data. The column names and data types are those previously defined in the corresponding Model layer's Entity or View object. By also dragging the `CreateInsert` action from that particular Model object's Operations folder, an Add button could also be added. When the user clicks the button, the grid should refresh without reloading the entire page. ADF makes this kind of partial page rendering simple with the Partial Triggers property. By selecting this property of the ADF table, the developer can click Edit and be presented with a list of page components that should trigger a reload of the ADF table.

Page Layout

ADF page rendering is generally visually appealing by default. Still, complex component placement can be a challenge. For example, while designing a basic data entry form is simple, designing one in the manner of Blueprint Cascading Style Sheets (CSS) or some other grid layout can be quite challenging. To that end, it is possible to extend ADF's UI components and provide renders that allow the developer to control exactly what Dynamic Hypertext Markup Language (DHTML) is generated. That kind of customization isn't for everyone or every project, but at least it is possible when users simply must have a certain layout. This becomes an important feature in Forms conversion if users demand a similar look and feel of the legacy Forms application. To embrace ADF fully, similar result can be achieved by nesting layout containers and skinning.

Other powerful layout components are also available from the ADF palette. The Panel Form component is good for keeping labels and fields aligned on a page. The Panel Group component allows for horizontal or vertical positioning of its child components. And the Panel Stretch component is definitely a welcome addition from the Swing package collection of objects allowing Top, Bottom, Right, Left, and Center areas to be filled in by content. That is by no means the entire list of available rich client components, but merely a sample of those that are more generally used.

ADF page design is a wide enough subject that it makes sense to become familiar with the applications for which each component is and is not suited. Figure 12.4 shows the default page layout for our example.

OTHER FORMS-TO-ADF MAPPINGS

Now that we have covered some basics, we can expand on those concepts with additional Forms-to-ADF-specific mapping scenarios. Please keep in mind that this not a complete list, just several examples of situations commonly seen in Forms applications and how to work with them in ADF. The complete list of patterns for Forms conversion to ADF is beyond the scope of this chapter.

Table-based Search/Edit

For the simplest type of screen, typically used to maintain administration data (e.g., lists of countries or product types, etc.), the UI pattern we use in an ADF application is very similar to the pattern used in the Forms application. The main difference is that a separate component is used to perform the search.

If you are familiar with the ADF 11g framework, you know that the simplest way to provide CRUD capabilities is to create an entity based on the table being edited. A View object would then be created for that entity and exposed to the user in the page. To provide the search capability to the user, the developer would create a set of view criteria. These view criteria are then used to create an ADF Query Panel that the user of the application will use to search the data. To take advantage of the benefits of the ADF Query Panel, you need to include the Query Panel on the page.

FIGURE 12.4

UI and Tabs

In order to alleviate any unnecessary button clicks, the ADF Panel Query is provided fully disclosed. The user can then search and see the results on the same screen. Edits to the returned data can be performed in the table itself, and records can be deleted from the returned results. When the user wants to add a record, the user simply clicks the Add button which will insert an empty row into the table, and then he or she can enter data directly into that row.

The task flow for this type of search and edit functionality in Figure 12.5 explicitly shows the messages being set and cleared to indicate to the user that an action has been successfully performed.

Users of the original application normally react well to a change such as this. Though the UI has changed from the original form, it provides them some additional functionality that they did not have before through the ADF Query Panel. If you were to use the Oracle Metadata repository, users could even save their favorite queries using this panel.

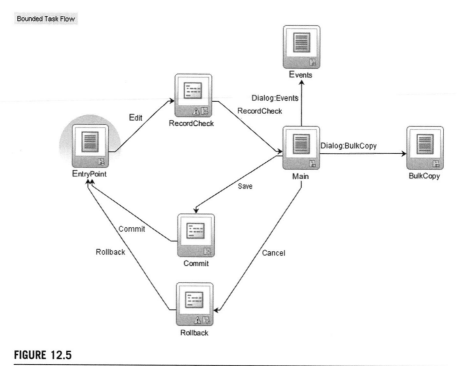

FIGURE 12.5

Search and Edit Task Flow

List of Values versus Drop Downs

Forms applications use a lot of LOVs. Newer applications have a mix of LOVs and drop downs. Many times when an application used an LOV, after the user selected a value from the list, a description field would be populated.

ADF 11g provides an easy way to produce this same behavior, but you can also just as easily display the description instead of the key when a value is selected, or show the key and the description when a value is selected. The ADF 11g LOV components also provide some more enhanced search functionality.

For short LOVs, consider replacing them with single-choice selects. For longer lists, use pop-up LOVs to postpone the initial query that retrieves the list until it is actually needed. In the case of static LOVs, replace them with entity-based LOVs where feasible. This allows you to cache the list and have it be able to change without changing the application.

Post-Query versus View

Post-query triggers in Oracle Forms applications can be used for many things, and depending on what function that trigger was performing in the form, implementing the same functionality in ADF 11g can be quite similar or very different.

In the previous section, we mentioned LOVs with description fields that are populated based on the key from the LOV. Those description fields are normally populated in a post-query trigger on the form. In fact, Oracle Forms allows you to make an awful lot of database calls in a very short period of time and have minimal impact on the performance of the application. This makes populating a description field via a post-query trigger an acceptable option.

This option has more of a performance impact for applications built in other frameworks, including ADF. There is a better method to accomplish the same task in ADF. When you create an LOV and add a transient description field from another entity, ADF will create a join in the query for the view that contains the description field so that the field will be populated at the same time the rest of the data is retrieved from the database. This eliminates the need for a separate call, and even a separate call per row of results returned, in some cases.

This is a very common and simple example, but at the same time, it illuminates a point that should be recognized. The performance of your application is going to be greatly affected by how many database calls are made. Watch out for situations where you might be executing a query per row of a result set, and try to reduce that access as much as possible.

> **WARNING**
> Oracle Forms (Client/Server version), like all 4GL technologies, can have an excessive amount of database calls and not experience a significant impact on performance. This is because the application runs on a PC that is in close proximity to the database server and there are only two tiers—thick client PC and database server. In a Web or cloud environment, you have three tiers—thin client Web browser, application server, and database server—that can physically be literally anywhere in the world. When moving to ADF, the amount of database access for small lists of data must be minimized. This means moving this logic from the presentation tier (JSP or DHTML pages) into the application server tier. The authors recommend combining multiple SQL queries into joins where possible in order to minimize the number of database calls made by the application.

Keystrokes and Menu Items versus Buttons

In a lot of older Forms applications, users are used to a lot of keystroke commands to execute certain functions. You can almost mimic some of this behavior with shortcuts on buttons, but no matter what you do, the functionality is almost certainly going to be replaced by buttons. Adopting a self service approach instead of a manual data entry is ideal when migrating to ADF.

Forms applications are also very good at keeping track of context, knowing where the cursor is in the UI and executing the right event depending on the field that has focus. For example, if there is a master record and several detail tables, clicking Add will add a record to the right place depending upon what block had focus when the button was clicked. While this can be achieved in ADF 11g, it makes the application more complex, sometimes unnecessarily so, and it has the effect of not being intuitive for new users. Instead, put your detail tables inside a panel header group and add a toolbar with Add/Delete buttons to the header's toolbar facet. This puts more buttons on the page, but it makes their use very intuitive.

> **TIP**
>
> Look to reuse your existing business logic and flow using ADF 11g by analyzing and extracting those processes from your legacy application. This extraction and exposure through ADF will position your application for higher integration ability with other applications in the enterprise.

CASE STUDY: MANUFACTURING AND LOGISTICS

Vgo Software has conducted more than 30 Oracle Forms conversions to Java EE technologies around the world. This particular case study is interesting in that the end-state application architecture is Oracle ADF 11g, the application has an international user base, and the use of the application is elastic, from an end-user perspective; the total utilization fluctuates based on world events, market drivers, and overall demand. With that being said, it is, by its nature, an excellent candidate for cloud deployment. The cloud hosting environment allows for more processing power when necessary, and the 24/7 uptime means the system is available to end users at all times.

Background and Challenge

Vgo Software completed a modernization project on an aging, but mission-critical, Oracle Forms 10g application for a large multinational organization. The application manages logistics for a globally distributed and supported mechanical assembly.

The system was originally authored in the 1980s using Oracle Forms technology. The client routinely upgraded the application until its final upgrade to Oracle Forms 10g. While the software was physically upgraded, the actual business processes, logic, and rules architecture were never improved or optimized, underleveraging the investment in technology. As is typical with the majority of modernization efforts Vgo has conducted, little to no rationalization, process reengineering, or optimization was conducted during the life of the application by the client. The existing application consisted of 137 Oracle forms and 28 Oracle reports.

Business drivers were influencing the direction of the application. Requirements demanded fluid scalability to remote sites and to a variety of devices. A finer degree of separation between the application and data layers of the architecture, reusability of business logic to multiple, related applications, and a reduced business risk of sunsetting technology and knowledgeable staff also drove the need to modernize this critical application.

Vgo was asked to perform the following activities:

1. Assess, catalog, and rationalize the existing business processes.
2. Conduct and document the legacy Oracle Forms application and associated database.

3. With the business partner, recommend appropriate technology implementation alternatives for the legacy application.
4. Design, implement, test, and roll out a modernized application.

Vgo used its Evolutions methodology to engage with this client. The methodology delivers a holistic approach for modernizing legacy applications; it views business process and operations in equal measure to technology transformation. Using this holistic approach to modernization, Vgo worked with both the business community and the technology staff to ensure a complete solution to the client.

Working with the client's business partners, Vgo documented and mapped the new business process flows to the legacy application flow, identifying gaps and enhancements to be made in the modernized application. Once the gaps and business requirements were thoroughly understood, the team identified several alternatives to technology implementations of the Forms application. This due diligence was conducted to put a weighting factor on strategic, personnel, and cost factors indicated as priorities by the client.

Vgo recommended that the Oracle Forms application be modernized to Oracle ADF v11 for the following reasons:

- The existing staff was able to adopt/learn ADF.
- The staff was able to integrate ADF with new architectures such as service-oriented architecture (SOA)-based cloud computing.
- Oracle provided stability and long-term support.
- With an experienced team, the time required to modernize to ADF from Forms is quicker than with other Java-based frameworks.
- ADF is based on Java, a technology already in use by the client's IT staff.

The recommendation for Oracle reports was to convert them to an open source reporting suite, known as Business Intelligence Reporting Tools (BIRT). This recommendation was made for the following reasons:

- The functionality of existing reports could be implemented easily.
- BIRT is easy to learn.
- It is easy to integrate BIRT with other Web technologies.
- The open source implementation of BIRT is free.

Analysis and Design

Vgo's ART product was used to collect metadata within the Forms application. ART is an application portfolio assessment product that extracts metadata from an existing application and provides deep insight into the structure, code, and components within. The metadata can then be mined directly in the ART repository, or through a variety of reports in the ART product itself. This data is then presented with existing business logic, providing an accurate association of the Oracle form flow from the user interface, all the way back to the database.

> **WARNING**
>
> Beware of the requirement "I want this application to be exactly like the old application."
> In projects where this is a dominant requirement, it typically signifies a "technology-driven
> modernization effort," which usually aims to "simply" move from one architecture to another.
> These projects are not generally looking to really advance and benefit business processing,
> but to essentially stay the same, albeit in a new environment. So, why is that bad? It's not
> necessarily "bad" to have this type of project, but the question comes up as to "why do it in the
> first place?" These projects, even in the best cases, are somewhat costly and time-consuming,
> respective to the complexity of the application. If you spend a significant amount of money to
> modernize, why end up with what you had when you started? This isn't a terrible situation, but
> it is something to watch for as your business clients will look for an "exact" look, feel, and
> performance of the original application.

Assessing Complexity

The first step in the Evolutions process was to use the ART complexity analysis to
determine the level of effort required to modernize the existing forms to ADF.
Figure 12.6 shows a sample of the complexity output from ART. From the report, the
score for each form is used to determine how many hours of effort are required in
a modernization project. The score itself is determined from an algorithm based on
the values of certain key aspects of the gathered metadata.

ART generates a series of reports, including the complexity analysis previously
mentioned, that are used during the analysis phase of the project in determining the
project plan and what needs to be covered in the architecture design for the application. Though it was determined before the project started that ADF would be the
framework of choice for the application, any existing functionality of the application
that may require special attention, or may need to change, can be determined from
ART output such as the Built-Ins report shown in Figure 12.7.

The Built-Ins report from ART indicates Oracle Forms built-in functionality that
is used to conduct operations requiring a "Web-world" equivalent in order to
preserve functionality. In most cases, these equivalents require design input, or

Form	Canvases	Blocks	Form Trigg	Control T	Procedures	Code	Score	Select	Update	Insert	Delete
TRACKING	5	12	14	35	20	1325	2367	42	8	22	4
ASSIGNMENT	2	13	3	39	9	1885	2173	49	0	6	0
LOG	3	7	6	27	15	1591	2073	45	1	11	1
LOGB	1	11	5	39	9	1561	1700	34	2	4	0
STATUS	2	7	6	41	16	1434	1673	34	4	3	0
FIELD_REPORT	3	10	3	60	11	1585	1662	26	0	2	8
FACTBOOK	3	6	3	27	13	1416	1559	34	1	2	0
IMPACT	5	7	8	64	17	1074	1509	21	0	13	4
MEMO	2	3	5	17	17	1023	1508	34	9	2	0
CHANGECONTROL	1	6	5	45	15	1192	1335	25	0	3	2

FIGURE 12.6

Sample ART Complexity Analysis

Vgo Software

Form Name	Procedure / Trigger	Module Name	Sub Call	Built-In
CONFIGURATION	WHEN-NEW-FORM-INSTANCE			SHOW_ALERT
CONFIGURATION	WHEN-BUTTON-PRESSED			WEB.SHOW_DOCUMENT
CONFIGURATION	WHEN-BUTTON-PRESSED			WEB.SHOW_DOCUMENT
COST	WHEN-NEW-FORM-INSTANCE			SHOW_ALERT
STATUS	WHEN-NEW-FORM-INSTANCE			SHOW_ALERT
STATUS	WHEN-BUTTON-PRESSED			WEB.SHOW_DOCUMENT
STATUS	WHEN-BUTTON-PRESSED			WEB.SHOW_DOCUMENT
CONTROL	WHEN-NEW-FORM-INSTANCE			SHOW_ALERT
CONTROL	KEY-PRINT			PRINT
PARAM1	WHEN-NEW-FORM-INSTANCE			SHOW_ALERT
PARAM1	WHEN-BUTTON-PRESSED			WEB.SHOW_DOCUMENT

FIGURE 12.7

ART Built-Ins Sample

choice, from an architect; simply automatically generating one alternative when three options are available is not a viable direction.

It was evident from the Built-Ins report that the only special functionality that Vgo needed to account for was the calling of Oracle reports, and the upload and download of certain types of files. The team consolidated these, and similar, design considerations for the client and recommended solutions appropriate to the end state.

Other ART reports provided input for the schedule and design as well. A Form-to-Form Dependency report was used to help construct "work units," which provided a basis for scheduling of the project. Work units are logical groupings of forms (or other legacy programs) that support a specific business process, such as inventory resupply which may contain 13 forms, for example. Each work unit can then be assigned to a developer, or group of developers, for modernization. Work units are then brought together to conduct integration testing later in the project.

A Code Re-Use report was used to determine where redundancies existed in the application across forms. In cases where these redundancies were in the program unit code, they were extracted and coded as part of a base object or utility class that could be shared by all the components that needed it. In comparison to a "convert everything in the form" approach, Vgo advocates proper application design through reuse of existing programmatic assets. This creates a very stable, highly maintainable and high-quality ADF application.

TIP

Whether using ART or not, consider investing the time to assess the utilization of Oracle Built-Ins in your Forms application prior to attempting to modernize. Taking a proactive approach to understanding the complexities in your application will dramatically decrease the risk of the project running late or missing functionality.

Mapping Forms to ADF with ART

ADF Design Specification (Figure 12.8) documents produced per form by ART provided guidelines and suggestions for Vgo's developers to follow as they

---

Evolution Form to ADF Detailed Design For Manufacturing Logistics

CHANGE_CONTROL

ADF Model Layer for CHANGE_CONTROL

The first step is to create the model layer for the CHANGE_CONTROL form. You will need to create ADF Business component objects for all of the blocks based on the database (all non-control blocks). The components you will need to create are all listed in the following tables.

Entity Objects for CHANGE_CONTROL		
Package:	com.raytheon.lms.model.entities	
Entity Name	DB Object	DB Type
Master	MASTER	
Part	PART	Table
Id	ID	Table

To do that, right click on the Model project in JDeveloper and choose Create ADF Business Components from Tables. Make sure that the schema is set to the correct schema and move each db object listed in the above table from "Available" to "Selected".

On the next screen create Updateable View Objects for each of the entities. The following table show which Updateable Views need to be created, but you will not necessarily be able to create all of them at this point. At this point just make sure that you create at least one Updateable View per Entity Object created. You may need to change some of names if there was not a Block with a name matching the database object name for each. If there are any other Updateable Views to be created which will happen if more than one block was based on the same database object, you will create them later.

Updateable View Objects for CHANGE_CONTROL						
Package:		com.raytheon.lms.model.changecontrol.views				
View Name	Entity Name	Update	Insert	Where Clause		Order By
PartView	Part	true	false			
	Attribute	Label	Control	Update	Column	Type	Length	Mandatory
	DATE_ORIGIN	Date Orig	Text Item	true	DATE_ORIGIN	n/a	n/a	false
	DOC_ID		Text Item	true	DOC_ID	n/a	n/a	n/a
	DATE_REVIEW	Date	Text Item	true	DATE_REVIEW	n/a	n/a	false
	SIGN_RVW	Logistics	Text Item	true	SIGN_RVW	n/a	n/a	false
	ORIGIN	Originator	Text Item	true	ORIGIN	n/a	n/a	false
	PB_SEARCH		Push Button	true	n/a	n/a	n/a	n/a
	SIGN_PE_RVW	PROD ENGR	Text Item	true	n/a	n/a	n/a	false
	DATE_PE_APPROV	Date	Text	true	n/a	n/a	n/a	false

FIGURE 12.8

ART ADF Design Document

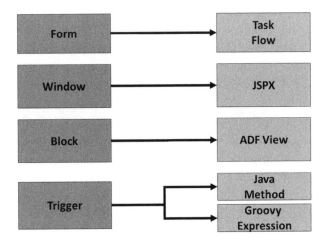

FIGURE 12.9

Forms-to-ADF Mappings

worked their way through the evolutionary process of converting to the modernized application. The documents outlined the ADF entities, views, view links, and LOVs that needed to be created for the Model layer for each particular form. These documents were used as the basis of development for each form.

Figure 12.9 shows a sampling of some of the common mappings used when converting an Oracle form to ADF 11g. These are not concrete rules, but rather guidelines to be followed and a good starting point when conducting a Forms modernization project.

In addition to describing the ADF Business Component layer, the ADF Design Specification documents outline all the PL/SQL logic that was accounted for in the modernized application. As the ADF framework is entirely different from Forms, many of the PL/SQL functions either need not be converted, or are converted not into coded routines, but outlined by properties of the Model layer itself. For example, audit fields were automatically populated by the ADF BC layer by simply specifying them as such in the Entity object. Using the instructions provided by the ART ADF Design Specification, developers can use JDeveloper to quickly create the Model layer and then fill in the business logic as necessary.

Project Results

The complete project took about four months to modernize the 137 forms to ADF 11g and reports to BIRT with a team of four resources (two developers, one project manager, and one analyst). The client added a six-week user acceptance test (UAT) cycle and then conducted a global rollout to production. Keep in mind that business rules were repurposed and redeployed in optimized business processes through the reengineering effort. So a degree of "new development" was conducted in this time period as well. Using the Evo product, the Vgo team was able to apply the existing logic in the new, reengineered business processes. During the UAT period, the team supported the customer in resolving any outstanding issues with the application, as well as preparing the application and infrastructure (Oracle WebLogic 10.3.2 deployment and tuning). The application will support approximately 100 users, both internal and external customers.

Having made this move to ADF, Vgo and the client are partnering on innovative ideas to maximize efficiency and effectiveness in the application. One example is the creation of a dynamic home page that, based on the user's role, would show metrics in the system such as how much work has been completed for the period and how much is outstanding. Using ADF's data visualization components, the system is able to provide user-friendly insight into this data. ADF's rich set of components and flexible development environment now make these types of enhancements a reality to the client.

Lastly, Vgo Software trained the client's IT staff on ADF development using JDeveloper. To date, Vgo Software has trained about 12 of the client's staff members during three training sessions that ranged from beginning ADF to working specifically with the code that was written for their application.

ADF IN THE CLOUD

"ADF in the Cloud" really means "Oracle WebLogic in the Cloud," since very little in the way of adjustment is required to get an ADF application functional in a cloud environment. Run the ADF application on a virtual machine (VM) provided with cloud services and you've brought your ADF application to the cloud.

Amazon and Oracle Cloud Templates

Deploying ADF in a cloud environment is most feasible when a cloud service provider such as Amazon, Terremark, or Savvis makes available the templates already created by Oracle for that purpose. These templates provide preinstalled applications such as Oracle WebLogic, Oracle Enterprise Linux, and Oracle JRockit.

TIP

The most straightforward template to use can be downloaded from https://edelivery. oracle.com/oraclevm if you are using your own Oracle Virtual Server instance. When creating an Amazon instance, follow the instructions at www.oracle.com/technetwork/ middleware/weblogic/wlsovm-ref-133104.pdf. This document also contains instructions for configuring and starting Oracle WebLogic.

Templates should provide a Linux environment with the following software:

- Oracle WebLogic Server 10.3.0.0
- JRockit JDK 6.0 R27.6
- Oracle Enterprise Linux 5.2, JeOS-1.0.1-6, a secure, headless (command-line control instead of UI-managed operating system) and minimized version of the Oracle Enterprise Linux OS

It is important to note that a headless Linux operating system requires that command-line utilities be used instead of the more familiar GUIs. A jumpstart utility in the template is automatically invoked after the first login. Details about the configuration of the VM are included in the referenced PDF document at www.oracle.com/technetwork/middleware/weblogic/wlsovm-ref-133104.pdf. The jumpstart tool will help configure the Oracle WebLogic server.

WARNING

The most difficult part of working with Oracle WebLogic 10.3 on Amazon's cloud is the ability to work with the instance from within JDeveloper.

When a developer tries to deploy to an external IP address, such as ec2-18?-??-???-???.compute-1.amazonaws.com (the question marks would have your specific IP address numbers), the internal IP address is different, such as 10.???.??.???, and the subsequent deployment is rejected.

The fix for this problem is as follows (at least on Amazon EC2):

1. Start the Oracle WebLogic console (with an edit session).
2. Go to **[Your domain name]** | **Environment** | **Servers** and select your SOA deployment server.
3. On the **Configuration** | **General** tab select the **Advanced** section at the bottom of the page.
4. Enter your AMI IP (e.g., **ec2-18?-??-???-???.compute-1.amazonaws.com**) in the **External Listen Address** field.
5. Restart your server(s).

All in all, deploying the template and configuration should take well under an hour. If you wish to install and configure your own Oracle VM locally, start here:

- http://blogs.oracle.com/alison/2008/04/installing_oracle_vm.html

---

NOTE

Deploying ADF applications in the cloud is relatively straightforward given that Oracle provides a lot of information to configure the environment. Take the time to try out different configurations using the templates and you will find success based upon your organization's cloud strategy.

SUMMARY

Oracle Forms customers have historically been somewhat constrained in their options for modernization: either upgrade to the newest Forms release, or rewrite the application from scratch using a newer technology. With the release of Oracle ADF v11g and JDeveloper, Oracle Forms users have a very viable path to get to a scalable, flexible, and enterprise-ready application architecture.

ADF 11g provides a feature-rich development framework made usable by the Developer development environment. Among these features, the ability to encapsulate and work with business rules and interact with the data model with application modules, a refined transaction architecture using task flows, and comprehensive wizards provide a sound alternative to the components and mechanics of Forms. These features were missing in earlier releases of ADF.

So, how do you get to ADF 11g from Forms? The answer is that there is a good hybrid approach between writing from scratch and properly reusing the business rules inherent in the legacy Forms application. Remember that even though the technology has become dated, in many cases the business logic and processing rules are still very valid. With new ADF features, and operating capabilities inherent in Web, SOA-based cloud architectures, business processing optimization opportunities are also present; be open to adapting to these new architectures to best position your business to succeed.

We also presented a case study where the key takeaways are that conversion from Forms to ADF:

- Is achievable in a reasonable amount of time
- Is a reliable, scalable alternative to other technologies
- Is a viable career/training path for existing Forms developers
- Can achieve better business results than staying on your legacy Forms environment
- Can be done in a manner that retains the positive aspects (business rules) of a legacy application while providing an opportunity to optimize processes

Lastly, we discussed how you would be able to deploy an ADF application to the cloud. Oracle makes this straightforward as well by providing you workable templates and excellent development virtualization and Linux environments in which to experiment.

So, in this chapter, you've learned that ADF is the best modification route for your Forms application, that the actual modernization to ADF from Forms can be very successful, and that the application can then be deployed in the cloud.

Application Migration: PowerBuilder to Oracle APEX

INFORMATION IN THIS CHAPTER:

- Oracle Application Express Overview
- Why Migrate PowerBuilder to APEX?
- Background on Carter's, Inc.
- The OMNIA Sales Order Management Pilot Project
- Legacy System Characteristics and Technical Architecture
- Legacy System Challenges
- Carter's Priorities
- Migration Options Considered
- Pilot Project Results
- The OMNIA2 Project
- The New OMNIA2 Architecture
- APEX in the Cloud

This chapter comprises a case study that describes how baby and children's clothing company Carter's, Inc., modernized a large-scale, mission-critical client/server business application to Oracle Application Express (APEX). The chapter reviews the legacy system architecture, the new technology stack and architecture that was utilized, and the approach the company took in the modernization effort. Oracle APEX, the new core of the target Oracle technology stack, is covered in detail. Oracle APEX is a free technology from Oracle that is embedded in the Oracle database and is built for cloud computing.

The modernization and rearchitecture efforts were led by JSA^2 Solutions LLC, an Oracle partner. JSA^2 has considerable expertise in business application design and delivery, as well as the Oracle technology stack. The JSA^2 team includes people with experience in large-scale system development, and all have worked previously at major software vendors and consulting firms.

ORACLE APPLICATION EXPRESS OVERVIEW

Oracle Application Express (APEX), a feature of Oracle Database 11g, combines rapid Web application development with the Oracle database. APEX is a browser-based

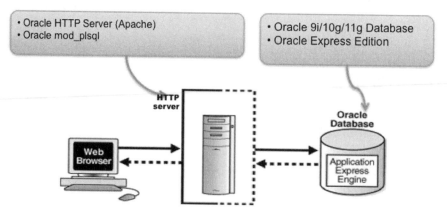

FIGURE 13.1

Oracle APEX Architecture Components Using Apache HTTP Server

application builder that allows both developers and nonprogrammers to develop and deploy data-driven Web applications. Most of the development can be done using drag-and-drop wizards, but it can be extended using JavaScript, PL/SQL, SQL, HTML, and Web services. All the application "code" is stored in a metadata repository in the Oracle database. Figure 13.1 depicts both the typical development and runtime architecture of Oracle APEX.

Figure 13.1 shows the Web browser that is used to develop, deploy, and run APEX applications. The free Apache-based Oracle HTTP Server can be used to handle APEX client requests. The Oracle WebLogic Application Server could also be used to handle APEX application communication. The Oracle HTTP Server contains a `mod_plsql` plug-in to communicate with the Oracle Database Application Express Engine to pass Oracle APEX requests from the HTTP Server to the Application Express Engine in the Oracle database. The Application Express Engine can run in Oracle Enterprise Edition or Oracle Express Edition for testing and development. The Oracle XML DB HTTP Server with the embedded PL/SQL gateway can be used instead of the Oracle HTTP Server. This setup is easier to configure, requires no separate HTTP server to install or manage, and includes all the components in the database. However, most customers would not allow this configuration in production, as users, and potentially hackers, would have direct HTTP access to the Oracle database. Allowing direct HTTP access to the Oracle database would cause the IT department to fail most internal or external company security compliance audits.

WHY MIGRATE POWERBUILDER TO APEX?

One of the best uses of APEX within an organization is to bring in all the disparate, older Microsoft Excel or Access applications that tend to run wild across many companies. Organizations have hundreds or thousands of applications deployed across their enterprise that are written in Access, Oracle Forms, Microsoft Visual Basic, and PowerBuilder. These technologies are very hard to manage and scale as organizations grow or more people use them. Further, regulatory and internal audit compliance can be very difficult to apply to a set of applications developed in disparate technologies and distributed across multiple locations and users. The emergence of regulations such as the Sarbanes-Oxley Act of 2002 (SOX) and the Health Insurance Portability and Accountability Act of 1996 (HIPAA), as well as increased investor scrutiny on audits and controls, means even more serious implications for poorly managed departmental applications.

APEX is a centralized application hosting environment, so it would make sense that companies looking to consolidate departmental applications would turn to it. APEX scales incredibly well and can easily handle applications of varying complexity: from small departmental needs to large-scale enterprise systems supporting thousands of users. It takes advantage of the well-known features of the Oracle database, including backup and recovery, security, auditing, scalability, and a wide variety of deployment platforms. Since it is completely browser-based, there are no client-side deployment prerequisites or dependencies. APEX can be accessed using any Web browser, including mobile devices such as the Apple iPhone and iPad.

WARNING

Running Oracle APEX in a public cloud or private cloud that has the potential of thousands of current users hitting the Oracle database-based Oracle APEX installation will require an Oracle database built for scalability and performance. Oracle Real Application Clusters (RAC) and other Oracle database scalability features and options such as partitioning and Multi-Threaded Server (MTS) should be considered.

BACKGROUND ON CARTER'S, INC.

With nearly $2 billion in annual sales, Carter's, Inc., is the largest branded marketer of apparel exclusively for babies and young children in the United States. It owns two of the most highly recognized and trusted brands in the children's apparel industry: Carter's and OshKosh. Established in 1865, the Carter's brand is recognized and trusted by consumers for high-quality apparel for children from newborns to size 7. In 2005, Carter's acquired OshKosh B'Gosh, Inc. Established in 1895, OshKosh is recognized as a well-known brand that is trusted by consumers for its line of apparel for children from newborns to size 12. When large, well-established companies such as Carter's and OshKosh merge as the result of an acquisition, many migration projects often occur as overlapping technology solutions are combined.

THE OMNIA SALES ORDER MANAGEMENT PILOT PROJECT

The OMNIA application is a comprehensive sales order management application which was developed in conjunction with Fruit of the Loom and has since been installed at several large organizations, including Stride Rite and Genesco, along with a number of other, smaller organizations. Carter's purchased the OMNIA application in 1998; the Carter's system implementation was completed and went live in 1999. All of Carter's sales orders are processed through this application. OMNIA includes the following capabilities:

- Optimized for high-volume transaction loads. Given the nature of the apparel industry, several distinguishing factors require optimized performance. One factor includes seasonality: spring, fall, "back to school," and Christmas are times when large volumes of sales orders are placed. Another factor is data density and complexity: A single order line may include a number of different colors and sizes (stock keeping units or SKUs). For example, a baby sleeper ordered in 3-, 6-, 9-, 12-, and 18-month sizes means that a sales order with 10 lines would actually include 40 SKUs. The vast majority of system operations are performed at the SKU level, including inventory allocation, pricing, and fulfillment.
- An advanced optimizing inventory allocations engine that handles finished goods, work in process, and in-transit inventory.
- Inventory management and accounting functionality supporting any number of warehouse, distribution center, and third-party logistics providers.
- A comprehensive pick release processing function that conveys the necessary fulfillment information to the warehouses, distribution centers, and third-party logistics providers. This includes detailed order information, special instructions, and packing requirements.
- Shipment interfaces which capture all the details of the fulfilled orders, and are used to generate necessary vendor-compliance-related documents including advanced ship notices (ASNs).
- An advanced invoicing module that supports standard and consolidated invoices (typically required by very large customers). Invoices can be routed electronically through the EDI810 standard, or they can be printed.
- Financial interfaces to send and receive data to supporting applications including accounts receivable and general ledgers.

Initially, Carter's utilized the OMNIA application in its standard (base) form and only custom-coded it to support interfaces or extension points. Ultimately, as business needs changed and the IT staff became more comfortable with the architecture, technologies, and conventions, Carter's modified and enhanced the system. This practice became formal once the core OMNIA application was acquired by Geac Enterprise Solutions, which subsequently retired the application.

In addition to taking on ongoing modifications and enhancements to OMNIA, the Carter's IT team leveraged the OMNIA database and application in several other typical areas. These included:

- **Reporting and analytics**   Carter's utilizes Business Objects from SAP as its standardized reporting tool. Over the years, hundreds of reports have been created that leverage transactional and historical information from the OMNIA database.
- **Integration**   Carter's utilizes Informatica for data integration, extract-transform-load (ETL), and integration. Dozens of maps and processes integrate OMNIA to various other enterprise applications at Carter's.
- **Data warehouse**   Carter's utilizes Netezza as its data warehouse infrastructure. Every aspect of sales, inventory, customers, shipments, and various other facts is fed into the data warehouse daily.

LEGACY SYSTEM CHARACTERISTICS AND TECHNICAL ARCHITECTURE

One of the challenges of maintaining and developing OMNIA over the years concerns keeping all the supporting technologies current and integrated. There has been considerable effort and, at times, difficulty in making all the layers in the technology stack work together during system upgrades. The application uses PowerBuilder, COBOL, IBM MQSeries, Informatica, and Business Objects on the software side. The hardware and operating system (OS) consist of IBM RS/6000 and IBM AIX. Legacy systems don't need to be mainframe-based to exhibit the characteristics of a legacy system, including multiple application languages, operating systems, hardware platforms, and integration solutions.

Legacy System Characteristics

The OMNIA legacy application supports all aspects of sales order processing. The multiple-terabyte database consists of more than 800 tables. Transactional data is archived and purged regularly for optimum performance and storage requirements. Several hundred users across several primary geographical locations in Georgia, Wisconsin, Connecticut, California, and New York have varying degrees of access to the system depending on their role and responsibilities in the organization.

The primary user interface of the legacy OMNIA application consisted of two Microsoft Windows 32-bit (XP, Vista, and Windows 7) applications in a client/server architecture. The first of these two Windows-based applications, OMNIA Order Management, was used by the vast majority of business and casual system users. This application consisted of the core transactional and inquiry type functions of the system. The second application, OMNIA Administration, was used by a much smaller number of users who managed configuration options and business rules that controlled the operation of key functions in the application.

The vast majority of business processing and logic resided in several hundred programs running on a large UNIX server. The client and external interfaces interacted with this business logic through message-oriented middleware (MOM). The OMNIA business processing continued on a full 24/7 operating schedule and had high availability (HA) requirements given the criticality of the system.

Legacy Technical Architecture

The overall architecture of the base OMNIA legacy system is that of a hybrid client/server. In a classic client/server architecture, you would see application code and logic running on the client with the database running on the server. The server might also include some supporting logic in the form of database stored procedures, functions, or packages.

The OMNIA legacy architecture provides more core system functionality on the server tier than is typical of a client/server architecture, for performance, scalability, and modularity reasons. Although there was some degree of duplication between the client and server tiers, most compute and I/O-intensive logic resided on the server in application programs and was invoked via messaging requests from the clients, as depicted in Figure 13.2.

The following technologies were utilized in the OMNIA legacy system:

- **User interface** The two Windows 32-bit executables were developed using Sybase PowerBuilder. This included dozens of application PowerBuilder libraries (PBLs) and hundreds of objects to support approximately 250 individual screens and menu choices.
- **Server logic** The application server logic was developed using Micro Focus COBOL. This included several hundred COBOL programs and even more COBOL copybooks. COBOL copybooks contain the file record definitions or common COBOL functionality leveraged across multiple COBOL programs. The COBOL programs utilize complex business rules defined in the database to drive all application logic. Further, the COBOL programs have been optimized extensively to yield a very high rate of transactional performance. These programs varied from service providers to small transactional units of work (e.g., allocate a single order) to large batch-type processes that ran on a schedule (optimize allocations across the entire order pool).
- **MOM** IBM MQSeries (also known as IBM WebSphere MQ) was utilized for several purposes: first, to invoke server-side logic from the client asynchronously for maximum UI performance and responsiveness, and second, to minimize duplication of code across the client and server tiers. In the base application package configuration, some degree of inbound and outbound interfacing and ETL was also done via messages, although this proved to have scalability problems for complex transactions. Because the base OMNIA system was designed and delivered before the creation of XML, messages consisted of fixed-length record formats delivered across queues specifically designed to receive a business transaction request. Examples of these requests include allocate order, credit

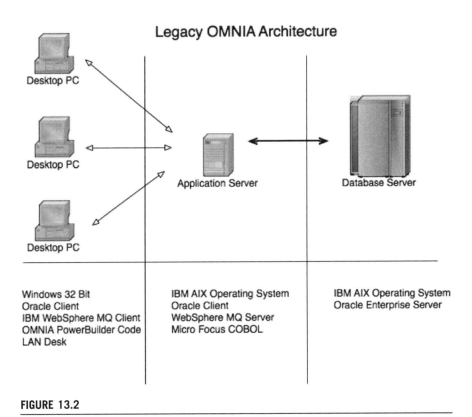

Legacy OMNIA Architecture

Windows 32 Bit Oracle Client IBM WebSphere MQ Client OMNIA PowerBuilder Code LAN Desk	IBM AIX Operating System Oracle Client WebSphere MQ Server Micro Focus COBOL	IBM AIX Operating System Oracle Enterprise Server

FIGURE 13.2

Legacy PowerBuilder Architecture

check order, cancel order, pick release order, receive inventory, ship inventory, and other business processes. These messages were categorized as "triggering" requests and performed very well in contrast to the previously mentioned ETL type of requests.

- **Server host system**   The database, server logic (COBOL), and MOM tiers (IBM MQSeries) were all collocated on a large IBM pSeries (RS/6000) machine running the AIX operating system.
- **Database**   The database tier utilized Oracle Database 10g Enterprise Edition that consisted of more than 800 tables in the application schema. A secondary, smaller schema of approximately 50 tables contained application and security infrastructure code (menu definitions, users, groups, and authorities).

LEGACY SYSTEM CHALLENGES

Carter's growth in sales revenues meant that data transaction volumes were also growing at a very high rate. As new customers were acquired and market conditions changed, new functionality was required for either service, competitive, or compliance reasons. This all translated into changes to the system. Further, as Carter's grew, so did the OMNIA system user base. This presented several challenges to Carter's, the largest of which were the following:

- **Client performance** Increased transaction volume and system users meant more load. The client tier, given the volume of data being transmitted between the client and server, began to experience response delays in some geographic areas. The response delays worsened as additional remote locations with limited network bandwidth were introduced. Carter's did try, with some success, to utilize Citrix to mitigate these concerns. Ultimately, this was viewed as a stopgap measure since the business users really wanted completely new views of the OMNIA data and enhanced functionality, not just a rehosted UI.
- **Server performance** Just as the client tier suffered from performance issues, some of the large server-side processes struggled under the increased load. Progressively larger, more powerful hardware was continually installed and the software was continually monitored and enhanced to perform acceptably at peak times.
- **Client software distribution** The client software distribution comes in two forms: system prerequisites and application code. System prerequisites included installing an Oracle and MQSeries client on each PC running the OMNIA application (hundreds of PCs). The PowerBuilder code consisted of an initial InstallShield-based installation for the two Windows applications and their supporting PBDs. InstallShield is a product used by software developers to package software so that IT personnel or users can install client/server software easily and safely on PCs; it can also be used to uninstall a software product. PBDs are PowerBuilder libraries analogous to Windows dynamic link libraries (DLLs). For code updates, changed PBDs had to be distributed to each PC. As a result, Carter's had to invest in a software distribution system in an effort to keep hundreds of PCs up-to-date with the latest code. This was not always successful, which caused applications to work improperly. Note that InstallShield provides the developer with templates and prebuilt interface objects that make it easy to package the software. Users who receive software packaged with InstallShield are assured that it will be installed quickly and without affecting other applications or system characteristics.
- **IT skills** The Carter's in-house technical team had several members with solid COBOL experience. Only one full-time Carter's employee had any PowerBuilder experience. A few had basic IBM MQSeries skills. Most of the Carter's developers were comfortable with basic SQL queries and Data Manipulation Language (DML) functions in Oracle. A mix of adequate skills and limited skills in other areas combined to mean longer development times for modifications and enhancements to the system.
- **Upgrades/staying current** Obviously, a production application as critical as OMNIA needed to be in a valid support state for all its technical components.

Vendors introduce security fixes, performance fixes, and bug fixes, and they retire versions as new versions are released. Given the number of different vendor components in the OMNIA technology stack, this proved challenging and expensive over time. On the client side, Windows, PowerBuilder, Oracle client, and IBM MQSeries client code needed to be kept up-to-date. On the server side, IBM AIX, IBM MQSeries, Oracle Database, and Micro Focus COBOL needed to be kept up-to-date and interoperable. Over the years, several large projects involved technology upgrades across the OMNIA technology stack. Each one took from three to six months and required extensive involvement from the Carter's IT and business communities along with considerable resources to set up parallel testing environments.

CARTER'S PRIORITIES

While the business community was generally happy with the capabilities of the system, Carter's did have a lengthy "wish list" of new functionality it desired. A concern was how responsive IT could be in delivering new functionality given the complexity of the legacy architecture and their ongoing production system support responsibilities. Further, at peak times there were processing delays that impacted operations to a limited extent.

An incredible amount of valuable information is contained in the OMNIA application database; however, much of it was only being presented on hard-copy reports or spreadsheets. It was clear that there was a deficiency in parts of the legacy OMNIA system when it came to presenting this information to the user.

The business wanted better information available to users as they worked to improve customer service levels. The IT team wanted fewer moving parts to manage and the ability to have more depth in terms of development and support resources.

MIGRATION OPTIONS CONSIDERED

The Carter's team considered a number of options, including finding a viable packaged software replacement (commercial off-the-shelf or COTS solution) for OMNIA. They evaluated available solutions in the market and weighed features/functions, technologies, and cost. They also considered rewriting large portions of the critical functionality in-house using newer technologies such as .NET or Java EE (J2EE). JSA[2] proposed a hybrid approach that would modernize OMNIA and reduce the complexity of the supporting software stack. Rather than a complete rip-and-replace project, which would have resulted in much more time, money, and risk, the team chose to modernize using a rearchitecture approach and automated tools, which provided benefits much more quickly. JSA[2] delivered the new software iteratively, usually every six to eight weeks, which allowed the business to benefit from the project almost immediately.

The packaged software options either lacked essential functionality or were cost-prohibitive. The time and effort to ramp up the in-house IT team on .NET or J2EE (even to a basic level of proficiency) seemed daunting, especially considering how these people would still have production support responsibilities. Ultimately, the team decided to conduct a pilot modernization project led by JSA[2].

As a long-term partner to Carter's, JSA[2] had a unique understanding of the company's business needs, IT skills and strengths, and culture. While JSA[2] has team members who have experience with many development languages including J2EE, JSA[2] ultimately recommended Oracle APEX. Oracle APEX is relatively easy to install and configure and is an incredibly productive environment for developers with solid Oracle SQL and PL/SQL development skills. JSA[2] felt that APEX would allow the developers to focus on business functionality and provide quick access to all the valuable information already contained within the OMNIA database. Oracle APEX was also a zero-cost solution: free with the Oracle Database.

The project team asked the user community to select an area for the JSA[2] team to focus on for the pilot project. The user community selected the Style Administration application. This application provides support for the definition, maintenance, and reporting of styles (items/products) in the system. The objective of the pilot was to migrate this part of the legacy OMNIA system into Oracle APEX.

In order to get up and running quickly and not impact any of the existing Carter's systems, all pilot development was conducted in the cloud using Amazon Web Services (AWS). JSA[2] quickly configured an instance using one of the prebuilt Oracle 11g Amazon Machine Images (AMIs) that had Oracle APEX installed. The base AMI configuration was altered so that the Oracle Database data files were located on separate Amazon Simple Server Storage (S3) and therefore could be remounted to another Oracle Database instance should the need arise. The project team then ported data from the Carter's environment to the AWS environment in order to begin development. The project team was ready to begin development work in just a few hours.

The use of the AWS cloud environment demonstrates the power of using the Oracle database and APEX in the cloud. Both the database and the development environment can be up and running in a matter of hours. Typically, standing up a pilot hardware and software project can take weeks or even months. In addition, a large monetary investment needs to be made for hardware and software that will only exist for the life of the pilot project.

As the four-week pilot progressed, the project team worked iteratively with the business users. Rather than a simple "as is" migration, however, the team worked directly with the business users to see how they interacted with the system and identified deficiencies in OMNIA usability. These deficiencies were typically obvious by observing either a lot of tedious work or the need to go to another tool for information (report, spreadsheet, another entry screen). The approach was iterative as the project team frequently showed the users the new UI and solicited user feedback. Oracle APEX made the iterative process easy as it provides the ability for rapid prototyping and Agile development. Often, the project team would make minor changes while sitting with the users and get their feedback immediately.

In addition to UI functionality, Carter's wanted to migrate one legacy Power-Builder function to an Oracle Database PL/SQL stored procedure package. At Carter's, each year for every new season (e.g., fall 2011), new styles are created in a separate Product Data Management (PDM) system and then interfaced into the OMNIA style master. Customer service would then have to configure the style so that it could be sold as a separate product within the system: add it to a catalog, define pricing rules, designate exactly which sizes are available for sale, define units of measure, and so on. This was a manually intensive task that took two people up to a week each season. The pilot team sat with the business users and captured all the requirements, and coded a new rules-driven PDM interface as an Oracle PL/SQL package. The result was that the entire season of new styles was imported in less than five minutes, with no manual work required by the business team. The new PL/SQL package was developed by a senior JSA[2] developer over the course of a few days using Oracle SQL Developer.

TIP

The PL/SQL package and Oracle APEX development processes were so quick during this project because of the decades of experience within JSA[2] regarding PL/SQL and APEX. As with any migration project, engaging resources that have experience with migrations and with the target technologies will expedite the migration process. Even if you are not inclined to turn the entire project over to a third party such as JSA[2], you should strongly consider at least supplementing your staff with a service provider skilled in migrations to the cloud and Oracle.

PILOT PROJECT RESULTS

The pilot deliverables were presented to the Carter's team and their feedback was universally positive. The accomplishments of the pilot were:

- Development of a fully functional style administration module.
- Improvements in application usability, speed, and responsiveness.
- Inclusion of the business team in the review and design process, which gave the user community a sense of ownership in the newly developed application.
- Demonstration of the potential and value of modernizing the UI.
- Validation of Oracle APEX as a capable development tool that supports rapid, iterative development.
- Demonstration of the advantages of a Web-based solution by removing three items from the technology stack (PowerBuilder, MQSeries, and COBOL), eliminating software distribution requirements, and reducing interoffice communication infrastructure requirements.
- Demonstration of how complex legacy COBOL functions could be ported to PL/SQL packages.

- Development of a "Style Flash" inquiry in APEX that consolidated all information about a given style—inventory, configuration, pricing, work in process, images, and so on—onto one screen. This was received very enthusiastically by the business users and took an experienced APEX JSA[2] developer less than a week to complete.

A short time after the pilot project was completed Carter's management approved a project to modernize the OMNIA application. The CIO also recommended that APEX be the development tool of choice for other in-house projects. The new modernization project was to be known as OMNIA2.

THE OMNIA2 PROJECT

Following the pilot project, extensive meetings were held with the business team. Each area of the legacy system was identified and scoped. JSA[2] solicited input on desired functional and usability improvements. The JSA[2] team shadowed many of the business users to gain firsthand knowledge of how the legacy system was being used, and recorded use cases. The project team also identified areas where the workflow of the legacy system failed to add value and added cost to the business. These breakdowns in workflow efficiency were easy to identify as the user needed to refer to an external report, spreadsheet, or other system.

With the classification of the system functionality complete and the use cases captured, the project team consulted the business team regarding the priority of the modernization work. This was a collaborative effort that was based on the following key business drivers:

- Improved customer service
- ROI
- Cost reduction or containment
- Consolidation of rarely used functions (this driver provides the most significant ROI for the money invested)
- Compression of the technology stack (reducing the number of software vendor products)

Ultimately, Carter's and the project team had a prioritized list to work from functionally, and it was time to assemble the project implementation team. Carter's felt strongly that it wanted the team to comprise its IT people and JSA[2] resources. JSA[2] would provide overall architectural design and review, education and mentoring, and development resources. The Carter's IT team would ramp up on Oracle APEX, Oracle PL/SQL, and Web technologies. JSA[2] utilized the Feature Driven Development (FDD) approach to map out features for developers to work on.

FDD is an iterative and incremental software development process. It is one of a number of Agile methods for developing software and forms part of the Agile Alliance. FDD blends a number of industry-recognized best practices into a cohesive whole. These practices are all driven from a client-valued functionality (feature) perspective. Its main purpose is to deliver tangible, working software repeatedly and in a timely manner.

An initial week of education was conducted by the JSA^2 team for the Carter's team members. This included both APEX and PL/SQL subject areas. Also, regularly scheduled tech sessions were conducted by the JSA^2 team to continue to reinforce and introduce new concepts. JSA^2 led biweekly team calls to review issues, questions, and concerns regarding developer assignments.

Design Objectives

A set of design objectives, some business-related and some technical, were identified as part of the OMNIA2 project. Here are some of those objectives:

- **Protect Carter's investment and mitigate risk**   Carter's had invested heavily in getting the OMNIA legacy system to perform. Although 100 percent of the UI would be rewritten, many years of developer time had been invested in the server-side logic. Unless there was a compelling reason to rewrite the COBOL code, the initial focus would be on getting 100 percent of the UI into APEX. The "mitigate risk" part of this is that Carter's is passing almost $2 billion of business through this system, so any error or disruption has huge consequences and visibility.
- **Port COBOL to PL/SQL where appropriate**   If a particular COBOL program had either functional or performance problems, it was a candidate for fast-tracking the rewrite into PL/SQL. Likewise, all new development would be done in PL/SQL. Gradually, the dependency on COBOL will diminish; however, it is accepted as a phased approach given the preceding objective.
- **Refactor the database where appropriate**   The legacy OMNIA database did not employ referential integrity (RI) constraints. When the pilot modernization project of the system was completed, RI constraints had been introduced. In some cases, this involved introducing surrogate keys; in other cases, existing natural key columns were utilized.
- **Consolidate the two OMNIA legacy PowerBuilder applications into one browser-based UI**   This simplifies the UI by creating a customized view based on user functional and authorized tasks. A future function is to integrate a tab into the browser to request and view Business Object reports.
- **Consolidate user identification and authorization**   Rather than use a separate proprietary database-driven repository for user identification and authorization, security will be integrated into the corporate Microsoft Active Directory server. User credentials will now be authorized against Active Directory, providing a centralized mechanism for group membership and status validation. Application functional authority will be controlled by an access control list (ACL)-based mechanism designed and developed by JSA^2.
- **Use base APEX functionality wherever possible**   Users coming from a fat client user interface would have to adjust to a browser-based environment.

Although there are places where advanced UI techniques leveraging jQuery and JavaScript could be used to provide a richer user interface, the project team will try to work within the APEX framework whenever possible.

- **Separate UI from business logic** A big objective of OMNIA2 is to separate user interface logic from core business logic. Wherever possible, standard validation, customer, style, and code value lookups are to be conducted using standardized OMNIA2 PL/SQL packages. If a UI has a high degree of complexity or uniqueness, a UI helper package is to be developed to push the complexity out of the UI. This allows smaller, more incremental updates and enhancements since just the affected package needs to be installed, instead of the entire APEX application having to be deployed or redeployed.

- **Eliminate IBM MQSeries for ETL and "nontriggering" patterns** This was an objective for the Carter's IT team, and it has been largely successful. IBM MQSeries is still in use as a triggering and asynchronous request mechanism, but ETL operations have been migrated to Informatica, or are performed using XML or simple interface/staging database tables that other systems read from and write to.

- **Perform iterative development and delivery** Rather than delivering OMNIA2 in a "big bang" approach, the team delivered it in several incremental releases: generally every four to six weeks. This allows the business to benefit from enhancements during the life of the project. Deployment rollout went from several days to a few minutes. This is due to the fact that client software distribution has been eliminated because OMNIA2 is completely browser-based. As quickly as the updated APEX application can be deployed, it is available to all system users. Even when rolling large pieces of new functionality into production (involving new or changed tables, PL/SQL packages, or other components) deployment time is usually less than 30 minutes.

- **Deliver Flash Reports** Flash Reports were created when it was identified that users had to go to multiple sources to get an overview of data. "Is there a problem with this style?" and "What's going on with this customer?" are questions that used to take a lot of time to answer. Several different inquiries, a report, and maybe a phone call were all part of the manual "query" approach. Now there is a consolidated view to give the user the ability to see the information and drill down where appropriate.

- **Provide actionable views** Actionable views provide a meaningful view of analytical information with the ability to take direct action. For example, the following query can now be answered: "Show me all the orders for a given style and allow me to allocate them, since I know inventory just arrived." Previously, users would print reports and then have to log in, find the right function to perform, search for the entity (order, customer, etc.), and then take the appropriate action. Now, all of this is integrated into an actionable view. An actionable view presents either analytical or exception information a user might see in a report or data warehouse inquiry, but allows the user to immediately take action to resolve the condition or exception.

THE NEW OMNIA2 ARCHITECTURE

The OMNIA2 architecture is dramatically simplified over the legacy architecture on both the client and server tiers, as shown in Figure 13.3. The application UI is now 100 percent browser-based, and MQSeries is being phased out of the application. All new server-side development is conducted in PL/SQL packages, and a significant portion of the legacy COBOL code has been rearchitected into PL/SQL packages. The balance of the COBOL code will be rewritten over time based on priorities set by the business. This approach has improved overall performance significantly while simplifying deployment and application management.

Here is a recap of the new architectural components of OMNIA2 depicted in Figure 13.3:

- **User interface** This consists of Oracle APEX 4.0, along with leveraging dynamic actions, jQuery (and supporting plug-ins), and on-demand processes, custom templates, and Cascading Style Sheets (CSS), to support complex user interfaces.

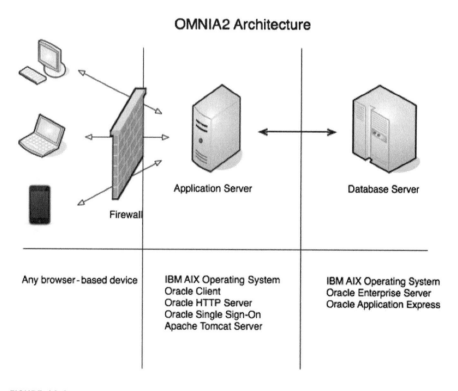

OMNIA2 Architecture

| Any browser-based device | IBM AIX Operating System
Oracle Client
Oracle HTTP Server
Oracle Single Sign-On
Apache Tomcat Server | IBM AIX Operating System
Oracle Enterprise Server
Oracle Application Express |

FIGURE 13.3

Oracle APEX OMNIA2 Architecture

- **Application server** JSA[2] developed a J2EE application that wraps legacy OMNIA COBOL programs and IBM MQSeries requests as Web services. These are consumed by the APEX user interface to mitigate risk and leverage Carter's investment in the OMNIA code base. It also provides an abstraction layer so that, as COBOL is rewritten into Oracle Database stored procedure packages, the migration is transparent to the consumer.
- **Security** Application security and auditing has been improved significantly. The initial delivery of OMNIA2 provided integration to the corporate Microsoft Active Directory server. A subsequent release provided integration to the Oracle Single Sign-On Identity server. Selected use of other Oracle technologies including Workspace Manager have provided enhanced auditing and compliance functionality. The result is a much more secure application that provides instant answers to auditor questions.
- **Database** Oracle 10g R2 — Because the source database contained no referential integrity contraints, a significant amount of rework and refactoring of the 800+ legacy tables was completed to introduce referential integrity constraints. More than 100 OMNIA2-specific Oracle Database packages were developed that encapsulate business logic as well as UI helper packages that help segregate presentation and business logic. JSA[2] has also delivered Java within the Oracle database to perform specialized tasks.

NOTE

Here are some guidelines for reworking legacy databases to an Oracle database:

- Developers should take maximum advantage of the Oracle database to enforce data and referential integrity. It has been said that applications come and go, but data lives forever. Applications are extended, rewritten, interfaced to, and used in ways never anticipated by the original developers. Using programmatic data integrity checks results in more code, is inefficient, and is risky. The database server can perform this checking faster and more consistently than handwritten code, and you are assured that data validation checks will always be done no matter what application is accessing the database. Defining these rules in the database leads to a self-documenting data model that shows interdependencies and relationships.
- As a general rule, tables should usually be defined with a surrogate key column (a named ID) that is a number data type and is populated from an Oracle sequence. Natural keys can be utilized provided they are immutable (they don't change after they are created) and compact (they are short in length). Natural keys consisting of several columns are generally less efficient than a single-column surrogate; think about joining multicolumn foreign keys in a where clause versus a single-column surrogate key join. Finally, surrogate key values should have no embedded values or implied meanings. Rather, surrogate keys should simply be unique numbers assigned from an Oracle sequence that may include gaps due to caching. Business logic should never be built based on the value of a surrogate key.
- All tables and table columns must be defined with comments. Comments are easily added via development tools such as Quest Toad and Oracle SQL Developer. They can also be added via COMMENT ON TABLE and COMMENT ON COLUMN statements.
- It may seem obvious, but all table columns should be defined using the correct data type. This means you should put numeric values in NUMBER, date values in DATE, and character strings in VARCHAR2 columns. Using the closest data type to the attribute you are modeling

> in the column improves data integrity and performance. Also, use the closest size appropriate for the requirement; don't define a column as VARCHAR2(4000) if you will never store more than 30 characters. Using the correct data type improves data integrity because you can utilize check constraints, as well as improve performance. For example, store a date in a date column as opposed to storing it in a VARCHAR2. Performance is improved because there are fewer type conversions and manipulations to work with the data in application code.

PL/SQL Emphasis When Using Oracle APEX

PL/SQL is a Third Generation Language (3GL) programming language that is part of the Oracle database. It is the most efficient language for data manipulation as it leverages tight coupling with the Oracle database. PL/SQL uses the same data types as the database and there is no conversion of rows and columns into ancillary constructs like copybooks or include files. The developer is protected from most changes in the database, such as a new column, and there are tremendous productivity benefits. A significant part of the Oracle E-Business Suite 11i, a major enterprise resource planning (ERP) application, is built using PL/SQL.

PL/SQL is a highly portable language and can run, unchanged, on any platform on which the Oracle database runs. PL/SQL can be invoked from COBOL, PowerBuilder, Java, .NET, and Informatica. Bind variables allow statements to be parsed once and executed. PL/SQL has full dependency management that leads to a self-documenting system if the developer designs it correctly. Given Carter's investment in Oracle skills and its IT depth of experience using the Oracle database, using PL/SQL was a natural fit.

TIP

In making the transition to PL/SQL programming, developers must work hard not to carry forward patterns and constructs from other programming languages. PL/SQL is a powerful language for manipulating Oracle data and has unique features that should be maximized. Here are some tips to help you minimize your ramp-up time when beginning to work with PL/SQL and maximize your efficiency:

- The fastest way to do something is to not do it at all. In other words, write the least amount of code possible. Don't create a cursor loop (and all the related code) to iterate over rows processing updates when a single UPDATE statement would do the same thing. Implicit cursors are also another example of maximizing PL/SQL strengths.
- When processing several rows think in terms of sets. For example, a copy order function could take advantage of inserting based on a SELECT statement to copy order lines.
- Stay within PL/SQL as long as possible when processing data. If an interface requires producing a flat file or integrating with Informatica, do as much of the processing with Oracle constructs as possible. Generate the flat or XML file in a specific procedure or function in which the only purpose of the procedure or function is to produce that output.
- When writing code, try to have your PL/SQL routines (functions and procedures) fit on a single screen. If they cannot fit on a single screen, they are probably performing more than one purpose. This is a basic modular programming practice; however, some developers still do not grasp this. Think in terms of modules and subroutines that perform a specific task in conjunction with other blocks of logic in your programs.

APEX IN THE CLOUD

Either by design or by coincidence, APEX is an incredible fit as the product for cloud-based systems from development to deployment/runtime. From a development perspective, APEX is a cloud development platform as all development is done in a Web browser. There are absolutely no development components to be installed on a client machine. All components that are developed in APEX can be exposed as Web services and can be consumed by other applications running on a private, public, or hybrid cloud. From a runtime perspective, all the end user needs in order to access the application is a URL.

The most well-known public cloud deployment, Amazon, supports Oracle APEX in the cloud in its Elastic Compute Cloud (EC2) environment. Amazon has partnered with Oracle to offer images with preconfigured software. One such image contains Oracle Enterprise Linux and Oracle Database 11g R1. Because Oracle APEX is an embedded feature of the Oracle database, you can easily create an Amazon EC2 Oracle Enterprise Linux and Database 11g image and be up and running on APEX in the cloud in minutes. We already discussed how this can be used in the "Migration Options Considered" section earlier in this chapter. One of the benefits of using the EC2 cloud is that pilot projects can be started or development environments can be set up in minutes.

Your company can also set up APEX in a private or hybrid cloud just as easily. In addition, any hosting provider that offers the Oracle Database as a Service (DaaS) is able to offer APEX in the cloud since APEX is a free component of the Oracle database. AppsHosting, IT Convergence Hosting Services, and Mythics are just a few cloud providers that offer Oracle APEX in the cloud. Another option for development and testing is to use apex.oracle.com to develop database-centric Web applications with Oracle APEX. Oracle provides apex.oracle.com as an evaluation service free of charge.

APEX addresses some of the biggest issues with public cloud application deployments: dynamic multitenant workload migration, management, and provisioning. This is because the APEX security, database, metadata, and application are all contained in the Oracle database. This means an APEX application from bits on disk, to network, to database, to the application can be managed, provisioned, and migrated as one workload. This type of end-to-end workload management, migration, and provisioning can only be achieved by using virtualization. With Oracle APEX, all these capabilities are provided without the need for and overhead of a virtual server.

The multitenant capabilities of Oracle APEX allow multiple users and their associated applications to coexist within one Oracle database, minimizing cost and management. Only one instance is needed, and users work in a dedicated work area called a workspace. The workspace is an important concept for APEX. An Oracle tablespace is a container for database data, and an APEX workspace is like a container for APEX applications and data. Usually a workspace is related to a database schema, and the APEX application's definition and data will be stored in

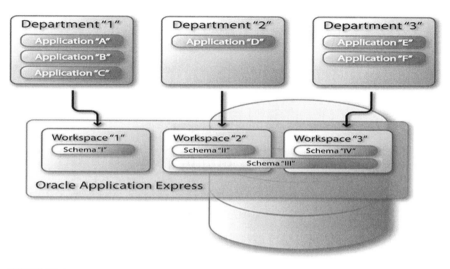

FIGURE 13.4

Multitenancy with Oracle APEX

the schema default tablespace or in a custom tablespace. Figure 13.4 shows the relationship among departments (or customers in a public cloud provider deployment), workspaces, and tablespaces.

Figure 13.4 demonstrates how Oracle APEX workspaces can be used to provide multitenancy by providing the following:

- **Single Oracle database for multiple applications** Each department or customer has his or her own workspace with only his or her application and security.
- **Virtual private databases** Using workspaces, each department or user can see only his or her data, and this database can be managed separately from the data of other customers or departments. To prevent the hardware, storage, or database failure of one database from affecting other databases, Oracle Real Application Clusters (RAC) and/or Oracle Exadata can be used to provide HA.
- **Self-service or IT managed provisioning** The customer or department data and applications can be managed and provisioned through a Web browser.

A secure APEX environment in the cloud can be achieved easily because the application and data are all in an Oracle database. However, you still need to make sure your database and HTTP Server are both behind a firewall and have secure communication, as shown in Figure 13.5.

Figure 13.5 shows how both SSL encryption and firewalls can be used to secure the Oracle HTTP Server and the Oracle database. If both the Oracle HTTP Server and the Oracle database are inside the same intranet firewall and are secured internally, perhaps SSL and a firewall are not required from the HTTP Server to the Oracle database.

Using Secure Sockets Layer (SSL) encryption

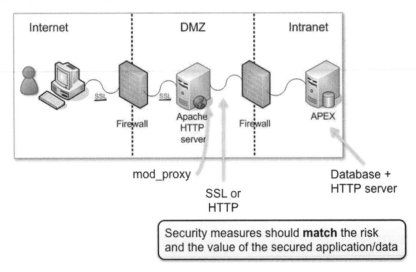

FIGURE 13.5

Oracle APEX Firewall Secured Architecture

Customers have also expressed concerns about the public cloud, as the cloud provider now has control of their application and database environment. Of course, the cloud provider has to turn over all your data, applications, and integration software if you choose to bring the installation in-house or move to a different service provider. In reality, this is not a trivial process, and therefore many customers feel they are locked in to their current cloud provider. With an APEX application, if you wish to migrate any applications developed on the cloud onto your internal systems, you simply need to ensure that the correct version of APEX is installed on the target server, export the APEX application, data schema, and data from the cloud provider, and then import them on the target server. This is possible because all the data, applications, and integration points are stored within the Oracle APEX metadata repository. Backing up your application environment is also easy with APEX as backing up a database also backs up the application source.

SUMMARY

Application modernization provides a number of benefits to an organization. Replacing a working enterprise application is a risky proposition for any company, and many of these projects fail to ever meet their functional or financial goals or ROI. Many companies cannot afford for their business teams to invest resources in modernizing applications as they are consumed with supporting and growing the company's business. Nor can they invest in training or replacing their technical teams. Application modernization provides many of the benefits of a system replacement at a lower risk and cost.

Oracle APEX is made for the cloud. It contains a cloud development environment, built-in multitenancy capabilities, and end-to-end disk-to-application management and migration. Disk-to-application management and migration allows for the entire system to be viewed as one integrated unit, which makes for easy application management and provisioning in the cloud. This case study showed the limitations and issues caused by legacy client/server applications including the issues associated with upgrading hundreds of client PC machines. Moving to the cloud where the application is located on a centralized server eliminates the cost and time associated with maintaining client machines.

Oracle APEX in the cloud provides many benefits for application developers and application development in general. Application developers only need to have access to a URL to begin developing using graphical wizards. Since all APEX applications and data are centralized, all developers, no matter where they are located, have access to the application code and can view what other developers are working on. If a developer does not have access to the Internet (the developer is on a plane or in a remote location), Oracle APEX, with Oracle Database Express Edition, is so lightweight that it can run on a laptop for development purposes.

In this case, cloud computing provided the pilot team with a quick, fully functional APEX development environment on the Amazon Elastic Cloud. JSA^2 has used this approach with several customers to develop and implement enterprise solutions. The approach is beneficial to the customer regardless of whether the customer ultimately chooses to deploy in the cloud or not. Many companies are using the Oracle AMI to quickly and inexpensively execute pilot projects or Proofs of Concept (POCs).

Challenges and Emerging Trends

INFORMATION IN THIS CHAPTER:

- Business Challenges in Database and Application Migration
- Technological Challenges in Database and Application Migration
- Emerging Trends in Database and Application Migration Technology
- Business Challenges in the Adoption of Cloud Computing
- Technical Challenges of Cloud Computing
- Emerging Trends in Cloud Services and Offerings

Acquisitions and consolidation in the IT industry drive the need for database and application migration as many older databases and application development frameworks are discontinued or simply face an uncertain future. Computing innovation is generally driven by a desire to address the most vexing problems that IT organizations are facing today, as well as technological advances such as faster CPUs and networks, and the miniaturization of technologies. Just as the success of Internet computing depended on the availability of the Internet, any new innovation will potentially require advances in technology which is easily available to all or which can leverage existing IT infrastructure. The success of any new innovation also depends heavily on the business value it provides, even if an upfront investment is required in order to adopt it. Innovations that cater to only a select user group may not be as widely adopted as expected. Similarly, innovations that address only a particular IT issue, such as developer productivity, will likely remain niche products or technologies that a majority of IT organizations will not adopt (an example of this is object-oriented databases). To understand trends in computing innovation it is essential to understand the current business and technical challenges that likely will be the driving factors for such innovations. In this chapter, we will first look at the challenges involved in database and application migration as well as the adoption of cloud computing, and then we will look at the trends in these two areas.

BUSINESS CHALLENGES IN DATABASE AND APPLICATION MIGRATION

Typically, businesses do not care which languages are used to develop an application or which database platform is being used by the IT department. They simply care about getting the job done by having access to the right information at the right time and at the lowest cost. However, any change to IT infrastructure, such as the acquisition of new hardware or software, involves a capital expenditure that needs to be approved by the business leadership. Therefore, for IT infrastructure changes, IT departments have to provide a business case depicting the business value in such terms as ROI and Total Cost of Ownership (TCO), along with the potential improvements the business will see, such as quicker turnaround time for generating important reports (from hours to minutes) and reduced batch cycle times. As businesses adopt new technologies and computing architectures, they face newer and different types of problems. As we discussed in Chapter 1, the advent of client/server computing and of Internet computing silos led to inefficiencies in data centers as a majority of data center servers were underutilized and required significant management effort.

With the interest in cloud computing gaining momentum, there will be challenges ahead for businesses that use cloud services as well as businesses that provide cloud services. Any improvement in the usability features of databases and applications, such as the use of a GUI instead of a terminal emulator, may not be considered a big change from a business perspective. However, if a new database or application can prove to the business that it can reduce deployment, management, and productivity costs, it will be very appealing to the business leadership. Major concerns with respect to database and application changes for business leaders include the following:

- Cost of the new platform
- Cost of migrating to the new platform
- Duration of the migration project
- Impact on existing users of the applications
- Impact on the IT staff (new hires versus retraining the existing staff)

The cost and duration of a migration project usually depends on the number of applications and databases being considered for migration as well as the complexity and migration approach adopted. Similarly, the impact on existing users (e.g., retraining users on the new platform) also depends on the migration approach selected. At a minimum, retraining database administrators to manage Oracle databases as a result of a database migration is essential.

TECHNOLOGICAL CHALLENGES IN DATABASE AND APPLICATION MIGRATION

To encourage database and application migration, platform vendors typically offer free tools that support the migration of various databases to their own database; examples include Oracle SQL Developer and the Microsoft SQL Server Migration Assistant. Usually, vendor-provided toolkits only support migration from the most popular databases to the vendor's own database, but some vendors' primary business is focused on developing tools and services that support migration to and from a variety of databases. Even considering all the migration tools that are currently available, database and application migration still cannot be automated completely. However, many new technologies are being developed to ease the migration effort. Database migration tools (for schema and data migration) have matured quite a lot, but as we saw in Chapters 7 and 8, much work still needs to be done to automate the migration of existing applications to support the Oracle database platform. The following are key technological challenges that influence migration projects at many organizations:

- **Lack of tools to migrate data from large databases in an automated and efficient manner**   Most IT organizations deploy a combination of tools and scripts to perform data migration. A majority of online data migration tools are either inefficient in migrating large volumes of data or inflexible in terms of configuration options for achieving optimal performance.
- **Lack of tools for automating the application migration effort**   As we discussed in Chapter 7, very few tools are available to automate application migration as a result of a database migration.
- **Lack of tools for automating testing scripts and use cases**   This tends to be the most common issue across all migration projects.

EMERGING TRENDS IN DATABASE AND APPLICATION MIGRATION TECHNOLOGY

Platform vendors and specialty migration tool vendors are constantly working to develop new solutions designed to make it easier for organizations to migrate from one platform to another and from applications developed using one language or development framework to another. Platform vendors are interested in developing efficient migration solutions to make it easier for new customers to migrate to their platform. As we discussed in the "Technological Challenges in Database and Application Migration" section, it is very important for platform vendors to develop new technologies and tools to reduce the migration effort, focusing specifically on tasks such as application porting and migration to convert embedded SQL statements and database APIs in addition to ensuring that the features and functionalities offered by other databases can be successfully migrated to their own database platform. Potential solutions to reduce the migration effort in general are:

- **Database platform feature standardization**   One way to reduce the complexity of database migration is to standardize the features and functionalities across database platforms, especially for relational databases, as they offer similar functionality yet differ widely in implementation. The wider the differences are among databases in terms of core features and functionalities, the more complex the database migration task will be (e.g., all relational databases follow the same object naming standards and a standard set of data types to manage various types of data). Similarly, if all databases were to offer similar functionality and support for general syntax in their procedural language extensions to SQL, such as PL/SQL in Oracle and T-SQL in Sybase/SQL Server, migration from one platform to another would be easier. This is certainly not a new concept, as Java application servers from different vendors incorporate similar functionality, making it easier to deploy Java applications on any standards-compliant application server.

- **Tool-based application code remediation**   The availability of tools that can migrate source database platform-specific code such as embedded SQL statements, database APIs, and error codes, and that can convert programs written to leverage call-level interfaces for specific databases to target database platforms, can make application migration and porting a lot easier. Oracle SQL Developer 3.0 has some capabilities in this area that currently support the scanning of Sybase CT-Lib/DB-Lib applications, and it has an extensible framework to add support for more databases and languages. System integrators and customers can easily extend the capabilities of the SQL Developer application migration tool by building rules for converting non-Oracle database SQL statements to Oracle.

- **Emulation technologies**   As we discussed in the "Migration Options and Solutions" section in Chapter 7, use of emulation technologies can be an effective way to facilitate a migration effort in terms of porting and migrating applications to an Oracle database. Emulation technologies can reduce the need for changes to application programs (especially client/server applications), which otherwise is a significant task in most database migration projects. These technologies can be a great option, especially for large corporations that have dozens or hundreds of applications and databases that need to be migrated, as they can avoid the migration and porting of each application to make it compatible with the Oracle database. Currently, support for Oracle databases is limited by the tools and technologies available and not much choice is available for customers.

- **Automatic generation of test suites**   In database migrations involving a large number of business logic implementations in stored programs, it is a big challenge to test all the migrated procedures for accuracy to ensure correct data manipulation and retrieval as well as code-path integrity. Currently, there are no tools for generating such test suites. Having tools that can generate appropriate test suites to ensure proper testing of the migrated code can significantly reduce the testing effort involved in migration projects. Oracle SQL Developer generates individual unit test cases for each stored procedure, but for large databases, it is a big challenge to generate a test case.

- **Data verification/quality testing tools**   Another area of focus for enabling migrations is data verification tools. Today there are few tools that can automate this task. Most tools that are in use are developed by migration service providers and are offered to customers as part of their migration services rather than as an independent product or tool that can be purchased directly by customers. The biggest challenge in the data verification task is to automate the process of identifying data elements that need to be verified between the source and target databases, such as numeric columns representing money, and the scheduling/execution/monitoring of background jobs on source and target systems. Traditional data quality and profiling tools can also be enhanced to support data verification and validation tasks.

BUSINESS CHALLENGES IN THE ADOPTION OF CLOUD COMPUTING

As businesses consider adopting cloud computing to reduce the costs of maintaining expensive IT infrastructure, they also encounter many challenges. Cloud offerings need to be evaluated on the basis of deployment models (private, public, and hybrid), service offerings (Infrastructure as a Service or IaaS, Platform as a Service or PaaS, and Software as a Service or SaaS), cost, audit and compliance features offered, and security services offered. Businesses also need to avoid potential vendor lock-in issues and decide which applications, databases, and other IT systems are good candidates for cloud deployment. Businesses also need to decide the future of existing data centers and plan to use them in some fashion to protect their current investments.

TECHNICAL CHALLENGES OF CLOUD COMPUTING

After an organization decides to deploy some or all of its IT systems onto a cloud infrastructure, its first major technical challenge is to decide where to start. Out of all the IT systems and solutions that are deployed in the data centers of large corporations, picking the first set of applications and databases that are good candidates for deployment on a cloud infrastructure is a big challenge, as a thorough assessment and inventory is required for all IT assets, and analysis of dependencies among applications and databases as well as other requirements such as security, auditing, and backup and recovery are essential. It is also important to identify applications and databases that have low-latency, high-throughput requirements that may not be suitable for deployment on a cloud infrastructure. Sizing of the cloud infrastructure is also important for these applications which can be easily expanded as needed by the virtue of cloud infrastructure elasticity.

IT departments also need to decide whether a private cloud infrastructure is suitable for their business needs, or whether a public cloud infrastructure would be better. How will audit and compliance requirements be met in public and private cloud environments? Most applications and databases typically leverage some sort of centralized security and identity management system to provide role-based access controls to IT resources. When moving some applications and databases to a cloud infrastructure, it is important to decide how security will be enforced and who will be responsible for managing the security infrastructure.

EMERGING TRENDS IN CLOUD SERVICES AND OFFERINGS

For customers planning to deploy applications and databases onto a cloud infrastructure, just the use of IaaS or PaaS offerings for the operating system, databases, and application servers may not meet all of their requirements. As most applications depend heavily on other systems within an IT organization for information exchange as well as to enforce security and role-based access control, it is essential for cloud service providers to enable such applications to integrate seamlessly with other applications and databases. Customers are also wary of potential vendor lock-in. Features and functionalities that can drive the faster adoption of cloud computing are:

- **Ability to switch cloud providers (PaaS/SaaS)**   With more offerings on the market from cloud providers, businesses may decide to switch their preferred cloud providers just as they switch database platforms, so it is important to dispel concerns around vendor lock-in. Cloud service providers that can provide tools and interfaces for customers to migrate from one cloud provider to another, involving complete environment migration (application and database) and including the specific configuration of the environment, will be of great help to customers.
- **Development and adoption of standard cloud APIs by cloud service providers and platform vendors**   Many software vendors are contributing to the development of standard APIs encompassing all aspects of cloud computing from infrastructure provisioning to application development. In 2010, Oracle submitted the Oracle Cloud Resource Model API, a subset of the Oracle Cloud API, to the Distribution Task Management Workforce (DMTF) as a consideration for inclusion in the proposed Cloud APIs for IaaS. Using these APIs, cloud providers can manage infrastructure running on the Oracle stack seamlessly, just as they can any other technology stack. Hence, development and support for standard cloud APIs is important to platform vendors, and can result in increased adoption of their technology stack. Similarly, leveraging standard cloud APIs instead of native or proprietary APIs can be beneficial to cloud providers as they don't need to develop or update their client interfaces (self-service portals) to support a new platform. This can, in turn, benefit the end users of cloud computing as they will have more choices for platform selection, even in the cloud.
- **Industry-specific cloud service offerings**   Many organizations are hesitant to deploy sensitive applications and databases onto a cloud infrastructure as they don't want to share data with different business units and departments deployed on a private cloud infrastructure as well as with other organizations in the public cloud. This is mainly due to concerns around data security and privacy. In some cases, organizations need to scrub their storage systems completely (and not just delete their data files) to remove any trace of their customer data to comply with federal regulations. In such circumstances, the goal is to prevent recovery of data even by expert hardware and software engineers with malicious intent. To increase the comfort level of customers with respect to deploying sensitive applications and databases on a cloud infrastructure, cloud service offerings may be targeted to specific industry verticals that can enable data security (encryption, scrubbing capabilities) at rest or in transit, as well as auditing capabilities required

by the specific industry verticals. Going one step further, cloud service providers can develop an infrastructure implementation that can comply with industry-specific regulations and government standards as a built-in feature. A good example is a cloud service offering targeted for defense and national security agencies that includes a data warehousing platform with encryption, compression, and data scrubbing features as well as strong analytics capabilities, and another offering for the health care industry that enables users to comply with legislation surrounding the Health Insurance Portability and Accountability Act of 1996 (HIPAA).

- **Solutions beyond PaaS and SaaS offerings** It is important for organizations that plan to leverage cloud computing to consider how they can meet integration and security requirements for all the applications and databases targeted for such deployments.

  - **Integration as a Service** It is just not enough to deploy some databases and applications to a cloud infrastructure and consider that as the last milestone in taking the greatest advantage of a cloud computing architecture. Most applications and databases need to integrate with other systems that are deployed either locally within the data center or in a cloud environment. Typical data integration needs are met by designing and implementing extract-transform-load (ETL) tasks using solutions such as Oracle Data Integrator and Informatica. For application integration, a common and standards-based approach is to use a service bus, or orchestration engine such as the Oracle Business Process Execution Language (BPEL), both of which facilitate application integration via Web services. To facilitate interaction with other systems in a loosely coupled fashion for data transformation, cleansing, and verification, the most common way to integrate applications and databases in a standards-based approach is to use Web services. For applications and databases that are deployed in a PaaS or SaaS environment, integrating with other systems outside the cloud environment can be challenging, as it may not be possible for these applications to discover and execute an integration task (data or application) outside their environment unless the solutions in the cloud environment are Web service-ready and the integration platform is Web service-enabled. To really take advantage of a cloud computing architecture, businesses must be able to use an integration infrastructure in an on-demand, pay-as-you-go model (SaaS). To enable use of an integration platform in the cloud, some vendors have launched Integration as a Service (not to be confused with Infrastructure as a Service or IaaS) offerings; notable among these companies are Informatica and Hubspan. These integration cloud offerings facilitate both data and application integration and support a host of databases and applications with prebuilt connectors out of the box. There are generally two types of offerings in this space. One is an extension to a PaaS offering where the integration platform is simply deployed in the cloud for use by customers on demand, like a database or an application server. The second option offers an integration platform as a service where customers pay to use the service only, similar to using SaaS applications. As such, Integration as a Service can complement existing SaaS offerings and enable seamless data and application integration in the cloud. Sooner or later, many other integration platform vendors are expected to offer such services as cloud computing becomes more mainstream and customers start to look for additional choices. It is important for integration platforms to provide SaaS offerings instead of just supporting the deployment of the platform in a cloud environment or just enabling Web service-based access to the platform.

- **Security as a Service** In any large organization, it is common to have an identity management and role-based access control system deployed to cover all IT systems. It is also a common practice to leverage a directory server based on Lightweight Directory Access Protocol (LDAP) standards, such as Oracle Internet Directory (OID) and Microsoft Active Directory, for managing user identities. The most important tasks performed in the area of identity and security management are the provisioning of user identities, access and role management, and reconciliation, as organizations need to bring new users on board quickly and remove the user identities of users who leave the organization. When moving some applications and databases to a cloud infrastructure, and leaving behind other applications and databases as well as the security infrastructure in the data center, it is essential to decide who will manage the security requirements of the applications and databases in the cloud, and how this will be done. It is possible that existing infrastructure used by an organization can be leveraged and customized to manage security for the applications and databases in the cloud as well, but this may not provide much benefit to the organization from a cost perspective. Also, customizing applications to change different security providers may require some work, depending on the development platform used. Organizations can also outsource the management of security infrastructure (IaaS/PaaS) and retain the management role governing security so that only they are responsible for controlling access to all IT systems (and not the cloud service provider). Alternatively, organizations can purchase security applications that are offered in the SaaS model, such as CloudGate from Managed Methods. This model can be appealing to some organizations that are satisfied with the service-level agreements (SLAs) offered by the vendors of such security systems and are not concerned about storing user identities and roles outside their own data centers, even if it is only for applications and databases in the cloud. Many security software vendors, among them McAfee and Symantec, already offer services for protecting Web traffic and providing e-mail security.

In addition to Integration as a Service and Security as a Service deployment, there is a Development as a Service offering which can provide a platform with frameworks for developing cloud-ready applications. Oracle Application Express (APEX) can provide a development environment in the cloud leveraging an Oracle database which is also multitenant-capable. Other vendors, such as SalesForce.com and

Google, provide a development platform and a framework for developing applications in the cloud.

SUMMARY

In this chapter, we covered some of the most pressing challenges in database and application migration and the adoption of cloud computing by many organizations. As a first step toward adopting cloud computing, many organizations are trying to leverage private clouds due to concerns around security in public clouds, although many public cloud providers have implemented robust security solutions to protect themselves from unauthorized access to data in the cloud. We also talked about services that complement public and private clouds in the integration and security space that are very important for many organizations. As adoption of cloud computing continues at a fast pace, there will be more and more offerings from platform vendors as well as other software vendors in the areas of development, business process management, and cloud management. All these efforts are also leading to the development of standard cloud APIs which can result in simplification of management, integration, and development in a cloud environment. SaaS-based applications will continue to provide maximum value to customers and will be the model for implementation for many services in the cloud, such as security, integration, and development. However, there will be exceptions to this trend due to organizations' specific need for security and isolation.

Index

Note: page numbers followed by f indicate figures and t indicate tables

Check out our extensive list of titles in the area of Digital Forensics